Ecological Principles and Environmental Issues

Peter J. Jarvis

Prentice
Hall

An imprint of **PEARSON EDUCATION**

Harlow, England · London · New York · Reading, Massachusetts · San Francisco · Toronto · Don Mills, Ontario · Sydney
Tokyo · Singapore · Hong Kong · Seoul · Taipei · Cape Town · Madrid · Mexico City · Amsterdam · Munich · Paris · Milan

Pearson Education Limited
Edinburgh Gate
Harlow
Essex CM20 2JE
England

and Associated Companies around the world

Visit us on the World Wide Web at:
www.pearsoneduc.com

First published 2000

ISBN 0 582 36971 1

British Library Cataloguing-in-Publication Data
A catalogue record for this book is available from the British Library.

Library of Congress Cataloging-in-Publication Data
A catalog record for this book is available from the Library of Congress.

Typeset by 32 in 10/12 Sabon

Printed and bound in Great Britain by
T.J. International Ltd., Padstow, Cornwall

Contents

Acknowledgements

For suggesting that I write this book, for her subsequent encouragement and perhaps most of all for her patience I wish to express my gratitude to Alex Seabrook, Senior Commissioning Editor at Addison Wesley Longman, now Pearson Education. Lynn Brandon, Shuet-Uei Cheung and Emily Pillars, also of Pearson Education, are also thanked for pushing me to completion in the end phase. Dennis Hodgson did a marvellous job of copy-editing. Ian Spellerbergs's noises of encouragement and sound advice are much appreciated. I am also pleased to acknowledge that the germ of the approach taken in this book came from John Barkham, to whom I am therefore once again indebted for facilitating my publishing career.

Many of the ideas and examples used in this book emerged while I taught in the School of Geography at the University of Birmingham, and I am grateful to all former colleagues who in one way or another helped in the development of some degree of understanding in the fields of ecology, conservation and environmental management. I am particularly appreciative of the opportunities provided by the late Rowland Moss, and the education that was sharing the course on Conservation, Planning and Resource Management with Michael Tanner, whose voice echoes through many parts of this text.

My five years at the University of Wolverhampton in the Division of Environmental Science (latterly Environmental and Analytical Science) within the School of Applied Sciences have been a joy, and it is a privilege to acknowledge the support and help of all my colleagues. Particular mention, however, must be afforded to Robin Stuttard, Ian Trueman, Eleanor Cohn, David Harding, Nick Musgrove and Chris Young. David Carter Baker, too, kindly supplied me with many newspaper reports of value.

I am also grateful for the feedback from the 8000 or so students who, for over 30 years, have served as critics of the work in progress that is now this book, encouraging me (I hope) to get the level and approach about right.

Much of the literature was to hand, thanks to Elsevier/Geo Abstracts, for whom I edited *Ecological Abstracts* over the period 1975–98. Particular thanks are due to Margaret Bass, Shane Harris and, especially, Jim Cooper for their editorial help over the years.

I appreciate being introduced to Ulrich Beck's ideas on risk by Bob Jarvis, and on being able to check on some biological terminology and definitions with Nicky Jarvis. Fran Ryland kindly lent me some books, otherwise unknown to me, on biodiversity and conservation.

My love and thanks to Kat Clifford, for all the usual without whoms and for a whole lot of others beside.

This book is dedicated with love and gratitude to my parents, Margaret and John.

St Barnabas Day 1999
Peter Jarvis

Every effort has been taken to secure permission to use copyright material, but apologies are offered to any copyright holders whose rights have been unwittingly infringed. I am grateful to the following to reproduce copyright material as indicated:
John Wiley & Sons Inc.: Fig. 1.4: P. Colinvaux, *Ecology 2* (1993); Fig. 1.7: W.M. Marsh and J.M. Crosson, *Environmental geography* (1996); Figs. 2.13 and 2.14: J.O. Nriagu (ed), *Copper in the environment: I* (1979); Figs. 7.4 & 8.1 and Tables 7.5 and 7.6: D.B. Botkin and E.A. Keller, *Environmental science* (1995); John Wiley & Sons Ltd: Fig. 2.11: B.Bolin and R.B. Cook (ed*), The major biogeochemical cycles and their interactions* (1983); Fig. 7.2: A. Warren and F.B. Goldsmith (ed), *Conservation in practice* (1974). Routledge: Figs 1.6-1.8 and 4.2: C. Park, *The environment* (1997). Fig 1.6 & 1.8: G. Dury, *Environmental systems* (1981). Fig 1.9: Simon and Schuster/Macmillan Publishing: R.H. Whittaker, *Communities and ecosystems. Ed 2* (1975). Fig 1.11:Unwin Hyman Ltd: A.S. Collinson, *Introduction to world vegetation* (1978). Fig 2.1 and Table 2.1: Ambio (Royal Swedish Academy of Sciences, 1994). Chapman & Hall Ltd.: Fig.2.3: C. Elton, *Animal ecology* (1927); Figs 2.4, 2.5, 2.12 and 4.6 and Table 2.2: A.Beeby and A.-N. Brennan, *First ecology* (1997); Fig 3.12: R.W. Furness and J.J.D. Greenwood (ed), *Birds as monitors of environmental change* (1993); Figs 6.11 and 6.12, Tables 6.1 and 6.2: B. Groombridge (ed), *Global biodiversity* (1992); Table 8.1: M. Williamson, *Biological invasions* (1996). Ecological Society of America: Figs 2.7, 4.8, 4.11, 5.15, 6.9 and 8.11. Blackwell Scientific: Fig. 5.17: M. Begon, J.L. Harper and C.R. Townsend, *Ecology: individuals, populations and communities. Ed. 3* (1996); Figs. 5.14 and 6.4: C.B. Cox and P.D. Moore, *Biogeography. Ed 5* (1993). Cambridge University Press: Figs 2.9 and 2.10: J.L. Chapman and M.J. Reiss, *Ecology: principles and applications. Ed 2* (1999); Fig. 3.5 (*Environmental Conservation*, 1992); Fig. 5.11: L.C. Bliss, O.W. Heal and J.J. Moore (ed*), Tundra ecosystems: a comparative analysis* (1981); Issues Box 6.3 (New Phytologist, 1998). Prentice-Hall Inc: Fig 2.15: N. Brady, *Nature and properties of soil* (1984). Elsevier Science Ltd: Figs 2.16, 4.1 and 6.3 (1987, 1990, 1998); Issues Box 5.1: B. Gopal, Aquatic plant studies. I. Water hyacinth (1987). Oliver & Boyd: Fig 2.17: J. Tivy and G. O'Hare, *Human impact on the ecosystem* (1981). American Society of Agronomy, Crop Science Society of America and Soil Science Society: Fig 2.18 *Journal of Environmental Quality*, 1975). Penguin Books: Fig 2.19: G. Conway, *The doubly green revolution* (1997). University of Chicago

xii ACKNOWLEDGEMENTS

Press: Figs. 3.1, 3.2, 6.6, 6.7, 7.11 and 8.5. UNEP: Fig. 3.7: *Environmental data report. Ed. 3* (1991). Oxford University Press Canada: Fig 3.8: C. Mungall and D.McLaren, *Planet under stress: the challenge of global change* (The Royal Society of Canada, 1990). Sinauer Associates Inc.: Fig 3.9: W.W. Murdoch (ed*), Environment: resources, pollution, society. Ed. 2* (1975); Figs. 8.13 and 8.14: M.E. Soulé and B.A. Wilcox (ed), *Conservation biology* (1980). Houghton Mifflin: Fig 3.10: T.C. Foin Jr, *Ecological systems in the environment* (1976). British Ecological Society: Figs 3.11, 3.13 and 6.5 (1970, 1970, 1999); Fig. 2.8: A. Watson (ed), *Animal populations in relation to their food resource* (1970); Table 9.1: J.M. Cherrett (ed), Ecological concepts (1989). American Association for the Advancement of Science: Fig. 3.14 and Table 7.8 (1982, 1969). Dr W. Junk: Fig 3.15 and Table 3.3: W.H. van Dobben and R.H. Lowe-McConnell (ed), *Unifying concepts in ecology* (1975). Addison Wesley Longman/Pearson Education: Figs. 4.3-4.5: J. Graves and D. Reavey, *Global environmental change* (1996); Fig. 4.10: G.N. Louw and M.K. Seely, *Ecology of desert organisms* (1982); Fig 4.13: C.J. Barrow, *Developing the environment* (1995). World Resources Institute: Fig 5.1 and 5.3: *World resources, 1994-95* (1994). US National Marine Fisheries Service: Fig 5.2 (1996). Munksgaard International Publishers Ltd: Figs 5.1, 5.14 and 5.16 (*Oikos*, 1981, 1983, 1983). Muzeum i Instytut Zoologi PAN: Fig 6.1 (*Acta Ornithologica*, 1996). IUCN: Fig 6.2 (World Conservation Strategy, 1980). RSPB: Issues Box 6.1. British Ornithologists' Union: Fig 6.10 (*Ibis*, 1995). HMSO: Fig 7.3 and Tables 7.3 and 7.4 (Crown Copyright 1992). Kluwer: Table 8.2: F. di Castri et al. (ed), *Biological invasions in Europe and the Mediterranean Basin* (1990). Fig. 8.12: M.P. McClaran and T.R. VanDevender, *The desert grassland* (The Arizona Board of Regents, 1995), reprinted by permission of the University of Arizona Press. Andromeda Oxford Ltd: Ecology Box 8.2: D. Macdonald (ed), *The encyclopedia of mammals* (1995).

Foreword

Humans have had to know something about ecology since their earliest evolution. To survive, primitive societies had to have knowledge, if not necessarily understanding, of how plants and animals interact with their environment (which is as useful a definition of ecology as any), and also of how human activities can modify or manipulate such interactions. Palaeolithic people had tools of stone to kill for food and other animal products; they collected fruits, seeds and nuts; and they used fire not just for warmth and cooking but also to alter the environment. Some late glacial animal extinctions almost certainly resulted, in part at least, from overhunting.

So early humans needed to know how and where plants lived and grew. They also had to know how they themselves interacted with the environment. They were, at some level, ecologists.

Today, we have a similar need to understand the living world and how each component interacts with other organisms and with the physical environment. We too need to know something about ecology, and we need to be able to understand the consequences of our actions affecting the biosphere – that thin layer on and close to the surface of our planet which contains the only known life in the universe.

Although we may have had to be ecologists during the 200 000 years or so since the emergence of *Homo sapiens* as a distinct species, and while the study of ecology goes back in practice well before 1869, it was only in this year that the word ecology was actually first proposed, by a German biologist, Ernst Haeckel. Even so, the science of ecology is really a twentieth-century phenomenon. It is just that many ecological principles and practices were known long before. The word 'ecology' derives from two Greek words, *oikos* and *logos*, meaning, respectively, 'house' (or 'living place') and 'word' (but incorporating the idea of 'study' or 'understanding'): it has come to mean the study of organisms in their 'home' or environment, the environment including other organisms. Hence, ecology is the science that examines the nature of the interrelationships between organisms and their environment.

Ecology at its core is clearly a biological discipline, since it deals with processes involving and interactions between plants, animals and micro-organisms of many different sorts. Inevitably, however, there are links with many other disciplines: biochemistry, chemistry and physics, for example, since the living components of the environment are made up of carbon-based compounds, and ecological and biological processes must obey physical laws such as those of thermodynamics. Geography and environmental science are also linked with ecology, because there are spatial and environmental implications of how and why ecological systems function. Psychology, too, where animal behaviour might be the focus of attention. In utilising living resources and their environment, humans also need to consider disciplines such as economics and resource management; politics in one form or another almost inevitably so; philosophy, even, where we consider issues of ethics and responsibility. At this stage, we are moving from ecology itself into looking at ecological and environmental issues, but in order to understand these issues we need to know something about ecological principles. And ecological principles can be illustrated by considering these issues.

This book aims to do just this. Chapter 1 introduces the reader to the biosphere, showing that the ecological structure and functioning of Spaceship Earth can be studied at different scales, and demonstrating how feedback mechanisms control how different land, air and water compartments interact at these different scales. The large scale of such interactions has implications for human activity, since they transcend national boundaries and are therefore difficult to study and control. As with all chapters, these ideas are set in train using a key example, in this case the fires that blazed throughout much of South-east Asia in 1997: here, issues include exploitation, management, environmental pollution and political control.

Chapter 2 looks at nutrient cycling together with energy flow in an examination of primary and secondary production. Food chains and food webs are exemplified, and the idea of ecological efficiency is mooted. These concepts are brought together by looking at agro-ecosystems, in particular reviewing issues of sustainability and feeding the expanding human population.

Chapter 3 pursues the idea of ecosystem stability by considering how pollution can affect ecosystem integrity. Ideas of stability, resilience, resistance and recoverability are examined in the context of oil pollution; and bioaccumulation of chemicals along the food chain is discussed using examples of how birds of prey themselves fall prey to lethal and sub-lethal concentrations of pesticides. There are problems of measuring pollution (for instance in identifying threshold levels of safety) and in perceiving the problems of pollution, where the cure may be more of an environmental problem than the cause.

Global warming is the issue used in Chapter 4 to examine two interacting ecological themes: how organisms might respond to the greenhouse effect; and limiting factors, which in many ways control where organisms can live and, with other environmental and historical factors, lead to particular regional and global patterns of distribution. Climate changes, both naturally and through human action, and this also has implications for species distribution.

The growth of the world's human population poses many problems, but it is important to examine population growth generally in terms of ecological principles, and this is done in Chapter 5, in particular looking at marine fisheries and how and why some organisms become weeds and pests. Species interactions are noted, paying particular attention to predator–prey relationships.

Chapter 6 reviews biodiversity, including notions of evolution and extinction, species diversity, species turnover and endemism. Here, too, the ecological and biogeographical background provides a basis for decisions concerning how we might conserve biodiversity, and how we have to prioritise what we target. Conservation receives a more generous treatment in Chapter 7 in the context of goal-oriented management, including discussion of rarity, endangered species, zonation and succession. The idea of wilderness is discussed, and options for management and legislation are noted, stressing the importance of an ecological as well as environmental awareness and understanding if we are to achieve success. Aspects of practical conservation are examined, focusing on reclamation and habitat creation, but doing so in the context of ideas on dispersal and colonisation, and on succession and zonation.

Comments on introduced species are made in Chapter 8, recapitulating ideas on ecosystem stability and on weeds and pests in the context of species life history, community structure, habitat, niche, competition and coexistence. The particular vulnerability of islands to biological invasions is explained, and island biogeography theory is described.

Chapter 9 recapitulates the message of the book by noting the fifty ecological concepts perceived, at least by British ecologists, to be the most useful and important, and identifying a set of ecological, professional and personal responsibilities that are needed in any agenda on the rational and sustainable management of environmental resources.

By the end of the book, the reader will have been introduced to a set of key ecological principles and shown why these are important in understanding how our environment works, how we have affected what goes on in our environment, and how we might manage our environment perhaps more carefully and wisely.

For up-to-date reviews of current work in ecology and on environmental issues, always scientifically sound yet written in an accessible style, read magazines available from newsstands such as the following:

BioScience
National Geographic
New Scientist
Science
Scientific American

Questions, exercises and discussion topics

The questions are opportunities for self-testing, using general knowledge and information provided in each chapter. Suggested answers are provided immediately after the questions.

The set of discussion topics and exercises allows the reader to use some of the ideas examined in the chapter, often in a different context. Readers with some general environmental knowledge should be able to discuss many of the issues without further preparation, but additional reading or research would be useful in most cases for informed debate in essays, seminars, workshops, etc. Many of the discussion topics could be undertaken as exercises.

Chapter **1**

The Biosphere: Global interaction of land, air and water

Summary

Life on Earth can be examined as systems at different scales of study, for example cells, organs, organisms, populations, communities, ecosystems and biosphere. The living world interacts with the non-living part of the planet, and interactions between the land, air and water compartments are demonstrated by examining feedback mechanisms in the context of tropical forestry and the ocean–atmosphere implications of El Niño. Photosynthesis and chemosynthesis are introduced as the means by which energy is converted into forms usable by living matter by green plants and microorganisms, respectively. The significance of water is indicated by a brief examination of the hydrological cycle and evapotranspiration. Links between global climate and major vegetation types (as biomes) are emphasised. The terms 'ecosystem', 'community', 'environment' and 'habitat' are explained and exemplified. Self-regulation (homeostasis) of systems via feedback mechanisms is a crucial property of systems, again exemplified using tropical forests. Issues in environmental management are explored using deforestation and burning in Brazil and Indonesia as case studies.

1.1 Systems, Gaia and the biosphere

The basis of life on Earth is energy from the Sun. This life (Ecology Box 1.1) can be viewed, at different scales, as systems. All systems possess four attributes: a structure; a set of functional relationships (structure reflecting function and *vice versa*); mechanisms that tend to maintain the system's *equilibrium*; and *dynamism*, which can modify or alter the system to allow adjustment to changing circumstances or to function more efficiently. The extent to which a system is successful can be viewed in terms of its persistence, although its form and function may alter through amendment or some form of development.

Cells and sub-cellular features are systems with these attributes. So too are collections of cells which make up tissues and organs. These in turn form a higher-level system, the individual organism. At this stage, we move from biology into ecology, since organisms of the same species make up a population system. Populations of different organisms make up a community system. Add the non-living component of the environment to a community and we have an *ecosystem*. A collection of ecosystems of similar features (frequently defined in terms of general climatic and vegetation characteristics) is a *biome*, for example tundra, hot desert, tropical moist forest and the deep ocean. At the larger scale of study there is the *biosphere*, the thin skin of life on our planet found between a few hundred metres below the Earth's crust and a few thousand metres above, all treated as one giant system. This reflects what James Lovelock has called 'Gaia' – named after the Greek goddess Mother Earth – the self-sustaining, self-regulating system that is our planet, equivalent to a single super-organism (see Ecology Box 1.2).

Gaia possesses exactly the same characteristics as other systems: its structure and function are interrelated; it has an inherent stability, but it has also evolved. There are feedback mechanisms that allow it to do this, and the whole system is much greater than the sum of its component parts. The biosphere is at the surface of Gaia, and is the component possessing this interdependence, or symbiosis, between living and non-living elements.

The interconnectedness of different components of the biosphere, and ways in which events have knock-on implications, can be exemplified by looking at the forest fires that raged in Southeast Asia during 1997 and 1998.

ECOLOGY BOX 1.1

The meaning of life

Life first appeared on Earth around 3.5 billion years ago. A living cell fixes and uses energy in a way that allows it to grow and reproduce. It is this replication that is a key to life, but some inorganic matter can also replicate – crystals, for example – so replication itself cannot be the sole criterion for defining life. A system of energy management (or metabolism), together with the ability to replicate, has in the past transformed inanimate matter into animate matter, which has subsequently evolved into more and more complex forms.

Life is nevertheless an intangible quality that defies simple definition. Some of the characteristics that, taken together, distinguish living from non-living things are:

Living things

- have a complex, organised structure based on organic (carbon) compounds;
- acquire material and energy from their environment and convert these into different forms;
- actively maintain their complex structure;
- respond to environmental stimuli;
- grow and reproduce themselves using a molecular blueprint (DNA);
- have the capacity to evolve.

ECOLOGY BOX 1.2

The Gaia hypothesis

In the early 1970s, James Lovelock introduced the idea of Earth as a self-regulating super-organism, at the same time suggesting how life has evolved as an integral part of the evolution of the planet. 'Gaia is not a synonym for the biosphere', warns Lovelock (1988: 19). 'The biosphere is ... that part of the Earth where living things normally exist. Still less is Gaia the same as the biota, which is simply the collection of all individual living organisms.'

Rather, the Gaia hypothesis supposes that 'the atmosphere, the oceans, the climate, and the crust of the Earth are regulated at a state comfortable for life because of the behaviour of living organisms ... The temperature, oxidation state, acidity, and certain aspects of the rocks and waters are at any time kept constant, and this homeostasis is maintained by active feedback processes operated automatically – by the biota' (*ibid.*). (The terms 'homeostasis' and 'feedback' are discussed later in this chapter).

As the Earth began to cool and life emerged from the primordial soup, a two-way process of adaptation began, essentially a symbiosis between organisms and the abiotic environment. Clearly, organisms only succeeded where they were able to evolve and adapt to what was happening within the Earth's system, but they themselves were a part of that system, and so both effected and were affected by change.

For example, life initially took advantage of hydrogen and carbon, but around 2 billion years ago these early life forms began excreting – as plants do today – a waste product, oxygen, in such quantities that survival depended on being able to tolerate this gas. The whole chemistry of the planet's surface then changed. The seas began to precipitate dissolved iron, and in doing so released more oxygen. Some lifeforms began not just to tolerate but to require this increasingly abundant gas, now a more efficient source of energy than the hydrogen and carbon of previous times.

Different organisms thus produced and depended upon oxygen. Oxygen supports life, but without life there would be no oxygen. Earth would be lifeless, an immensely hot and barren desert, with temperatures of 200–300 °C and an atmosphere comprising about 98% carbon dioxide.

Lovelock used the term 'geophysiology' to describe how life and the physico-chemical environment have co-evolved in what is essentially a single process, a rather different idea to the conventional view that organisms and their global environment have evolved independently.

1.2 Key environmental issue: forests and fires in South-east Asia and the El Niño effect

A combination of year-round warmth and high annual rainfall (over 2000 mm and commonly over 3000 mm each year) has led to many parts of the tropics having a natural vegetation of rain forest. The taxonomic diversity of the trees is very high at species, genus and family levels (see Ecology Box 1.3). This is true of such forests in South and South-east Asia, Latin America, West and Central Africa, and northern Australia. In Malaysia, for example, Whitmore (1975) has estimated that there are around 2500 tree species, although only 700 or so become large enough (basal girth 1.35 m) to be usable, and fewer than 150 of these are regularly exploited for timber.

For years, huge tracts of land have been logged, but only a few mature trees from the hundred or more that grow in each hectare are commercially useful. In average Malaysian dipterocarp forest (forest dominated by members of the family Dipterocarpaceae) about fourteen trees are felled per hectare. The land is therefore rarely clear felled, but the felling and extraction of the targeted trees cause damage to much of the remainder. Whitmore has suggested in his 'rule of three' that for every tree felled, another is killed or destroyed, and a third is so severely damaged that it will die in the near future. But in any case,

ECOLOGY BOX 1.3

Taxonomic divisions

Organisms are classified according to their degree of similarity (generally implying inability to reproduce and to breed true to the parental form) and degree of evolutionary relatedness. Traditionally, this has been according to key morphological features, although recent advances in genetics and biochemistry have forced taxonomists to reconsider the nature of many groups.

The living world contains at least five kingdoms, which are the broadest classificatory group. (Taxonomists have recently argued for the need to extend the number of kingdoms to include some particularly distinct microbial forms). Animals, plants and fungi probably evolved from protists, which in turn evolved from prokaryotes (bacteria). Bacterial cells lack a central nucleus, and DNA (the genetic material) is found throughout the cell. Protists are single-celled organisms, and like fungi, plants and animals their DNA is contained in the cell nuclei; these four kingdoms are eukaryotes.

The plant kingdom is divided into a number of divisions, which in turn are subdivided into classes (see below). Classes are subdivided into orders, which in turn contain a number of families. Families are divided into different genera (this is the plural of genus), and genera into species (which is both a singular and a plural noun). A similar taxonomic hierarchy is seen with animals, except that the term 'phylum' (plural phyla) is used in place of division. Examples from the Indo-Malaysian rain forest are:

Common name:	teak	orang-utan
Kingdom:	Plantae	Animalia
Division/Phylum:	Tracheophyta	Chordata
Class:	Angiospermae	Mammalia
Order:	Lamiales	Primates
Family:	Verbenaceae	Pongidae
Genus:	Tectona	Pongo
Species:	*Tectona grandis*	*Pongo pygmaeus*

much of the forest is also burned after logging, or sometimes instead of logging.

In the wake of the loggers come plantation owners and farmers, who clear the remainder of the forest for oil palms and cash crops. As elsewhere, agriculture destroys more rain forest than does logging. The quickest and cheapest way of clearing the remaining forest and its debris is to burn it. Traditional slash-and-burn (or swidden) agriculture has used fire in an environmentally sensitive way: the scale of the burning can be accommodated by the forest vegetation, the soil is temporarily enriched by the wood ash, crops can be grown for a few years, the settlement moves on, and the vegetation can recover. But

with large-scale burning of forest, a series of environmental problems commonly emerge. The exposed soil, for instance, is vulnerable to erosion following the heavy rains that characterise these regions. Also, clay particles move up through the soil by capillary action to be redeposited at the surface, forming a hard, impermeable layer that prevents water and plant roots penetrating. And plants are no longer available to return water to the atmosphere via evapotranspiration, so less water is subsequently available as rainfall (half of Amazonian rainfall, for example, is reputed to be generated through evapotranspiration), and the actual nature of the vegetation may therefore change.

In parts of South-east Asia, another problem emerged in 1997: the forest fires got out of hand. Hundreds died as the fires spread in the islands of Sumatra and Borneo. Smog, with its associated health hazards, covered hundreds of square kilometres (Figure 1.1), affecting over 70 million inhabitants of Indonesia, Thailand, Malaysia, Singapore and Brunei. In Kuching, Borneo (Malaysia), the air pollution index rose to 839 on a scale where any reading above 100 is considered to be unhealthy and above 300 very dangerous. In Sumatra, the crash of an airbus, with its crew of twelve and all 222 passengers killed, was attributed to the smoke- and particle-filled air, while the collision of a cargo ship with an oil supertanker (and the death of 28 crew) in the Strait of Malacca between Sumatra and peninsular Malaysia was certainly caused by poor visibility from the same source.

In early November, John Vidal reported that the smog had been drifting backwards and forwards across the six countries, in some cases for 20 weeks, and in places was worse than ever.

Singaporeans have seen the moon only once in four months, the Malaysian capital of Kuala Lumpur has fumed for most of the summer, and holidaymakers

at Thai resorts more than 1000 miles from the nearest fires have choked. In total, some 100,000 people across south-east Asia have sought medical help for respiratory problems.

(*Guardian Weekend*, 8 November 1997: 17)

Fires had raged through Indonesia before. During 1982–83, 3.7 million hectares of east Kalimantan were destroyed, but there was less problem with smoke and smog. Some of the rain forests have developed over deep peatlands, which are penetrated by fires that are impossible to put out. This is especially the case in central Kalimantan and the Riau region of Sumatra. Around 1 million hectares of peat is likely to burn underground for many years to come. It is probably this smouldering peat that, in 1997, exacerbated air pollution when the effects combined with dampened-down air convection currents to trap the smoke close to the ground (Pearce, 1998a).

But if things were bad in 1997, the following year saw a further 30 000 square kilometres (an area the size of Belgium) of forest destroyed, the fires lasting from late January to May, when the rains arrived. Almost all of Kutai National Park (eastern Kalimantan) and the Wein River orang-utan sanctuary have been destroyed, as well as

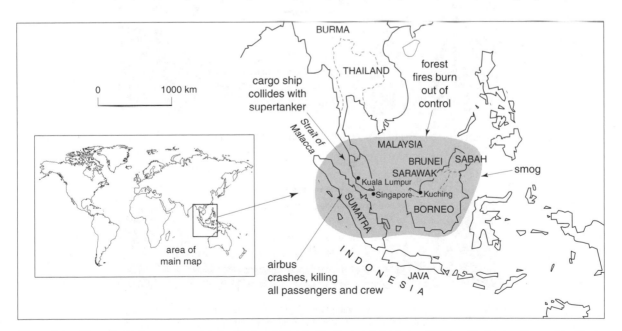

Figure 1.1   The extent of smog associated with forest fires in South-east Asia during 1997, with the locations of incidents mentioned in the text.

unique limestone forest in the north of the island. Most fires this time had apparently spread from illegal burning of ground and scrub vegetation in oil palm plantations (Pearce, 1998b).

At first sight, the fires appear to have been simply a case of human greed and a careless attitude to the environment, but another environmental factor also has to be brought into the story. The *El Niño–Southern Oscillation* is a naturally occurring climatological and oceanographic phenomenon, though one that has really only been studied by scientists for the last quarter of a century. Every few years, the surface of the eastern tropical Pacific Ocean warms up more than usual. This reverses currents and upwelling systems in the ocean (Figure 1.2), with knock-on effects on marine life, for example the death by bleaching of many Indonesian coral reefs as the algae living inside the coral polyps are expelled following rapid changes in water temperature. The warm sea also evaporates more than normal

to create thick clouds, which form in warmer than usual air. With changes in high- and low-pressure areas, atmospheric circulation is modified. Rain-laden clouds shift in direction, bringing unaccustomed precipitation to some regions, failing to deliver – and causing droughts – in others.

Climatologists agree that El Niño events are occurring more frequently; most argue that this is a consequence of global warming, itself a consequence of human activity (see Chapter 4). Recent El Niño disturbances have been in 1972–73, 1976, 1982–83 and the early 1990s. In 1997, El Niño caused the worst drought to have hit South-east Asia for half a century (Figure 1.3), drying out forests and delaying the monsoon rains, which might otherwise have put out the September fires. The drought also badly affected the rice harvest, a problem exacerbated in the northern Philippines and elsewhere by an infestation of rats, which consumed up to 15% of a

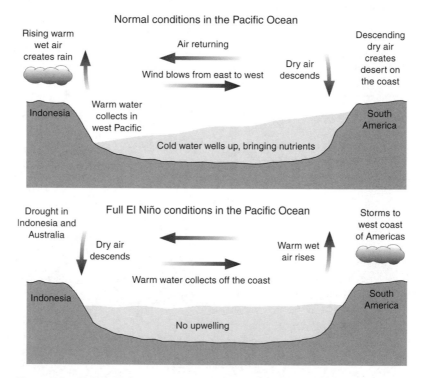

Figure 1.2   El Niño/Southern Oscillation (ENSO). Top: pattern of wind and ocean currents across the equatorial Pacific in a 'normal year'. Bottom: pattern of wind and ocean currents across the equatorial Pacific during an El Niño event.

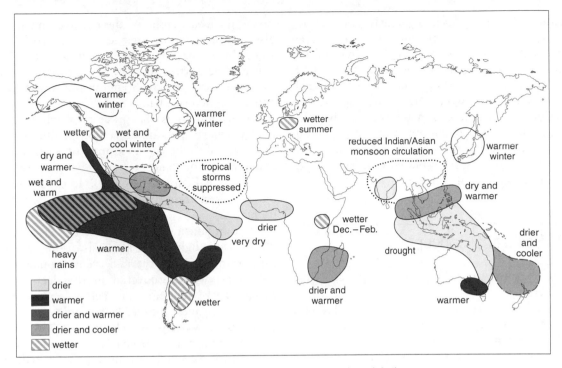

Figure 1.3   Some effects of the 1997 El Niño on global temperature and precipitation.

crop already reduced in yield by about a third (*The Guardian*, 3 March 1998: 12).

The fires in Indonesia reflect, at different scales, the interaction of different systems. A biological system, the rain forest ecosystem, has evolved in a particular way as the living world develops in response to its environment. It provides resources for humans – forestry, plantations and agriculture, which in their exploitation reflect not only a complex economic system but also expose socio-cultural and political systems. Meanwhile, the ocean system interacts with the atmospheric system in such a way as to have a number of consequences, one of which is drought in South-east Asia. The rain forest ecosystem begins to break down as a consequence of exploitation: areas that are not cleared are heavily damaged; other areas are so fragmented that the integrity of the ecosystem functions is compromised, and the system begins to lose its chance of recovery (see Chapter 2).

Indonesia has not been the only part of the world affected by fires triggered, in part, by El Niño. An idea of this is shown by the summary

Table 1.1   Summary of major regional fire events, 1997–98

Sept. 1997	Indonesian fires cause haze from Thailand to northern Australia
Oct. 1997	Fires in Peru, Central Asia, China, Western Australia and East Africa
Nov. 1997	Annual burning in Amazonia 50% above average
Dec. 1997	Bush fires across southern Australia more widespread than usual
Feb. 1998	Borneo fires resume, but with less smoke they are less reported
Mar. 1998	Northern Amazonia now burns
May 1998	Major fires in Canada and Siberia
June 1998	Over 1 million ha burns in Central America and Florida
July 1998	Fire sweeps over an area from Sardinia to Greece
Oct. 1998	Siberia burns again

For updates, see World Wide Web at http://www.gvm.sai.jrc.it/projects/fire/wfw/wfw.html

in Table 1.1. This scenario emphasises how ecological systems interact at different scales, even without discussion of levels below that of the ecosystem. Disturbance becomes so pronounced that irreparable damage is done: the feedback mechanisms that would normally operate in retaining the efficient functioning of the rain forest as an ecosystem simply cannot cope, and in many places the system begins to break down. Such ideas can now be explored in greater depth in terms of ecological concepts.

1.3 Ecological concepts

- The biosphere and the interaction of ecological systems
- Spatial/organisational scale of study: biomes, ecosystems and communities
- Environments and habitats
- Homeostasis and feedback mechanisms

1.3.1 The biosphere and the interaction of ecological systems

As indicated earlier, ecological systems can be viewed at different organisational and spatial scales, which, moreover, change through time. The biosphere represents all the ecosystems of the planet viewed as a whole: all the plants, animals and microorganisms; all the tangible consequences of life on Earth, including the products of decomposition; and all the air, water and soil in which life exists. The term 'biosphere' was invented by the nineteenth-century Austrian geologist Eduard Seuss to describe the 'thin green smear' on the Earth's surface, but it was first examined explicitly and in detail by the Russian Vladimir Vernadsky in 1926.

The biosphere is the arena within which a fraction of the energy from the Sun is captured by green plants, photosynthesised and used by all organisms – the plants themselves for growth and reproduction; animals that feed on plants and are in turn eaten by other animals; and microorganisms inside and outside the bodies of larger life forms but which also live high in the atmosphere,

in the greatest depths of the oceans, and indeed also within the skin of the crust of rocks, for some living bacteria have been found 3.5 km beneath the Earth's surface. The biosphere is also the stage through which energy flows and nutrients are cycled (see Chapter 2).

Photosynthesis is the process by which green plants (those containing chlorophyll), in the presence of light as a source of energy, can convert carbon and water into glucose and oxygen (see Ecology Box 1.4). It occurs where light can penetrate water (even as ice), as well as on land.

Some organisms, however, are associated with places where light is not the basis of life. In 1977, for example, hydrothermal vents (underwater volcanoes) were discovered in the deep ocean. Molten rock wells up from below, and cold sea water seeps into the fresh volcanic rocks and dissolves a variety of chemicals. The water becomes buoyant, is driven back up through the rock and is expelled as a hot (360 °C) hydrogen sulphide-bearing fluid. These features produce ecosystems with communities, including giant tubeworms and bivalve molluscs, which are ultimately dependent on bacteria capable of obtaining energy by oxidising the hydrogen sulphide. The bacteria are producing energy via chemicals, not light: this is called *chemosynthesis*. Chemosynthesis has also recently been found to occur a few hundred metres within crustal rocks, microorganisms again being capable of synthesising organic material from chemicals extracted from the mineral rock.

The atmosphere, too, contains life. Immediately above the surface of the land or water lies a zone where some animals may be found – active fliers such as bats, most birds and many insects, and those passively being transported by the wind, whether brine shrimps colonising saline desert ponds or spiderlings dispersing from their nest. Seeds, pollen and spores are also blown by the wind, a form of transport essential for many plant species: for example, the plumed seeds of the dandelion and the winged seeds of the sycamore enhance the chances of effective dispersal. Some of these aerial organisms, however, can reach considerable heights: spiderlings, for instance, have been observed at altitudes

ECOLOGY BOX 1.4

Photosynthesis, respiration and transpiration

Energy from the Sun enters the biosphere as visible light and is stored in green plants, which use the energy to convert simple inorganic molecules of carbon dioxide and water into complex organic molecules of glucose. This process, called photosynthesis, thus converts radiant energy (i.e. from the Sun) into chemical energy.

This change in the form of the energy is consistent with the first law of thermodynamics, which states that, while energy can neither be created nor destroyed, it can be converted from one form to another. Photosynthesis also obeys the second law of thermodynamics, which states that no transfer of energy is completely efficient, and some energy is always lost as heat during the transfer. In photosynthesis, the heat loss into the surrounding atmosphere is accompanied by the loss of carbon dioxide, water and nitrogenous compounds, which are then recycled within the ecosystem.

The basic formula for photosynthesis is

$$6CO_2 + 6H_2O \xrightarrow{\text{energy}} C_6H_{12}O_6 + 6O_2$$

i.e.   carbon dioxide + water $\xrightarrow{\text{light energy}}$ glucose + oxygen

As well as glucose and the by-product of oxygen, photosynthesis also leads to the production of free amino acids, proteins, fatty acids and fats, vitamins, various pigments and enzymes.

The chemical energy is thus stored as glucose, which in turn may be used to create other storage and structural compounds such as cellulose and starch. The stored energy can be released when the products of photosynthesis are oxidised, a process known as respiration, whose basic formula is:

$$C_6H_{12}O_6 + 6O_2 \longrightarrow 6CO_2 + 6H_2O$$

i.e.   glucose + oxygen $\longrightarrow$ carbon dioxide + water

The carbon dioxide needed for photosynthesis is readily available in the atmosphere. It enters the plant through stomata, which are guard cells on the leaf (occasionally the stem) with a hole (pore) between them which opens to allow the entry of carbon dioxide. The same pores allow the exit of oxygen. They also allow water vapour to escape, a process known as transpiration. This water has been absorbed from the soil by the roots and transported to the leaves via special tubes (xylem vessels).

of around 5000 m, radar has occasionally detected migrating birds at 6000 m, and some pollen grains and fungal spores have been identified at even greater altitudes.

The example of forest fires in South-east Asia shows how the three basic compartments of land, air and sea can interact. A more general way of showing this kind of interaction is by examining throughputs in the global system, for example of mineral nutrients (see Chapter 2), of gaseous elements and of water.

The *hydrological cycle* (see Figure 1.4) represents a major subsystem of the biosphere. Water *evaporates* from the ocean; it condenses onto hygroscopic particles and forms clouds; it falls as precipitation over the seas, lakes and land; on land it may infiltrate soil and rock to form groundwater reservoirs, or subsurface flow may take it into rivers or lakes; overland flow also collects to form lakes and rivers, which eventually take the water back to the sea, and the cycle continues (see Figure 1.4). Meanwhile, water is being taken up by plants and is being directly returned to the atmosphere as water loss through *transpiration* (see Ecology Box 1.4). The combination of direct evaporation and indirect

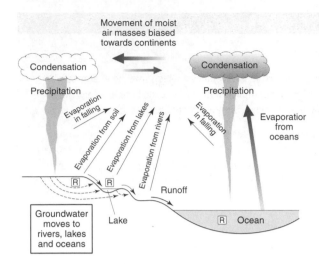

Figure 1.4 The hydrological cycle, without vegetation (from Colinvaux, 1993). ℝ = reservoir.

transpiration from plants is called *evapotranspiration*. Animals also use water and return it in one way or another to the system, for example through urine, sweat and decomposition. Just as the living world depends on water, so too it influences how the water moves through the hydrological cycle (see Ecology Box 1.5).

1.3.2 Global climate and biomes

Climatic variations reflect the orbit of the Earth around the Sun, the tilt of the Earth's axis, relationships between land and major water bodies, and – recently – the impact of human activities, which have led to the enhanced greenhouse effect and depletion of the ozone layer. Climatic variations lead to global-scale variations in temperature, precipitation (form, amount and seasonality) and light (including differences in day length). The Sun provides light and heat to the Earth. Rotation around a tilted axis gives both night and day and the seasonality found even at the equator but which gets more pronounced as one moves polewards. Energy from the Sun has more atmosphere to pass through before it reaches the Earth's atmosphere at higher latitudes, where it falls obliquely on the surface and, again, energy is dissipated more than at lower latitudes (Figure 1.5). Thus,

per unit of time, light and heat reaching the surface varies with latitude; indeed, the equator receives more or less twice as much energy as the Arctic or Antarctic (Woodward, 1987).

On top of this pattern is imposed seasonality resulting from the Earth's solar orbit. The apparent movement of the Sun, reaching its 'overhead' position at the Tropic of Cancer (23°30'N) at the Northern Hemisphere's summer solstice, and the Tropic of Capricorn (23°30'S) at the winter solstice, means that in theory the equatorial and tropical regions would show very little seasonality, but in practice this is not so: even minor shifts in the trade winds or the monsoons affect rainfall patterns, and clouds affect temperatures. At the poles, seasonality is so pronounced that the Sun never sets in summer (and total daily irradiance is higher than at the Equator, which receives half the amount of daylight), while in midwinter there is no daylight at all.

Differences in seasonality in terms of day length, incident radiation, temperature and precipitation lead to different climatic regimes, which in turn lead to different vegetation types. At a global scale, therefore, there are close similarities between maps of climate and maps of natural or potential vegetation, and indeed also with maps of major soil types (Figures 1.6–1.8). A reasonable correlation is evident in Eurasia, for example, between cool continental and transitional temperate climates, boreal (coniferous forest) and spodosols (podzolised soils). Similarly, as one would expect, dry (arid) climates, hot deserts and aridosols are closely associated.

Generalised relationships between vegetation types and climatic parameters are shown in Figures 1.9 and 1.10. As a very general rule, precipitation will tend to control vegetation form (for example, whether forest, shrubland or grassland predominates) while temperature will suggest a particular vegetation type (for instance, given an appropriate amount of precipitation for forest, whether rain forest, temperate deciduous forest or coniferous forest prevails). But if climate controls vegetation, so too does vegetation control aspects of energy (such as through heat exchange), even at regional and global scales (Hayden, 1998).

Particular vegetation types can be classified together, and they will contain characteristic

ECOLOGY BOX 1.5

The hydrological cycle at different scales of study

Although water moves between oceans, lakes, glaciers and groundwater, the volume actually moving at any point is low. It has been estimated that the atmosphere and rivers, where water movement is greatest, together only account for 0.0011% of the water of the biosphere (see table). The rest is in what are appropriately called 'sinks' - the oceans themselves, glaciers and deep subterranean reservoirs.

Estimated water budget for the biosphere

Compartment	Estimated water volume ($\times 10^6$ km^3)	Notional % age total
World oceans	1322.0	97.21
Glacier ice	29.2	2.15
Groundwater	8.4	0.62
Freshwater lakes	0.125	0.009
Salt lakes and inland seas	0.104	0.008
Soil water	0.067	0.005
Atmosphere	0.013	0.001
Rivers and streams	0.001	0.0001

after Strahler, 1969

When it falls onto soil, some water is retained in the soil's pore spaces, and some is absorbed onto minerals, particularly onto clays. The picture is complicated by the presence of living material, especially plants. Plants can intercept precipitation, amending the speed and rate at which it reaches the ground, and altering its chemistry as it trickles down as leaf-flow or stem-flow, losing and gaining minerals as it does so. Plants take up water from the soil – water that will provide nutrients in solution and turgidity for the plant cells. Transpiration rates affect the return of water to the atmosphere.

The amount of water present will reflect a balance between the amount and rate of water input and the amount and rate of water loss. Whether there is a net gain, a net loss or a steady state within the system depends not only on these inputs and outputs but also upon the nature of the system itself (for example whether rain forest or rain forest cleared for pasture), and crucially also on the temporal and spatial scale of study.

Water entering a mineral soil will contain dissolved nutrients that have been acquired from the atmosphere and from plant surfaces. Once in the soil, water acquires further nutrients from the mineral particles and from living and decomposing organic matter. Soil water is therefore a nutrient reservoir, but the extent of this reservoir depends on the nutrient-retaining abilities of the soil and its components (for example roots which pump nutrients into the body of the plant).

Plants therefore affect this part of the hydrological cycle through transpiration, water uptake by roots, and the presence of dead and decaying tissue. These processes work in different ways and are of different degrees of significance in different habitats in different biomes.

communities, not of the same species but often with similar growth forms and similar interactions: this is true of the animal, microbial and soil components as well as the above-ground vegetation. These are the *biomes*. Major terrestrial biomes, some key characteristics, and relationships with climate and other environmental factors are shown in Ecology Box 1.6. It must be stressed that biomes are conceptual features, convenient abstractions for ecologists to study the

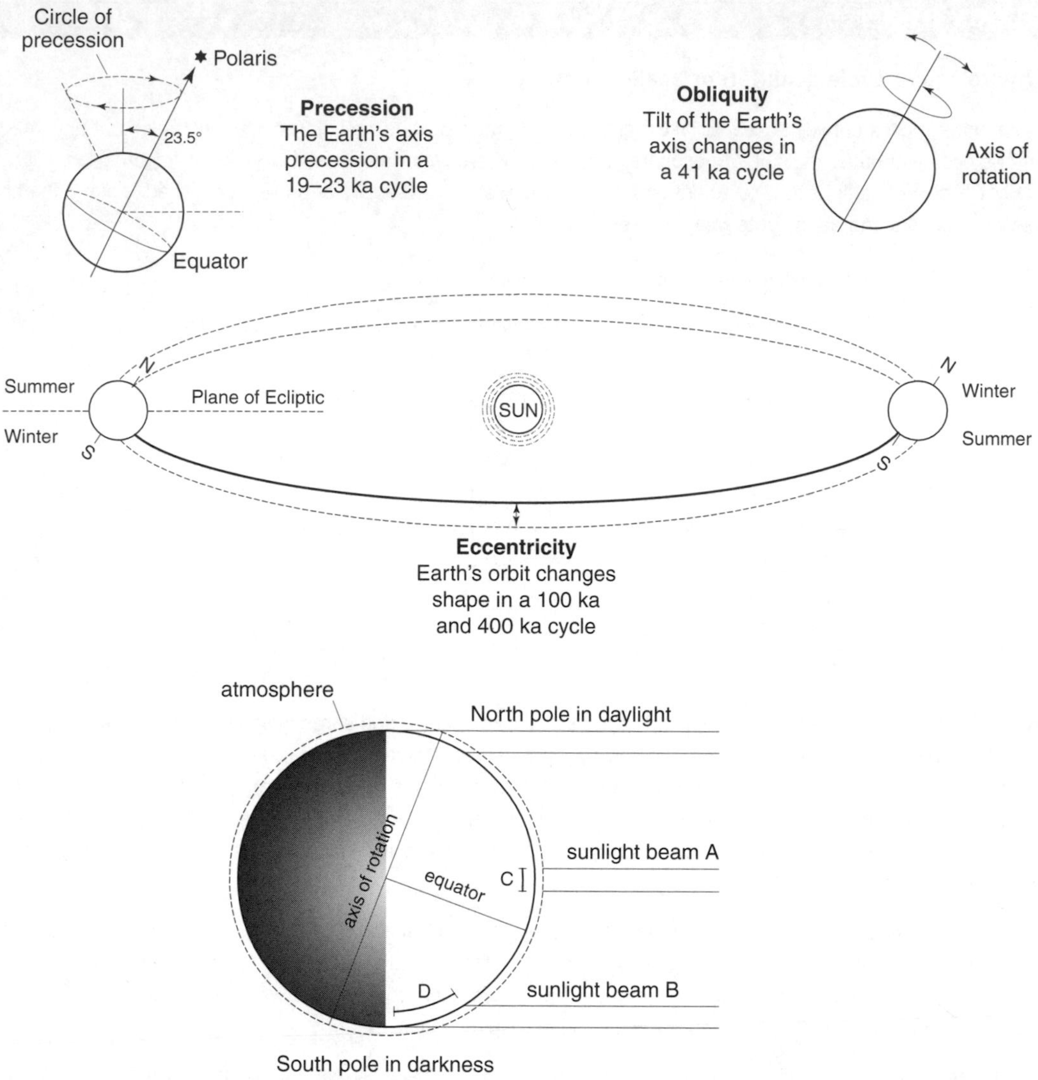

Figure 1.5 Orbital factors affecting the amount of solar radiation reaching the Earth's surface (top); differences between the poles and the Equator in terms of daylight and energy from the Sun (bottom).

world. There are no relationships between examples of the same biome: they simply have generally similar environmental and biotic characteristics.

These global-scale biomes, in which climate, soil, vegetation and animal communities more or less coincide, represent generalisations as well as convenient abstractions: they mask heterogeneities that become evident at smaller scales of study. Biomes, too, may be thought of as representing zones of natural vegetation, and some writers have referred to the essentially climatically controlled vegetation types as zonal vegetation. Within these zonal forms are 'azonal' vegetation types, with their own soil types and animal communities. Here the controlling factors are not climatic: salt marsh and heathland are examples (the latter being more complicated since in many places their origins and maintenance often rely on human activity), and these are discussed later as ecosystems, which is the more appropriate scale of study.

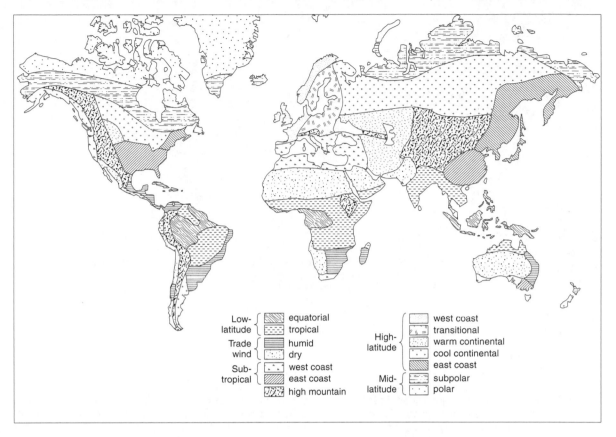

Figure 1.6   Global distribution of climate zones. The map shows a simplified distribution of climate types (after Figure 15.2 in Dury, G.H. (1981) *Environmental Systems*. Heinemann, London).

Biomes rarely have sharp boundaries but instead often merge into one another. In West Africa, for example, different kinds of savanna reflect increasing amounts and reliability of rainfall and merge with each other, more and more trees being found as one moves from the dry Sahel just south of the Sahara to the moister, tree-rich Guinea savanna north of the tropical moist forest. Similarly, there are few locations where a sharp forest–savanna boundary exists naturally, a pronounced boundary more commonly reflecting human activity in clearing the forest. Transitional border zones between biomes or distinct vegetation communities are called *ecotones*, and these often contain samples of species found in the adjacent part of the biome, together with some species unique to that ecotone. Ecotones are therefore often very species-rich areas.

Attempts to apply the concept of the biome to aquatic systems have also been rather unsatisfactory because again these are azonal systems, for example various coastal zones and coral reefs, better suited to study as ecosystems. Mountain areas are also azonal, since it is their topography that effects the climate, which in turn influences the vegetation. Latitudinal zonation of vegetation types is in many ways echoed by altitudinal zonation, although there are important differences in both the environmental controls and how these influence plant communities.

1.3.3 Ecosystems, communities, environments and habitats

It has already been suggested that the ecosystem represents an order of systems organisation below

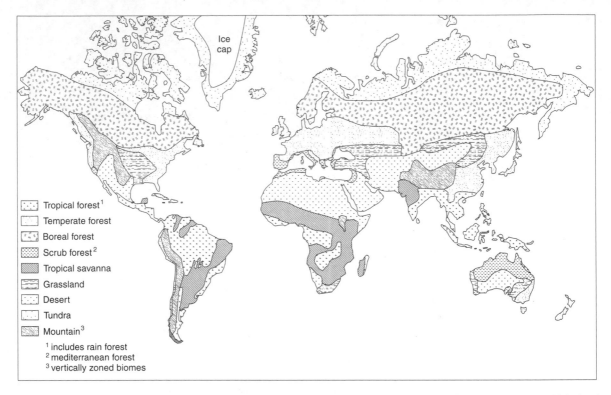

Ice
cap

Tropical forest[1]
Temperate forest
Boreal forest
Scrub forest[2]
Tropical savanna
Grassland
Desert
Tundra
Mountain[3]

[1] includes rain forest
[2] mediterranean forest
[3] vertically zoned biomes

Figure 1.7 Distribution of the major biomes. This simplified map shows the global distribution of terrestrial biomes, which closely reflects the distribution of the world's climatic zones (after Figure 4.8 in Marsh, W.M. and Grossa, J.M. (1996) *Environmental Geography: Science, Land Use and Earth Systems*. John Wiley & Sons, New York).

that of the biosphere, and that a collection of similar ecosystems – at regional and global scales of study – makes up the conceptual notion of a biome. The word 'ecosystem' was coined in 1935 by one of the founders of British ecology, Sir Arthur Tansley, to mean the whole community of organisms *and* their environment taken as a single functioning unit. *Communities* are interacting components belonging to the living world. Communities exist in *habitats*, which are the areas where organisms live, defined in terms of space and the environmental characteristics of that space.

The *environment* of an organism relates to those features which are operationally significant to that organism during part or all of its existence: those physical, chemical and biological features, in other words, which the organism needs or at least uses in order to survive. The environment thus includes abiotic characteristics such as atmospheric gases, temperature (ranges and changes), fire and wind, and components

such as mineral nutrients and water. It also includes food, both in itself and in terms of required nutrients. It includes the physical availability of places to rest, sleep, hide and reproduce. And it follows that it also includes other organisms, of the same species (for example the social environment regarding group behaviour and reproduction) and of other species (as grazers, predators, prey, parasites and symbionts).

There is no such thing as a homogeneous environment. Even in the laboratory, a test-tube wall possesses characteristics (and organism responses) that are different from the rest of the test-tube medium. Environmental heterogeneity depends on the scale of study and the size of the organism: a leaf may be the food and living quarters of a leaf-mining insect, but it is only a small part of a meal for an elephant. Environments contain within themselves gradients of conditions in space and time, and gradients of the resources needed for each member of the community. And the exis-

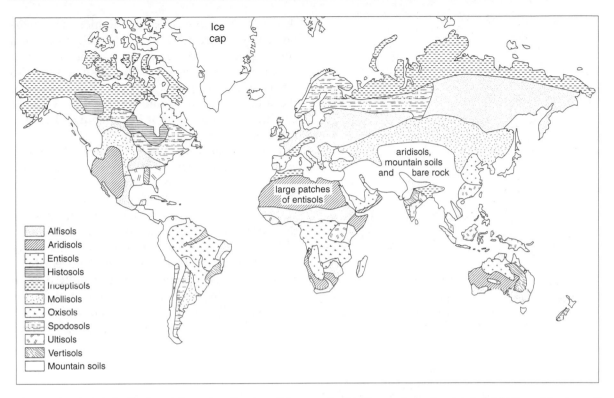

Figure 1.8 Global distribution of the main soil orders. This generalised soil map shows the global distribution of the ten soil orders (after Figure 20.8 in Dury, G.H. (1981) *Environmental Systems*. Heinemann, London).

tence of one individual immediately diversifies the environment for other organisms of the same or different species.

An organism therefore cannot exist in isolation. It exists in an environment that is the result of the complex interactions between biotic and abiotic components (Ecology Box 1.7). Environmental factors may change through time and will certainly do so in a cyclical manner following diurnal, lunar and seasonal changes. Environmental factors also generally change in relevance and importance as an organism grows, develops and reproduces. A seed, for example, can lie dormant until an appropriate environmental trigger, such as a change in temperature or light, initiates germination. The germinating seedling may require particularities of temperature, water and nutrients that are different from those of the adult plant, which in turn may have different requirements in its reproductive and non-reproductive states. Also, perennial plants often have to withstand seasonally stressful conditions, for

instance summer drought or winter cold, and will respond to different environmental characteristics in different ways. Similarly an embryo responds to a different environment in the egg or womb compared with the newly born offspring, with the developing young, and with the adult. Some animal groups, indeed, have pre-adult environments completely different to the adult one: amphibians, for example, and insects such as dragonflies, stoneflies and mayflies have larval forms which are aquatic, before metamorphosing into the terrestrial adult stage. Even in entirely terrestrial animals, the adult may differ radically in form and requirements from the pre-adult, for instance nectar-sipping butterflies contrasting with their leaf-eating caterpillars.

The extent to which an organism can survive, develop and reproduce in its environment, and its tolerance of (or requirements for) particular environmental conditions, will determine its status and distribution both within particular habitats and, together with other factors such as

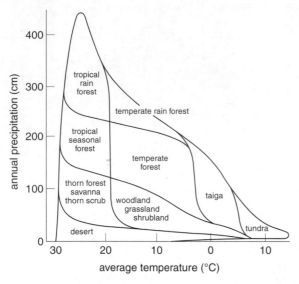

Figure 1.9 Pattern of world biome types in relation to mean annual precipitation and mean annual temperature (from Whittaker, 1975).

dispersal ability, its global distribution. The environmental requirements of a single organism, or a single species, are complex enough; since that organism is part of a broader community, with all its interlocking relationships, it follows that the study of the environmental relations within a community (and between communities) becomes very complex indeed.

These features may be exemplified by briefly examining the nature of tropical rain forest ecosystems. The warm, moist climatic conditions have already been mentioned. Soils are generally rich in organic matter at and close to the surface, a consequence of the high amounts of leaves, branches and, from time to time, trees themselves falling to the ground. This leaf litter and woody detritus, however, is rapidly decomposed by a huge microbial community in the soil, especially fungi and bacteria. This in turn releases nutrients for uptake by plants. The high

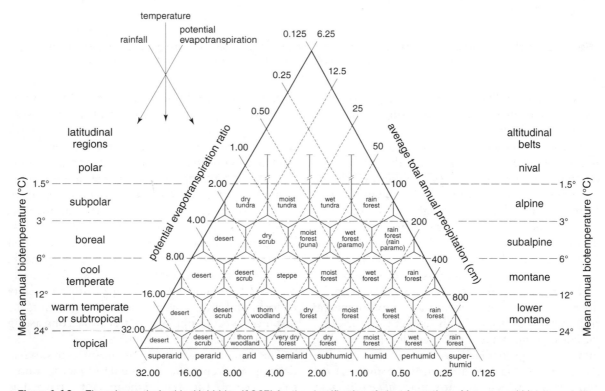

Figure 1.10 The scheme devised by Holdridge (1967) for the classification of plant formations. Mean annual biotemperature is calculated from monthly mean temperatures after converting means below freezing to 0 °C. The potential evapotranspiration ratio is the potential evapotranspiration divided by the precipitation, the ratio increasing from humid regions to arid ones.

ECOLOGY BOX 1.6

Major biomes

Biome	Climate and other environmental controls	Soils and other characteristics	Vegetation
Polar desert/high mountains	Freezing ground temperatures. Polar regions have precipitation (predominantly snow) of under 250 mm p.a. High mountains vary according to latitude, e.g. >3000 mm in Himalayas. Polar light alters according to season, mountain light according to aspect.	No soil. Rock, ice (including glacial) and snow.	Ice algae immediately under glacial ice. Lichens on rock surfaces and occasional vascular plants in cracks in rock.
Tundra	Freezing winter temperatures, short growing season with above-freezing temperatures, though rarely >10°C.	Soils frequently shallow and poorly drained. Permafrost (permanently frozen subsoil layer). Surface soil unfreezes in summer, often resulting in wet, boggy conditions.	Variable, reflecting different lengths of growing season, summer temperatures and precipitation. Slowly growing perennials, including mosses and lichens, take advantage of the short growing season. Treeless, although dwarf birch (*Betula nana*) and creeping willow (*Salix repens*) may occur. Sedges (*Carex*) are common.
Coniferous forest (Other names are: (1) boreal forest – 'boreal' is Greek for northern, but patches of coniferous forest do occur in the Southern Hemisphere; (2) Taiga – Russian. NB: different kinds of coniferous forest are found in other climates, e.g. in the US South-east).	Freezing winter temperatures but summer temperatures reach around 20°C. Longer growing season than tundra. Low winter precipitation (as snow), wetter summers.	Variable drainage. Often on free-draining, sandy or gravel soils, e.g. podzols, where mineral nutrients are leached through the soil and redeposited lower down, frequently creating an impermeable iron pan. Peats are also common. Gleying may be present, where waterlogging occurs above clay. Permafrost is present in northern reaches. Burn–regeneration cycles are important.	Dominated by coniferous trees, especially the evergreen pines (*Pinus*), spruces (*Picea*) and firs (*Abies*) or the deciduous larches (*Larix*), often with little understorey vegetation, although large tracts may have bog or heath vegetation. The evergreen habit allows leaf flush immediately spring temperatures are suitable. Needle leaves reduce transpirational water loss. Cones are wind-pollinated. Sloping branches reduce risk of breakage from weight of snow. A few broadleaved trees may occur, e.g. birches (*Betula*), willows (*Salix*) and poplars (*Populus*).

ECOLOGY BOX 1.6 (cont)

Biome	Climate and other environmental controls	Soils and other characteristics	Vegetation
Temperate deciduous forest	Cool or cold (continental) winters, warm summers, long growing season. Oceanic climates have year-round rain with a winter maximum; continental areas have summer maximum rainfall.	A variety of soils, ranging from free-draining brown earths through sandy podzols, which may have iron-pan impedance to drainage, to soils with waterlogged gley horizons.	Broadleaved deciduous forests characterised by such trees as oaks (*Quercus*), beech (*Fagus*), ash (*Fraxinus*), lime (*Tilia*), elm (*Ulmus*), hazel (*Corylus*) and hickory (*Carya*). Some broadleaved evergreens are found, e.g. holly (*Ilex*). Trees are predominantly wind-pollinated. Beech-dominated woodlands tend to have poorly developed understoreys, but other dominant trees or mixtures may possess species-rich shrub, field and ground layers.
Temperate evergreen forest	The wetter parts of mediterranean climate regions, with warm, moist winters and hot, dry summers.	Lightly leached dry forest soils.	Trees have evergreen broad leaves, which are often small, waxy and tough to minimise transpirational water loss and to reduce risks of herbivory.
Temperate rain forest	Cool maritime climates with abundant rainfall, although generally with a summer maximum. Low cloud and fog add moisture. Little temperature variation.	Variable, but often deep brown earth types.	Tall trees, e.g. the redwoods (*Sequoia*) of the Pacific North-west, mountain ash (*Eucalyptus regnans*) in Australia, and *Podocarpus* in New Zealand.
Tropical rain forest	More or less constantly warm with high annual rainfall and no dry season.	Shallow minero-trophic soils with rapid turnover of nutrients because of microbial decomposers (especially fungi and bacteria) and detritivores (especially ants and termites). Thus despite high litter input these are inherently nutrient-poor soils.	Canopy develops at ≥ 25 m, with emergents above this. Broadleaved evergreen trees often show synchronised flowering (for animal pollination), fruiting (for animal dispersal) and leaf shedding. High taxonomic diversity, though Dipterocarpaceae are characteristic of South-east Asia and Fabaceae/Mimosaceae of Latin America. Also palms, tree ferns, etc. Characteristic growth forms include buttress roots (support in shallow soils), drip tips on

ECOLOGY BOX 1.6 (cont)

Biome	Climate and other environmental controls	Soils and other characteristics	Vegetation
			leaves (rapid rain runoff to maximise opportunities for photosynthesis) and cauliflory (flowers/fruit growing directly on trunk/branch). Climbers, stranglers and epiphytes (plants growing directly on other plants, including orchids and bromeliads) are common. Aerial roots absorb nutrients from moist air. Small leaves on emergent trees reduce water loss; larger leaves in understorey cope with low light levels.
Tropical seasonal forest	Humid and constantly warm, high annual rainfall but with a pronounced dry season, e.g. as monsoonal rains withdraw.	Similar to tropical rain forest but with less litter fall and less rapid nutrient turnover.	Not as species-rich as tropical rain forest. Tree species often lose their leaves during the dry season, which causes a much more 'pulsed' phenology (seasonality of life-cycle events) than with rain forest.
Savanna	Year-round warm tropical temperatures. Less annual rainfall than tropical forest regions, with a pronounced dry season. Some savannas, however, apparently occur as a result of burning rather than through climatic controls.	Red and (in drier areas) black savanna soils and tropical red earths. Periodic fires burn off accumulated litter. Control of the vegetation types may be climatic or result from burning, the latter occurring naturally from lightning or as a result of human activity, especially where forest has been cleared for agriculture or pasture and subsequently abandoned. In the latter case, the forest–savanna boundary becomes sharp.	Essentially grassland, dominated by grasses (Poaceae) or sedges (Cyperaceae), but with tree growth possible, e.g. baobab (*Adansonia digitata*) and acacias in Africa, palms (Arecaceae) in Latin America and 'grass trees' (*Xanthorrhoea*) in Australia, which all have thick bark to withstand fire. Trees also tend to have small leaves and frequently have flat-topped ('umbrella') canopies, possibly a trade-off between avoiding mammalian browsers and reducing maintenance costs of excessive height in a seasonally stressed environment. The less the rainfall and the longer the dry season the fewer the trees, so true grassland may merge through areas with scattered trees to regions of wooded savanna.

ECOLOGY BOX 1.6 (cont)

Biome	Climate and other environmental controls	Soils and other characteristics	Vegetation
Temperate grassland (North America: prairie; Eurasia: steppe; Argentina: pampas; South Africa: veld)	Continental climate with cold winters, hot summers. Moderate rainfall (200–750 mm), with dry season. (Higher rains/shorter dry season allows forest; lower rains/longer dry season leads to semi-desert).	Prairie soils (grassland pedalfers, with leaching predominating over upward movement of soil water) in moister conditions merging through deep organic-rich black earths (Russian: chernozems), into chestnut and light brown prairie soils. Fire (including that from human activity) may maintain grassland, e.g. in parts of the prairies (anthropogenic pyroclimaxes), and often leads to pronounced artificial vegetation boundaries, in wetter parts, with forest. At the drier margins, grassland merges into semi-desert. Treeless contrast with tropical savanna may reflect influence of winter cold.	Treeless perennial grassland, though flowering broadleaved herbs (forbs) are often as important as grasses. Smaller broadleaves may flower in early spring (before grasses overgrow them), larger ones in late summer (when grasses die down) but general sequential flowering of herbs allows 'species packing', maximising insect pollination while minimising competition for pollinators. Grasses are wind-pollinated. In North America, tall-grass prairie (grasses 1–1.5 m height) is found in wetter conditions, with bunch grasses (e.g. common stipa, *Stipa spartea*) mixed with sward species (e.g. *Andropogon scoparius*, *Bouteloua curtipendula*). Moving through mixed prairie as conditions get drier, mid-height grasses are found (e.g. *Stipa comata*, *Agropyron smithii*) with some sward species (e.g. blue grama, *Bouteloua gracilis*; buffalo grass, *Buchloe dactyloides*). Short-grass prairie is found in the driest parts of this zone. Bunch grasses become more prominent elements as conditions get drier. Similar trends but with different genera and species are evident in Russian steppe.

ECOLOGY BOX 1.6 (cont)

Biome	Climate and other environmental controls	Soils and other characteristics	Vegetation
Temperate scrubland or broadleaved sclerophyll vegetation (California: chaparral; Chile: matorral; Australia: mallee; Mediterranean: maquis + garrigue; South Africa: fynbos)	Mediterranean climates with warm or cool moist winters and hot, dry summers, during which fire is common.	Pale, greyish-brown or grey soils poor in organic matter. Upward movement of soil water tends to predominate over leaching (pedocal or pedocal-like). Taller vegetation (e.g. maquis) on calcareous substrates, scrubbier vegetation (eg. garrigue) on sandy ones.	Vegetation grows during the winter rains and tolerates hot, dry summer conditions. In Mediterranean Europe, maquis – evergreen trees (e.g. holm oak, *Quercus ilex*; cork oak, *Q. ilex*, Aleppo pine, *Pinus halepensis*) and dense tall scrub (e.g. myrtle, *Myrtus communis*; heaths, *Erica*), and garrigue – low scrub (e.g. juniper, *Juniperus communis*; lavender, *Lavendula*), merging into temperate evergreen forest in wetter areas, (semi)desert in drier ones (e.g. Israel). Woody plants have thick, leathery leaves (sclerophylly), often waxy or hairy (pubescent). Chaparral includes sclerophyllous woodland, and Cape fynbos has a similar vegetation form (e.g. with species of *Protea* and *Leucadendron*). Chilean matorral is also characterised by maquis analogues, with *Quillaja saponaria*, *Kageneckia oblonga* and *Rhus caustica* almost universal. The belt of mallee scrub extends along the dry side of the forests of south-west and south-east Australia and is characterised by many *Eucalyptus* species 2–3 m in height. Hot summers possibly prevent trees from dominating (a physical constraint), while grasses are out-competed by the taller scrub, especially during winter growth (an ecological control): the combination of these mechanisms may lead to this particular lifeform.

ECOLOGY BOX 1.6 (cont)

Biome	Climate and other environmental controls	Soils and other characteristics	Vegetation
Hot desert and semi-desert	Absence of clouds means high irradiance and high temperatures during the day, massive radiation heat loss and low temperatures at night. Very low rainfall (extremely arid <60–100 mm p.a., arid 100–250 mm p.a., semi-arid 250–500 mm p.a.), with decreasing predictability (occurrence, amount, seasonality) leading to more pronounced desert conditions. Rain often falls as discrete storm events. Warm and cool semi-deserts are found where there are less temperature extremes but where rainfall remains low and unreliable.	Hot deserts are not just dunes of sand and plains of barren rock but also include areas where a thin organic layer may form, or where water may collect during the rains (pools, wadis) or permanently (oases).	There is enough moisture to support specially adapted plant species, including long-lived succulent perennials (storing water in leaves, stem or root), resurrection plants (which die down to a non-metabolic state, revived with moisture), geophytes (persisting underground as bulbs or corms), or ephemerals (persisting through seeds then using rapid germination, growth, flowering and seeding – 20–30 days in total – immediately after rains). Growth forms reduce stress of temperature and drought, e.g. cacti (fleshy body stores water, green photosynthetic stem, needle leaves reduce transpirational water loss and discourage browsing, hairs encourage cooling wind, fluting does the same and channels moisture to the roots, orientation of leaf pads (cladodes) maximises photosythesis at dawn and dusk but minimises heat stress at noon). Other succulents (e.g euphorbias, aloes) store water in leaves, have sunken stomata (reduces water loss), and salt excretion (white leaf surface alters albedo, reflecting sunlight). In all perennials, long roots tap groundwater, and shallow subsurface spreading 'rain roots' maximise water uptake following rain. Shrubs are spaced out in a regular pattern to allow shallow roots to maximise water uptake. Many species use the C_4 photosynthetic pathway or crassulacean acid metabolism (see Chapter 4) to optimise carbon uptake, minimise water loss.

ECOLOGY BOX 1.7

The organism and its ecological context

The autecology of an organism addresses interactions with its environment – what it needs in order to live, feed and breed. This includes examination of any environmental constraints on the organism, together with ecological aspects of the organism's shape and behaviour. A collection of individuals is a population, the study of which is often referred to as demography, which includes examination of age and sex structure, birth and death rates and density. The population level is also appropriate for studying social relationships within the group (intraspecific interaction), and dispersal and migration. Setting an individual or population into the context of other living components of the environment leads into community-level studies, often called synecology; these are interspecific interactions, and the community is sometimes known as the biocoenosis. By adding the abiotic components of the environment we reach the ecosystem level, or biogeocoenosis.

For example:

Organism: Malayan pangolin, *Manis javanica* (order: Pholidota; family: Manidae)
(The name pangolin comes from the Malayan 'peng-golin', meaning the roller, from its habit of rolling into a ball as a means of defence).

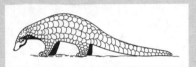

Autecology: Nocturnal, sticky long-tongued ant- and especially termite-eating mammal covered, apart from its underside, by horny body scales (with basal hair) which are periodically shed and replaced. Body is under 1 m in length, elongated with a stout tail. Powerful limbs with claws (used to dig out termite nests), protected by walking on the outer edges of the front feet with claws tucked inwards, leading to a shuffling gait, but speeds of 4 km/hour achieved by rearing up and running on hindlegs using the tail as a counterbalance. Thick lids protect eyes from termite bites, and for the same reason special muscles close nostrils during feeding, and ears are sunken. Usually terrestrial, but can climb. Solitary, but scent (faeces, urine marking, anal gland secretion) communicates dominance and sexual status within the home range. Young born underground with soft scales; first carried outside on the mother's tail at 2–4 weeks old.

Demography: Limited intraspecific interaction. Longevity unknown. Sexually mature at 2 years old. Births usually November–March. Usually one young, occasionally two or three, each year.

Community: Little interaction with other animals. Dominates ground termite-eating community. By curling into a ball its scales provide protection against predators.

Ecosystem: Grasslands, subtropical thorn forest, rain forest and barren hill areas.

Distribution   Malesia (Malaysian and Indonesian region); see map.

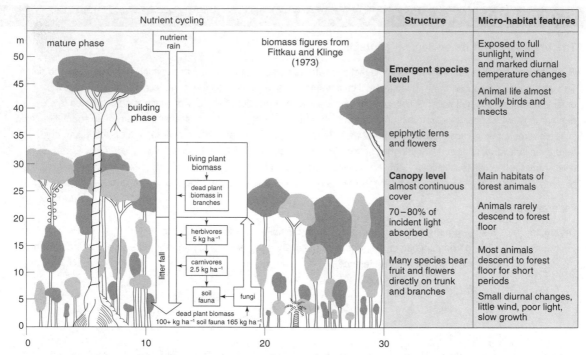

Figure 1.11   Tropical lowland evergreen rain forest, showing structure, microhabitat features and nutrient cycling. A strangler vine, rooted in the ground, has entwined the emergent tree on the left, which also has an epiphytic plant growing in the crown, its air roots extracting moisture directly from the damp atmosphere.

species diversity of rain forests has also already been noted. Trees germinate in treefall gaps to grow through a building phase to mature specimens at a height of 25–30 m, with some emergent species pushing further towards the sunlight. Vines grow from the ground, encircling the trees and sometimes effectively strangling them. Epiphytes (plants growing *on* other living plants), parasitic plants (growing *from* and using nutrient material from other living plants) and saprophytes (growing on dead plants) are frequent (Figure 1.11).

The plants are fed on by grazing animals, which in turn often become prey. The grazers include many specialist feeders, for example wood-eating termites, but many are more generalist and indeed may be omnivorous. To take some examples from South-east Asian mammals, the stump-tailed macaque (a large monkey), found in Indo-Malaysia, feeds on the leaves, fruit and roots of many species, while the proboscis monkey of Borneo lives off leaves, flowers, fruit and shoots of a variety of plants

found along river banks and in mangrove forest. The siamang, largest of the gibbons, favours figs, but it takes other fruit, together with flowers, leaves and shoots, as well as insects and occasionally birds' eggs. Sun bears eat fruit, honey and coconut palm, and prey on jungle fowl, small rodents, and insect adults and larvae. Many of these species are opportunist, grabbing what they can. Generalist mammalian predators in South-east Asia include large cats such as tigers and leopards, hunting dogs such as the dhole, and members of the weasel family, as well as specialist consumers such as the termite-eating pangolin (see Ecology Box 1.7). Fruit bats, including the flying foxes, pollinate many plants and disperse their seeds. And as with mammals, so too with other animal groups – none isolated; all interconnected in some way. Competition is reduced by partitioning the food and habitat resources, for example by occupying different parts of the forest and by eating at different times of the day (Figure 1.12).

Rain forest communities are therefore complex

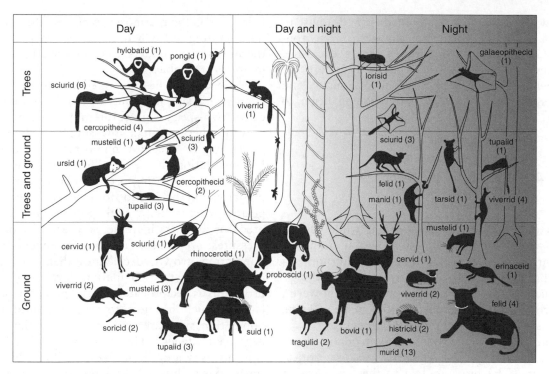

	Day	Day and night	Night
Trees	hylobatid (1), pongid (1), sciurid (6), cercopithecid (4)	viverrid (1)	galaeopithecid (1), lorisid (1)
Trees and ground	mustelid (1), sciurid (3), ursid (1), cercopithecid (2), tupaiid (3)		sciurid (3), felid (1), manid (1), tarsid (1), tupaiid (1), viverrid (4), mustelid (1)
Ground	cervid (1), sciurid (1), rhinocerotid (1), viverrid (2), mustelid (3), soricid (2), tupaiid (3), suid (1)	proboscid (1), tragulid (2)	cervid (1), viverrid (2), bovid (1), histricid (2), murid (13), erinaceid (1), felid (4)

Figure 1.12   Vertical distribution and activity period of mammals (excluding bats) in lowland rain forest in Sabah, Malaysia (after MacKinnon, 1972). Hylobatids belong to the gibbon family and include the siamang; cercopithecids are Old World monkeys, including macaques; pongids are great apes, here represented by the orang-utan; sciurids are squirrels, including flying foxes; viverrids are mongooses; lorisids are lorises; galaeopithecids are flying lemurs (restricted to Malesia); ursids are bears; mustelids belong to the weasel family, tupaiids are tree shrews; felids are members of the cat family; manids are pangolins; tarsiids are tarsiers (again limited to this region); cervids are deer; soricids are shrews; rhinocerotids are rhinoceroses; suids are pigs; proboscids include the elephants; histricids are porcupines; murids belong to the mouse family; and erinaceids belong to the hedgehog family, here represented by a moonrat.

interacting components within the ecosystem, whether at the scale of the whole forest or in microhabitats such as tree holes, which fill with water and contain both microorganisms and larval forms of larger animals such as mosquitoes and tree frogs.

Rain forests tend to be stable habitats, yet they are often stressed. Water is generally available, but the demand for water is so great that at times there may actually be a water deficit. Most nutrients in the rain forest are stored in the plants themselves, and relatively small amounts are stored in the soil. Demand for nutrients is high and turnover of nutrients is rapid, so nutrient stress is also not uncommon. Often it is a single essential nutrient that, because of its marginal

availability, becomes potentially limiting to plant growth, and thus to the success of the whole ecosystem. In Sabah, Malaysia, for example, Nykvist (1997) found that calcium in particular was found in very low concentrations in the soil. This became particularly significant after clear-felling, which led to 19% of the available calcium disappearing, meaning that sustainable forestry was impossible without fertilisation. Logging represents a major disturbance of the rain forest equilibrium, as well as initiating nutrient stress and, by opening out the forest, exposing the system to the microclimatic stresses of increased temperature and insolation.

The inherent stability of ecosystems derives from a series of feedback mechanisms which allow the system to accommodate and adjust to most naturally occurring changes in environmental conditions. If perturbation is excessive, however, these feedback mechanisms are no longer able to exercise this kind of control, and the system's structure and functioning begin to alter.

1.3.4 Homeostasis and feedback mechanisms

It is important to emphasise that while ecosystems have structures, functions and an ability to maintain a state of dynamic equilibrium via feedback mechanisms, they are not 'living things' as such: ecosystems possess properties, however, which allow the sustained participation of living things as inherent components of them.

The ability of ecosystems to maintain themselves through self-regulation is a critical property. The term applied to the tendency for ecosystems (and systems generally) to resist changes and to remain in (or return to) a state of equilibrium is *homeostasis*. Ideas from cybernetics (the science of controls) are useful in providing a way of looking at mechanisms of homeostasis. If an ecosystem is viewed as a control system, then control depends on feedback, which occurs when output (or part of it) feeds back as input. When this feedback is positive it accentuates or accelerates the output, much as in banking, where compound interest is generated by the principal sum of money but in turn becomes part of the principal. This *positive feedback*, being 'deviation accelerating', is necessary for an organism's growth, but is not by itself beneficial to equilibrium at the ecosystem level. To achieve homeostasis there must also be *negative feedback*, or 'deviation counteraction'.

An everyday example of negative feedback loops is the thermostat/air conditioning in a home heating system. If the thermostat is set at a desired temperature of, say, 20 °C and the room air temperature rises above this, then the thermostat will signal the air conditioning to cool the air until the desired temperature is reached once again. Similarly, if the room cools

below 20 °C the thermostat will start the heating unit, cutting off when 20 °C is reached. The thermostat counteracts change, keeping the air temperature stable.

Feedback can be illustrated in an ecological context in a simple (if unrealistic) density-dependent, two-species predator–prey system. Low prey numbers mean a low supply of food for predators, so predator numbers are also low. Low predation, however, allows prey numbers to increase; increasing prey numbers then allow predator numbers also to increase: these are positive feedbacks by both populations. But as predator numbers increase, so greater predation pressures are placed on prey numbers, their population growth decelerates then eventually declines, and the population level begins to drop; this is reciprocated by the predator population, which has less to feed on, until both population sizes are low once again: these are negative feedbacks. The cycle starts again. There is in this way a cyclic state of stability – homeostasis exists, but it oscillates around a mean population state for both species. In nature, such a simple system would not exist. For instance, the prey species (whether itself a herbivore, carnivore or omnivore) will also depend to an extent on its food sources; the prey will probably be consumed by more than one predator species; the predator will almost certainly have more than one prey species; predator numbers and predator population growth rate will probably be lower than those of the prey; and the influence of external environmental fluctuations cannot be ignored. But the principle of such feedback mechanisms holds, how ever complex the system. An example of feedback relationships between soil nutrient system factors is shown diagrammatically in Figure 1.13.

The more complex the system the greater the number and interaction of the feedback loops and the more inherently stable the system tends to be, although complexity itself is not the cause of this. Rather, good homeostatic control tends to be associated with ecosystems whose components have had a long evolutionary history during which structural adjustments and functional fine-tuning have taken place. Recently evolved ecosys-

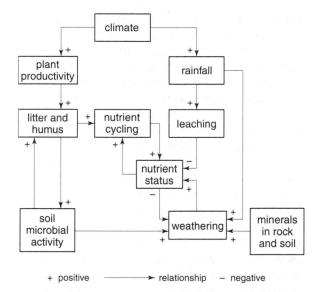

+ positive ——→ relationship − negative

Figure 1.13 Positive and negative feedback relationships between soil nutrient system factors. Weathering and leaching are likely to be high in the wet tropics, and plant productivity, litter decomposition, microbial activity and nutrient cycling all high under warm, damp environmental conditions such as are found in tropical rain forests.

tems, including those of human origin such as plantation forestry ecosystems and agro-ecosystems, tend to lack this inherent stability to adjust and are therefore more susceptible to disturbance and perturbation.

This can be seen in the rain forest example outlined earlier. The rain forest ecosystem usually has a number of checks and balances. Rain forests have a long evolutionary history, and the complex of interactions maintains a state of dynamic equilibrium. In Sabah, unlogged rain forest has been estimated to contain 400 Mg (metric tons) of biomass per hectare, 17% of this being underground (Pinard and Putz, 1996). Previous work has suggested that about 1% of above-ground plant material falls to the ground each year. This means that in this forest there is about 3.3 Mg of litterfall each year in each hectare. The Malaysian example may represent a rather low amount of litterfall. Near Manaus, in central Amazonia, for example, the estimated litterfall is $11 \, Mg \, ha^{-1} \, year^{-1}$.

This litter, however, is rapidly assimilated by the soil microorganisms to become available as nutrients to the forest plants. Nutrients cycle through the animal sector, as well as the microbial community, as they feed on plant material and on each other (see Chapter 4 on energy flow, nutrient cycling, productivity and food webs). The rain forest can withstand disturbance from treefall gaps – indeed, like all forests, it relies on such gaps for its long-term survival as a dynamic system with a series of patches of different ages, reflecting different times since treefall on that site.

Small clearings for agriculture are analogues of such treefall gaps, and the forest can accommodate these small-scale perturbations. With large-scale clearance, however, whether burned or not, and whether for logging or conversion to agriculture or pasture, the system breaks down. The feedback mechanisms can no longer return the system to equilibrium. Ideas on ecosystem stability, resilience and recoverability are discussed and exemplified in Chapter 2.

The problem of creating stable, self-perpetuating ecosystems can be seen with the failure of Biosphere 2. Biosphere 2 aimed at providing a self-sustaining microcosm of key ecosystems found on Earth (i.e. *the* biosphere, or Biosphere 1) with a 1.8 ha glass-and-steel construction in the Sonoran Desert, Arizona. An attempt was made to construct self-regulating ecosystems representing tropical rain forest, savanna, thorn scrub, hot desert, freshwater marsh and a marine system, together with an area devoted to intensive agriculture, and comprising 3800 plant and animal species together with a microbial community of unknown size. In September 1991, eight ecologists/biologists were sealed into Biosphere 2. Shortly after, however, carbon dioxide levels began to fluctuate rapidly and, overall, to exceed the capacity of the system to recycle the gas. By March 1993, oxygen concentrations had dropped from the normal level of 20.9 to 14.5% and, despite pumping extra oxygen into the microcosm, levels continued to decline by around 0.25% each month until the end of the experiment in the following September. Much had been learned, including a lesson on how difficult it is for us to repeat on a small scale what Biosphere 1 does naturally.

1.4 Issues in environmental management

The consequences of burning rain forest in Brazil and Indonesia illustrate how many of these basic ecological ideas translate into real situations on the ground. Interactions between different compartments can be seen at different scales, and the integrity of the ecosystem breaks down as insupportable pressures are placed on the environment. But the ecological situation also involves real environmental issues, and these in turn indicate how economic, political, social and perhaps ethical factors must be considered in examining the environment and the utilisation of environmental resources.

1.4.1 Politics, investment and environmental disaster in Brazilian rain forests

Burning of rain forest is not unique to South-east Asia. In January 1998, for example, the Brazilian government admitted that in Amazonia 6 million ha of rain forest had been destroyed in the period 1995–97, most of it being burned, a return to levels previously seen in the 1980s. The amount of forest destruction, in absolute terms, remains higher in the Amazon basin than in any other rain forest in the world. In Brazilian Amazonia (which accounts for two-thirds of the forest area of the basin) the average *rate* of clearance, while showing great inter-annual variation, has actually accelerated overall during the 1990s from about 1.1 million ha in 1991 to over 2 million ha per annum from 1995 to 1997, peaking at 2.9 million ha in 1995 (Laurance, 1998).

During the 1970s and 1980s, the Brazilian government had actively encouraged clearing and burning of rain forest for cattle ranching. This conversion of forest to pasture has been a feature of many Latin American countries, much of the beef being sold to North American fast-food chains, a process which has been called 'hamburgerisation' of the rain forests (Myers, 1981). The pastures become degraded after a handful of years, and one in three in Brazil is abandoned, generally reverting to degraded scrub or even (ironically in such a part of the world) semi-desert.

In the 1980s, the Brazilian government injected over £6 billion as incentives to clear the rain forest, yet it also joined with other countries with land in this region in an Amazon Pact, which declared 'the importance of genetic and biotic conservation' along with 'sustainable use of natural resources'. They established a Special Commission on the Amazon Environment, one of whose tasks was to prevent the deterioration of the area's natural resources, particularly where this caused deforestation and soil erosion. In 1989, partly as a response to an international outcry about the scale of destruction, President José Sarney announced a new initiative, 'Our Nature', which managed to reduce the impact of subsidies by getting a ban placed on new licences. Formerly acquired licences, however, were maintained, and illegal burning continued. Brazil's Environmental Agency (IBAMA) has only eighty environmental inspectors to police its forests, in which over 80% of clearances are illegal, and has had the task of monitoring an area the size of Western Europe for illegal fires using six rented helicopters. Bureaucracy, inefficiency, corruption and the problem of finding absentee landlords exacerbated the problem.

Pressure to reduce this environmental rapine came from environmentalists within Brazil, at the cost of lives of activists such as the union organiser Chico Mendes in December 1988; from other Latin American nations; and from the developing as well as the developed world. There are now major Thai and Malaysian investments in logging in Brazilian Amazonia, over US$500 million, for example, having been invested in the Brazilian timber industry in 1996 by Asian companies. Many nations have therefore retained their demand for timber products, and there are other reasons for exploiting the forest lands, particularly mining for such minerals as gold, tin and iron. The iron mine at Grande Carajas, the richest source of iron in the world, is supported by loans from the EC, USA and Japan and since 1985 has destroyed large tracts of rain forest from access routes as well as around the mine itself, but in particular because its smelters convert ore into pig iron using charcoal acquired from the surrounding forests (Harmon *et al.*, 1990).

Just as forest fires have led to atmospheric pollution in South-east Asia, so too do they affect the skies over Brazil. The main burning season by farmers in the forests and savanna grasslands of Amazonia is usually September, yet by the end of 1997 clouds of black smoke were still blocking out the sun in many areas, with airports closed, heavy deposits of particulate matter, and an increase in the numbers of people being hospitalised with respiratory illnesses. These fires – fuelled by strong winds and the worst drought for 30 years – had clearly

got out of control by the start of 1998, and by March a 400 km-wide fire line existed in Roraima state, with an area the size of Wales largely destroyed in a region itself the size of Great Britain (Figure 1.14). These were the worst fires in almost a century. The eleven fire engines in the state were, unsurprisingly, of little consequence. A state of emergency had been declared early in the year, but no government aid was forthcoming, although the state governor, Nuedo Campos, had repeatedly asked President Henrique Cardoso to release $2.4 million already approved to rent 22 Russian and American fire-fighting (water-dumping) helicopters. Only on 19 March was approval given for the use of two such helicopters brought in from Argentina. Most local people, including the already endangered 'stone-age' Yanomami tribe, whose entire reserve was threatened, could only pray for the April rains, yet at the same time

Figure 1.14   Location of Roraima state, Brazil and the extent of the Yanomami Indian Reserve.

some farmers were still actively burning their land (Associated Press, 16 March 1998; *The Guardian*, 21 March 1998: 1, 3).

Nevertheless, in December 1997 President Cardoso did announce a plan to increase the area of protected forest by an additional 25 Mha, an initiative which would have the effect of tripling the total area of national parks and similar reserves from 3.8 to 10% of the Brazilian Amazon by the year 2000 (Laurance, 1998). Implementation, however, has almost inevitably faltered in the face of logistic and political problems and, perhaps, a lack of will to succeed.

In August 1998 the fires were back, spreading through the southern Amazon region and destroying 420 000 ha of forest and savanna, with 2900 ignition points being identified via satellite images. Jaguars, monkeys, anteaters, deer and a variety of bird species died in the nature reserve of Ilha de Bananal, the world's largest river-bound island, where 1800 indigenous people also live. Farmers were again the prime culprits (*The Guardian*, 29 August 1998: 16).

1.4.2 Forestry and politics in Indonesia

The Indonesian government has been accused of hypocrisy in the past over its stance on forest conservation (Hurst, 1990). Granting concessions to timber companies to fell 1 million ha of high forest each year certainly runs counter to promises of a more sustainable forest industry. There have also been allegations of turning official eyes away from further illegal logging enterprises, and certainly the government appears to be ignoring its own rules on appropriate replanting. Even allowing farmers and plantation owners to burn their forests is in breach of Indonesian law. To his credit, forestry minister Djamaludin Suryohadikusamo named 176 plantation, timber and construction companies suspected of deliberately firing forest land during the mid-1990s, but action was taken against only one, and the government withdrew only 66 permissions to cut more wood (and has not revoked anyone's 20-year concessions to log).

John Vidal reports the forestry minister admitting 'low-level corruption' and quotes him as saying 'Collusion between local-area government officials and companies is one reason for open violation of laws by forest companies. Fires are set partly because it is easier and cheaper than clearing away secondary vegetation, old plantations and sometimes also primary forest.' Fires also cover up illegal logging and blur the lines of concession boundaries, allowing plantation owners greater access to land (*Guardian Weekend*, 8 November 1997: 20). A Worldwide Fund for Nature report of May 1999 claimed that government figures on logging should be at least doubled because of continued illegal clearance, especially in the forests of Sumatra (*The Guardian*, 5 May 1999: 15), and it is over-optimistic to believe that the picture will change much until there is too little forest remaining for forester or farmer to be interested.

The victims of this greed – a greed of the plantation owners, some members of the government, industrialists and the markets of the Western world – are themselves many. Victims directly affected are those in Indonesia itself, including local tribespeople, many already dispossessed of their land. But beyond the boundaries of Indonesia others are also suffering the health consequences of the fine particulate-laden smog, with asthma, bronchitis, pulmonary diseases and almost certainly cancers. The Worldwide Fund for Nature has estimated the economic cost of the fires to be around $20 billion (Pearce, 1998a). Tourism in South-east Asia fell by a third during the latter part of 1997. Lost business to the Malaysian national airline alone was £2 billion. And beyond the region, too, there were consequences: just as the Mount St Helen's eruption in Washington State in 1980 spewed particulates beyond the troposphere, demonstrably affecting global climatic events, so too did the fires of South-east Asia.

Indonesia declared a national disaster as a consequence of the 1997 fires, and Malaysia notified a state of emergency.

But the fires in Southeast Asia are a disaster for the whole world, and an inevitable consequence of its twisted values: indifference to pollution, powerful

---

ISSUES BOX 1.1

Sustainable management of forests: relationships with ecology and conservation

(a) In 1992, one of the outcomes of the United Nations Conference on Environment and Development, often referred to as the Rio Conference or the Earth Summit, was a Declaration on Environment and Development, which included a Statement of Principles for Sustainable Management of Forests. These principles included

- Forest resources and forest lands should be sustainably managed to meet social, economic, ecological, cultural and spiritual needs of present and future generations.
- Forest policies should be integrated with economic and trade policies.
- The right of states to exploit their own resources is recognised, but this right has the responsibility that activities should not cause environmental damage to other states.
- There should be international cooperation in meeting costs of achieving benefits of conservation and sustainable development.

(b) Draft principles proposed by the Forest Stewardship Council for sustainable forestry in 1993 included

- Minimal impact on wildlife biodiversity and water resources.
- Plantations should not replace natural forests.

(c) In the United Nation's Food and Agriculture Organisation's 'The Challenge of Sustainable Forest Management' (1993), priorities included

- Maintaining the environment, integrity and benefits of forests.
- Reducing as quickly as possible actions leading to the deforestation and degradation of forests.

---

multinationals, lack of law enforcement, official corruption. And fuelling it all, an inexhaustible, unfathomable greed.

(David Harrison, *The Observer*,
28 September 1997: 11)

1.4.3 International agreements and sustainable forestry

Even where a country's policies and actions are environmentally disastrous there is very little that can be done to monitor, police or enforce more sustainable and less damaging activities, despite international agreement and media spotlight (Issues Box 1.1). For example, after all the fine words at the Rio Conference in 1992, the Rio Plus Five summit held in New York in 1997 noted that in fact little had changed, and once again the United Nations was unable to get an agreement on how to use the global forest

resource in a sustained manner, with enforceable standards and sanctions.

It might in any case be argued that it is big business rather than national governments that call the tune. In 1996, the Environmental Investigation Agency (EIA) named the worst environmental offenders in the world's timber industry, among which were Georgia Pacific (USA) and Mitsubishi (Japan). The EIA also accused Japanese and Indonesian companies of corruption, and South Korean and Malaysian commercial organisations of illegal forestry operations. Logging companies were simply using their financial powers to undermine national forestry bodies.

1.5 Conclusions

This chapter has outlined a number of basic ecological principles, focusing on and illustrating the interrelatedness of compartments (land, air and water), and looking at interactions between components of the environment within and between particular ecosystems. What is also evident is that ecological interactions are greatly affected by human activity, and *vice versa*.

But in order to understand the environmental consequences of human activity it is essential to begin looking at issues of how and why certain decisions have been taken – issues of national and international political will, of social demands and controls, of the sustainable use of resources, and of perception and judgement. For judgements to be wise they need to be informed, and an understanding of ecological principles is part of that information.

Further reading

Aiken, S.R. and Leigh, C.H. (1995) *Vanishing rainforests: the ecological transition in Malaysia* (Oxford: Oxford University Press).

Barrow, C.J. (1995) *Developing the environment: problems and management* (Harlow: Longman).

Botkin, D.B. and Keller, E.A. (1995) *Environmental science: Earth as a living planet* (Chichester: Wiley).

Bradbury, I.K. (1998) *The biosphere* (second edition) (London: Wiley).

Colinvaux, P. (1993) *Ecology 2* (Chichester: Wiley).

Cunningham, W. and Phillips, G. (1998) *Environmental science: a global concern* (fifth edition) (Maidenhead: McGraw-Hill).

Enger, E. and Smith, B. (1998) *Environmental science: a study of interrelationships* (sixth edition) (Maidenhead: McGraw-Hill).

Golley, F.B. (1993) *A history of the ecosystem concept in ecology* (New Haven, Conn.: Yale University Press).

Goudie, A. (1993) *The human impact on the natural environment* (fourth edition) (Oxford: Blackwell).

Hecht, S. and Cockburn, A. (1989) *Developers, destroyers and defenders of the Amazon – the fate of the forests* (Harmondsworth: Penguin).

Hurst, P. (1990) *Rainforest politics: ecological destruction in South-east Asia* (London: Zed Books).

Jackson, A.R.W. and Jackson, J.M. (1996) *Environmental science: the natural environment and human impact* (Harlow: Longman).

Jepma, C.J. (1995) *Tropical deforestation: a socio-economic approach* (London: Earthscan).

Kemp, D. (1998) *The environment dictionary.*

(London: Routledge).

Lawrence, E., Jackson, A.R.W. and Jackson, J.M. (1998) *Longman dictionary of environmental science* (Harlow: Longman).

Longman, K.A. and Jenik, J. (1987) *Tropical forest and its environment* (second edition) (Harlow: Longman).

Lovelock, J. (1979) *Gaia: a new look at life on Earth* (Oxford: Oxford University Press).

Lovelock, J. (1988) *The ages of Gaia. A biography of our living Earth* (Oxford: Oxford University Press).

Margulis, L. and Lovelock, J.E. (1989) Gaia and geognosy. In M.B. Rambler, L. Margulis and R. Fester (eds) *Global ecology: towards a science of the biosphere* (London: Academic Press) 1–30.

Mabberley, D.J. (1992) *Tropical rain forest ecology* (second edition) (London: Blackie).

Menotti, V. (1998) Globalization and the acceleration of forest destruction since Rio. *The Ecologist*, **28**: 354–62.

Park, C.C. (1992) *Tropical rainforest* (London: Routledge).

Pickering, K.T. and Owen, L.A. (1997) *An introduction to global environmental issues* (second edition) (London: Routledge).

Stolz, J.E., Botkin, D.B. and Dastoor, M.N. (1989) The integral biosphere. In M.B. Rambler, L. Margulis and R. Fester (eds) *Global ecology: towards a science of the biosphere* (London: Academic Press) 31–49.

Tudge, C. (1991) *Global ecology* (London: Natural History Museum).

Tunnicliffe, V., McArthur, A.G. and McHugh, D. (1998) A biogeographical perspective of the deep-sea hydrothermal vent fauna. *Advances in Marine Biology*, **34**: 353–442.

Watson, A. (1991) Gaia. *New Scientist*, 6 July – Supplement: *Inside Science*, No. 48.

Whitmore, T. (1998) *An introduction to tropical rain forests* (second edition) (Oxford: Oxford University Press).

Wilson, E.O. (1992) *The diversity of life* (Cambridge, Mass.: Belknap Press of Harvard University Press; London: Penguin).

Also undertake key word and key phrase searches of the World Wide Web. The following web sites are particularly useful:

http://www.ucmp.berkeley.edu/help/taxaformold.html (provides an index of all taxa from virus to humans, with a synopsis of characteristics, and links to cognate sites).

http://www.york.biosis.org (provides an index to the world literature on zoology).

QUESTIONS BASED ON CHAPTER 1

Q1. On what three factors does the continuation of life on Earth depend?

Q2. If water is one of the most abundant resources on Earth, why are we concerned about its availability in the future?

Q3. Rank the taxonomic categories given below from highest to lowest, and link each level with the appropriate name associated with dog rose, *Rosa canina*, and domestic dog, *Canis familiaris*.

class, family, kingdom, species, phylum, species, order, division

Rosales, Trachaeophyta, Canis familiaris, Plantae, Rosa, Animalia, Chordata, Angiospermae, Canis, Carnivora, Mammalia, Rosaceae, Rosa canina, Canidae

Q4. Which biomes are ill-suited to agriculture, and why?

Q5. Which aquatic ecosystem can be compared with tropical rain forest? Why?

ANSWERS

A1. Solar energy, cycling of matter and gravity.

A2. Increased demand for good-quality (unpolluted, non-saline) fresh water means concern for quantity and quality. Massive use of water in agriculture and industry has placed tremendous pressure on groundwater resources, and water tables are often the lowest they have ever been in historical times. Water used for irrigation is prone to salinisation. Sufficient quantities of clean water for human consumption is another problem as urbanisation rates increase, especially in the developing world. In arid and semi-arid parts of the world there may be international conflict over water rights. Deforestation leads to sedimentation of rivers and lakes, interfering with water flow and therefore its availability. Channelisation increases speed of flow, so water may be more difficult to extract.

A3.

Kingdom	Plantae	Animalia
Phylum/Division	Trachaeophyta (division)	Chordata (phylum)
Class	Angiospermae	Mammalia
Order	Rosales	Carnivora
Family	Rosaceae	Canidae
Genus	Rosa	Canis
Species	*Rosa canina*	*Canis familiaris*

A4. Hot deserts, polar deserts, tundra and mountains. These are biomes with extremes of temperature and a lack (and, in the case of hot deserts, unreliability) of precipitation or available water, together with characteristically thin, nutrient-poor soils.

A5. Coral reefs. Like tropical rain forests they are found in physical environments which impose few constraints, where energy availability is high, where biomass and species diversity is high, and where environmental stability over millennia has allowed many co-evolutionary interactions (including many mutualisms) to have evolved.

Discussion topics

D1. If we assume that the Earth is a self-regulating super-organism capable of maintaining conditions necessary for the continued survival of life (the Gaia hypothesis), does this mean that we can alter the environment as much as we want, knowing that feedback mechanisms will correct any damage and maintain an equilibrium?

D2. What arguments might be advanced for Antarctica to be considered a distinct and separate biome? What environmental differences are there between Antarctica and high mountain regions such as the Himalayas?

D3. Too much disturbance is likely to be damaging to an ecosystem. But under what circumstances can an *absence* of disturbance also be damaging in the long term? Give examples, and explain your ideas in terms of ecological principles.

D4. Choose a recent environmental catastrophe (flood, wildfire, earthquake, etc.) and discuss how human activities might have contributed both to the catastrophe itself (if at all) and to its consequences. How might we learn from this experience?

D5. How valid is it to consider towns and cities as ecosystems?

EXERCISES

E1. Some of the information used in Chapter 1 comes from newspaper reports. Examine national and international environmental issues covered by quality newspapers and by other media such as radio and television for a week (or longer). What kind of environmental issue do you think makes a good news story? Group the stories into different kinds of issue, for example pollution, global warming, nature conservation, and environmental hazards such as fire, flood and hurricane. To what extent do environmental issues in the media show (if only by implication) interactions between different ecosystem components?

E2. Compare local news sources and reports on environmental issues with their national and international counterparts. What differences are there in topic? What differences are there in the treatment of environmental concerns? What levels of explanation and discussion of implications are there in these different reports?

E3. What actions can *you* personally take to help to preserve the world's tropical forests? Visit a DIY superstore and ascertain the source(s) of hardwood timber and timber products. Does the store have an environmental policy on its wood products?

Chapter **2**

Food, energy and nutrients

Summary

The acquisition of food, which provides nutrients and energy, and the avoidance of being another organism's food are prerequisites for survival in plants, animals and microorganisms. There are risks and costs in feeding, as well as gains, and there is often a need to behave in ways that optimise future food resources as well as to respond to immediate feeding needs and opportunities. This is as true for humans as it is for other animals, as exemplified by consideration of sustainable agriculture and an evaluation of recent green revolutions. Agriculture, however, is essentially based on converting sunlight, directly or indirectly, into profitable tissue, and the ecological core of this chapter examines how energy and nutrients pass through ecological systems. This is done by examining food chains and food webs, and the feeding relationship between different positions in these constructs (trophic levels and trophic structure), looking at herbivores, carnivores, omnivores and detritivores. Energy is fixed into living weight, or biomass, and its flow reflects the metabolic demands of the individual and the community, as well as the productivity of the system. The notion of ecological efficiency is introduced. Carbon, oxygen, nitrogen, phosphorus and copper are used to exemplify nutrient cycles and biogeochemical cycles. Agriculture can usefully be viewed as constructing different kinds of ecosystem – agro-ecosystems – which possess the same inherent characteristics of energy flow and nutrient use as natural systems, although a number of differences in degree are highlighted. A brief history of environmentalism in the 1970s and 1980s introduces the argument that humans need to integrate a reduction in environmental degradation, increased productivity, a more equitable distribution of food production and a slowing down of global population increase. Among other things, the 1992 Earth Summit heralded Agenda 21 and the implementation of programmes aimed at increasing sustainable use of the world's resources, including those of food.

2.1 Agriculture: risks, costs and benefits of manipulating the environment for food

This chapter is basically about food. Living organisms need supplies of nutrients and the provision of energy in order to survive, grow and reproduce, and these requirements both drive and are driven by characteristics and properties of the ecosystem. Humans are no exception, and, while hunting (including fishing) and gathering still occurs, the basis of our food provision lies with the deliberate production of plant and animal material. Whether this enterprise is commercial or subsistence, whether it takes place in a field or on open rangeland, what farmers and pastoralists are doing is optimising the conversion of solar energy to useful plant material or, via useful plant material, to useful animal material. Food is not always the end-product of farming, for example the production of industrial crops such as flax, or at least not the only end-product, for example rearing cattle for hide and horn as well as milk and meat, but the predominant aim of most farms is to maximise benefits (yield) while minimising costs (losses).

Gain can be short-term, but increasingly the need for longer-term *sustainable agriculture* is being seen as important for future human prosperity. The general idea of sustainability has become increasingly important in the last decade, and indeed was a central issue at the Rio Conference in 1992. Agriculture is viewed by Barrow (1995) as 'stretching' nature, pushing environmental and biological opportunities to increase production, although it might be more useful to think in terms of 'squeezing' nature to maximise production of a limited component of the environment. Certainly, agriculture involves environmental manipulation. These opportunities and manipulations, however, also carry risks, with undesirable environmental (and economic) consequences. Environmental risks include the exacerbation of pest and disease damage, soil erosion, over-extraction of water, and loss of genetic variability.

Agriculture is an open system that receives energy naturally by way of solar radiation and nutrients via weathering and precipitation. Into this system also come inputs from human activity: usually the desired plants and animals themselves, together with chemicals such as fertilisers and pesticides, water manipulation through drainage and irrigation, and additional energy, whether from human labour or hydrocarbon-fuelled machinery. The system loses energy and production as harvested crops and marketed livestock (including waste products), and it also loses material through soil erosion, leaching and water loss.

Throughout history, new products have been found or old ones modified through breeding or genetic engineering. Technological advances have allowed humans to use previously unusable land (although definitions of marginal land are usually based on economics, i.e. profitability, rather than on biology, i.e. feasibility of growing something), or to intensify production on land already being used. But the world is finite, and the human population is growing. The spectre of Thomas Malthus (that amounts of food will increase at an arithmetic rate, while population growth will outstrip food production by increasing at a geometric rate) has merely been deferred. There remains plenty of food for all in today's world, and in tomorrow's: famine and starvation reflect allocation, not total amounts. Nevertheless, in order to fulfil current needs without taking away from the needs of future generations (a standard definition of sustainability) it is necessary not only to rationalise food production in cultural and economic terms, for example by looking carefully at what we grow, where we grow it and how we distribute it, but also in biological and environmental terms. This chapter therefore reviews issues relating to sustainability in agriculture and examines the ecological basis of this by considering the flow of energy and the transfer of nutrients within the ecosystem.

2.2 Key environmental issue: world food supply

People need food to eat. The 5.77 billion people in the world in 1996 showed an increase of 69 million over 1995, made up of about 1.7 million new individuals per week minus 0.4 million deaths. Although the annual rate of growth has declined from around 2% in 1960 to 1.4% by the late 1990s, world population reached 6 billion in 1999, and is predicted to reach 9.4 billion by 2050 (United Nations Population Fund, 1998). Agriculture in its broadest sense is the main provider of food. In the early 1960s, most countries were self-sufficient in food; today only a few are (Kendall and Pimentel, 1994). To provide minimum Word Health Organisation health standards on calorific intake, we need to produce over 3.5 million tonnes of food each day, increasing at a rate of 83,000 tonnes daily to accommodate the global rate of natural increase. All of this is to be achieved on the 11% of the land surface that can be used for agriculture (Miller, 2000).

Even so, while in theory 2–4 billion ha is cultivable, only 1.5 billion ha is actually being used, providing <0.3 ha per person (and declining, in part because of environmental degradation such as soil erosion, desertification and salinisation), while around 0.5 ha per person has been estimated as the minimum amount for there to be an adequate diet for all – bearing in mind the grossly over-simple assumption of equal shares for all (Meadows et al., 1992; Southwick, 1996).

Issues relating to world food supply therefore involve, primarily, the production and distribution of sufficient food to feed the human population. Despite droughts and floods, diseases and war, there is – at least for the moment – no technological problem in providing enough food. Access to food resources is another matter. So, too, are the economics associated with this, for example the politico-economic justifications for 'food mountains' of 'surplus' resources. In 1998, the Nobel Prize for Economics was awarded to Amartya Sen, Master of Trinity College Cambridge, who argues that food production is not the fundamental cause of famine but rather the way in which global food resources are marketed and distributed.

Whether or not we are growing the most nutritious or energy-efficient foods is another issue: for example, as is discussed in Section 2.3, a meat diet adds another stage in the food chain, energy use is therefore less efficient, carrying capacity is lower, and land area needs are all the greater. Different societies favour different proportions of different foods (Table 2.1). What sustainability means in an agricultural context, and what the methods might be to introduce and retain any

Table 2.1 Consumption of foods and feed grains in the USA, China and the world (kg per capita per year)

Food/feed	USA	China	World
Food grains	77	239	201
Vegetables	129	163	130
Fruits	46	17	53
Meat & fish	88	36	47
Dairy products	258	4	77
Eggs	14	7	6
Fats & oils	29	6	13
Sugars & sweeteners	70	7	25
Food total	771	479	552
Feed grains	663	100	144
Grand total	1374	605	696
Kcal./day (per capita)	3600	2662	2667

such sustainability, also needs to be examined critically.

The number of undernourished people in the world has declined since 1970, reflecting greater per capita food energy supplies and improvements in food distribution, but this has not been the case in all regions. The number of chronically undernourished people in Africa increased from 101 million in 1969–71 to 168 million in 1988–90, even though, because of a rapid rise in population, this reflected an actual decline in the *proportion* of undernourished people in the total population. Over the same period, Asia saw the greatest decline in the proportion of people suffering from malnutrition (from 40 to 19%) but still supported the largest absolute population of the undernourished at 528 million people in 1990 (FAO, 1992; McCann, 1994). Some 20–25% of the world's human population do not receive an adequate diet in terms of either calorific value (energy) or nutrition (Kendall and Pimentel, 1994). Over 180 million children suffer from being underweight and show evidence of nutrient deficiency (IFPRI, 1994). Even in the USA, 12 million children and 30 million adults go hungry, yet within that country there is an overall food surplus, and obesity resulting from excessive intake of high-sugar, fat-rich foods is also a general problem (Southwick, 1996).

Famines such as those in Ethiopia, Somalia and Sudan in 1983 and the 1990s are the most dramatic, media-evident consequences of climatic marginality, environmental degradation, civil strife and inefficient infrastructures. Starvation of whole populations is horrific enough, yet famines also exacerbate what in many parts of the world is the endemic problem of malnutrition, and that is an ever-present indictment of us all. Malnutrition may involve insufficient intake of energy, measurable in calories and evident in the wasting away of fat and muscle (in Africa called *marasmus*); or insufficient protein, especially evident in bloating of the stomach or indeed the whole body, and particulary found in children (*kwashiorkor*); or both. Normal growth and functioning also require an appropriate suite of vitamins, minerals and fats.

Malthus predicted that population size would outstrip food supply, yet from 1950 to around 1980 world food production actually increased at a higher rate than did the human population, with per capita grain production actually peaking in 1984 (Figure 2.1). During 1950–84, world population growth was 1.8–2.1% per annum, while food grain production increased at an annual rate of 1.9%, i.e. grain production per person increased by almost 40%. Likewise, over the same period, soya bean production had an

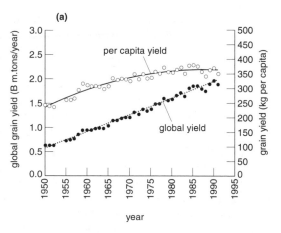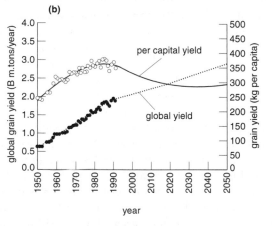

Figure 2.1 World grain yields from 1950. (a) World grain yields, total and per capita, 1950 to 1991. A linear least square fit to the total yield, made to guide the eye, has a slope +1.5% yr⁻¹ in 1989 (shown). (b) Data and projections of world grain yields, 1950–2050. After 1992 the global production rises at 0.7% yr⁻¹, according to the busines-as-usual scenario discussed in the text. The per capita yield employs the UN medium growth case.

annual rate of increase of 5.1%, meat 3.4% and fish catch 4.0% (Miller, 2000; Brown *et al.*, 1993; 1994). Yet per capita food production has not risen everywhere; for example, grain production fell by 22% in Africa between 1969 and 1990, and if we adopt a 'business-as-usual' scenario (i.e. change nothing from what we are doing today) this will happen globally (Figure 2.1).

Although global food production outstripped global population growth in the 1950s through to the 1980s, the situation has now changed, partly as population growth continues to accelerate, partly because of a drop in overall agricultural production. In 1991, global agricultural production fell for the first time since 1983, attributable to reduced harvests in North America, Australia, Eastern Europe and the former USSR, since in the developing world gross agricultural production continued to increase (FAO, 1992; McCann, 1994).

Most of the increase in per capita food production in the latter half of the twentieth century has come from two 'green revolutions'. The first began in the first decade after the Second World War though the widespread use of a new range of agricultural chemicals, in particular selective herbicides and inorganic fertilisers. The second dates from the 1960s, following the development of new strains of cereals, particularly wheat and rice. These new cereals possessed characteristics such as faster growth, higher yield and greater resistance to disease. High-yielding varieties (HYVs) of wheat came on the market in 1961, HYV rice in 1965 (with the very important IR-8 variety released in 1966), and HYV barley in 1969. With genetic engineering, the 1990s may be seeing the advent of a third green revolution. Associated with these biotechnological breakthroughs were improvements in water management, developments in agricultural machine technology, rationalisation of farm layout, and the distribution and marketing of new commercial agricultural products.

India, for example, became self-sufficient in wheat between 1961 and 1980. Its food grain production rose from around 50 million tonnes year^{-1} in 1947 to 170 million tonnes year^{-1} in 1989, a 240% increase at a time when population rose by 140% (Davidson *et al.*, 1992). Similarly, Indonesia moved from being a rice importer to a rice exporter by 1986.

All of these improvements have had limitations, risks and costs associated with them. The downside of pesticides is examined in greater depth in Section 3.2.2. There are also many current concerns about the introduction and use of the results of advanced genetic techniques in husbandry, for example cloning (as with Dolly the sheep) and genetic engineering, such as with the use of bioengineered soya in food products and possible 'genetic pollution' risks attached to the cultivation of transgenic crops in open fields.

Yet while these HYVs reduced the reliance by the developing world on grain originating from developed countries they also introduced new dependencies – on imported seed (since HYV seed generally cannot be saved by the farmer), on agrochemicals, on machinery and on fuel. Farmers who had often previously been subsistence croppers, and who certainly had little cash, now had to find the money to buy these commodities. Furthermore, there was a reduction in genetic diversity, as traditional crop varieties fell into disuse, together with an even greater move than previously into monocultural cropping. The resilience and resistance of traditional crop strains to drought, frost, pests and diseases were no longer found, and a number of harvest failures did result. For example, the HYV rice IR-8 suffered from a bacterial blight during 1968–69 and 1970–71, affecting much of Southeast Asia.

Environmental stresses have also followed as a result of the use of HYVs. For instance, many of the new strains are very water-dependent, but increased irrigation has often led to waterlogging and salinisation of soils, a rapid and substantial lowering of the water table in already drought-prone semi-arid regions, and an increase in waterborne diseases. Machinery compacts the soil, wasting precious water by reducing water infiltration and increasing surface runoff, and not infrequently accelerating soil erosion. Machinery also requires initial purchase, continued maintenance and purchase of fuel, the latter all the more expensive after the 1973 oil crisis (Barrow, 1995).

Improvements have only affected cereals, with no equivalent interest shown in vegetables, fruit or other staple crops of different parts of the developing world. Also, the use of other plant foods may be reduced as HYV grain is used, for example a reduction evident in the cultivation of protein-rich legumes such as beans and lentils in parts of South and South-east Asia. The green revolution was also geographically partial: Africa, for example, places more emphasis on root crops and much less reliance on cereals than Asia and Latin America, and has therefore received few of the benefits from advances in cereal crop breeding.

The nutritional quality of the new varieties of cereal is often lower than traditional strains. HYV cereals are also often difficult to store, because their high moisture content reduces their keeping quality and makes them susceptible to mould, all the more serious a problem given that 30% of food produced in the developing world is destroyed by pests during storage.

The higher yields of HYV crops come from high (and expensive) inputs, together with appropriate manipulation of environmental conditions, and clearly there are socio-economic and environmental costs associated with their use (Shiva, 1991). New biotechnology may provide at least a partial solution, but it is increasingly believed that often it is a return to traditional labour-intensive, low-input agriculture that holds the key to the future. In many ways, this would be a progressive rather than a retrogressive step, because modern knowledge and technology can be harnessed to earlier ideas of organic farming, permaculture and agroforestry, and used to improve yields, increase crop variety and sustain both the environment and the economy. Moreover, these ideas can be translated back into agricultural practices in Western societies (Pretty and Howes, 1993). Implementing such changes reflects a shift in philosophy as well as a change in technology: the philosophy is to do with sustainability, which is examined more explicitly in Section 2.4.3.

In an important sense, maximising or, rather, optimising agricultural production without reducing the efficiency with which this is accomplished is simply an extrapolation into an economic system of what is basically an ecological system: optimising the conversion of sunlight into profitable tissue. The ecological concepts in Section 2.3 therefore examine in more detail how energy and nutrients pass through ecological systems.

2.3 Ecological concepts

- Food chains and trophic levels
- Food webs
- Standing crop biomass and metabolic rate
- Trophic structure and ecological pyramids
- Energy flow and productivity
- Energy allocation and ecological efficiencies
- Energy flow through communities and pyramids of energy
- Nutrient and biogeochemical cycles
- Agro-ecosystems

2.3.1 Food chains and trophic levels

Ecology Box 1.4 showed how solar energy is fixed by green plants, which convert carbon and water into stored energy by the process of photosynthesis. Plants are eaten by some animals (*herbivores*), which may in turn be eaten by other animals (*carnivores*). Some animals eat both plant and animal material (*omnivores*). At each stage of consumption, there is a transfer of stored energy and nutrients.

'Trophic' is a term deriving from the Greek for food. Green plants are examples of *autotrophs*, the term meaning organisms that 'feed themselves', which they do in the sense of not requiring organic compounds as their source of energy. Green plants, requiring light in order to photosynthesise, are *photoautotrophs*. Algae (viewed by some taxonomists as separate from plants), some bacteria and all cyanobacteria (sometimes known as blue-green algae) also photosynthesise. Where organisms use chemosynthesis, by which energy is obtained from the oxidation of inorganic material in the absence of light, they are known as *chemoautotrophs*. These are restricted to prokaryotic organisms.

Organisms that require already existing organic compounds as their source of energy are known as *heterotrophs*. These include all animals, whether herbivore or carnivore, and some parasitic organisms, including plant parasites which do not have green leaves (and therefore cannot photosynthesise) and rely on their hosts for all their nutrition. Broomrapes (*Orobanche*), for example, make contact with the roots of their hosts, dodder (*Cuscuta epithymnum*) with the stem, stimulating a growth which penetrates the transport cells in the host's tissues, from which sugars and other nutrients are then extracted.

Heterotrophs ingest their food. Digestion is followed by absorption, then either assimilation (for use in storage, for growth or to fuel other activities) or excretion (of excess or waste material). Egestion may also take place, using regurgitation (for example by owls of pellets containing undigested feathers, fur and bones of their prey) or elimination in faeces (for example, plant fibre is egested in an undigested form by humans).

Since herbivores eat plants, carnivores eat herbivores, and indeed some carnivores eat other carnivores we can view these feeding relationships as a *food chain*. The positions along this food chain at which organisms feed are *trophic levels*. Autotrophs represent the first trophic level, herbivores the second, and carnivores the third, fourth or even fifth. Yet another way of viewing the food chain lies with what an organism uses as its source of energy. Since they convert solar energy into organic matter, autotrophs can be called *primary producers*. Herbivores rely on plant material and are therefore *primary consumers*. Carnivores at the third trophic level are then distinguished as *secondary consumers*, and at higher trophic levels as *tertiary consumers*, and so on.

Trophic levels are a useful way of characterising the structure of a community in terms of energy flow. Bearing in mind the second law of thermodynamics (Ecology Box 1.4), that no transfer of energy is completely efficient and that some energy is always lost as heat during any transfer, at each stage of energy transfer via feeding some energy is lost to the environment. Within an ecosystem, progessively less energy is

therefore available at each trophic level, and the relative paucity of available energy at higher trophic levels may be a key reason why there are rarely more than five or six trophic levels in any ecosystem Figure 2.2). Other explanations involve the inherent stability of the system (see Sections 2.3.4 and 2.3.5).

The picture is complicated further by the fact that not all energy is stored, used internally, respired or subsequently eaten by another organism. Waste products themselves may be consumed, and dead organic matter is also food for a number of organisms. To the standard food chain, therefore, must be added a system which deals with decomposition.

The simplest self-sustaining community needs both primary producers and decomposers.

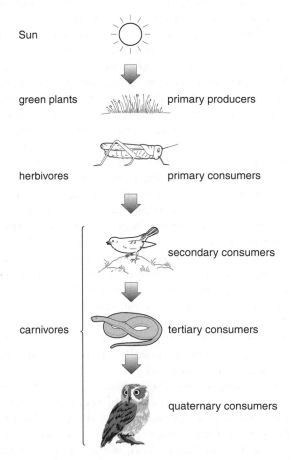

Figure 2.2   Trophic levels in a simplified terrestrial food chain.

Without producers there could be no herbivores or carnivores, but no decomposers either; and without decomposers the remains of dead plants and animals would simply accumulate, or at most desiccate and be dispersed via weathering. Decomposers convert organic waste products and dead material into inorganic substances needed by plants as nutrition. Without decomposers, the Earth would eventually run out of essential gases such as carbon dioxide and inorganic substances essential for life.

Detritus is organic material that has fallen to the ground or (in water) sediment. Many decomposers are therefore *detritivores*, although detritivory is also pursued by many invertebrates. By definition, detritivores are heterotrophs. *Saprotrophs* feed on dead organic matter, which they ingest as small particles or absorb in solution. Most decomposition is carried out by saprotrophic fungi, bacteria and invertebrates.

Another complication of using trophic levels to examine community structure is that carnivores and parasites can feed at more than one trophic level, and omnivores by definition do so. Also, cannibals 'move up' a trophic level when they eat conspecifics. Another dilemma occurs with some bacteria. For example, ruminant animals such as cattle and sheep require certain gut bacteria for the digestion of their food, particularly in breaking down cellulose, a complex carbohydrate that is the main constituent of plant cell walls, while the bacteria can only live in the stomachs (technically, the rumens) of the animals. (This interdependence in organisms that live together is a *symbiosis*). In one sense such bacteria are herbivores, grazing on unbroken-down plant matter, but not at the second trophic level, and in another sense they are saprotrophs. Cattle are clearly herbivores, but they digest material after they have been processed by the rumen bacteria, so are cattle also technically carnivores that rely on herbivorous bacteria?

Food chains are thus often a useful starting point for considering how energy and material move through a community, but there are limitations when translating each stage in a food chain into a trophic level. Also, while some animals (*monophages*) feed on only one plant or animal species, most consumers rely on at least a few species (*oligophages*) or feed on many (*polyphages*). Another criticism of the idea of a food chain is therefore the fact that each component (individual or species) generally either feeds on, or is food for, a number of other species. It becomes more realistic, therefore, if extraordinarily difficult to disentangle and represent graphically, to think of the feeding relationships of a community in terms of a complex *food web* rather than a simple food chain.

2.3.2 Food webs

In a sense, a food web represents a collection of interacting food chains. It identifies the feeding relationships between all the components of the particular ecosystem, even if some components are large groups rather than individual species (Figure 2.3). Components can be shown visually, even where they occur at different trophic levels. Omnivores, for example, can be represented in a way that they cannot in a food chain diagram. Even a simple food web, however, can look complicated when shown diagrammatically, and it shows nothing of actual energy flow other than its 'direction' through the components of the web, or of the relative importance of different components to each other, since one 'route' may represent anything from a small amount to virtually all of an animal's actual food intake. Finally, to construct a realistically accurate food web an ecosytem has to be studied in great depth, and rarely can we be sure that all components and relationships have been identified.

2.3.3 Standing crop biomass and metabolic rate

The living weight of an organism or group of organisms is known as its *biomass*. The energy fixed in plant tissues is the standing crop biomass, which can be expressed as either the total dry weight or total calorific value of organisms present at any one time. The amount that can be supported by a regular flow of energy through a food chain largely depends on the size

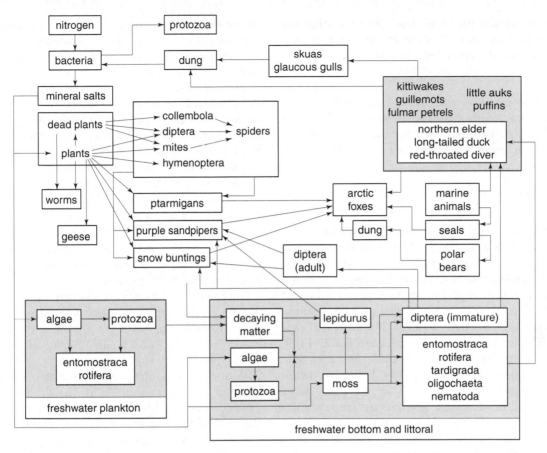

Figure 2.3 An early food web (or food cycle) among the animals of Bear Island, in the Arctic Circle (from Elton, 1927).

of the individual organism, and this ties in with the organism's metabolism and the metabolism of the whole community. *Metabolism* represents the sum of all the chemical reactions that occur within the cells of living organisms by which either complex molecules such as proteins, fats and carbohydrates are manufactured from smaller molecules (*anabolism*), or whereby complex organic compounds are broken down into simple molecules (*catabolism*). The *metabolic rate* of an organism reflects the amount of energy it needs per unit time. The basal metabolic rate (BMR) is the minimum amount of energy needed by an organism while at rest (so energy is not needed for activities) in a thermoneutral environment (so no energy is required to thermoregulate) some time after eating (so minimal energy is being used in digestion). Energy expen-

diture needed above BMR for various activities and physiological processes allows measurements such as daily energy expenditure to be made, and this is usually about 1.5 to 3.0 times BMR under non-extreme conditions.

Some activities and situations will lead to at least a temporary increase in energy requirements and therefore in actual metabolic rate, for example where hunting by predatory mammals (and avoidance by the prey) involves running, or when temperatures rise or fall to levels where an animal has to respond to offset stress, for example by panting or shivering. The most important factor affecting metabolic rate, however, is usually the size of the organism, although the relationship is not a directly proportional one. An animal ten times heavier than another does not need ten times as much food (energy intake) per day. The actual relationship between biomass and metabolic rate is expressed as an *allometric equation*, in which

$$\text{metabolic rate} = a(\text{biomass})^b$$

The exponent b is what relates metabolic rate to body mass. Although the relationship is not a directly proportional one, we can transform the values on each side of the equation logarithmically, so that

$$\log(\text{metabolic rate}) = \log(a) \\ + b(\log[\text{body weight}])$$

When shown graphically, this log–log equation is represented by a straight line, and from such a graph a can be shown to represent the metabolic rate when body mass has a unit value of 1, and b represents the slope of the line, i.e. the rate at which one factor changes in relation to the other.

Measurements over a range of taxa reveal that the value of b generally lies between 0.5 and 0.9, whatever the units of measurement for each side of the equation (Kleiber, 1947; Peters, 1983; Reiss, 1989). That $b < 1.0$ shows that larger organisms need to use less energy (and acquire less energy) each day relative to their body mass than is the case with smaller organisms. It is important to remember that it is the weight-specific metabolic rate that decreases with increasing size, not the total metabolism of the individual. An adult human, for instance, requires more total food than a child, but less food per unit of body weight.

Even so, different organisms of the same body weight often have different metabolic rates. Warm-blooded animals (*endotherms* or *homoiotherms*), i.e. mammals and birds, need more energy per unit of biomass than cold-blooded animals (*ectotherms* or *poikilotherms*), since the former need to use energy to maintain a constant and relatively high body temperature. Indeed, endotherms may need to spend over 90% of their energy income simply in maintaining their body temperature. Ectotherms maintain their body temperatures by using external sources of heat, whether directly from the Sun or indirectly, for example using a Sun-warmed rock. The downside for ectotherms is that removal of the heat source makes them sluggish and less capable of movement or less efficient in their physiological processes. In turn, both endotherms and ectotherms use less energy per unit of biomass than single-celled organisms.

Another way of expressing the implication of the allometric equation is that since the smaller the organism the greater the metabolism per unit of biomass, then the smaller the organism the smaller the amount of biomass that can be supported at a particular trophic level. The converse is also true: the larger the organism the greater the standing crop biomass. The biomass of bacteria present at any one time in an ecosystem will therefore be much smaller (even though numbers are much higher) than the biomass of, say, mammals, where the energy use is the same for both groups.

The biomass–metabolism relationship holds for plants as well as animals, since plants also require energy to function, but it is sometimes difficult to decide what constitutes an individual. Odum (1971) points out that while a single tree is by definition an individual, its leaves may usefully be regarded as 'functional individuals'. Similarly, seaweed species with thin or narrow fronds (and thus with a high surface-to-volume ratio) have a higher rate of metabolism per unit of biomass than do species with thick fronds; thus the fronds are the functional individual, not the whole organism, which could include several fronds attached to the substrate by a single holdfast.

2.3.4 Trophic structure and ecological pyramids

The interaction between the energy loss at each transfer of energy along the food chain and the size–metabolism relationship results in each community having a particular trophic structure, which is often characteristic of particular ecosystems. The trophic structures of different coniferous woodlands, for example, are more similar to each other than to a set of trophic structures belonging to savanna grassland. Trophic structure can be described either in terms of the standing crop per unit area or in respect of the energy fixed per unit area per unit time at each trophic level.

Trophic structure, and also trophic function, can be represented diagrammatically using *ecological pyramids*, in which the first (producer) level is shown as the base, and successive layers move through subsequent trophic levels to the last one, which appears as the apex. There are three general types of ecological pyramid: pyramids of number (depicting the number of individual organisms per unit area at each trophic level in a community); pyramids of biomass (based on a measure of the total amount of living matter, e.g. total dry weight or total calorific value per unit area); and pyramids of energy (in which the rate of energy flow, or productivity, is shown at each level as energy per unit area per unit time) (Figure 2.4).

The numbers pyramid may be entirely or partly inverted, for example where many invertebrates occur as grazers on a few large trees, or where a number of parasites depend on a small number of hosts. The biomass pyramid is also occasionally

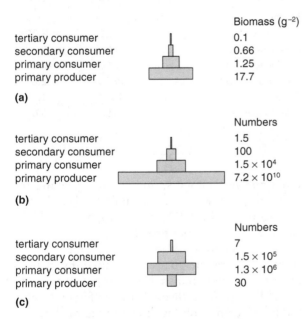

(a)

(b)

(c)

Figure 2.4 Ecological pyramids showing plots of (a) biomass and (b) numbers of individuals with most terrestrial habitats, both showing conventional pyramids with broad base and narrow apex. In some cases, however, for example on a tree, (c) large numbers of herbivores can be found on a single primary producer, so an inverted pyramid will be found when considering numbers (but not biomass).

inverted, for instance in parts of the oceans, where rapid reproduction by phytoplankton (microscopic plant life) can support a more slowly reproducing zooplankton (microscopic animals): the rapid turnover of plant life provides enough food for the grazers, but at any one time there may well be a greater number of the latter, and the biomass pyramid is therefore inverted.

Pyramids of number are of less value in describing or explaining community interactions than the other two types. The numbers pyramid may be difficult to depict graphically on the same scale, because numbers could be orders of magnitude apart when comparing different trophic levels or when making comparisons between different pyramids, where the shape will also vary, depending for example on whether the producers are small (phytoplankton or grass, for instance) or large (giant kelp or trees).

A biomass pyramid is often difficult to compile, but it can more usefully indicate the trophic relationships within the community. This is also the case with pyramids of energy (see Section 2.3.7).

2.3.5 Energy flow and productivity

Energy is the capacity to do work, and it obeys the laws of thermodynamics (see Ecology Box 1.4). Life is accompanied by changes in energy, although no energy is created or destroyed (first law of thermodynamics). The energy that enters the Earth's surface as light is balanced by the energy leaving the planet as invisible heat radiation. Between radiant energy input and heat output, life involves a flow of energy in various forms that allows the synthesis of complex organic matter, growth and duplication. The behaviour of energy in the living world can be thought of as an energy flow, because transformations of energy are one-way, in contrast to materials, which are cycled.

Living organisms receive radiation from the Sun, together with long-wave thermal radiation from nearby surfaces (including clouds, rocks, soil, water and vegetation). Only a small amount of solar radiation can be used in photosynthesis. Sunlight reaches the biosphere at a rate of around

2 Gcal cm^{-1} min^{-1}, but in passing through the atmosphere it is dissipated (attenuated), and at most 1.34 Gcal cm^{-1} min^{-1} reaches the Earth's surface on a clear day, much less when the radiation has to penetrate cloud, water and vegetation (Gates, 1962). For most of the biopshere this translates into a radiant energy input of 3000–4000 kcal m^{-1} day^{-1} (1 kcal = 4.2 kJ). It is this amount that is used by green plants in photosynthesis. The *primary productivity* of a biological system is the rate at which radiant energy is stored by photosynthetic activity. Gross primary productivity (GPP) is the total rate of photosynthetic storage, including the organic material used in respiration during the period of measurement. GPP thus represents the production of dry matter per unit area per unit time. The amount of actual dry matter produced in this way is the gross primary production. During respiration, however, some of the stored energy from GPP is reconverted to carbon dioxide and water; the overall gain of dry weight per area per unit time, i.e. GPP minus respiration, is known as net primary productivity (NPP).

In terrestrial systems GPP is generally around 2.7 times NPP, but this value falls to about 1.5 in oceanic systems (Whittaker, 1975), so that the 72% of the globe covered by water is responsible for only 35% of global NPP. Table 2.2, however, shows that within terrestrial biomes there are considerable differences in NPP, a reflection of a number of confounding factors, including light levels (e.g. degree of cloudiness), water availability (including the effects of evapotranspiration, see Section 1.3.1), temperature, length of growing season and nutrient availability.

Some of the energy acquired as NPP is used by the plant itself; the plant may die and the energy be transferred through decomposers, but some or all of the tissue might instead be consumed by herbivores. Energy is thereby transferred to the second trophic level, and indeed perhaps beyond. Again some energy is always lost as heat during such transfers (second law of thermodynamics). The rate at which energy is stored at consumer level is *secondary productivity*. Because consumers only use energy (food) already produced by plants and convert this energy to different tissues by a single process, secondary productivity is not divided into

Table 2.2 Mean global net primary productivity and mean biomass of major ecosystems

Ecosystem type	Mean net primary productivity (g m^{-2} per annum)	Mean biomass (kg m^{-2})
Continental		
Tropical rain forest	2200	45.0
Tropical seasonal forest	1600	35.0
Temperate evergreen forest	1300	35.0
Temperate deciduous forest	1200	30.0
Boreal forest	800	20.0
Woodland and shrubland	700	6.0
Savanna	900	4.0
Temperate grassland	600	1.60
Tundra and alpine	140	0.60
Desert and semi-desert scrub	90	0.70
Extreme desert, rock, sand, ice	3	0.02
Cultivated land	650	1.00
Swamp and marsh	2000	15.00
Lakes and streams	250	0.02
Mean continental	773	12.3
Marine		
Open ocean	125	0.003
Upwelling zones	500	0.02
Continental shelf	360	0.01
Algal bed and reefs	2500	2.0
Estuaries	1500	1.0
Mean marine	152	0.01
Grand total	333	3.6

gross and net amounts, and strictly speaking the total energy flow at heterotrophic levels (which is analogous to the GPP of autotrophs) should be called *assimilation*, not production.

Net community productivity is the rate of storage of organic matter not used by heterotrophs (i.e. NPP minus heterotrophic consumption). Energy flow through the different trophic levels of a community is shown in Figure 2.5.

2.3.6 Energy allocation and ecological efficiencies

Some energy is lost during transfer from one organism to another, and the consumer assimi-

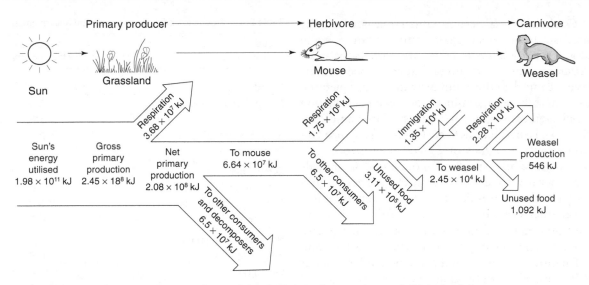

Figure 2.5 Loss of energy as it passes along a simple food chain. Energy values are in kilojoules (kJ).

lates the remainder. Much of the assimilated energy (A) is used in metabolism, with the energy used in respiration (R) lost as heat. The amount of energy expressed as the difference between A and R can be used in the production of new tissue or growth (P_g) or to produce the reproductive material of gametes, i.e. sperm or eggs (P_r). Thus: $A - R = P_g + P_r$.

The allocation of energy resources will vary according to environmental circumstances, for example whether food or water is in short supply (i.e. where there is a limit on assimilation) or whether a reproductive season is approached (in which case greater emphasis will be on P_r. The allocation of energy to growth and reproduction in an animal is shown diagrammatically in Figure 2.6, but it should be pointed out that similar 'decisions' are made by plants, and that a similar diagram could be used to describe the allocation of other environmental resources, for example nutrients.

Various measures of efficiency are used in ecology. *Photosynthetic efficiency* is the proportion of available solar radiation that is used in photosynthesis, while *assimilation efficiency* is the animal equivalent, *viz.* the amount of energy assimilated (A) divided by the amount of energy consumed (C), i.e. A/C. *Production efficiency* is the percentage of the energy assimilated that is used for production, i.e. $(P_g + P_r)/A$, although

some authorities prefer to use $(P_g + P_r)/C$. Certainly, *growth efficiency* is P_g/A, i.e. the percentage of the energy assimilated that is used for growth (P_g) rather than reproduction (P_r) or respiration (R); and *reproductive efficiency* is P_r/A, i.e. the percentage of the energy assimilated that is used for reproduction (P_r) rather than for growth (P_g) or respiration.

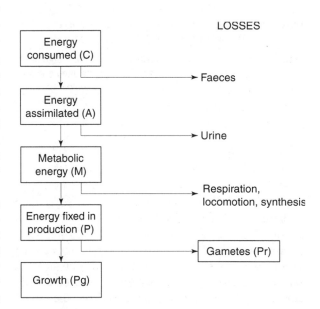

Figure 2.6 Allocation of energy to growth and reproduction in an animal.

Production efficiency, which excludes energy used in respiration, again differs with position along the food chain, and also differs between different groups of animals at the same trophic level (Table 2.3). For animals with similar metabolism, herbivores again have the lowest production efficiency, carnivores the highest. For example, in terrestrial invertebrates herbivores have production efficiency values of 21–39%, carnivores 27–55%. Generally speaking, cold-blooded animals (ectotherms) have production efficiencies of 10–55%, while warm-blooded animals (endotherms) have efficiencies of only 1–3%. Table 2.4 shows that, in non-social insects for instance, herbivores average a production efficiency of 38.8% and carnivores 55.6%, with detritivores in between at 47.0% (Beeby and Brennan, 1997).

These measures of ecological efficiency lead into two others. *Exploitation efficiency* is the percentage of the production of one trophic level that is ingested by the next higher trophic level. Anything not ingested in this way is either consumed by decomposers or accumulates in or is transported out of the system. *Trophic efficiency* is the efficiency of energy transfer from one trophic level to the one above. For example, the trophic efficiency of herbivores equals the percen-

Table 2.3   Production efficiency of selected species at Wytham Wood (data from Figure 2.8)

Group	Trophic position	Percentage of consumed energy converted to production
Herbivores		
Winter and tortrix moths	2	11.3
Voles and mice	2	1.2
Parasite		
Tachinid fly	3	21
Predators		
Spiders	3	25
Predatory beetles	3	10
Shrews	3	0.9
Blue and great tits	2 and 3	0.7
Owls	3	0.6

Source: Varley (1970)

Table 2.4   Production efficiencies of different animal groups

Group	Production efficiency (%)
Endotherms	
Mammalian insectivores	0.9
Birds	1.3
Small mammal communities	2.5
Other mammals	3.1
Ectotherms	
Fish and social insects	9.8
Non-insect invertebrates	25.0
Non-social insects	40.7
Non-insect invertebrates	
Herbivores	20.8
Carnivores	27.6
Detritivores	36.2
Non-social insects	
Herbivores	38.8
Detritivores	47.0
Carnivores	55.6

Source: Humphreys (1979)

tage of NPP converted to herbivore production, and the trophic efficiency of secondary consumers equals the percentage of production of herbivores (primary consumers) that is converted to the third trophic level.

Table 2.5 shows the trophic efficiencies of two important early studies in Minnesota, USA (Juday, 1940; Lindeman, 1942). The trophic efficiency of the primary producers is equivalent to their photosynthetic efficiencies. The Lake Mendota data were indeed used as the basis of

Table 2.5   Trophic efficiencies of different trophic levels in two lakes (after Lindeman, 1942)

Trophic level	Lake Mendota	Cedar Bog Lake
Producers	0.4%	0.1%
Primary consumers	8.7%	13.3%
Secondary consumers	5.5%	22.3%
Tertiary consumers	13.0%	–

Lindeman's law of trophic efficiency – that the efficiency of energy transfer from one trophic level to the next is about 10% – although this is more of a generalisation than a true law which would lead to accurate scientific predictions.

Organisms further along the food chain tend to have higher assimilation efficiencies, largely because of the higher energy value of their food. Thus a high proportion of a herbivore's food is likely to be cellulose, which requires bacteria in the stomach or rumen for digestion (see Section 2.2.1), and assimilation efficiency tends to be rather low, often below 10% and rarely much above: this is why herbivores must eat large quantities of food in order to meet their energy requirements. Since carnivores consume energy-rich, easily digested proteins and fats they have much higher assimilation efficiencies, which, together with the high nutritional quality of their food, means that meat eaters need to eat less food and/or to eat less frequently.

2.3.7 Energy flow through communities and pyramids of energy

Although carnivory is a more energy-efficient strategy than herbivory, so much more plant biomass is available in the biosphere that considerably more energy is available to plant eaters than to meat eaters. Ecological efficiencies also help to explain why there are relatively few trophic levels, since available energy decreases so rapidly at each transfer.

Figure 2.7 shows the energy flow established in a classic study undertaken by Howard Odum at Silver Springs, Florida, over the period 1952–55, one of the earliest quantifications of energy flow through a natural community. Most of the primary production came from phytoplankton such as diatoms and algae, in the water itself, on the sediment surface and also covering the leaves of larger plants (macrophytes), in particular arrowhead *Sagittaria*. Herbivores included snails,

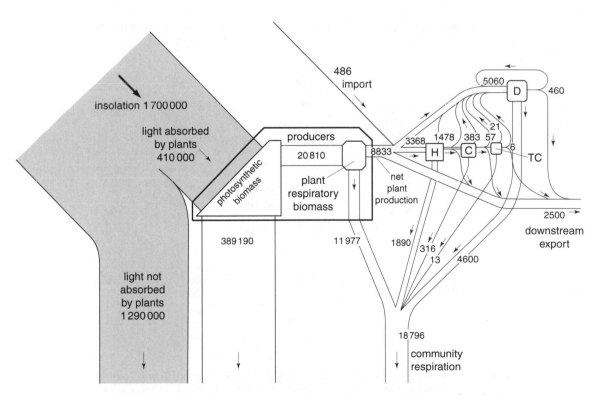

Figure 2.7 The energy flow in the Silver Springs community. The units are kcal m^{-2} yr^{-1} (1kcal = 4.2 kJ). H = herbivores: C = carnivores: TC = top carnivores: D = decomposers (from Odum, 1957).

insect grazers such as midge and caddis fly larvae, fish and turtles. Carnivores were largely fish, including the top carnivores (at the fourth trophic level) of gar and bass. One fish (stumpknocker) was omnivorous, and parasites occurred on all animals whatever their trophic level.

Examination of the data shows that photosynthetic efficiency was 1.2%, although the efficiency relative to incoming light of useable (rather than total) wavelengths reaching plant level was 5.3%. The trophic efficiency of herbivores was 15.9%, of secondary consumer carnivores 4.5%, and tertiary consumer carnivores 9.0%. The energy entering the system from solar radiation was 1.7 million kcal m^{-1} $year^{-1}$, yet only 6 kcal m^{-1} $year^{-1}$ was stored in the top carnivores, i.e. the fourth trophic level possessed a mere 0.000035% of the total incoming energy per unit area per unit time; similarly, the top carnivores stored only 0.007% of NPP, i.e. energy stored by the plants.

The system included some energy imported as plant material coming from outside the water body, and while most of the production went into respiration about 12% was exported downstream in the form of particulate material. Bacteria consituted a relatively small part of the standing crop biomass but next to green plants were the main consumers in terms of energy use.

A similar situation is shown in a terrestrial British example (Figure 2.8; see Table 2.3) although of necessity the food web and energy flow have been simplified. Photosynthetic efficiency was around 2.5%. The efficiencies of different animals, however, varied considerably, with ectotherms (such as earthworms and insects) having efficiencies about an order of magnitude greater than endotherms (birds and mammals). However, trophic position, or position within the food web, had apparently little to do with ecological efficiency in this example.

Pyramids of energy indicate the energy flow

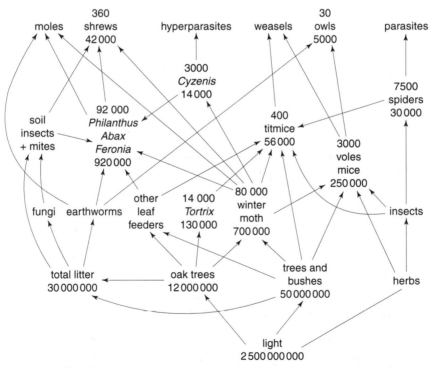

Figure 2.8 A simplified description of the energy flow at Wytham Wood, Oxford. The figures below a group of organisms give their rates of consumption in kcal ha^{-1} yr^{-1}. The corresponding figures above the organisms give their rates of production in kcal ha^{-1} yr^{-1} (after Varley, 1970).

through a system by representing the rate of energy flow, or productivity, at each trophic level. Since values represent rates of flow through a community, the units of measurement are energy (kcal or kJ) per unit area per unit time. Following the second law of thermodynamics, pyramids of energy cannot be inverted, since there is always a loss of energy into the environment (as respiratory heat) at each transfer (Figure 2.9).

2.3.8 Nutrient and biogeochemical cycles

Not only do organisms require energy in order to function and reproduce but they also need nutrients. Nutrients comprise elements that are chemically bound in different ways to make the (macro)molecules upon which all life depends. For most plants, the only source of raw materials that are used as nutrients are minerals. For most animals, nutrients come directly or indirectly from plants. The elements that form nutrient molecules are essentially unalterable and so pass from one trophic level to the next, and indeed for much of the time may be removed from the living system altogether, particularly following decomposition. They may be stored in the abiotic environment (water, air and the inorganic part of the soil) but are nevertheless always potentially available for subsequent uptake and recirculation. We therefore do not talk about a flow of nutrients but of *nutrient cycles*, and nutrient cycles are themselves part of *biogeochemical cycles*, in which elements circulate through the non-living as well as living compartments on Earth.

It is convenient to distinguish between *macronutrients*, which are present in various chemical forms and in large quantities in the environment, and are generally also in demand in large quantities by living organisms: examples are carbon, nitrogen, phosphorus and potassium; and *micro-*

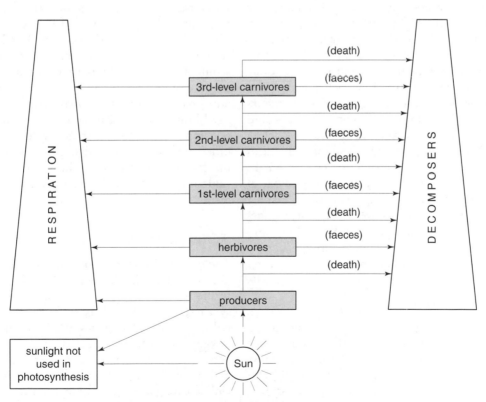

Figure 2.9   The flow of energy through a generalised food web.

nutrients, which are present in much lower quantities, often as *trace elements*, and while the actual quantities used by organisms may be small, these amounts are nevertheless often necessary for those organisms to thrive or even survive: examples are copper, zinc, manganese and cobalt.

Energy and nutrients are linked because both are transferred via feeding, but more than this the global movement, or *flux*, of nutrients is largely determined by the amount and availability of the energy needed to drive key ecological and environmental processes. Thus the energy acquired by photosynthesis fuels the metabolic processes that take up and utilise macro- and micronutrients. The availability or otherwise of nutrients will affect the distribution, activity and ecological relationships of individual species, communities and whole ecosystems.

Different elements cycle through the biosphere at different flux rates, depending on their physical form and chemical properties as well as the uses to which they are put by living organisms. The geochemical components of biogeochemical cycles include gaseous, aqueous and sedimentary compartments. In the sedimentary compartment, elements may be 'locked up' as rock for millions of years until, following erosion or volcanic activity, for example, they become available to the living world once again. Biogeochemical cycles thus include 'storage compartments' – *reservoirs* or *sinks* – which in time become *sources* and allow the elements to re-enter the active cycling process. Movement through the biogeochemical cycle thus can involve tectonic forces (e.g. earthquakes and volcanic activity), geomorphological processes (such as erosion), gaseous transport (especially through the atmosphere), water transport (e.g. as precipitation, stream flow and oceanic currents), and movement through uptake and transfer by living organisms as food.

2.3.8.1 The carbon cycle

Carbon is particularly important to the living world, as all organic material contains this element. Around half the dry weight of most animals consists of carbon, for example 48% in humans (Rankama and Sahama, 1950), and in plants the proportion is much higher. The carbon

reservoir in the atmosphere is around 7.5×10^{14} kg (see Figure 2.10). The atmosphere is the most important source of carbon for the living world, even though it is found in only low concentrations there: carbon dioxide (CO_2) is the most abundant form, for instance, yet comprises only 0.03% of the atmosphere. Green plants provide the major route, photosynthesis, by which carbon is removed from the atmosphere; because they represent the highest total biomass, marine phytoplankton and the world's major forests make the most important contributions.

Carbon becomes stored in sediment and rocks in many forms, for example coal, oil and gas deposits derived from ancient plants, or as calcium carbonate ($CaCO_3$) in chalk and limestones derived from the shells of myriads of marine organisms. Decayed and decaying organic matter is also found in soil humus and peat, where microbial activity provides a major source of carbon dioxide. Land and sea together provide carbon storage 40 000 times greater in amount than in the atmosphere, but it is the carbon in the latter that is generally most available, especially to plants. The carbon stored in rocks has a very long *turnover time* of about 413 million years (Kempe, 1979), i.e. it has been estimated that it would take 413 million years for all the stored carbon atoms to move to an atmospheric, aqueous or biological compartment.

Although carbon can be released via microbial decomposition, the carbon cycle differs from other nutrient cycles in that green plants can take up carbon directly from the atmosphere in the same form, CO_2, as it is excreted by organisms in respiration.

2.3.8.2 The oxygen cycle

The oxygen content of the atmosphere is inextricably linked to the development and continuation of life on Earth (see Ecology Box 1.2) via photosynthesis (which releases it) and respiration (which uses and depletes it). The link between oxygen and life is reflected by a tight linkage between the oxygen cycle and the carbon cycle, and indeed with other global nutrient cycles. Unlike carbon, oxygen is much more abundant in the atmosphere (21%).

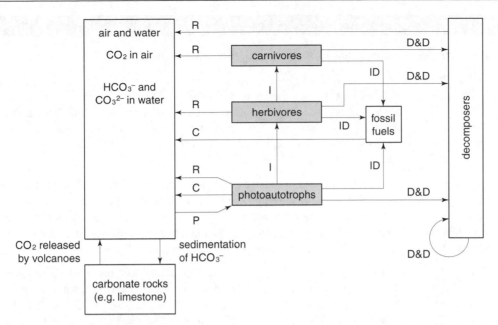

Figure 2.10 The carbon cycle. I = ingestion of organic compounds containing carbon: P = uptake of CO_2 in photosynthesis: R = release of CO_2 in respiration: C = release of CO_2 in combustion: D & D = passage of organic compounds containing carbon to decomposers via death and decay: ID = conversion of organic compounds into fossil fuels via incomplete decay.

2.3.8.3 The nitrogen cycle

Around 78% of the atmosphere comprises nitrogen, and after carbon and oxygen, nitrogen is weight for weight the next most abundant element in biological molecules such as proteins, chlorophyll and nucleic acids. However, moving from the atmosphere into the biological system is not simple, because atmospheric nitrogen is largely in the molecular form (N_2), which is unusable by most living organisms and difficult to convert to forms that can be used. Most organisms cannot afford the energy needed to split the nitrogen molecule, and the biochemical means of doing this have therefore not evolved.

The most important form of nitrogen used by plants as a nutrient is nitrate (NO_3^-). Huge discharges of energy such as from lightning can convert N_2 to NO_3^-, but only small amounts enter the soil in this way, and conversion by nitrogen-fixing organisms is a far more significant source of nitrate to plants (Ecology Box 2.1). Some of these microorganisms are free-living, for example cyanobacteria (also known as blue-green

algae, but they are neither true bacteria nor true algae) and true bacteria such as *Thiobacillus*, but many microbial taxa, for instance bacteria such as *Rhizobium*, fix nitrogen only in symbiotic associations with plants in which energy costs are shared.

Nitrate, however, is a highly soluble form of nitrogen, which makes it vulnerable to being washed (leached) through soil, and this may make nitrogen as a nutrient in short supply in areas where there is free-draining soil and heavy rainfall.

The amount of nitrogen in its various forms present in the living system is negligible compared with the amount held in the atmosphere (4×10^{18} kg) and in rocks (2×10^{20} kg) (Figure 2.11). Annual rates of nitrogen fixation by terrestrial bacteria are only about 1.4×10^{11} kg. In terrestrial ecosystems, around 97% of the nitrogen is found in the non-living part of the soil – as soil organic and inorganic matter and in the litter – leaving a mere 3% in plants and animals (Rosswall, 1983). Nitrogen fertilisation, however, can be efficient: for permanent pasture a recovery

ECOLOGY BOX 2.1

Nitrogen fixation, nitrification, denitrification and ammonification

Nitrogen fixation involves the reduction of atmospheric nitrogen (N_2) to ammonium (NH_4^+). Most biological nitrogen fixation from the atmosphere is performed by free-living or plant-symbiotic bacteria and cyanobacteria, which occur in both terrestrial and aquatic environments. These microorganisms contain *nitrogenase*, an enzyme (specialised protein molecule) responsible for splitting N_2 and combining it with hydrogen to form ammonia (NH_3). The ammonia immediately dissolves in the cell's water and picks up a proton to become ammonium. (Ammonia is the non-ionized form, ammonium the dissolved, ionized form.)

In turn, ammonium may have oxygen added to it by the microorganisms (such oxidation benefiting them by releasing energy, which can be used for growth) so that ammonium is converted to nitrite (NO_2^-), which in turn can be converted to nitrate (NO_3^-). These last two chemical reactions represent a process known as *nitrification*. Most plants take up the majority of their nitrogen in the form of nitrate, but many plants also absorb ammonium, although often this will then be converted to nitrate (Mauseth, 1991; Stewart, 1991).

The commonest group of nitrogen-fixing bacteria belong to the genus *Rhizobium*. Such bacteria form symbiotic associations in the root nodules of certain plants, particularly members of the pea family (Fabaceae) – including many nitrogen-fixing plants of agricultural importance such as peas, beans, clover, lucerne, sainfoin and groundnut. Rhizobia can also fix nitrogen in some members of the elm family (Ulmaceae) and also some grasses (Poaceae), although not as yet (pending success via genetic engineering) any commercial cereals. The symbiosis benefits both the rhizobia, which receive protection in the plants, which also provide a carbon source for the bacteria, and the plants, which have nitrogen made available in a usable form. A similar symbiotic relationship can also be found between nitrogen-fixing actinomycete fungi of the genus *Frankia* and plants such as alder (Betulaceae) and buckthorn (Rhamnaceae). Cyanobacteria such as *Anabaena* and *Nostoc* can also form symbiotic associations, for example with relatively primitive plants such as cycads and *Azolla* ferns. Some free-living bacteria and cyanobacteria can fix nitrogen for their own use. This ability can give cyanobacteria a competitive advantage in fresh water, where available nitrogen is often in short supply, even when other nutrients are abundant (Mauseth, 1991).

The oxidation of ammonium to nitrite is often undertaken by bacteria of the genera *Nitrosomonas*, *Nitrosospira*, *Nitrosococcus* and *Nitrosolobus*. Subsequent oxidation of nitrite to nitrate takes place with bacterial genera such as *Nitrobacter*, *Nitrospira* and *Nitrococcus* (Hamilton, 1988).

Denitrification is the process by which nitrate (NO_3^-) is reduced to nitrous oxide (N_2O), nitric oxide (NO) or molecular nitrogen (N_2) by some *aerobic* (oxygen-dependent) bacteria, which use the nitrate for respiration. Some *anaerobic* bacteria, for example *Clostridium* and *Pseudomonas*, can convert nitrate to nitrite under non-oxygenated, waterlogged conditions. Also, plants lose small amounts of nitrogen to the atmosphere as gaseous ammonium, N_2O, NO_2 and NO.

Finally, *ammonification* occurs when organisms die or excrete nitrogenous waste, and when bacteria and fungi convert nitrogen into ammonium to use in the synthesis of protein and other organic compounds for their own use. Some of the ammonium is lost into the surrounding soil and can be taken up by other microorganisms and plants.

of 67% of applied nitrogen is usual, partitioned between herbage, stubble and roots (Dilz, 1988; Jenkinson and Smith, 1988). Nitrogen relationships in all plants reflect the interaction between this and other nutrients, light and water availability, and this in turn is reflected in yield, i.e. production of biomass (Montieth *et al.*, 1994).

2.3.8.4 The phosphorus cycle

Unlike carbon, oxygen and nitrogen, phosphorus is not found in the atmospheric compartment. Phosphorus occurs mainly as phosphates (PO_4^{3-}), which are insoluble compounds that are slowly weathered from rocks but are also found in the

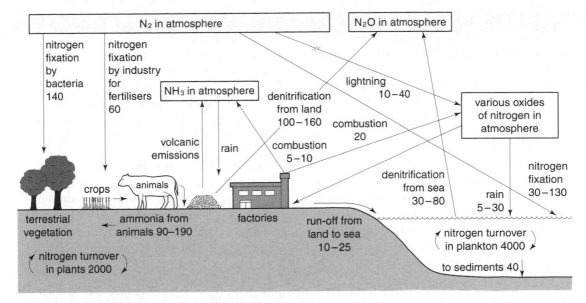

Figure 2.11   Global nitrogen cycle, with estimates of the annual rates of flow (as 10^{12} g).

oceans, where they are much more accessible (Figure 2.12). Indeed, a major source of phosphorus for terrestrial organisms is from marine waters via plankton, fish and fish-eating seabirds. When these birds defecate on land they create phosphate-rich deposits, or *guano*, which can

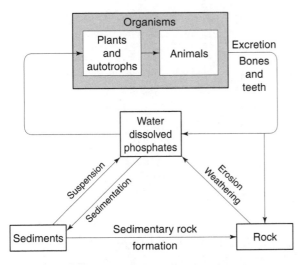

Figure 2.12   The phosphorus cycle. Phosphorus occurs mainly in the form of phosphates – insoluble compounds that are slowly weathered from rocks or resuspended from living organisms. This cycle differs from most of the others as it lacks a significant atmospheric phase.

accumulate to considerable depths, and in parts of the world guano has been 'mined' as a rich source of fertiliser.

Phosphorus largely enters the food chain via phytoplankton and, on land, higher plants, which are then eaten by animals. Plants obtain phosphorus from the soil either as dihydrogen phosphate ($H_2PO_4^-$), when the soil is acid or, more slowly, as hydrogen phosphate (HPO_4^{2-}), in non-acid soils. Both plants and animals bioconcentrate phosphate in their tissues. On death, the phosphorus either continues to cycle rapidly through the food chain or decomposer system, or enters soil or sediment, where it can become inaccessible and therefore unavailable for thousands or even millions of years, for example until erosion transports it back to the sea, where the cycle can continue more rapidly.

Phosphorus is an essential nutrient for proteins, nucleic acids, cell membranes, bones and teeth, and it is crucial in many intracellular biochemical processes, especially as a constituent of adenosine triphosphate (ATP), which is essential for the transfer of energy. However, phosphorus is the key limiting nutrient in many ecosystems because of its insolubility.

As with nitrogen, a number of bacteria and fungi are important in making phosphorus available to other organisms. Of particular importance are the symbiotic relationships forged between some plants and a group of fungi known as *mycorrhizae* (from the Greek words for 'fungus' and 'root'). These fungi grow either around the plant root (*ectomycorrhizae*) or around and inside small spaces in the root (*vesicular-arbuscular mycorrhizae*, VAM). The plant provides nutrients (including carbon) for the fungus, while the fungal network of thread-like pseudo-roots (mycelia) extending outside the root explores the soil and scavenges for phosphorus, as well as some ammonium, nitrate, potassium and micronutrients, which are thereby made available to the plant (Hayman and Mosse, 1972; Robinson, 1991). VAM also provide additional moisture to the host plant, increasing the latter's resistance to drought.

2.3.8.5 *The copper cycle*

Copper is required in relatively small concentrations by many organisms. When even this requirement is not met organisms suffer from a nutrient deficiency. Copper, however, is also an example of an element that can occur in excessive amounts in living tissue, when it can become toxic and therefore an example of a pollutant. Many other micronutrients become heavy metal pollutants when found in quantities that an organism finds intolerable, the commonest being iron, zinc, manganese, molybdenum, nickel, cobalt and selenium.

Figure 2.13 shows the global copper cycle, while Figure 2.14 gives a general view of the annual cycling of this element in the soil. The copper associated with soil organic matter globally (2.4×10^{12} kg) is roughly 36% of the copper burden in soil. A residence time of 860 years has been estimated for copper in the soils of the upper Thames basin (Bowen, 1977). The global copper load in litter is estimated at 1.3×10^9 kg, in plant biomass 2.9×10^{10} kg, and animal biomass 2.4×10^{10} kg (Nriagu, 1979).

Copper in the soil is more strongly bound to organic matter than are most other trace elements,

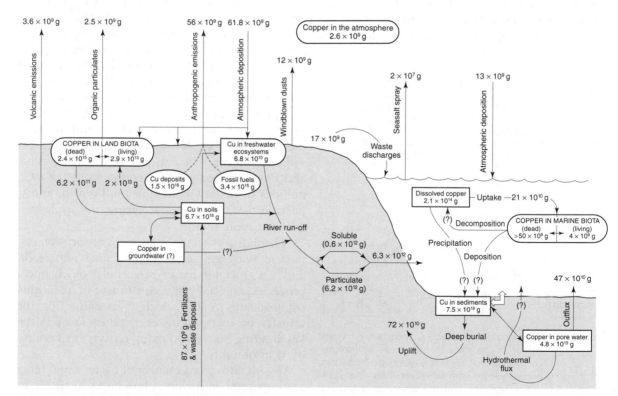

Figure 2.13 The global copper cycle on a 1-year time frame.

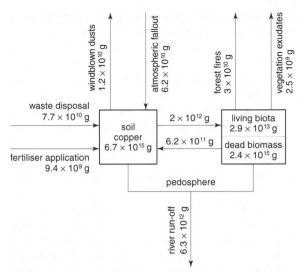

Figure 2.14   The annual cycling of copper in the pedosphere.

and it is also generally strongly held on inorganic compounds. As a result, much of the total copper content of soils is not available for uptake by plants, although more is available from mineral soils than from organic-rich ones such as peat. Copper deficiencies in crops and plants generally may be due to an inherently low copper content of the soil but may also reflect the small amount actually present in an available chemical form. Deficiencies may be exacerbated by relatively large uptake by microorganisms. In agriculture, use of nitrogenous and phosphatic fertilisers may also lead to copper deficiency (Thornton, 1979).

Copper deficiency in livestock may again reflect low copper concentration in the soil, but it also commonly results from an excess of another trace element, molybdenum, and an interaction between copper, molybdenum and sulphur which reduces the availability of copper. A minimum dietary requirement for cattle of 10 μg Cu g^{-1} has been recommended in the UK (Agricultural Research Council, 1965). Uptake of copper from pasture depends not only on the amount and chemical form of the copper in the soil but also on plant species, stage of growth, season and fertiliser application. Leguminous plants such as clover tend to take up larger amounts of copper than grasses. Mixed pasture herbage rarely contains >20 μg Cu g^{-1} in the dry matter, and usually <10 μg Cu g^{-1}. Copper taken up by

grasses may be preferentially stored in the roots, and this may hinder transfer from soil via plants to grazing animal (Jarvis, 1978).

In woodland systems, soil animals are important in the copper cycle, but different animal groups possess different abilities to assimilate this element; for example, earthworms tend to contain little copper compared with gastropods (slugs and snails), which in turn acumulate rather less than woodlice. Many such animals will, of course, be eaten, so copper proceeds through the food chain, but faeces are also very important in distributing copper through the food web (Wieser, 1979).

2.3.9 Agro-ecosystems

Energy and nutrients pass through crop and pasture, perhaps through livestock, and eventually to humans (Figure 2.15). Energy and nutrients also pass through other plants and animals, a few of which may be designated weeds or pests because of their real or perceived adverse effects on crops and stock. Particular systems may closely mimic natural systems, for instance extensive livestock grazing on open rangeland, or they may be very artificial, heavily subsidised, for example, by chemicals and hydrocarbon-based

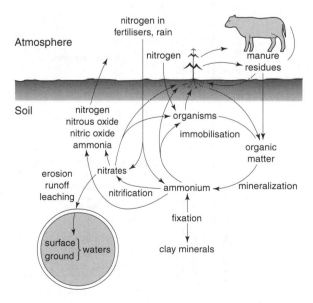

Figure 2.15   The nitrogen cycle in soil, crops and livestock.

energy inputs, but in all cases we are looking at different kinds of ecosystem, albeit ones with heavy human influences (Loucks, 1977; Odum, 1984). These are *agro-ecosystems*.

The definition of an agro-ecosystem by Coleman and Hendrix (1988) as 'an ecosystem manipulated by frequent, marked anthropogenic modifications of its biotic and abiotic environment,' while curiously context-free (since the definition is true of other highly human-modified ecosystems, for example urban ecosystems), rightly stresses the importance of human influence. Tivy (1990) emphasises that 'the farmer is an essential ecological variable in influencing or determining the composition, the functioning and the stability of the system.' Conway (1987) similarly defines an agro-ecosystem as 'an ecological and socio-economic system, comprising domesticated plants and/or animals and the people who husband them, intended for the purpose of producing food, fibre or other agricultural products.' 'It takes little effort,' continues Conway, 'to recognize agricultural systems, such as the ricefields of northern Thailand, as modified ecological systems' (Figure 2.16).

Major distinctions between agro-ecosystems and natural ecosystems include:

- As well as energy derived from incoming solar radiation, additional energy inputs to agro-ecosystems come from human and animal labour and fuel-powered machinery. Additional water, fertilisers and pesticides may also be provided.
- Artificial selection produces the dominant plants and animals, whose genetic base is also generally more limited than would occur in nature.
- Biodiversity in agro-ecosystems is reduced to maximise yield (expressed as biomass or economic profit). There are fewer plant species because of crops or pasture being sown and undesirable species (weeds) minimised, and fewer animal species because of livestock being grazed and numbers of undesirable species (pests) reduced.
- Food chains are simplified, so energy is channelled along fewer and often shorter routes than in many natural ecosystems.
- Energy use is more 'efficient', and the biomass of large herbivores (cattle, sheep, pigs, etc.) is much greater than that of their equivalents in unmanaged ecosystems.
- Less energy passes through the decomposition compartment of an agro-ecosystem, and a

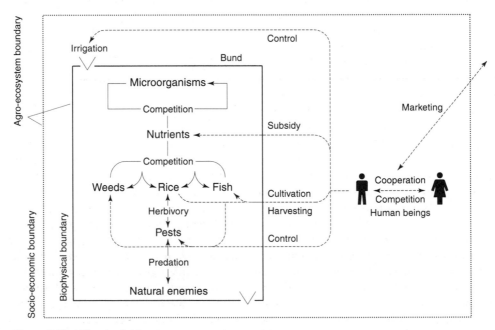

Figure 2.16   The rice field as an agro-ecosystem.

higher proportion of plant biomass is consumed by livestock or exported from the system following harvest.

- Because profitable plant and animal tissue is exported from the system, nutrients are also taken away. (Even residue such as stubble may be burned off rather than allowed to decay or be ploughed back into the soil.) Such a loss of nutrients from the system thus needs replenishment by the periodic introduction of fertilisers by the farmer.
- For the same reason, nutrient cycling tends to be more rapid than in natural systems, and nutrient amounts are pulsed as fertilisers are applied and harvesting takes away the crops, which are using (but not replenishing) the nutrients.
- Agro-ecosystems are often considered to be inherently less stable than natural systems because they lack the species diversity and functional interactions of the latter. While the concept of ecosystem stability is examined more fully in Chapter 3, it is worth pointing out that such comparisons may be invalid because the stability of an agro-ecosystem depends on how well the farmer manages the system.
- Agro-ecosystems are generally more open systems than natural systems, with a greater number and larger quantities of inputs (gains) and outputs (losses). In terms of inputs, agro-ecosystems are subsidised by the additions of energy noted earlier (Figure 2.17) (Tivy, 1990).
- At a landscape scale, agro-ecosystems usually incorporate (semi)natural habitats – for example, farmland may include woodland areas, hedgerows (a woodland edge/scrub analogue) and verges (herb-rich grassland) – which do increase overall biodiversity and make ecosystem structure more complex.

Smith and Hill (1975) identify biological diversity, the nature and intensity of management, and net energy balance as key features by which different ecosystems can be distinguished and characterised (Figure 2.18). Clearly, though, boundaries between different ecosystem types vary, and Coleman and Hendrix (1988) plausibly

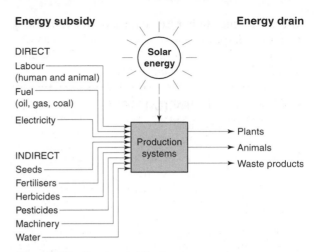

Figure 2.17 Energy subsidies in agro-ecosystems.

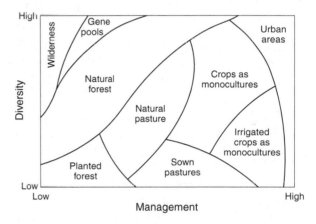

Figure 2.18 The relationship between agro-ecosystem diversity (species, habitat) in terms of management intensity.

argue that 'perhaps it is best to drop the now timeworn distinction between natural and human managed ... ecosystem. The extent and timing of the disturbances is what sets managed systems apart from nonmanaged ones.' The chief difference between such systems is the imposition in managed systems, including agro-ecosystems, of immediate, short-term economic goals. Agro-ecosystems are managed to maximise net production, while most natural ecosystems have a production/respiration ratio close to 1 (Odum, 1971; Coleman *et al.*, 1976). Agriculture has indeed been described as artificially maintaining a site at an early successional (low maturity) stage to exploit the high rate of productivity, thereby accumulating biomass.

2.4 Issues in environmental management

A business-as-usual scenario – a continuation of present trends, patterns and activities – 'suggests that the world is unlikely to see food production keep pace with population growth... The world will experience a declining per capita food production in the decades ahead... A tripling of the world's food production by the year 2050 is such a remote prospect that it cannot be considered a realistic possibility. Fertility and population growth in numerous developing countries will then be forced downward by severe shortages of food, disease and by other processes set in motion by shortages of vital resources and irreversible environmental damage' (Kendall and Pimentel, 1994).

Global commitment is therefore needed to integrate three policies: a reduction in environmental degradation (including a less profligate use of resources); an increase and rationalisation of food production and distribution; and a slowing down of global population increase (which in practice means focusing on birth rates in the developing world). Despite the resolutions of the 1992 Rio Conference and some action resulting from these, governments on the whole remain lacking in vision and commitment. It is nevertheless useful to review what the Rio Conference set out to do, what it did achieve then and what it has achieved since.

2.4.1 Before Rio: environmentalism in the 1970s and 1980s

The Rio Conference did not take place in a strategy vacuum. The preceding decades had seen a number of ideas, both philosophical and practical, converging on the common goals of social equity and sensible, sustainable use of environmental resources.

During the 1960s and early 1970s, the emergence of the idea (and with satellites and spacecraft, the image) of Spaceship Earth developed into a greater awareness of the vulnerability of the global environment. In 1972, Stockholm hosted the United Nations Conference on the Human Environment, attended by 113 countries and nineteen intergovernmental agencies. As well as leading to the initiation of many national conservation and environmental policies and agencies, the Stockholm Conference legitimised the place of environmental issues in international relations (Thomas, 1992).

Also in 1972, two publications initiated major and often radical rethinking about how we use our planet. *Blueprint for survival* (Goldsmith *et al.*, 1972) popularised the opinion that infinite growth cannot be sustained by using finite resources (non-*renewable* resources such as minerals, or – with the same end-result and therefore amounting to the same thing – profligately used and therefore non-*renewed* resources such as timber). *The limits to growth* (Meadows *et al.*, 1972) was a more substantial report produced for the Club of Rome, an informal international group concerned for the present and future predicament of humankind (Barrow, 1995).

This latter publication used a complex systems dynamic approach to model past and probable future behaviour of the global environment between 1900 and 2100. It was nevertheless presented in a non-technical manner and was therefore accessible to and assessable by a concerned public. The format used was of a series of scenarios: assuming a set of conditions and trends, an assessment was made of likely consequences. The assumptions, and how one used them, were inevitably the subject of furious debate (e.g. Cole *et al.*, 1973), with advocates pursuing the idea of zero economic growth, a completely free market and all positions in between (O'Riordan, 1976; Freeman and Jahoda, 1978). Twenty years later, Meadows *et al.* (1992) claimed that some of the 'limits' described and defined in 1972 had already been exceeded, although catastrophe could still be avoided were there to be a common will to modify our approaches to economic development and resource management.

Completed in 1979 by the Council of Environmental Quality, an advisory branch of the US government, *The Global 2000 Report to the President* made a pessimistic prognosis:

> If present trends continue, the world in 2000 will be more crowded, more polluted, less stable ecologically, and more vulnerable to disruption than the world we live in now. Serious stresses involving population, resources, and environment are already visible ahead
>
> (Barney *et al.*, 1982)

Although the conclusions of this report were refuted by a number of economists, the general points do seem to have been sustained.

Between 1973 and the early 1980s, however, global concern was generally more aimed at the energy crisis that followed the raising of oil prices by OPEC (the Organisation of Petroleum Exporting Countries) than at population growth, environmental degradation and resource depletion. Nevertheless, in 1980 another environmental strand was promoted by the *World conservation strategy: living resources for sustainable development* (IUCN, UNEP and WWF, 1980) which stressed that conservation is not the opposite of development. Its three major objectives can be summarised as:

- Essential ecological processes and life-support systems must be maintained.
- Genetic diversity must be preserved.
- Any use of species or ecosystems must be sustainable.

The *World conservation strategy* was the first publication in which the phrase 'sustainable development' reached a wide audience. There were also environmental implications behind the Brandt Report (Independent Commission on International Development Issues, 1980), which indicated the socio-economic contrast between 'North' (the more developed world) and 'South' (the developing world) and stressed the need to recognise the interdependence and mutual interest of both 'halves'.

The Bruntland Report, *Our common future* (World Commission on Environment and Development, 1987) reiterated the need for sustainable development, emphasising that any understanding of the issues behind sustainability and any attempt to implement a solution needed to integrate economics with ecology. The environmental message of the politician Gro Harlem Bruntland, prime minister of Norway, was forcibly reiterated by the economist David Pearce and colleagues in their *Blueprint for a green economy* (Pearce *et al.*, 1989) and subsequent publications (Pearce and Turner, 1990; Pearce, 1991). These were polemical texts that initiated a new relationship between the social sciences, the natural sciences, economics and policy making (Barrow, 1995).

In 1991, the same organisations behind the *World conservation strategy* produced *Caring for the Earth* (IUCN, UNEP and WWF, 1991). Its subtitle indicated its aim – to define 'a strategy for sustainable living'. More specifically (and recapitulating the Bruntland Report) it defined two requirements:

- To secure a widespread and deeply held commitment to a new ethic, the ethic for sustainable living, and to translate its principles into practice
- To integrate conservation and development: conservation to keep our actions within the Earth's capacity, and development to enable people everywhere to enjoy long, healthy and fulfilling lives.

Earlier, and more explicitly on agriculture, the World Resources Institute had published *To feed the Earth: agro-ecology for sustainable development* (Dover and Talbot, 1987). The idea was

> not to abandon the methods of industrial agriculture that have been so successful in the economic and ecological conditions for which they were designed, but to determine where such methods as mechanisation, use of agricultural chemicals, and monoculture are and are not appropriate, and to develop alternative systems better suited to tropical climates and developing economies
>
> (Dover and Talbot, 1987)

The last five words, however, indicate a weakness in this otherwise valuable publication, because, while the aim of feeding the world must certainly focus on problems in the developing world, much also needs to be done to make Western farming in temperate latitudes more sustainable and less environmentally damaging.

2.4.2 The Earth Summit 1992: Agenda 21 and sustainability

The United Nations Conference on Environment and Development was held in Rio de Janeiro, Brazil, over the period 3–14 June 1992; it has also become known as the Earth Summit or simply the Rio Conference. It was a response to and a demonstration of a greater global and national awareness and willingness to discuss environmental and development issues and the socio-cultural, -economic and -political implications of these issues. A rapprochement was needed between the developed and developing world, yet it was apparent even before the summit that some of the latter, at least, would have to take steps towards development that would have both goals and paths rather different from those taken by the more developed countries (Holmberg *et al.*, 1993).

The Earth Summit brought together representatives of 178 national governments, including over 100 heads of state and government leaders. There were almost 10 000 official delegates, added to whom were several thousand representatives of environmental groups and other non-governmental organisations.

Major agreements reached at Rio included a Framework Convention on Climatic Change (see Chapter 4); a Convention on Biodiversity (Chapter 6); Forestry Principles (including the principle that forest resources and forest lands should be *sustainably* managed to meet the social, economic, ecological, cultural and spiritual needs of present and future generations); and Agenda 21, an action plan or agenda for the twenty-first century by which conservation and development can be reconciled and sustainable development achieved (Koch and Grubb, 1993). Another outcome of the summit was the Rio Declaration of 27 principles, which placed greater emphasis on issues of development and less on ecological concerns than the Stockholm Conference 20 years earlier. The very first principle, for example,

declared that 'human beings are at the centre of concerns for sustainable development' and are 'entitled to a healthy and productive life in harmony with nature' (United Nations, 1993).

Agenda 21 reflects consideration of both general issues relating to development and sustainable use of rather more specific resources. It also addresses how individual action plans could be implemented and what the roles of various groups, organisations and governments might be. Agenda 21 was not a binding treaty, but it has carried authority as 'a collection of agreed and negotiated wisdoms' (Koch and Grubb, 1993). Each country is to translate Agenda 21 into 'terms appropriate for its own circumstances' (Mather and Chapman, 1995). In the UK, for example, action and implementation has been devolved to local authorities, hence Local Agenda 21 (LA21). At the global level, however, the UN General Assembly has established the Commission on Sustainable Development to review progress in the implementation of Agenda 21 by each signatory nation.

A number of useful resolutions were therefore agreed at Rio, even if their implementation has often been tardy or even non-existent, but delegates balked at firm recommendations or agreements over one key issue – population control.

> The long-term consequences of human population growth must be fully grasped by all nations. . . Rapidly increasing demands for natural resources, employment, education and social services make any attempt to protect natural resources and improve living standards very difficult. There is an immediate need to develop strategies aimed at controlled world population growth.
>
> (Sitarz, 1993)

It can be seen from the above that a key component in much of what was agreed at Rio, at times implicit but often explicit, was the idea of sustainability, in particular the notion of sustainable development. Sustainable development was cleverly defined in the Bruntland Report as 'development that meets the needs of the present without compromising the ability of future generations to meet their own needs' (World Commission on Environment and Development, 1987). The report continued: 'Perceived needs are culturally determined, and sustainable development requires the promotion of values that encourage consumption standards that are within the bounds of the ecological [*sic*] possible and to which all can reasonably aspire.'

More usefully, perhaps, the UN Food and Agriculture Organisation defines sustainable development as:

> the management and conservation of the natural resource base, and the orientation of technological and institutional change in such a manner as to ensure the attainment and continued satisfaction of human needs for present and future generations. Such sustainable development ... conserves land, water, plant and animal genetic resources, is environmentally non-degrading, technologically appropriate, economically viable and socially acceptable.

(FAO, 1992).

Even with such definitions, however, sustainability remains in many ways a rather vague, bland and possibly meaningless concept, although these very qualities may well have allowed it to become an acceptable notion to many governments (Mather and Chapman, 1995). Turner (1993), however, proposes that a range of approaches is legitimate and merely reflects different world views, from the ecocentric to the technocentric.

2.4.3 Sustainable agriculture

Conway (1997) argues that 'agricultural sustainability is the ability of an agroecosystem to maintain productivity in the face of [environmental] stress or shock.' One way of improving sustainability is to protect the agro-ecosystem from such shock, for example nomadic pastoralists moving livestock to avoid drought, or farmers reducing pest infestations using biological (rather than chemical) means of control.

Productivity, ecosystem stability and sustainability are linked, although sometimes inversely, for instance where irrigation initially increases productivity (crop yield) but in the longer term reduces stability and sustainability, through salinisation for example (Figure 2.19).

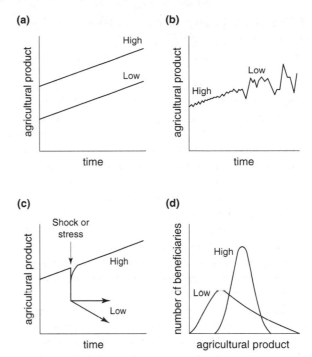

Figure 2.19 (a) Productivity, (b) stability, (c) sustainability and (d) equitability in agro-ecosystems.

Agricultural techniques that tend to enhance sustainability include:

- **Intercropping** – growing two or more crops on the same piece of land at the same time. Benefits may come from crops exploiting different resources, for example drawing water up from different soil depths or placing different demands on soil nutrients. Crops may also interact to mutual advantage: leguminous plants such as clover might fix nitrogen for another crop, for instance, or one plant may deter pest insects from another by virtue of its scent. Interactions may also help to control weeds: Carruthers *et al.* (1998), for example, showed that intercropping maize with combinations of soya beans, lupin, clover and forage ryegrass could reduce weed biomass and density by 73–100%. The 'intercrop' may indeed be a non-crop plant, whose aim is purely to attract potentially damaging pests away from the actual crop plants. Intercropping often increases the yield per unit area over that obtained from a monoculture (Table 2.6). Yield can be 20–50% higher

Table 2.6   Yield of grain (kg ha^{-1}) in monocrop and interplanted stands of corn and pigeon pea

Treatment	16 weeks*	24 weeks†	24-week total‡
Corn	3130	–	3130
Pigeon pea	–	1871	1871
Mixed intercrop	2025	1710	3735
Row intercrop	2606	1854	4460

* Corn harvest; † pigeon pea harvest; ‡ corn and pigeon pea harvest

when the mixture is one of annual plus perennial crop species (Tivy, 1990).

One variant is relay intercropping during part of the life cycle of each crop: a second crop is planted after the first has reached its reproductive stage of growth but before it is ready for harvesting.

- **Rotation** – growing two or more crops in sequence on the same piece of land, with similar benefits to intercropping. Avoiding use of the same crop year after year also reduces the chances of a build-up of soil pathogens.
- **Agroforestry** – a variation on intercropping but with perennial trees or shrubs interspersed with annual crops. Again different soil resources may be exploited. Trees provide fruit, nuts, leaf fodder and fibre; leaf-fall can serve as a mulch; benefits from shade in tropical areas tend to outweigh any reduction in photosynthetically active radiation; and roots help to bind the soil to reduce the risk of erosion (see Issues Box 2.1).
- **Silvo-pasture** – combining trees with grassland and other fodder species. A mixture of grazing on grass and herbs and above-ground browsing on trees may permit stocking of different livestock animals, partitioning the food resource.
- **Green manure** – legumes and other plants fix nitrogen, sustaining the fertility of the soil, but rather than being harvested they then may be dug or ploughed into the soil to be used by the next crop. Similarly, cereal stubble can be incorporated into the soil rather than being burned off.
- **Conservation tillage** – minimum, shallow or zero tillage in which seeds are placed directly in the soil reduces the amount of disturbance

and the risk of soil erosion by wind or water. Minimal turning over of the soil may also reduce weed germination and emergence. On the other hand, soil turnover may help with nutrient cycling and reduce the chance of less permeable crusts forming on the topsoil.
- **Minimal use of machinery** – conventional wisdom suggests that, as well as the expense of using machinery (and its fuel), large and heavy machinery compacts the soil, making it more difficult for roots and water to penetrate, and encouraging erosion of the soil by greater amounts and concentrations of surface runoff. In some cases, however, light compaction actually reduces the risk of erosion.
- **Biological control** – using natural enemies to control weeds and pests (see Chapter 5) rather than chemical methods (see Chapter 3), or if chemicals are used then this is done as part of a programme of *integrated pest management* where, for example, pesticides are used sparingly together with biological or cultural methods of control.

Sustainable agriculture is also about reducing, avoiding or substituting many farming practices that rely on heavily subsidised, quick-fix solutions to increase productivity. In its action plan for sustainable agriculture, the World Resources Institute prescribed four key areas for consideration (Dover and Talbot, 1987):

1. **Soil quality** – maintain and improve soil quality by maintaining plant growth of some sort for as long as possible during the year, using cover crops, appropriate crop rotations or multi-cropping, retention of residues (e.g. stubble), mulching, and minimal or zero tillage.

2. **Ecological efficiency** – for example, recycling nutrients and using organic fertilisers, optimising energy efficiency, and using biological control.

3. **Agro-ecosystem stability** – using short negative feedback loops, e.g. use of natural enemies in the biological control of weeds and pests.

ISSUES BOX 2.1

Agroforestry

Agroforestry refers to 'land-use systems and technologies where woody perennials (trees, shrubs, palms, bamboos, etc.) are deliberately used on the same land management unit as agricultural crops and/or animals, either in some form of spatial arrangement or temporal sequence' (International Council for Research in Agroforestry).

Agroforestry uses trees as a major component of a multi-crop production system that echoes more natural multi-layered ecosystems. The trees provide shade. Competition for soil water and nutrients is minimised since tree roots use these resources from a lower soil depth than do crops, although use of some water-demanding tree species (e.g. eucalypts) has in places led to a lowering of the water table. Roots can actually draw nutrients up into the topsoil, where they become available to crop plants. By binding the soil with their roots and protecting the soil from the impact of heavy rain by their crowns, trees also reduce the threat of soil erosion.

Agroforestry includes:

- *alley cropping*, in which annual crops are cultivated between lines of trees that provide mulching and fodder material, particularly from leaves, and possibly fuelwood;
- *orchards*, in which trees provide fruit (or other commodities, e.g. medicines) where the ground Is cropped or grazed;
- mixed growth of *permanent crops* (e.g. coffee or cacao) between timber trees;
- growth of crops in fields sheltered by tree *windbreaks*;
- growth of *scattered trees*, especially in pasture land, to improve soil conservation and provide shade, fuelwood and timber;
- *plantation system*, where the ground layer may be grazed by livestock;
- arguably, also *shifting cultivation* systems, where small plots are allowed to revert to forest after a number of years of cropping.

One of the most intensive agroforestry systems is that of the 'gardens' around Kandy, Sri Lanka. These are small farms based on a close association of coconut, kitril and betel palms; with spices such as cloves, cinnamon and nutmeg; small tree fruit such as citrus, mango, durian, rambutan and breadfruit; a lower stratum of bananas and pepper vines; and a peripheral ground layer of maize, cassava, beans and pineapples (Tivy, 1990).

---

4. **Diversity** – complex spatial arrangement of crops can make the best use of nutrients, water and sunlight. Crop diversity can extend growing seasons and ensure ground cover.

From these areas of consideration, Dover and Talbot (*ibid.*) identified measurable criteria by which to judge the success of sustainable agriculture:

- replenishment of soil nutrients removed by crops
- maintenance of the soil's physical condition
- constant or increasing humus level in the soil
- no build-up of weeds, pests or diseases
- no increase in soil acidity or toxic elements
- control of soil erosion
- minimisation of off-farm contamination of the environment
- maintenance of adequate habitat for wildlife
- conservation of genetic resources.

A useful way of looking at the efficiency of agricultural production is to consider its energy budget. Two examples illustrate this. Figure 2.20 shows the number of calories of energy needed to be put into a food production system for each calorie actually produced. A ratio below 1.0 indicates a net gain: range-fed beef, intensive corn (maize) cultivation and low-intensity egg production appear just below this threshold, with low intensity rice farming emerging as the most energy-efficient method of farming. Above the line, i.e. with inputs of energy greater than output, are grass-fed dairy and beef cattle, fishing and feedlot (stall-fed) livestock production. Much

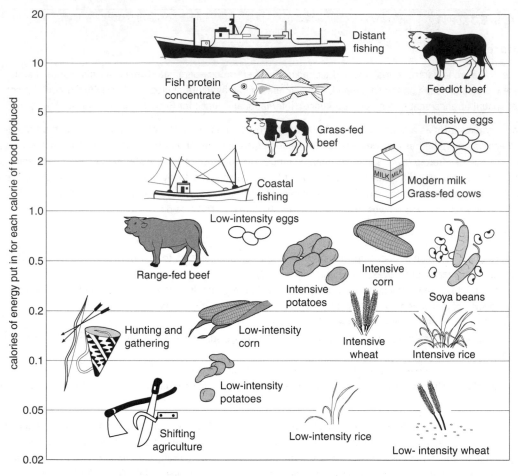

Figure 2.20   Calorie input–output ratios for different kinds of food production.

of the energy cost reflects the input of machinery (and its fuel) and the factory production of inorganic fertilisers. Table 2.7 contrasts the energy costs of modern methods of producing rice and maize in the USA with traditional methods in the Philippines and Mexico, respectively. Again, the energy 'profligacy' of Western agriculture is shown: yields are higher, but energy inputs are so much greater.

These energy inputs are more usefully viewed as energy subsidies, and they have their natural analogues, for example the effects of wind and rain entering a rain forest ecosystem, or tidal energy in an estuary (Odum, 1971). Energy subsidies reduce the energetic costs of internal self-maintenance of an ecosystem, and in so doing increase the amount of energy (the energy already present in the system plus the introduced subsidy)

that can be converted to production. 'Nature maximises for gross production, whereas man maximises for net production' (*ibid.*)

2.5 Conclusions

Plants, animals and microorganisms interact in a number of ways related to food, whether feeding on each other, avoiding being another organism's food or competing for food resources. Feeding relationships are important to understand because, among other things, they link community structure and community interactions with energy flow and nutrient cycling.

In theory, there is sufficient food for humans that none need go hungry. In practice, such a utopian

Table 2.7 Commercial energy used in the production of rice and maize by modern and traditional methods (10^6 joules per hectare).

	Rice		Maize	
	Modern (USA)	Traditional (Philippines)	Modern (USA)	Traditional (Mexico)
Machinery	4 200	173	4 200	173
Fuel	8 988	–	8 240	–
Nitrogen fertiliser	10 752	–	10 000	–
Phosphate fertiliser	–	–	586	–
Potassium fertiliser	605	–	605	–
Seed	3 360	–	621	–
Irrigation	27 336	–	351	–
Insecticides	560	–	110	–
Herbicides	560	–	110	–
Drying	4 600	–	1 239	–
Electricity	3 200	–	3 248	–
Transport	724	–	724	–
Total	64 885	173	30 034	173
Yield (kg ha^{-1})	5 800	1 250	5 083	950
Energy input per kg of output (joules $\times$ 10^6)	11.9	0.14	5.91	0.18

Source: FAO (1977) *The State of Food and Agriculture, 1976*, Rome, p. 93

situation can probably never exist. Nevertheless, greater efficiency *is* possible in agriculture and livestock rearing, and less environmental degradation need be associated with farming activities, provided that thought and effort go into practices that lead to sustainability. In turn, this requires government support and action, together with the implementation of international agreements such as were reached in Rio de Janeiro in 1992.

Further reading

Cohen, J.E., Briand, F. and Newman, C.M. (1990) *Community food webs: data and theory* (New York: Springer-Verlag).

Holden, J., Peacock, J. and Williams, T. (1993) *Genes, crops and the environment* (Cambridge: Cambridge University Press).

Kidd, C.V. (1992) The evolution of sustainability. *Journal of Agricultural and Environmental Ethics,* **5**: 1–26.

Mansfield, T., Sheppard, L. and Goulding, K. (eds) (1998) *Disturbance of the nitrogen cycle* (Cambridge: Cambridge University Press).

Moore III, B. and seven others (1989) Biogeochemical cycles. In M.B. Rambler, L. Margulis and R. Fester (eds) *Global ecology: towards a science of the biosphere* (London: Academic Press) 113–41.

Postgate, J.R. (1998) *Nitrogen fixation* (third edition) (Cambridge: Cambridge University Press).

Schlesinger, W.H. (1992) *Biogeochemistry: an analysis of global change.* (London: Academic Press).

Soulé, J.D. and Piper, J. (1992) *Farming in Nature's image: an ecological approach to agriculture.* (Washington DC: Island Press).

QUESTIONS BASED ON CHAPTER 2

Q1. Why is the concept of a food web generally more useful than that of a food chain?

Q2. Are there any circumstances that permit an inverted pyramid of energy?

Q3. Could a sustainable ecosystem contain only producers and consumers? Only consumers and decomposers? Only producers and decomposers? Explain your reasons.

Q4. At what trophic level(s) do the following organisms occur?

vampire bat	mistletoe
zebra	lion
blood parasite	seaweed
parrot	fungus-farming ant

Q5. Why are there fewer lions than grass mice in the savannas of Africa?

ANSWERS

A1. Food chains show trophic levels and can be useful in indicating energy flow through the biotic components of an ecosystem, but their descriptive power is weak. Food webs indicate specific feeding relationships between different taxonomic groups (species or otherwise), including which taxa are monophagous, oligophagous or polyphagous; identify which taxa have more than one animal grazing or preying on them; and can delineate omnivory and where predation occurs at more than one trophic level.

A2. No. The transfer of energy between trophic levels is less that 100% efficient, because at each transfer some of the energy is transformed to heat energy and is 'lost' to the surrounding environment, obeying the second law of thermodynamics.

A3. Producers and decomposers only. Producers are needed as the basis of any food chain, whether photosynthesisers or chemosynthesisers. If they did not decompose on death, accumulation of necromass (dead tissue) would soon prevent growth. Consumers are not needed for the success of either producers or decomposers. Therefore an ecosystem could exist, in theory, consisting only of producers and decomposers.

A4. Vampire bat – third or higher (it drinks blood from other animals, equivalent to predation. If the other animal is a herbivore, the bat is at the third trophic level; if a predator, the bat is at the fourth or a higher trophic level).
Mistletoe – second (a plant parasite that acquires nutrients from another plant).
Zebra – second (a grazing animal, or herbivore).
Lion – third or higher (a predator that catches herbivores or other predators).
Blood parasite – third or higher (see vampire bat; the fact that this is an internal parasite is irrelevant to its position in the food chain).
Seaweed – first (seaweed are algae, which are photosynthesising plants).
Parrot – second (parrots eat fruit and/or seeds).
Fungus-farming ant – second (these ants cultivate fungi, which they treat as a crop).

A5. Lions are large and carnivorous (secondary consumers). They need to eat a large quantity of biomass, and their food is energetically expensive to acquire. Grass mice are small and granivorous (primary consumers, i.e. feeding at a lower trophic level than do lions). A lion therefore needs greater amounts of food and energy than a mouse, yet less energy is available at the third (or higher) trophic level than at the second (pyramid of energy). Fewer lions can therefore be supported by the food resources of the habitat.

Discussion topics

D1. Discuss how aquaculture is more similar to agriculture than it is to open-water fisheries.

D2. Which is more likely to enhance global sustainability, a world in which more and more of its population is found in towns, or one in which cities become less important and

most people live in suburbs or scattered in rural communities?

D3. Discuss the view that genetic engineering of crops will lead to a third 'green revolution'.

EXERCISES

E1. Construct a (simple) food web for your garden or a local park. Identify how human activities have contributed to the components and structure of your web.

E2. Note the food you eat during one day. Construct a diagram showing the food chain linkages you have made. On the diagram, indicate the biomass (in grams, g) and energy (in kilocalories, kcal) of each item you have eaten. Assuming that your net production is 10% efficient in terms of your energy intake, calculate how much additional energy you might have stored during the day. Using a figure of 5 kcal/g, calculate the weight gain associated with your food. (Don't panic – you will have expended lots of energy as well!) Calculate the amount of vegetable matter you have eaten. If vegetation is 1% efficient in converting sunlight into organic matter stored as net primary production, how much sunlight (in kcal) was needed to provide the vegetation you consumed? (If you want to convert kcal into kilojoules, then 1 kJ = 0.24 kcal).

E3. Contact your local authority or equivalent local government organisation and find out what contributions to Local Agenda 21 are being introduced in your local area. Which local government departments, which local community groups and which business organisations are involved in these? Do you feel that fine words are being put into good practice?

Chapter **3**

Ecosystem sustainability and chemical pollution

Summary

The idea of sustainability is taken forward from the specific case of agriculture to that of ecosystems in general. Characteristics of sustainable ecosystems are described, and the idea of interactive controls mooted. The integrity of ecosystems is defined in terms of different meanings of stability, resistance, resilience and persistence, all of which can be affected by environmental perturbations, some of which are the result of human activity. Pollution is an important example of this, as is exemplified by looking at oil pollution and the polluting effects of chemical pesticides, the latter in particular demonstrating adverse effects of bioaccumulation. A distinction is drawn between *chronic* and *acute* forms of pollution. The idea of environmental risk is introduced in the context of human activities, and ways of monitoring and reducing such risks are outlined. Ultimately, human decisions on risk avoidance and management are affected by perception and can only be effected in the context of political decisions.

3.1 Ecosystem sustainability

This chapter develops some of the points made earlier about ecosystems, particularly the extent to which some may be considered inherently stable. The key environmental issues relate to pollution, which can be viewed as a particular kind of disturbance of or interference to ecosystem structure and functioning. This again ties in with ideas on stability and is part of the broader notion of ecosystem sustainability.

A *sustainable* ecosystem is one that, 'over the normal cycle of disturbance events, maintains its characteristic diversity of major functional groups [groups of species that have a similar effect on ecosystem processes], productivity, soil fertility, and rates of biogeochemical cycling' (Chapin *et al.*, 1996). Ecosystem sustainability has become a key issue with many ecologists as they witness the accelerating impact of global environmental changes resulting from human activities. The idea of sustainability has largely been linked to socio-economic enterprises such as fisheries, forestry, farming and range management, and to environmental consequences of such activities as desertification following overgrazing or loss of soil following inappropriate logging methods. Recently, however, ecologists have begun to consider the concept of sustainability in relation to natural ecosystems.

Time scale is important in examining ecosystems. Even stable ecosystems, however they are defined, are rarely sustained for more than a few tens of thousands of years. This is because the factors that mould ecosystems themselves change, often dramatically, over such time scales: physical environmental factors such as climate and soil, and biological factors such as gene pools and (in relation to environmental requirements and dispersal abilities) species distributions. Ecosystems may not simply be a collection of organisms that happen to share particular environmental conditions, although this case has been argued (Engelberg and Boyarsky, 1979), but the species composition, structure and functions of any ecosystem are not indefinitely sustainable (Chapin *et al.*, 1996). Nevertheless, it is relevant to examine ecosystem sustainability, especially but not only within the sorts of time periods – decades and centuries – that reflect human activities, all the more so given the impacts that humans have had in destroying, modifying and creating ecosystems.

Ecosystems are not static constructs: they change in response to random events and develop as internal processes also lead to change through what might be described as autogenic community effects and their interactions with the environment.

In some ecosystems, for example savanna grassland, semi-arid scrub and some mature forest types, wildfires are a predictable event – not predictable with respect to a particular year but in the sense that sooner or later a fire will break out naturally, for example following a lightning strike, and that the periodicity of such an event falls within a specific range of years, even if this is a century or two. Over a relatively brief time scale, therefore, as a result of fire, major changes occur in species content, ecosystem structure, productivity, and nutrient availability and cycling. After the disturbance, however, the ecosystem does not remain static. Development occurs, for example through plant succession as species respond to their own modification of the environment (see Chapter 7), and this development reflects a response to the environmental situation and opportunities found within the wider region. At the landscape scale, then, and over longer periods of time, the ecosystem is persistent. And while structure and function may change in response to random events, sustainable ecosystems do so within stable bounds (Figure 3.1).

Chapter 1 showed how ecosystem properties are controlled by both internal interactions and a suite of external factors. Jenny (1941) identified five independent *state factors* that largely determine soil development. Parent material, climate, topography and biota are fairly obvious factors, to which Jenny added time as a discrete factor, greater time allowing greater opportunity for soil development, which, by definition, is a dynamic process. To these factors we should perhaps add human intervention. Chapin *et al.*, (1996) develop Jenny's ideas by introducing the idea of interactive controls, which both control and respond to ecosystem characteristics (Figure 3.2).

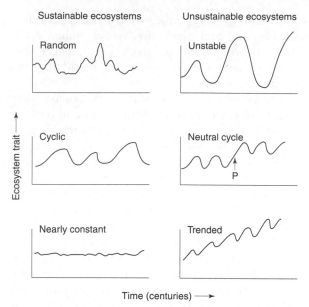

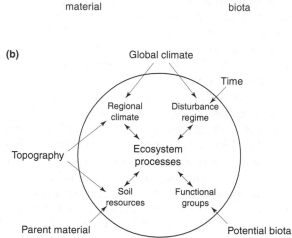

Figure 3.1 Temporal fluctuations in ecosystem traits in sustainable and unsustainable ecosystems. P = time of an external perturbation.

Figure 3.2 The relationship (a) between state factors and ecosystem processes, and (b) between state factors, interactive controls and ecosystem processes.

- **Climate** – climate is not simply an independent state factor: rather it is the interactive control that most strongly affects ecosystems at a broad geographical scale. A continuum exists between global- and local-scale climate, but whatever the scale climate and ecosystems do interact, and environmental changes affect the nature and consequences of such interactions. Field *et al.* (1992) describe changes in carbon dioxide, temperature, pollutants, nutrient deposition and solar radiation as environmental forcing factors, which are mediated through the atmosphere to influence the function of terrestrial ecosystems (Figure 3.3). Changes in the local and regional climate as tropical rain forest is converted to pasture, for example, were mooted in Chapter 1, through which water balances are also amended, productivity is affected, biogeochemical cycling is altered, and species composition and interaction are changed.
- **Soil resources** – the supply of soil resources determines the maximum and actual productivity of vegetation and strongly influences its structural complexity. Vegetation productivity,

nutrient cycling and water movement are all causally linked to the nature and availability of soil resources. In a particular climate, soil water and nutrients are effected by the other state factors of parent material, topography and soil biota (especially by the activity of nitrogen-fixing organisms), but are also affected by processes such as weathering, erosion (the actual movement of the weathered material) and leaching (removal of material including nutrients via water movement through the soil). Changes in soil resources are 'perhaps the most widespread mechanism by which human activity has altered ecosystem sustainability' (Chapin *et al.*, 1996), for example through deep ploughing, overgrazing or clear-felling, which initiate or accelerate loss of soil by erosion.

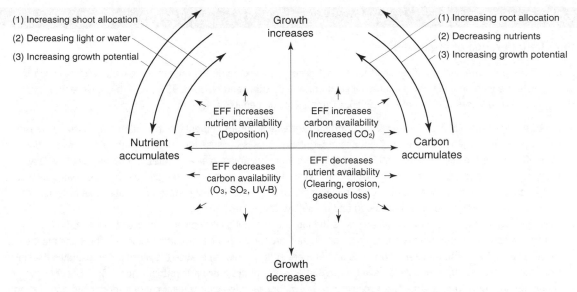

Figure 3.3   Conceptual model for the responses of individual plants to direct efforts of environmental forcing factors (EFFs). Effects of each EFF tend to push plants away from the centre point, which represents the status of a plant prior to the imposition of an EFF. Effects of all EFFs fall into one of four quadrants, depending on whether they tend to increase or decrease the availability of carbon or one or more nutrients, relative to the other resources. Plant responses to any EFF, or combination of EFFs, range from effects only on growth (movement up or down the vertical axis), with no change in tissue composition, to effects only on resource accumulation (movement left or right along the horizontal axis), with no effects on growth. The factors that determine where a plant moves within a quadrant are: (1) the extent to which changes in allocation compensate for the resource imbalance, (2) the availability of the resources not affected by an EFF, and (3) each species' maximum potential growth rate.

The equivalent of soil resources as an interactive control in aquatic ecosystems is water quality, which again controls productivity and biological complexity, and which again is often affected by human activity, such as nutrient enrichment associated with fertiliser runoff.

- **Disturbance regime** – Sousa (1985) discusses environmental disturbance as a 'discrete, punctuated killing, displacement, or damaging of one or more individuals (or colonies) that directly or indirectly creates an opportunity for new individuals (or colonies) to become established'. His definition can be extended to communities and ecosystems, since disturbance resulting from natural or human action – fire, for instance, could be either – will have significant effects on structure and function, whatever the scale of study. Climate and soil resources strongly interact with disturbance regime, and changes in the nature, intensity or frequency of disturbance often cause long-term ecosystem change.

- **Functional groups of organisms** – groups of species that have similar effects on ecosystem processes (see Ecology Box 3.1) not only influence climate, soil resource and disturbance regime but are themselves going to react to changes in these other interactive controls. Changes in functional groups can result from major natural disturbances but are also particularly vulnerable to introductions or extinctions resulting from human activity.

Interactive controls vary in space and through time, yet ecosystems can sustain themselves over long periods of time. The key to such persistence lies with negative feedback mechanisms, as described in Chapter 1. Sometimes, however, such is the impact of an environmental perturbation that the negative feedbacks break down. The system can no longer sustain itself, at least in the short term. The extent to which an ecosystem can recover is tied in with ideas about stability. Useful examples of such environmental perturba-

---

ECOLOGY BOX 3.1

Functional groups of organisms

Functional groups are 'groups of species that are not necessarily taxonomically related but which perform similarly in an ecosystem based on a set of common biological attributes' (Gitay and Noble, 1997), and that have similar effects on ecosystem processes (Chapin *et al.*, 1996). Examples of such effects are:

• *Endotherm* (warm-blooded) *terrestrial herbivores* (plant eaters) return nutrients to the soil in a form that increases their availability to other organisms, including other plants. This is because the animals' high rates of respiration burn off most of the carbon contained in their food material. Evergreen trees and shrubs, however, possess leaves that are available to capture carbon throughout the year. These leaves in turn often possess anti-herbivore defences – physical ones such as toughness, and chemical ones, which make the leaf distasteful, indigestible or toxic. Leaf litter, too, is generally chemically defended and is usually slow to decompose.

• In coniferous forest, *moss* biomass increases as the forest as a whole develops and changes through time (i.e. through succession), but increases in primary production are not as great as might be expected, because the greater moss cover reduces soil mineralisation rates and nutrient supply. This is because the moss cover insulates the soil from the input of summer heat, and because moss litter is itself not particularly nutrient-rich.

• Again in coniferous forest, some *late-successional trees*, for example black spruce, contain more resin and are more flammable than are trees found at an earlier stage in the forest development. Build-up of litter in such forests also makes the system more prone to devastation from fire. The probability of disturbance through burning thus increases as the forest matures.

• *Nitrogen-fixing plants* by definition have a major influence on the ecosytem. Introduction of nitrogen-fixing plants such as *Myrica faya* to Hawaii by humans, for instance, has altered the species composition of much of the tropical forest, partly by competition, partly by changing the supply of soil-based nitrogen, and overall productivity of these forest systems has greatly increased.

---

tion and the extent to which both perturbation and ecosystem affect stability can be found by looking at examples of pollution. The environmental issues examined in this chapter concern oil pollution and some adverse consequences of pesticide application.

3.2 Key environmental issue: pollution

Pollution has been defined as 'the adverse effect on the natural environment, including human, animal or plant life, of a harmful substance that does not occur naturally, e.g. industrial and radioactive waste, or the concentration to harmful levels of a naturally occurring substance, e.g. nitrate' (Robinson, 1996). It can be argued that excessive quantities of a substance deriving from a natural catastrophic event can be viewed as a pollutant, for example debris following a

volcanic eruption or in rivers during flood conditions, but in defining pollution it is usual to consider only those environmental perturbations derived from human activity. Such an opinion is reflected, for example, in the definition given by a former UK chief government scientist: 'the introduction by man [*sic*] into the environment of substances or energy liable to cause hazards to human health, harm to living resources and ecological systems, damage to structures or amenity, or interferences with legitimate uses of the environment' (Holdgate, 1979).

Pollution, then, may involve intangible phenomena such as heat and noise, and may adversely affect human use of the environment. This chapter, however, focuses on tangible forms of pollution and on harmful or adverse impacts on the environment, however difficult it often is to define the threshold beyond which such harm begins.

Pollution may also be viewed as a particular kind of environmental perturbation that weakens or destroys the negative feedback mechanisms. The system may be destroyed. More often, though, it is modified to such an extent that the system no longer functions efficiently or effectively – so much so that we can say that the pollution has an adverse impact in some definable way. Pollution is often caused by a deleterious substance or combination of substances previously unknown to the system. Usually, however, it is caused by the introduction into a system of material in excess of normal amounts or concentrations. In all cases, the level of the pollutant(s) exceeds the tolerance limits of the system, and it begins in some way to break down. The breakdown will involve physical, chemical and biological changes in the ecosystem. The biological changes may involve the appearance or disappearance of species; changes in community structure and functioning; changes in behaviour and demography; and changes in production, energy flow and nutrient cycling. Heavy pollution will produce changes that are unequivocably deleterious, but there exists a continuum of impact, and it is often human judgement that decrees the threshold at which an adverse impact is made.

We legislate to identify 'permissible levels of pollution', often couched in terms of being levels acceptable for human health. For example, public water systems in the USA must have a maximum nitrate concentration of 45 mg L^{-1} to remain within the public health standard.

Most studies on pollution remain attached to individual species and the changes effected by particular concentrations or combinations of pollutants to such characteristics as growth, fertility and mortality (see Ecology Box 3.2). The relationship between toxin concentration and effect can be shown as a dose–response curve (Figure 3.4). A common test in animals, for example, is the LC$_{50}$, the concentration of a pollutant that, under specified conditions over a set period of time, kills half of the sample population: thus the lethal concentration (LC) that produces a 50% mortality (LC$_{50}$) over 96 hours (96 h LC$_{50}$) can be determined experimentally. Nelson and Roline (1998), for example, show the 24-hour and 48-hour LC$_{50}$s for the water flea *Brachionis calyciflorus* (under defined laboratory conditions) to have mean values (in μg L^{-1}) of

169.7 and 127.7 for zinc; 19.6 and 18.3 for copper, and 132.0 and 78.2 for cadmium. The toxic threshold is lower for the longer test period, indicating that longer exposure time may make a population more vulnerable to chronic as well as acute forms of pollution, and also suggesting that any individual water fleas remaining after any test period are likely to be moribund.

Such tests, then, tell us little about the effect of the pollutant. There are questions not only about the state of the half of the population remaining after the test period but also about what happens in more natural conditions where a species is only one in an interacting community in often fluctuating environmental conditions, and where a changing variety of pollutants may be involved.

Where a number of pollutants are simultaneously present in an environment, the effects of each may simply need to be added together to indicate what the overall effect might be – an *additive* effect. Occasionally, one pollutant may cancel out or reduce the impact of another – an *antagonistic* effect. Often, though, pollutants (especially chemical pollutants) combine in such a way that the environmental and ecological effects are greater than would be expected additively – a *synergistic* effect. Synergism is thus where the whole is greater than the sum of its parts.

Pollution may derive from a point source (for example, a sewage outlet) or a number of such sources (for instance, chimney stacks), or it may seep into the environment (as with fertiliser runoff into a stream via overland flow and groundwater seepage). It may occur as a discrete event, a series of regular or irregular pulses, or more or less continuously. Pollutants can be spread by flowing waters or by flowing air, and in these ways many pollutants have been found in environments that might be expected to be pristine, for example the highly volatile toxic chemicals such as polychlorinated biphenyls (PCBs) that have travelled thousands of kilometres through the atmosphere from their source in temperate or even tropical lands to the Arctic and Antarctic (Pearce, 1997a).

It is convenient, if oversimple, to think of pollution as being acute or chronic. *Acute pollution* occurs where a large amount of waste matter enters the environment, usually from a point

ECOLOGY BOX 3.2

Measuring the toxicity of a chemical

Responses commonly measured in short-term tests on individual taxa under laboratory conditions:

1. mortality – e.g. LC_{50};
2. growth rate;
3. population increase;
4. measures of metabolic state or activity, e.g.

- RNA/DNA ratio
- Amounts of high-energy compounds such as lipids and glycogen
- ^{14}C amino acid incorporation into proteins
- Respiration rate (this is particularly useful for measuring soil microbial activity)
- Photosynthesis, e.g. by CO_2 uptake rate or root extension rate
- Microtox test, which uses the natural luminescence of the marine bacterium *Phosphobacterium phosphoreum*.

It is important to attempt to scale up laboratory results to predict responses under more natural conditions. Problems that may need to be considered include:

1. The test substance may act over a long time.
2. Species other than that being tested will almost certainly also be affected, but not in the same way at the same levels of pollutant.
3. Environmental conditions will be different from and will almost certainly fluctuate compared with those in the laboratory.
4. The test chemical will interact with other chemicals (natural or pollutant) in the environment.
5. The test organism's behaviour may be altered by the chemical in such a way as to affect its response to its environment, including other components of the community.
6. Interactions between species may alter their response to the chemical.

Sources: Newman (1993) and original

source, often as a one-off accidental event, and commonly having a toxic effect on the biota. After the pollution event, the ecosystem begins to recover and in time generally returns to a resemblance, at least, of the original system. An oil spill is an example of this. *Chronic pollution* reflects low-level input into the environment, but it occurs either more or less continuously or as frequent pulses. The environment is thus constantly under stress, albeit a light stress; the ecosystem does not have an opportunity to recover; and there is often a cumulative effect that eventually can have a greater impact on the ecosystem, or elements of the ecosystem, than an acute pollution event. An example of this is the

impact of pesticides on the demography and status of birds of prey. Oil spills and pesticide impact are examined in the next two sections.

3.2.1 Oil pollution

Crude oil is a blend of tens of thousands of chemical compounds. These fall into four groups: *aliphatic* (saturated) and *aromatic hydrocarbons*, *polar compounds* and *sulphurated compounds* (see Ecology Box 3.3). Non-volatile fractions are degraded by microorganisms, degradation taking place more rapidly at higher temperatures and in more nutrient-rich waters. This is why oil tends

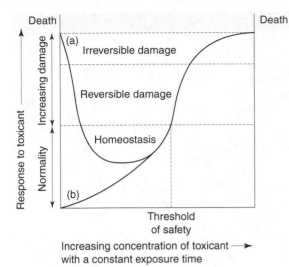

Figure 3.4 Dose–response curve, showing the relationship between observed effects and the concentration of a pollutant: (a) observed effects of a substance essential to life at low concentrations; (b) observed effects of a non-essential substance.

to persist for longer in polar and temperate waters compared with those in the tropics.

All components of the community are affected. Around 90% of sunlight is intercepted by oil in a slick, reducing photosynthesis at and near the ocean surface. Division of algal cells is inhibited at oil concentrations as low as 0.01 ppm, and photosynthesis at 0.02 ppm, yet 0.02 ppm is the average value for the present petroleum hydrocarbon content of the water off the Atlantic coast of Canada, and three to four times the concentration found as a matter of course in parts of the

Gulf of Mexico off the Texas coast. Prolonged exposure to oil, even at chronic levels, will lead to a decline in primary productivity and a shift in the composition of the phytoplankton (microbial plant) community.

Food chains are modified. Seabirds are affected by a reduction in preferred prey or prey biomass, but they are also exposed to the physical, carcinogenic and mutagenic effects of oil components (Jarvis, 1993). The acute impact of oil on birds derives from external contamination, ingestion and embryotoxicity (Leighton *et al.*, 1985). The most obvious effect of external contamination is to reduce the integrity, insulating properties and water repellency of the feathers, which become matted and waterlogged: birds become chilled, lose their buoyancy and drown. In attempting to preen, birds ingest oil, which may be toxic or clog up the respiratory and digestive systems. Inability to digest efficiently and forage effectively leads to a rapid depletion of fat reserves and energy. Reproductive impairment, reduced growth rate in juvenile birds, changes in osmo-regulation (related to the excretion of excess dietary salts), depressed kidney and liver functions, and anaemia are among other stress and toxic effects of oil.

Similar consequences occur with marine mammals, with interference of the metabolic system, genetic damage, and a wide range of disorders of the brain, liver, heart and central nervous system having been reported. With hepatic recycling, hydrocarbons in ingested oil circulate between the intestines and the liver until the latter organ is completely destroyed. There is

ECOLOGY BOX 3.3

The chemistry of crude oil

- *aliphatic hydrocarbons* include compounds such as hexane and octane. They are built around long chains of carbon atoms;
- *aromatic hydrocarbons* include benzene and toluene. They are structured around rings of carbon atoms;
- *polar compounds*, such as ethanol, include pairings between oxygen and hydrogen atoms, which impart small positive and negative charges to parts of the molecule;
- *sulphurated compounds* generally form very bulky compounds such as benzothiopenes.

The hydrocarbons, especially the aromatics, have the greatest toxicity to marine animals.

even a suspicion that sea otters (*Enhydra lutris*), seals and sea lions were attracted to the scent of unevaporated toluene following the *Exxon Valdez* spill, exhibiting symptoms of a kind of euphoria that drew them into the slick. Aromatics almost certainly affect the nervous system of fish, producing a short-term narcosis that impairs swimming. With oil-induced damage to the immune system, vertebrates become more susceptible to parasitic and bacterial infection, and there is an increased likelihood of leukaemias and viral diseases developing (Dayton, 1989).

Certainly, the *Exxon Valdez* has become a key example of what happens following a major inshore oil spill. On 24 March 1989, this 300 m supertanker hit a submerged rock in north-eastern Prince William Sound, Alaska, a wilderness location celebrated for its scenery and wildlife. The tanker had left the designated shipping lane to avoid ice broken off a nearby glacier, but it hit a charted reef. The grounded tanker spilled 38 000 tonnes (11.2 million gallons, 232 000 barrels) of crude oil, about 20% of its total cargo, into the coastal waters. This represents the largest oil spill in the USA's history. Three days of calm weather followed the incident, but little was done to contain or clear up the oil. Strong winds then arose, driving the oil in a generally south-westerly direction, dispersing it on the water and on to beaches. After two months some oil was traced to waters off the southern Kodiak archipelago and Alaskan Peninsula 750 km from the spillage site (Figure 3.5). About 35% of the oil had evaporated, 40% was washed ashore within Prince William Sound, and 25% entered the Gulf of Alaska, where it became beached or was lost at sea (Galt *et al.*, 1991). The level of beach pollution often varied greatly over short distances depending on the configuration of the shoreline. In places, oil penetrated gravel and shingle beaches to depths greater than 1 m. Some oiled shorelines were buried under new coastal material within a few months, reducing opportunities for clean-up. Perhaps 1500 km of coastline was affected.

Both the oil itself and the clean-up operations affected wildlife, for which it is impossible to give more than rough estimates of mortality. Piatt *et al.* (1990) estimated that 100 000 to 300 000

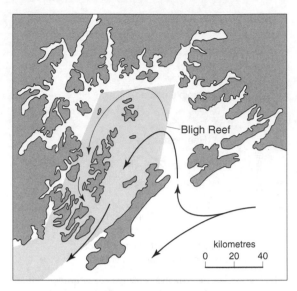

Figure 3.5 Prince William Sound showing the position of Bligh Reef (the site of the grounding), the area affected – though to varying degrees – by the oil spilled from the *Exxon Valdez* (fine stipple), and the surface currents.

seabirds were killed, but other sources suggest 580 000 birds (Miller, 2000). For guillemots (common murre) *Uria aalge*, 20 000 carcasses were collected after the spill, on the basis of which some US government biologists have extrapolated deaths of this species alone as possibly being 300 000 (Pain, 1993). Similarly, an estimated 2650 (and possibly as many as 5000) sea otters out of 6550 were killed by the oil in Prince William Sound (Garrott *et al.*, 1993). At least 22 whales and 30 seals, together with incalculable numbers of fish, also died. Consequences to invertebrate, plant and microbial life must also have been severe. The clean-up took three years and cost over $2.1 billion. The restoration strategy and other management issues are examined in Section 3.4.

The *Exxon Valdez* spill, however, was not the only major incident off North American waters, nor was it the largest marine spillage in the world. Other examples are shown in Table 3.1. The *Torrey Canyon* was important in the UK, both by stimulating release of government funds for research into oil spill prevention and restoration and for providing many lessons about what not to do. The spill not only killed many seabirds,

Table 3.1 Some major oil spills in the marine environment

Tanker/oil platform/pipeline	Location	Date	Spillage (tonnes)
Torrey Canyon	Scilly Isles	1967	118 000
Santa Barbara (undersea pipe leak)	California coast	1969	up to 7000
Argo Merchant	Massachusetts	1976	25 000–30 000
Ekofisk	North Sea	1977	
Amoco Cadiz	Brittany	1978	220 000
IXTOC I (blowout)	Gulf of Mexico	1979	435 000
Exxon Valdez	Alaska	1989	38 000
Sea Empress	Pembrokeshire	1996	65 000

with television bringing the evidence of this to millions of viewers, but also oiled long stretches of beach along Cornwall. The spill took place on 18 March 1967, and tremendous pressure was placed on the government to clean the beaches before the descent of thousands of holiday-makers to the seaside. Emulsifiers (about three-quarters solvent mixture, one-quarter detergents and emulsifying agents) were applied with varying degrees of effectiveness in clearing up the oil, but ironically caused more ecological damage than would have been the case with the oil alone (Nelson-Smith, 1968). Left alone, the oil would have disappeared naturally as the result, among other things, of sunlight, oxygen reaction and microbial activity (Figure 3.6), but this would have taken two or three years and, understand-ably, the tourist industry – never mind the local population – would have found such a time scale intolerable. One consequence was the subequent development of less environmentally damaging detergents such as Corexit 8666.

Even so, lessons continue to be taught. There were real fears that the *Braer* in early 1993 would become another British coastal disaster, but rough seas dispersed the oil rapidly enough to prevent a major incident. The reverberations of the *Sea Empress* incident, however, were much more important. This tanker hit rocks on the approach to Milford Haven, south-west Wales, on 15 February 1996, spilling 65 000 tonnes of crude oil. Bad weather postponed salvage opera-tions, the tanker breaking free and regrounding

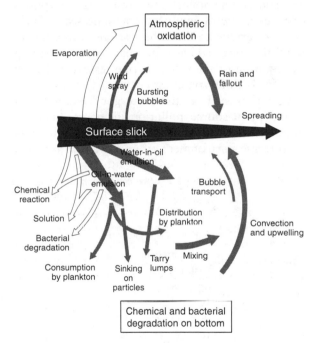

Figure 3.6 Processes bringing about the dispersal and degradation of oil spilt at sea.

on two occasions in the following four days. Only by day six could the tanker be refloated and towed to dock.

The coast around Milford Haven has suffered a number of oil spillages since the opening of the terminal in 1960, when the *Esso Portsmouth*, the first tanker to berth, caught fire and released much of its cargo of crude oil to avert an explo-sion. The coastline is part of a national park, and oil from the *Sea Empress* reached a number of sites along the Pembrokeshire coast which are important nature reserves and sites of special scientific interest. Wintering seabirds such as red-throated divers (*Gavia stellata*) were yet to fly north for the summer, while summer visitors were just about to arrive. (Ironically, the stormy weather that hindered salvage also, fortunately, slowed down the speed of bird in-migration). Particularly at risk were the 33 000 pairs of gannets (*Sula bassana*) found on the second largest gannet colony in the world on the small island of Grassholm. The island of Skomer is one of only three marine nature reserves in the UK and is home to a number of rare corals, sponges and sea anemones, as well as porpoises (*Phocaena phocaena*) and common seals (*Halichoerus grypus*). Altogether, strong winds drove the oil along 100 km of coast, even reaching Lundy (one of the other marine reserves), 18 km off the north Devon coast.

Oil spills such as these are good examples of acute, point-source pollution incidents, but it is important to stress that more pollutant oil enters the marine environment from sources other than supertanker and oil platform accidents. Ordinary tanker operations and (illegal) bilge pumping together put more oil into the world's seas than do accidents, and municipal and industrial waste entering the seas from estuaries and offshore pipes are even more significant (Table 3.2). Overall, it appears that the amount of oil entering the marine environment has declined in recent years, from over 6.11 million tonnes per annum in the early 1970s to around 2.35 million tonnes per annum in the mid-1990s. And while the extent of spillage following tanker accidents varies greatly from year to year (Figures 3.7 and 3.8), a small number of large spills – which is the norm – will bias the figures, and the impact that even a major spill has on overall figures is less than is generally realised.

It is also important to remember that major oil spills have happened on land and in freshwater areas as well. The most serious has been the 60 000 tonnes of oil spilled from a ruptured pipeline in the Komi region of Siberia between 17 August and 6 September 1994. The Russian oil industry is thought to lose 1–3% of its annual output in pipeline breakages. The 50 km pipeline

Table 3.2 Sources of oil in the marine environment (thousands of tonnes)

Source	1971	1980	1989
Amount of oil transported	1 100 000	1 319 000	1 097 000
Transportation:	1080	700	159
Tanker operations	250	30	4
Dry docking	3	20	30
Terminal operations	500	300	254
Bilge pumping accidents	300	420	121
Total from transportation	2133	1470	567
Offshore production	80	50	n/a
Municipal/industrial wastes	2700	1180	n/a
Natural sources	600	250	n/a
Atmospheric emissions	600	300	n/a
Total from non-transportation	3980	1780	n/a

Note that the oil spilled from tanker operations expressed as a proportion of the total oil transported is extremely low: 0.098% in 1971, 0.053% in 1980 and 0.014% in 1989. The *impact* of the oil, however, is often high because of the point source of the pollution and its concentration along a particular stretch of coast.
Sources: various, from Mitchell (1995; 1997)

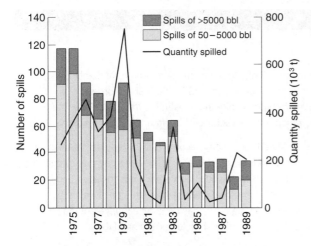

Figure 3.7   Oil spills resulting from accidents involving tankers, combination carriers and barges, 1974–89 (*Source:* International Tanker Owners Pollution Federation Limited, 1990, unpublished data).

had been a source of concern for its 20-year lifetime. It had been leaking periodically since 1988, but in August 1994 it sprang 23 holes, some 10 cm wide, in just one month. Oil broke through a containing dike and seeped into the Pechora, Usa and Kolva rivers. The hot oil penetrated the permanently frozen subsoil (permafrost zone) and in places has persisted for a number of years. More immediately, fishing grounds and local water supplies were badly contaminated (*The Guardian*, 26 October 1994: 12).

3.2.2 Pesticides as pollutants

It is important to stress that pesticides have saved many human lives and have been a major element in postwar increases in food and other organic products. Benefits have been considerable in terms of a reduction in the impact of weeds and pests, improved harvests, fewer storage losses, and the control of human, livestock and crop diseases.

Inappropriate use, however, has often led to an adverse impact on the environment, the economy

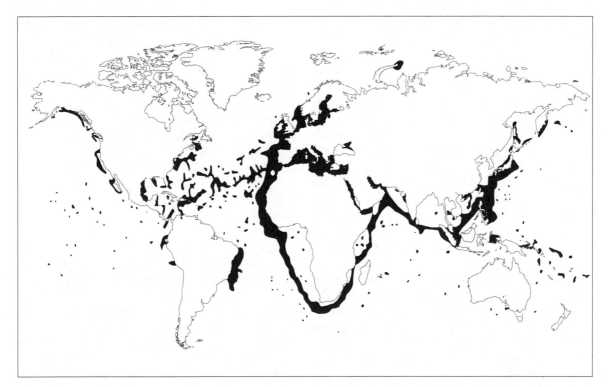

Figure 3.8   Distribution of major oil slicks throughout the oceans (shown in black). There is a striking coincidence of oil spillage and major shipping routes, for example off the west coast of Africa (after Mysak and Lin, 1990).

ECOLOGY BOX 3.4

DDT and its derivatives

DDT (chemically 1,1,-trichloro-2,2-bis[*p*-chlorophenyl]-ethane, or **d**ichloro**d**iphenyl**t**richloroethane, hence DDT) was first synthesised in 1874, but its insecticidal properties were discovered only in 1939. The first major field demonstration of its efficiency was when it was used to prevent a typhus epidemic in Naples, Italy, in 1943: the Neapolitan population was dusted with DDT to control lice, which are the vector of this often fatal human disease.

DDT is relatively insoluble, nor is it or indeed other chlorinated hydrocarbons readily decomposed by reducer organisms in natural ecosystems, so they are very persistent in the environment. Chlorinated hydrocarbons, however, do readily dissolve in fatty animal tissue, which is one of the factors important in their role as insecticides, since they must be absorbed through the fatty chitin exoskeleton of insects to be effective. They then commonly disperse through an ecosystem by selective concentration as they pass through successive stages of a food chain. DDT may remain unchanged or may be modified to substances of similar chemical structure and activity. Derivatives of DDT include DDD and DDE.

In 1971, the Environmental Protection Agency banned the use of DDT in the USA.

and human health. Pesticides are highly toxic chemical substances deliberately introduced into an ecosystem in order to kill or reduce the population size or growth of particular pests or weeds – organisms perceived to cause economic or other damage to human enterprise. The term 'pesticide' is here used as a general term: with more specific targets we can instead use terms such as 'insecticide', 'acaricide' (against mites), 'herbicide' (against weeds), 'fungicide', 'molluscicide', and so on.

Before the Second World War, weeds and pests were controlled by a few 'natural' chemicals, such as nicotine and pyrethrum, the latter being obtained from *Pyrethrum* flowers and used as a contact poison against domestic insects; or by chemicals such as sodium arsenite, lead arsenate and various mercury salts. These pesticides had an immediate but very temporary effect, and since they were broad-spectrum chemicals (i.e. not target-specific) they tended to kill harmless or even beneficial organisms as well as the pests.

During the Second World War, new kinds of synthetic organic insecticide were developed, the most significant being DDT and its various derivatives (Ecology Box 3.4). DDT is an example of a *chlorinated hydrocarbon* or *organochlorine*. Other examples are aldrin, dieldrin, endrin, lindane, chlordane and heptachlor. These are nerve toxins that attack any organism with a central nervous system. They are broad-spectrum

(non-specific) toxins, which cause convulsion, paralysis and death. They remain in the environment for a long period (Figure 3.9), however, and accumulate or work their way through the system in such a way as to become toxic to non-target organisms – in other words, to become a pollutant. The persistence of chlorinated hydrocarbons in the environment reflects both their chemistry and the fact that, because they are synthetic organic chemicals, natural ecosystems do not possess organisms that can use them in their metabolism and in doing so break them down or degrade them into new chemical forms.

However, this contrasts with the herbicides 2,4-D and 2,4,5-T, which are *chlorophenoxy compounds*, the chemical structures of which resemble those of naturally occurring plant-producing growth suppressants (*auxins*). There therefore exist a number of reducer organisms which readily switch from natural to synthetic compounds of this type, so 2,4-D, for example, is broken down in soil in a matter of days.

The other main groups of pesticides are the *organophosphates* (such as malathion and parathion) and the *carbamates* (such as sevin). Although these are highly toxic to humans, they are environmentally sounder than the chlorinated hydrocarbons since they are *biodegradable* and non-persistent – they are readily broken down by reducer organisms in natural ecosystems (as well

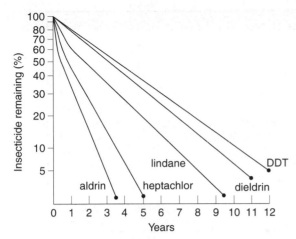

Figure 3.9 Pesticide disappearance rates in soil. The straight-line basis of predicted loss is unrealistic, however.

as anthropogenic ones such as agro-ecosystems). These chemicals also attack the nervous system, but in a different way to chlorinated hydrocarbons: they attack an enzyme that controls nerve impulses, causing the organism to twitch violently before death from organ failure. They are often used as systemic insecticides, being taken up and circulated through plant tissues, where they remain toxic to pest herbivores for a long period.

DDT and other chlorinated hydrocarbons were seen as wonder chemicals when their pesticide properties were demonstrated, and there was understandable pressure to put them on the market before sufficient long-term testing had been undertaken. The persistence, bioaccumulation and lethality of the chemicals were therefore unsuspected until a few dramatic examples showed that more care and caution were needed.

One such case was at Clear Lake, northern California, a scenic water body popular for recreational fishing that in the late 1940s was plagued by gnats (*Chaoborus asticipus*). Although this is a non-biting species the swarms were considered to be a nuisance, and a programme to eliminate them was initiated using DDD. The first treatment was carried out in 1949 using a DDD concentration of only one part in 70 million parts of lake water (0.014 ppm). A second treatment was undertaken in September 1954 using one part DDD per 50 million parts of water (0.02 ppm). In December

that year, a hundred or so western grebes (*Aechmophorus occidentalis*, a fish-eating diving bird) were reported dead in and by the lake, with further mortality evident in 1955. The gnat population, however, kept returning, and a third DDD treatment was made in 1957, again at 0.02 ppm. Once more, three months later, a large number of dead grebes was noted. This time, autopsies revealed that DDD was present in fatty tissue at 1600 ppm. Not only had some of the insecticide moved from the water into the bodies of the grebes but its concentration had increased by a factor of at least 80 000, a *concentration ratio* that provided a lethal dose.

In fact, it had done so in a series of stages. Further assays showed that plankton – the microscopic plant and animal life of the lake – had accumulated an average of 5.3 ppm DDD, plankton-eating fish in turn had higher concentrations of DDD in their fatty tissue, piscivorous (fish-eating) fish such as largemouth bass had 1550–1700 ppm, and western grebes, whose diet included bass, averaged 1600 ppm (Hunt and Bischoff, 1960) (Figure 3.10). DDT and its derivatives have some of the highest fat solubilities ever measured, which facilitates the bioconcentration process.

At each stage in what might be thought of as a food chain (discussed in the next section) the concentration of the insecticide increased, and in the later stages of the chain this bioaccumulation becomes insupportable and the organism dies. The gnats, however, remained. The interference to the ecosytem structure and the nutrient enrichment caused by the pesticides led to algal growth, so the waters of Clear Lake became cloudy. And the fishermen now caught fish containing levels of DDT that far exceeded the US Food and Drug Administration's maximum permissible dose of 7 ppm.

Subsequent experimental work elsewhere showed that a one-off application of DDT soon disappears from surface water, but residue levels remain in bottom sediments for well over a year. Similarly, less than 1% of pesticides sprayed on land actually reaches the target pests, the remainder being distributed in other compartments of the environment, often being transported from the application site via surface or

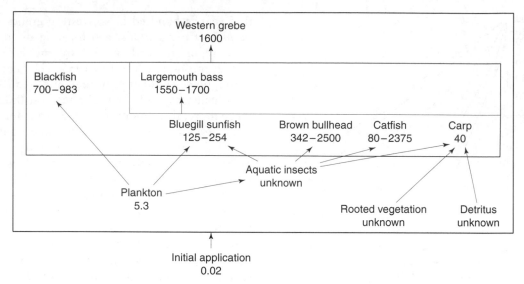

Figure 3.10 Clear Lake, California: an example of trophic web concentration of DDD. Units are in ppm.

groundwater. DDT also disperses widely geographically: Tatton and Ruzicka (1967) found DDT and its derivatives in non-migratory penguins, skuas and other birds in Antarctica, where the insecticide has never been used. These birds, however, were eating fish that did contain these chemicals, and the fish had possibly dispersed from lower latitudes such as South America, where pesticides may have entered coastal waters via rivers or particulate drift in air.

In the Antarctic, DDT has also been found in penguin eggs, another aspect of pesticide pollution whereby sub-lethal effects may, in the long term, have a greater impact on the status of a species than chemicals present in lethal concentrations. DDT had become commonly used in both the USA and the UK by the early 1960s. A group of organochlorine compounds known as cyclodienes (dieldrin, aldrin and heptachlor) was also extensively used, particularly in the UK. The toxic cyclodienes were targeted at pests via seed dressings rather than as a spray (with dieldrin also popular as a sheep dip), so harmful side-effects on non-target organisms were not anticipated.

In 1961, the British Trust for Ornithology found that breeding numbers of peregrine falcons (*Falco peregrinus*) had fallen dramatically from the stable level of around 800 pairs censused before 1940. Peregrines tend to use the same nest sites year after year, yet occupation of these sites in 1961 was only 68% of the prewar level; in 1962 this fell to 56%; and in 1963 to only 44%. But even in sites where breeding pairs were found it became evident that breeding success had been greatly lowered: there were behavioural changes such as non-completion of nests and agitation while incubating, reflecting effects of chemicals on the central nervous and hormone systems; an increased propensity for eggs to have thinner shells; and malformations in embryos and fledglings that made survival unlikely. No evidence was found to link this pattern with weather, habitat change, food, disease or persecution by humans. However, high residue levels of DDE (the stable metabolite of DDT) and HEOD (the metabolite of aldrin and dieldrin), were found both in the fatty tissues of peregrine carcasses and in eggs. The highest residue levels were associated with the highest use of these compounds (particularly dieldrin) as seed dressing, in arable-dominated southern and eastern England, where the most pronounced declines in peregrine numbers had been noted. Such eggshell thinning occurred in a number of raptor species and coincided with the first widespread use of DDT in 1947 (Figure 3.11).

Ratcliffe (1967; 1970) was able to link these postwar population declines in birds of prey (raptors) with the growing use of pesticides by

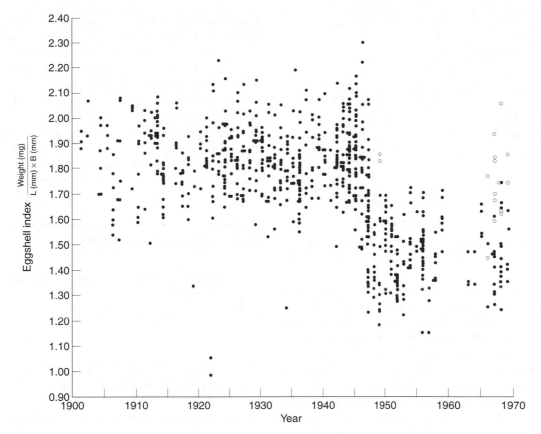

Figure 3.11 Change in time of eggshell index (relative weight) of peregrines in Britain:
○ = eggshells from the central and east Scottish Highlands.
● = eggshells from other districts

reference not only to these geographical and temporal coincidences, and not only by correlations between residue levels and decline, but also by using experimental work which confirmed cause and effect, with a generally clear dose–response relationship (Figure 3.12). Pesticide residues led to hormone changes, which affected the metabolism of calcium carbonate (which comprises 99% of the eggshell) by the mother, who then laid eggs prematurely or with lighter (thinner) shells. Shell thinning made damage to the egg more likely, and eggshell breakage reduced breeding success, contributing to population decline (Figure 3.13).

As with the western grebes, once again it was a group of birds at the end of a food chain that suffered mortality. Agricultural seeds were treated against insects and soil pests, particularly with the cyclodienes; the dressed seeds would be eaten by grain-eating (*granivorous*) rodents and birds such as wood pigeons (*Columba palumbus*); and these in turn would be preyed upon by raptors. In highland Britain, carcasses of sheep dipped in dieldrin would similarly have been taken up by scavenging birds of prey such as buzzards (*Buteo buteo*) and golden eagles (*Aquila chrysaëtos*). Once again, the residues became concentrated in fatty tissue and many adults died. But there were also sub-lethal effects: the loss of eggs and chicks meant that raptor populations did not have the chance to recover. While emphasis in the Clear Lake example has been on western grebe deaths, reproductive success in this species has also been inhibited (Rudd, 1975).

After an acute pollution event such as an oil spill many birds (and other animals) die, but after a year or two numbers generally recover because the remaining birds can still breed. The chronic

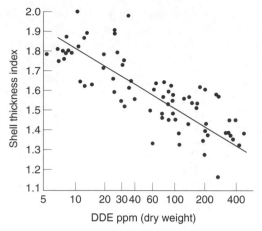

Figure 3.12 Eggshell thinning in relation to egg DDT levels in peregrines.

effects of sub-lethal poisoning seen with pesticides, however, are more insidious and ultimately more threatening because they include taking away from the population the opportunity to recover, because of low breeding success. Pesticide amounts not deadly to an individual may nevertheless ultimately be lethal to a population.

The use of such pesticides has gradually been phased out in North America and Western Europe: for example, DDT was banned in the

United States in 1971. Subsequent monitoring has shown a decline in residue levels in tissues and eggs, and a recovery of numbers and breeding success in birds of prey (Figure 3.14). Elsewhere in the world, however, legally or otherwise, many of these chemicals remain in use. Thus DDT is still being produced in the USA for use in the developing world, for example to control malaria-spreading mosquitoes. Over 30 000 tonnes of DDT is still used every year (World Health Organisation, cited in Botkin and Keller, 1995).

3.3 Ecological concepts

- Ecosystem stability, resistance, resilience and persistence
- Biomagnification and concentration factors

3.3.1 Ecosystem stability, resistance, resilience and persistence

So far, we have examined how pollution can destabilise populations, communities and ecosys-

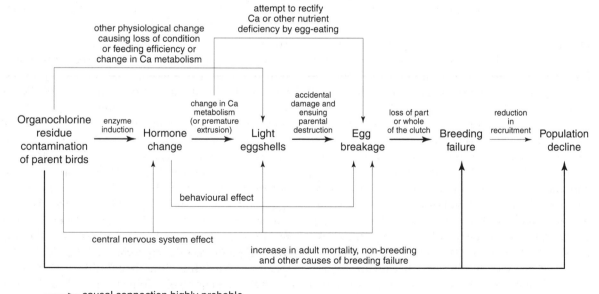

Figure 3.13 Possible relationships in a causal chain induced by organochlorine residues.

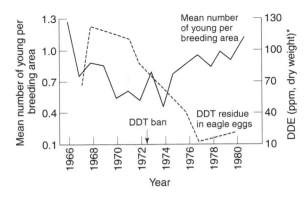

* DDT is converted to DDE in the birds' bodies

Figure 3.14 Comparison of the number of successful bald eagle offspring with the level of DDT residues in their eggs, showing how reproductive success improved after DDT levels decreased.

tems, without actually defining what we mean by stability. The *stability* of a system is a measure of its sensitivity to disturbance or perturbation. Stability reflects the ability of a system to return to an equilibrium state after a (temporary) disturbance. The faster the return, with the least fluctuation, the greater the stability. The actual return to an equilibrium state of any specific example depends in part on the external pressures placed on the system, but the degree of stability is an intrinsic property of the system itself.

Stability closely reflects and is often confused with resistance, resilience, elasticity and persistence. *Resistance* reflects the extent to which a system avoids change or prevents it from having an impact. *Resilience* is a measure of the ability of a system to absorb changes (Holling, 1973). Begon *et al.* (1996) argue that resilience describes the speed with which a system returns to its former state after it has been perturbed and displaced from that state, but this characteristic is better described by the term 'elasticity' (Orians, 1975). Strong resistance and resilience generally lead to *persistence*: the system will have a low probability of extinction (Holling, 1973).

Stability is also often linked with the diversity and maturity of a system, the latter (as discussed in Chapter 1) commonly reflecting greater opportunity for feedback mechanisms to have evolved. For example, spatial environmental diversity (heterogeneity) usually increases species diversity; temporal environmental heterogeneity may

increase or decrease diversity and stability (Jacobs, 1975). Environmental stress is often negatively correlated with diversity, i.e. increasing the stress reduces the number of species that can tolerate such conditions. Increased diversity of resources will lead to an increased resistance to changes in those resources but no significant change in resilience.

The relation of resistance and resilience to each other depends both on the underlying characteristics of negative feedback to population change and on the sensitivity of the growth rate to the environment. Strong feedback mechanisms that are independent of the environmental factor causing the stress will increase both resilience and resistance to that stress. If the feedback mechanism makes the population growth rate sensitive to the environmental factor, however, the amount of resilience and resistance under changes in that factor will be inversely related.

It was at first believed that there is a direct causal effect between system complexity and system stability, but recent work has suggested that, at least in community ecology, stability is linked with complexity simply because of the way the analysis is undertaken. Studies showing positive stability–diversity relationships have generally used a single class of stability (or, rather, instability) measure, *viz.* temporal variation in aggregate community properties such as biomass or productivity. Doak *et al.* (1998) demonstrate that for such measures stability will always rise with species diversity simply because of the statistical averaging of the fluctuations in species abundances.

Orians (1975) sees persistence as reflecting the survival time of a system, or some component of it. He also defines a number of terms that are useful in exploring how systems respond to environmental stresses or other changes (Table 3.3; Figure 3.15). *Constancy* reflects the lack of change in some parameter of a system, for example the number of species, taxonomic composition, lifeform structure of a community, or feature of the physical environment. *Inertia* is the ability of a system to resist external perturbations; it takes into account elements of both resistance and resilience. *Amplitude* is defined as the range of parameters or states ('ecological area')

Table 3.3   Environmental factors and phenotypic characteristics of species that increase different kinds of stability (see also Figure 3.15)

A. Persistence
  1. Environmental heterogeneity in space and time
  2. Large patch sizes
  3. Constant physical environment
  4. High resource utilisation thresholds of predators

B. Inertia
  1. Environmental heterogeneity in space and time
  2. Greater phenotypic diversity of prey
  3. Multiplicity of energy pathways
  4. Intraspecific variability of prey
  5. High mean longevity of individuals of components species (Frank, 1968)

C. Elasticity
  1. High density dependence in birth rates
  2. Short life cycles of component species
  3. Capacity for high dispersal
  4. Strong migratory tendencies
  5. Generalised foraging patterns

D. Amplitude
  1. Weak density dependence in birth rates
  2. Intraspecific variability of component species
  3. Capacity for long-distance dispersal
  4. Broad physical tolerances
  5. Generalised harvesting capabilities
  6. Defence against predators not dependent on a narrow range of hiding places

E. Cyclic stability
  1. High resource utilisation thresholds
  2. Long lag times in response of species to changes in resource availability
  3. Heterogeneity of environment in space and time

F. Trajectory stability
  1. Strong organism-induced modifications of the physical environment
  2. All factors increasing elasticity

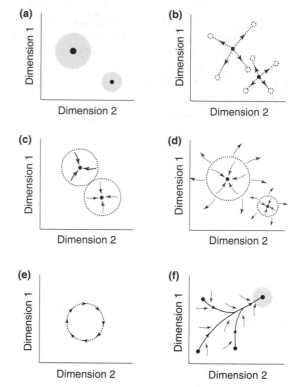

Figure 3.15   Graphic representation of some concepts of stability (see also Table 3.3).

amplitude). *Cyclic stability* is the property of a system to cycle or oscillate around some central point or zone. *Trajectory stability* is the property of a system to move towards some final end-point or zone despite different 'starting points' and is seen, for example, in some models of vegetation succession (see Section 7.3.5).

An ecosystem or community that is stable only within a narrow range of environmental conditions, or for a very limited range of species characteristics, is said to be *dynamically fragile*, in contrast to a system that is stable within a wide range of conditions and characteristics, which is *dynamically robust* (May, 1975).

Many of these ideas can be incorporated into the characterisation of what might be called 'ecosystem health', defined in terms of system organisation (diversity and number of interactions between components), vigour (using measurements of activity, metabolism or primary productivity) and stability, especially resilience. Ecosystem health has been particularly useful in

over which a system is stable. Amplitude can be used to distinguish between *local stability*, which describes the tendency of a system to return to its original state following a small perturbation (low amplitude), and *global stability*, where the same tendency occurs after a major perturbation (high exploring the responses of regional ecosystems to various kinds and combinations of human impacts on the environment, and also in examining the consequences of ecosystem health on human activity, including human health, economic opportunity and sustainability (Rapport *et al.*, 1998).

3.3.2 Biomagnification and concentration factors

Biomagnification occurs when an element or chemical compound moves from one compartment to another and occurs at a higher concentration in the second. Biomagnification may occur by three methods.

1. *Physiological magnification* occurs when residues are stored and accumulated by particular tissues within the bodies of individual organisms. A nearly straight-line relationship occurs between fatty (lipid) fractions of a tissue and the amount of residues contained.

2. *Biological magnification* occurs where residues move from an external medium directly through the skin or respiratory surface; the external medium can be water, and this method is indeed common in aquatic environments.

3. *Trophic magnification*, or food-chain magnification, occurs because one organism feeds on another: stored residues accompany ingested foods and are assimilated and stored in the grazer or predator. This is the case with organochlorines and birds of prey.

The element or compound could be a nutrient but, as has been shown with pesticides, it could also be a pollutant. Thus a pollutant would have a higher concentration in a plant than in the soil, in a herbivore than in its plant diet, and in a predator than in its animal diet. Biomagnification can be measured as a *concentration factor* (CF) where CF = (concentration of the pollutant in the consumer ÷ concentration of the pollutant in the diet). Biomagnification occurs where CF > 1. If both

the diet and water are taken into account as a source for aquatic organisms (as with the example of Clear Lake) then *bioaccumulation* is said to have occurred. The term 'bioconcentration' should strictly be used only when it refers specifically to uptake having been from water alone.

These terms, however, should be used with caution for they are all time-dependent, and pollutant levels in both the diet and (usually) in the consumer change continually. In making comparisons between trophic levels, we should consider only whole-body pollutant burdens, yet pollutants often accumulate in fatty tissues such as the brain, liver, kidney and heart, and these organs will represent different proportions of the body mass of different species. Moreover, pollutants that are stored in bones, shell and hair may not be consumed by predators, and are therefore not transferred. Problems also occur where an animal is preyed upon by different predator species, and where a predator consumes different prey species, especially with omnivores that feed at different trophic levels.

For a CF > 1, its rate of (pollutant) uptake must exceed its rate of (pollutant) loss, and this is not always the situation. Also, larger animals tend to eat more, thereby consuming a greater mass of a pollutant, yet will often lose that pollutant (by excretion or internal detoxification) more slowly. The pollutant itself may or may not be readily degraded. Differences in assimilation, degradation, excretion and storage between pollutants and organisms thus all complicate the picture. And large animals at the end of a food chain may have a higher concentration of a pollutant simply because of their size rather than their trophic position.

3.4 Issues in environmental management

3.4.1 Risks, hazards and costs

It is a truism that everything we do involves some kind of risk, and much human activity poses some kind of potential threat to the environment, whether it is a mild form of environmental modification that (as far as can be judged) is of no real consequence or a major perturbation that results in widespread and long-term environmental destruction. What becomes important is an awareness that a risk exists: what that risk is, what it involves, what the likelihood is of occurrence, what its consequences might be, what can be done to reduce the risk, what the costs of such reduction or of failure to prevent damage might be, what the cost–benefit balance is likely to be, and what alternatives are feasible. We thus need knowledge about the actual risks and costs, judgement about tolerable levels of, for example, environmental degradation in relation to perceived benefits, and decisions that are essentially political.

Beck (1992) considered that

> the social production of wealth is systematically accompanied by the social production of risk ... The debate on pollutant and toxic elements in air, water and foodstuffs, as well as on the destruction of nature and the environment in general, is still being conducted exclusively or dominantly in the terms and formulas of natural science ...The pollution debate conducted in terms of natural science correspondingly moves between the false conclusion of social afflictions based on biological ones, and a view of nature which excludes the selective afflictions of people as well as the social and cultural meaning connected to it.

Beck, though, is wrong: 'social affliction' is hardly ever discussed solely on the basis of biological damage, and many decisions to reduce, mitigate or indeed even allow pollution damage, for example, are based on (often short-term) human gain or acceptable levels of loss of social well-being at the expense of short- and long-term environmental damage.

Risk assessment involves identifying what hazards might exist and assigning probabilities of their occurrence:

- **Hazard identification** – the type and location of a (potential) pollutant; its mode of entry into the environment; and known or likely effect or impact.
- **Dose–response assessment** – the relationship between amount (quantity, concentration,

length of time of exposure) and adverse effect.
- **Exposure assessment** – vulnerability of an individual, population, community or ecosytem to exposure, again considering dose–response but also including additive, antagonistic or synergistic effects; and individual health and vulnerability or population/community vulnerability.
- **Risk characterisation** – the probability of an adverse effect, combining data from dose–response studies and exposure assessment.

Risk assessment has to be evaluated with environmental, socio-cultural, -economic and -political considerations. In turn, this will identify options for risk management involving control, alleviation or mitigation, bearing in mind (bio)technological knowledge and availability, cost–benefit ratios, public opinion, legislative regulation and monitoring opportunities.

For many economic enterprises today, environmental impact assessments and environmental risk assessments have, by law, to be made. In the UK the Environment Agency and in the USA the Environmental Protection Agency (EPA) are prime agencies for this. Proposed EPA guidelines have three phases – problem formulation, analysis and risk characterisation, the last phase predicting the environmental effects of the stress factor(s) to the likely presence and concentration in the environment.

Cost–benefit analysis is an important method of identifying probable costs, whether of damage itself or of mechanisms introduced to avoid or minimise damage. Even when used as an economic tool, accurate cost–benefit analysis is difficult. Economic costs in particular are difficult to predict accurately. For example, in the early 1970s, the petroleum industry predicted that the cost of phasing out leaded petrol in the USA would be $7 billion per annum, but the actual cost turned out to be less than $500 million (Raven *et al.*, 1998). Environmental costs are nigh on impossible to calculate, and most attempts at converting cost into actual monetary values are simplistic, for example in trying to put a price on ecosystem simplification, the extinction of a species, a reduction in scenic quality or a decline in human health. Nevertheless, attempts at costing must be made where compensation is required. Also, environmental benefits are often the avoidance of environmental costs, for instance in *not* constructing a new road or in *not* ploughing up a Site of Special Scientific Interest.

Risk assessment depends on good scientific data, but it also relies on a number of assumptions, preferred goals and the perception of both the public and the politicians.

3.4.2 Perception and political action

The perception of risk by the public, legislators and indeed scientists is important to consider. People often ignore major risks (or work on the 'it won't happen to me' principle) but become concerned over minor ones. Smokers, for instance, have an average life expectancy eight years less than that of non-smokers, and almost a third of smokers die from diseases caused or exacerbated by smoking. However, even when the risks are known they are often offset by perceived benefits or the (incorrect) argument that they are more likely to be killed in a road accident before they die from smoking. Risks of developing a cancer from eating pesticide-sprayed food are very much lower, yet (although again understandably) many smokers are more concerned about this than the consequences of their habit.

In risk assessment of employment in power generation industries for actuarial purposes it has been shown, taking the whole workforce in an industry into account, that there is a greater risk of death or serious injury per employee in the wind-generated power industry than in the coal industry, although most people would intuitively view the latter as the more dangerous because they consider only a small but very vulnerable component of the total workforce, the coalface worker. Similarly, the nuclear power industry is, for the employee, safest of all, yet the use of nuclear fuel worries many members of the public: the risk of a major accident is very low (although Chernobyl did happen), but radionuclide pollution following an incident would be spread widely by the wind, the public would have few opportunities to avoid the consequences, and sub-

lethal effects are difficult to identify since radiation can have long-term impacts on health and may increase the propensity for other diseases to develop. Risk here extends beyond a workforce into the general domain.

The perception of pollution risk by the public is often based on particular incidents. Point-source incidents such as major oil tanker spills produce demands that 'something must be done'. Tanker owners do not want accidents either, and over recent years some important technological advances have been made (Issues Box 3.1). Most accidents have involved human error: technology thus has to reduce the chances and consequences of such an error, whether on the vessel itself (for example in the use of double hulls and multi-compartmented tankers) or in cleaning up the spillage, whether on the sea or the coast.

Gut-reaction demands by the public, however, do not always make sound environmental or ecological sense. TV pictures of oil-drenched seabirds bring home to viewers one of the consequences of an oil spill, but it is actually more humane to kill moribund birds than to attempt to clean off the oil. There are major problems in de-oiling: application of detergents will often damage the fine structure of the feathers, destroy the natural oils that the birds need for water-proofing and affect the insulating properties of the plumage, and treated birds risk drowning and chilling. If seabirds such as species of auk are kept out of water while treatment takes place they often develop problems supporting their weight, leading to arthritis and bone deformities. Furthermore, survival of cleaned birds is very low. In one study, the number of days between release and carcass recovery of three species of seabird was 5–100 times lower than for non-oiled birds that had been captured, ringed and released as a control, and post-release life expectancy of de-oiled guillemots was only 9.6 days, with long-term recovery rates 10–20% those of non-oiled birds (Sharp, 1996).

Bird rescue, cleaning and treatment are costly: after the *Exxon Valdez* spill $41 million was spent dealing with only 800 birds. 'Cleaning and treatment do not provide effective mitigation for and cannot be considered as even partial restoration of damage ... Oil spill response planning and resources

---

ISSUES BOX 3.1

Supertanker design

Supertankers (or very large crude carriers, VLCCs) are the largest self-propelled machines ever built. Fifty years ago, few tankers had a deadweight (a measure of cargo capacity) of more than 16 500 tonnes. Today, VLCCs can be over half a million tonnes (the *Seawise Giant*, launched in 1990, has a deadweight of 565 000 tonnes), although most lie between 250 000 and 280 000 tonnes. Use of high-tensile steels reduces weight by 15% compared with mild steel, cutting costs but making the tanker more susceptible to fatigue stresses and fracturing. Once underway, VLCCs have difficulty in stopping or even manoeuvring when cruising at 15 knots.

In August 1990, President Bush signed the Oil Pollution Act, but this did not define standards for anything other than vessel design, important though this was. All new supertankers ordered after 30 June 1990 had to have a double hull. However, existing single-hulled vessels could operate until the year 2010. US legislation also made tanker owners operating in US waters liable to unlimited claims for compensation for damage caused by spillage. Equivalent laws in the UK regarding double hulls date from July 1993, with single-hulled VLCCs permitted in UK waters until 2023. The *Sea Empress* was single-hulled.

Double hulls involve a 3 m gap between the external hull and the oil tank. Nevertheless, a 3 m gap would be breached at a collision speed of just over 4 knots, and even a 6 m gap would be vulnerable at 7.3 knots. Greatly increased construction and maintenance costs are other issues with the use of double hulls. The 'mid-deck' design has also been suggested as a safety measure, where a horizontal division of the oil tanks is made, compartmentalising the oil to reduce the chance of the whole cargo being lost following a breach. Even small design improvements can make major differences. Halving the volume of oil that is spilled, for instance, will reduce the length of the slick hitting a coastline by ten to fifteen times.

A further suggestion has been to take advantage of hydrostatic balance by stopping filling a tanker while the hydraulic pressure of the cargo is less than that of the sea: if a hull is breached water will then flow in rather than oil seep out. However, this would not only mean carrying less oil and therefore reducing profits but may make the tanker less stable in high seas with oil moving around inside the compartments, unless some of the compartments contained seawater ballast.

Sources: National Research Council, 1991; Cross and Hamer, 1992

---

should be redirected to the prevention of damage, rather than focusing on ineffective attempts at rehabilitation after the damage has occurred' (*ibid.*). Nevertheless, many countries maintain facilities for cleaning oil-damaged animals, and in July 1997 the world's largest such centre opened in Santa Cruz, California, able to handle up to 125 sea otters and 100 birds at any one time.

The overall clean-up bill following *Exxon Valdez* was over $2.1 billion (Weiner *et al.*, 1977), and these costs, together with compensation for damage to natural resources, needed to be recovered from the individuals and corporations responsible for the spill. The principal statute invoked was the Comprehensive Environmental Response, Compensation, and Liability Act of 1980, which uses scientific data in a legally precise but scientifically unusual way. Natural resources (land, air, water and their living components) are included in a codification of 'public trust doctrine', which declares that government holds in trust for the people a duty to protect and make available certain natural resources for specific uses for the benefit of society as a whole. Violations of this doctrine require both compensation and restoration. Damage assessment studies determine the extent of environmental loss or damage; this loss is valued in terms of money; legal action follows to recover compensation; and damages thus obtained are used to restore the damaged ecosystem (Shaw and Bader, 1996).

Assessment of damage to natural resources, however, requires comparing baseline (pre-damage) conditions with later (post-damage) conditions. Four obvious problems exist here: the inevitably inadequate state of knowledge of pre-damage environmental conditions; the fact that in any case no static baseline can exist, since we are looking at dynamic ecosystems responding to natural fluctuations; problems of describing and quantifying environmental damage; and the problem of putting both a value and a price on such damage.

On 8 October 1991, the US District Court approved a plea agreement and a civil settlement ($900 million to be paid over 10 years) that avoided a trial between Exxon Corporation and the state and federal governments, although this was subsequently increased to $5 billion. However, this meant that restoration, beyond immediate clean-up, could proceed. One of the key elements of this has been the acquisition of habitat for management and protection: nearly 170 000 ha of private land (including some existing wildlife refuges) have now been bought and placed in public ownership, where they are being managed in such a way as to facilitate recovery of damaged resources (Weiner *et al.*, 1997).

In early 1999 the *Exxon Valdez*, understandably banned from Prince William Sound, was seen transporting oil in the Firth of Forth, Scotland, but under a new name – the *Sea River Mediterranean*.

After every major pollution incident recommendations are made to improve safety and reduce risk. The inquiry by Lord Donaldson into the 1993 *Braer* oil spill, for example, made thirteen specific proposals of this kind. One recommended formal identification of environmental high-risk marine areas where vessel masters would have to exercise particular care; it has been further suggested that only double-hulled vessels should be allowed to ply such waters. However, governments are reluctant to confront the powerful oil and shipping industries. Indeed, the British government has argued that the issue of double-hulled tankers is a matter for the International Maritime Organisation alone. A further issue is that of registrations of conveni-

ence, and fears of lower safety standards and denials of liability. The *Torrey Canyon*, for example, was owned by a Bermudan company on charter to a British one, flying the Liberian flag. The (single-hulled) *Sea Empress*, too, was registered to Liberia.

A year after the *Sea Empress* spill, costs were estimated at £10 million, yet no one was at that time formally held accountable. The Environment Agency had investigated a possible criminal action under the Water Resources Act (1991), Section 85 of which makes it an offence to allow noxious substances into the sea. The Department of Transport's Marine Accident Investigation Branch inquiry was held in secret, and there was no cross-examination of witnesses. This was in sharp contrast to the Donaldson Inquiry, where all events and actions were closely and publicly scrutinised. It does appear, however, that as well as a lack of proper charts and accurate local information on tides, on which refloating the tanker depended, there was a lack of a proper chain of command back to government in White-hall. Also, there were no tugs near the refinery capable of intervening, yet another recommendation of the Donaldson Inquiry that had not been implemented.

In February 1999, however, Milford Haven Port Authority was fined $4 million for its role in the incident. Yet the *Sea Empress* salvage and clean-up cost around £60 million; losses to tourism and fisheries have been anything between £13 million and £50 million; court costs were £2.7 million; the actual accident reports cost another £2.7 million; and repairing the vessel added a further £20 million. This total of £98 million does not attempt to include the cost of the environmental damage, nor does it cost time and effect by volunteers, who made a major input to the clean-up. Most of these costs will eventually be met by the International Oil Pollution Compensation Fund (*The Guardian*, 24 February 1999: Society 6).

Dramatic point-source events such as the oil spills discussed here, or Chernobyl, reach public attention and find official reaction largely because they are unambiguously examples of pollution with obvious (as well as less obvious) consequences for the environment. However, it has already been shown that most oil spillage comes from activities other than major tanker accidents. Similarly, potential pollution from pesticides affects the environment over time, over a wide space, and generally with less readily apparent environmental effects. Only when crusading scientists such as Rachel Carson publish books that become best-sellers do the risks of such forms of pollution receive critical attention from the public. Certainly, Carson's *Silent Spring* (1962) – the title reflecting the absence of birdsong following pesticide-derived deaths – was seminal in bringing the consequences of liberal, uncritical chemical application to public attention, causing media outcry, scientific re-evaluation and government action.

Some incidents involving pesticides, however, have had point sources. In 1976, for example, there was an explosion near Seveso in northern Italy when a reactor overheated at a pharmaceutical factory manufacturing trichlorophenol, which is used as a bacteriocide. The pollutant cloud, which included 2,3,7,8-tetrachlorodi-benzo-*p*-dioxin, a toxic and persistent pesticide, settled over 18 km^2 in which around 37 000 people lived. About 2000 people were treated for dioxin contamination, and 90 abortions and a significant rise in birth defects were reported in the following year. Over 81 000 domestic animals were killed or had to be destroyed. There were delays in reporting and responding to the incident, with nine days elapsing before the risks were acknowledged. The top 20 cm of soil had to be removed from the most heavily impacted area; some was burned locally, the rest stored in barrels, the last of which being incinerated (in Basle, Switzerland) in 1984. Compensation amounts are unclear, but disposal costs of toxic soil and other material alone were $150 million (Newson, 1992; Barrow, 1995).

An even more serious disaster occurred at Bhopal, in Madya Pradesh, India, in December 1984 at a Union Carbide chemical and fertiliser plant when 36 tonnes of methyl isocyanate (MIC) gas, which is used to produce carbamate pesticides exploded from an underground storage tank into which water had leaked, causing a violent chemical reaction. MIC itself is toxic, but reacting with the atmosphere some MIC was further converted into the even more toxic hydrogen cyanide. The deadly cloud covered 78 km^2, killing about 2500 people straight away, but with eventual deaths double that figure. Up to 60 000 locals subsequently suffered from serious respiratory, intestinal, neurological and reproductive problems. In 1989, Union Carbide (which argued that the incident was a consequence of sabotage) offered a compensation payment of $470 million, with over $100 million also set aside to build a hospital for the victims. The Indian government, however, argued for negligence and claimed $10 billion. By 1993, only 2747 of 15 000 claims for compensation for death had been settled. Most claims for injury or family deaths are not expected to have been met by the year 2000 (Weir, 1988; Shrivastrava, 1992).

3.5 Conclusions

This chapter has indicated some of the problems of identifying what additions to the environment might become pollutants and predicting the consequences of introducing pollutants into different environments. It has also outlined some of the problems associated with identifying costs and agreeing responsibilites.

However much care and control are exercised, pollution accidents will always happen; some individuals, companies, institutions and perhaps even governments will always deliberately release or dump toxic waste; and permissible levels will always legitimise a certain quantity of substances in water, air, soil and organic bodies, including humans. Also, thresholds of acceptable levels of pollution that satisfy scientists as well as politicians and the public change periodically and exacerbate the problems of waste production and disposal.

Further reading

Adams, J. (1995) *Risk* (London: UCL Press).
Carson, R. (1962) *Silent spring* (Harmondsworth: Penguin).

Hardman, D., McEldowney, S. and Waite, S. (1993) *Pollution: ecology and biotreatment* (Harlow: Longman).

Mason, C.F. (1996) *Biology of freshwater pollution* (third edition) (Harlow: Longman)

Natural Resources Defense Council. (1993) *After Silent Spring: the unsolved problems of pesticide use in the United States* (Washington DC: Island Press).

Neely, W.B. (1994) *Introduction to chemical exposure and risk assessment* (Boca Raton, Fla: Lewis Publishers).

Rodicks, J.V. (1992) *Calculated risks: the toxicity and human health risks of chemicals in our environment* (Cambridge: Cambridge University Press).

Schmidt, K. (1997) A drop in the ocean. *New Scientist*, **154**(2080) (3 May): 40–4.

Walker, D. (1989) Diversity and stability. In J.M. Cherrett (ed.) *Ecological concepts: the contribution of ecology to an understanding of the natural world* (Oxford: Blackwell Scientific) 115–45.

Wellburn, A. (1994) *Air pollution and climate change* (second edition) (Harlow: Longman).

QUESTIONS BASED ON CHAPTER 3

Q1. Which of the following are examples of pollution? In the case of pollution, are they point sources or non-point sources?

Sewage from a boat

Urban runoff from storm sewers

Thermal (hot) water from a power plant

Steam from a coal-fired power station

Fertiliser runoff from farmland

Erosion of sediment following deforestation

Q2. In general, what effects would you expect pollution to have on the species diversity and actual species content of a community?

Q3. What is the best way to reduce the use of oil, slow down the rate of global warming and improve air quality?

Q4. Atmospherically, what do canaries and lichen have in common?

Q5. Environmentally, what are the three least desirable ways of disposing of hazardous waste? How are 71% of hazardous wastes in the USA officially handled?

ANSWERS

A1. Sewage from a boat – point source.

Urban runoff from storm sewers – the runoff containing pollutants is non-point source, but the storm sewer outlet represents a point source.

Thermal water pollution – point source, however much or quickly the heat is dissipated. Thermal shock to rivers receiving heated water makes heat a pollutant in this context.

Steam from a coal-fired power station – steam by itself is not a pollutant, since the water vapour disperses and cools rapidly (the visible consequence of this being the steam) and will have no adverse environmental impact. Of course, other pollutants may be emitted into the air from the power station, but that was not what was asked about. The fact that the power station is coal-fired is irrelevant to the example.

Fertiliser runoff from farmland – non-point source.

Erosion of sediment following deforestation – This is context-dependent. If the material is redeposited in a way that is not harmful to the natural or anthropogenic environment it is not a pollutant. Assuming that the sediment enters a water body and has some kind of deleterious effect, then it will have become a pollutant and will have had a non-point source. That sediment is a natural material is irrelevant, since it is human activity that has displaced the sediment and has caused it to have an adverse effect.

ANSWERS (cont)

A2. Some pollutants at low levels can increase species diversity, causing no or few species losses, but allowing new species to enter a community (with a net gain in species numbers over losses), for example the nutrient enrichment causing cultural eutrophication of sewage, or small temperature increases with discharges of heated water. Beyond critical thresholds of pollutant concentration or degree, however (and indeed it may be argued that until that point is reached pollution has not occurred), we would expect to find a reduction in species diversity (a response to stress), the loss of taxa unable to tolerate the changed environmental conditions, and possibly the entry into the community of new species that can thrive in the altered conditions.

A3. Improve the energy efficiency of motor vehicles (about 10% of the energy in petrol is used to move a motor vehicle powered by an internal combustion engine, the other 90% being lost to the environment as waste heat); use public transport where feasible and inexpensive; and walk rather than drive over short distances where possible.

A4. They have both been used as indicators of air quality. Nineteenth-century coal workers took caged canaries into the mines. When the birds stopped singing it was probably an indication that air quality had deteriorated and was dangerous for the miners. Similarly, some lichens can indicate the presence or absence of air pollution; for example, many species of *Usnea* are intolerant of sulphur dioxide, while *Lecanora conizaeoides* thrives under such acid conditions, and *Ramalina* species are damaged by nitrate and fluoride salts.

A5. Buried in deep wells, ponds or landfills; incineration; and ocean dumping. In the USA, 64% of all hazardous waste is buried in wells, ponds and landfills, and 7% is incinerated.

Discussion topics

D1. What would be the constitution of the simplest stable ecosystem that you can think of?

D2. The risk of death or serious injury is far greater for road travel (per unit distance travelled) than for air travel. Why, then, are more people afraid of flying than driving or being driven? What similar attitudes are evident in the context of environmental risk?

D3. Most countries have legislation concerning clean air and water quality. Should there also be legislation for 'clean soil'? What would be the benefits and difficulties associated with any such legislation?

D4. Do the benefits of chemical pesticides outweigh the environmental risks?

D5. Which of the uses of chemical pesticides indicated below are most important to humans? Rank your results and give reasons for your decisions.
  Production of blemish-free fruit and vegetables
  Controlling damage to timber plantation trees by insects
  Controlling damage to crops by insects
  Controlling damage to crops by weeds
  Controlling damage to garden plants by weeds
  Controlling malaria
  Controlling vegetation on roadsides to maintain lines of sight for drivers

EXERCISES

E1. Find out what your water company does to ensure that your domestic water is drinkable, paying particular attention to physical and chemical processes. What other chemicals might be added to domestic water, and why? What other environmental responsibilities does your water company have?

E2. Undertake an audit of the ecosystem health of your garden, the grounds of your educational establishment or a local public park. What changes might improve the ecosystem health of your site?

Chapter 4

Species distributions and climatic change

Summary

Climate is a key environmental factor that changes through time, affecting among other things the geographical distribution of living organisms. Relatively rapid climatic change has occurred on a number of occasions throughout Earth's history, but current changes are more pronounced than at any other time in the last 2.4 million years, a consequence of human activities, in particular those contributing to an increase in the production of greenhouse gases (leading to global warming) but also including those thinning or destroying parts of the ozone layer. Focusing on the greenhouse effect, this chapter examines some of the actual and potential consequences of climatic changes on temperature and precipitation, sea levels, fresh water, soil, plants, animals and agriculture. The significance of environmental gradients is indicated, leading into discussion of ranges of tolerance and limiting factors, which affect the local distribution of species as well as their geographical range. A number of environmental factors, many of which show rhythmic diurnal and seasonal changes, regulate how organisms live, and many species have evolved a biological clock to anticipate their responses to predictable periodic environmental changes. Geographical distributions reflect geological and evolutionary history, geographical barriers and species interactions as well as the attributes and requirements of each individual species. Global warming will influence many aspects of human life, including patterns of disease. Means of reducing (or reducing the impact of) global warming, and problems of agreeing on the implementation of any such means, are discussed in the context of individual, institutional and governmental responsibilities.

4.1 Species distributions

The present-day distribution of species reflects the interaction of a number of factors, including the evolutionary history of the species, changing geographical barriers, interactions with other species and response to the environment, including the consequences of human activity. All organisms have a set of environmental requirements and preferences, and these determine where species are, at least in theory, able to survive, and where they cannot. The responses of organisms to different environments become more complicated to disentangle when it is remembered that environments change through time and the species themselves are capable of responding to such changes not only through changes in distribution but also by changes in tolerance and environmental demands. Climate (the long-term prevailing or average weather conditions of an area) is one of the key environmental factors that not only differs geographically but also changes through time, and this chapter focuses on what some of these changes have been and some of the plant and animal responses to such changes. Comments are also made on the implications of climatic change, particularly global warming, for human activities. Species distributions and activities are also examined with reference to limiting factors.

4.2 Key environmental issue: climatic change

The Quaternary record shows that migration has been the usual response of organisms to environmental change. This record also reveals that forecast future climate changes are of a magnitude and in a direction unprecedented in recent earth history: the rate of these changes is likely also to surpass that of any comparable change during the last 2.4 million years.

(Huntley, 1995).

The 1995 report of the Intergovernmental Panel on Climate Change declared that 'The balance of evidence now suggests that there is a discernible human influence on global climate' (IPCC, 1996). This conclusion reflects measurement of trends in such climatic features as temperature and such driving variables as carbon dioxide concentration, which demonstrate statistically significant changes. It is also symptomatic that, for example, 1997 was the warmest year, globally, since records began in the late nineteenth century. In England, the five warmest years witnessed since records began in 1659 have all been since 1975. Predicted climatic changes include a rise in global mean temperatures, regionally variable but significant changes in the amount of precipitation, and in many places important shifts in seasonal characteristics, especially in the length and timing of wet and dry seasons.

In the United Kingdom, the Climatic Change Impacts Review Group has anticipated a number of changes in climate that will have important consequences for vegetation and wildlife (CCIRG, 1996):

- Temperatures will rise rather more than the global average, since temperate latitudes are more likely to have pronounced temperature effects than tropical latitudes.
- Winters will be milder, with fewer frosts.
- There will be a greater frequency of warm summers, with an increased likelihood of heat waves.
- Rainfall will generally increase by around 10%. Most of this increase will be in the northern and western parts of the UK, but winter rainfall will also increase in the southeast.

- Nevertheless, summers will become much drier – especially in southern Britain – and drought conditions will be prevalent in some regions.
- There will also be an increase in extreme weather events such as storms, and average wind speeds will increase, especially at the time of the spring and autumn equinoxes.

4.2.1 Climatic change as a natural phenomenon

Climatic variation, however, is a natural phenomenon, occurring on a time scale of many thousands of years, as seen with the major glacial periods but also evident over centuries and indeed decades. External factors that promote climatic change include variations in solar output, changes in the Earth's orbit and continental drift (Ecology Box 4.1).

Global warming is a serious issue of concern today, evidence now essentially pointing incontrovertibly to this as a consequence of human activity. However, climatic change – including global warming – occurs naturally. The so-called 'climatic optimum', for example, occurred in the mid-latitude Northern Hemisphere between around 8000 and 5000 years ago, with conditions averaging 2.5 °C warmer than today over much of Europe, North America and East Asia. Climatic deterioration, especially in terms of cooling, became pronounced after about 2500 years ago in both hemispheres and continued up to about the tenth century AD. There then followed, certainly in the Northern Hemisphere, a phase that has been called the 'Little climatic optimum', or 'mediaeval warm period' – a warmer and drier period lasting from about AD 900 to 1300. This was a period that allowed the cultivation of vines in southern England, Viking colonisation of Greenland and beyond, and Anasazi Pueblo Native Amercans to practise dry farming in the now arid US South-west.

From about 1880 on, summer and winter temperatures have tended to rise in many parts of the temperate Northern Hemisphere, a trend that has also been seen more globally since the 1920s, probably as a consequence of higher levels of greenhouse gases (discussed later) and a relative absence of major volcanic eruptions (Wallen, 1986; Bradley and Jones, 1994).

ECOLOGY BOX 4.1

External factors promoting natural climatic changes

- **Solar activity**. Historical data suggest that colder conditions in Europe, such as the so-called Little Ice Age of about 1450–1850, coincide with periods of reduced or even no sunspot activity. There is also a roughly 9–13-year (average 11 years) cycle of sunspot activity, which appears to be reflected by a parallel cycle in precipitation, with years of maximum precipitation corresponding with periods of greatest sunspot activity.

- **Earth's orbit**. Three interacting variations appear to trigger climatic changes:
  shape of the *elliptical orbit* of the Earth round the Sun (a 21 000-year cycle);
  tilt of the Earth's *rotation axis* (a 42 000-year cycle);
  time of year when the Earth is closest to the Sun (*perihelion*) (a 21 000-year cycle).

  The pattern of these variations are known as Milankovitch cycles, after the Yugoslavian astronomer who first calculated them The procession of these cycles is associated with the timing of glacial and interglacial periods (Bartlein and Prentice, 1989).

- **Continental drift**. Shifts in the tectonic plates upon which the continents rest have taken place in geological time (and are continuing), breaking up an original super-continent (Pangaea), which existed 200–250 million years ago, into the distribution of land masses we have today. The changing disposition of land and sea, together with changes in the distribution of mountain areas, has led to long-term changes in climate.

Such changes in climate have had important consequences for plant and animal distributions and for human activities such as agriculture and forestry. In Scandinavia, for example, greater warmth in the 1930s resulted in a northerly advance of many plant and animal species. In Finland, there was an increase of 1.5 °C in the mean annual temperature in the 1930s. More significantly, winters in Finland in this period were warmer by over 1 °C, especially towards the Arctic, and remained so until 1966–70, when winter temperatures became markedly lower, followed by higher temperatures again from the 1970s through to the present. The coldest phase of winter shifted from December/January during the 1960s to November/December during the 1980s. This meant that not only were there higher mean temperatures during the growing and breeding seasons but also that these seasons began earlier. Increased productivity by vegetation was translated, through feeding relationships, into improved breeding success in animals. Complementing these changes in temperature were very variable trends in precipitation, although there has been a very general trend of a precipitation decrease during the twentieth century (Heino, 1978).

Great care needs to be taken when interpreting changes in plant and animal distribution in terms of climatic change. Von Haartman (1978), for example, observed that the degree of spread and increase in numbers of many bird species often greatly exceeded the northward displacement of isotherms (mapped lines of equal temperature) in Finland, and he concluded that changes in land use represented a more important reason for the changes in bird distribution than did climatic change. A similar study also suggested that, while climatic amelioration might account for some population changes in Finnish birds, abandonment of forest grazing, an increase in the extent of spruce though afforestation and extensive clear-felling, together with a consequent increase in 'edge' habitat, as well as other habitat changes and changes in interspecific interactions were in themselves sufficient to explain all the long-term trends in bird populations (Järvinen and Väisänen, 1979).

Another example of both natural climatic change and the problems of disentangling causes of a particular environmental effect is desertification in the Sahel, a band of semi-arid landscape in Africa running east–west between the Sahara Desert to the north and moister regions to the south. In the late 1960s and early 1970s, the drought in the Sahel received a great deal of media attention. The reduction in rainfall, however, was actually not as pronounced as it had been earlier this century, yet the rate and extent of desertification were greater. This was largely because a series of years in the 1940s and 1950s had had unusually high and less variable rainfall, tempting farmers and pastoralists to push further into these parts to take advantage. In doing so they effected a number of environmental changes, for example clearing the land of what little natural vegetation there was, including destroying the sparse tree cover for fuelwood and other purposes. When the climate reverted to something approaching the norm, agriculture and permanent pasturage were no longer viable, and people starved. At the same time, the landscape that had been cleared in many places now reverted not to scrub but to true desert. Drought in the Sahel, then, is the norm, and desertification is exacerbated if not actually caused by human activity (Jarvis, 1994).

The Sahel drought also has to be set into a wider geographical context of climatic change. In the mid-1920s, winter and spring rains north of the Sahara and in the Middle East had decreased, in places to a minimum of 16% below average; summer rainfall, however, was 16% above average. Since the 1920s, the pattern has been reversed, although with some exceptions, for example during parts of the 1950s. In other words, North Africa has become wetter, the Sahel has become drier, and the desert of the Sahara has been drifting southwards at a rate that has averaged 9 km per annum since 1960. The decrease in rainfall since 1960 was indeed considered (even before the greenhouse effect was identified) to be part of a more widespread, natural climatic change that was predicted to continue until 2020 (Winstanley, 1973). And while 1972 has been identified in retrospect as a critical year for the Sahel, at this time there were also severe droughts in India, the Soviet Union, Australia and elsewhere.

With the growth in the human population and changes in the nature and spread of technology, the impact of humans has become an increasingly important factor in local, regional and global climate. However, because human activity is only one of a number of factors, it is difficult to identify the actual extent to which climatic changes are anthropogenic. Nevertheless, it has become increasingly evident that changes in the emission of certain so-called greenhouse gases as a result of human activity have made a major contribution to the current phenomenon of global warming.

4.2.2 The greenhouse effect

Incoming solar radiation is of short wavelength, but because the Earth is a much cooler body than the Sun it radiates energy at much longer wavelengths. This long-wave (infrared) energy is stored in the atmosphere, trapped by gases that slow down the rate at which the energy returns to space. The trapped long-wave energy heats the atmosphere: the temperature of the surface of the Earth would be about $-23\,°C$ were it not for the atmosphere, which warms the surface instead to a temperature of around $15\,°C$. This is a natural greenhouse effect .

Earth emits radiation at $4–100\,\mu m$, with a peak at around $10\,\mu m$. A number of atmospheric gases absorb radiation at wavelengths $>4\,\mu m$, and 94% of the outgoing long-wave radiation is absorbed by these. Particularly important are carbon dioxide (CO_2), methane (CH_4) and water vapour (H_2O).

4.2.2.1 The greenhouse gases

The pre-industrial global average concentration of carbon dioxide was around 260 ppm (parts per million) by volume (Wigley, 1983). The 1988 level averaged about 350 ppm, rising to 360 ppm in 1995, a rate of increase approximating 1.3 ppm each year, although some estimates are of 1.8 ppm (Watson *et al.*, 1992). Models of climate change use different scenarios but, for example, the model developed by the Goddard Institute for Space

Studies (GISS) has predicted a level approximating 600 ppm by 2065 (Houghton *et al.*, 1990). Other scenarios have suggested 850 ppm by 2100. Much current research on likely impacts of carbon dioxide enrichment works on a predicted eventual figure of 700 ppm (i.e. $2\times$ the approximate current ambient CO_2 concentration). Two of the many uncertainties that enter into modelling atmospheric carbon dioxide concentrations are future burning of fossil fuels and (particularly tropical) forests (see Section 1.2) – such burning representing the main sources of carbon dioxide released into the atmosphere – and the extent to which carbon dioxide will be absorbed by the oceans (Henderson-Sellars, 1990). It has been estimated that around 500 000 million tonnes of carbon dioxide were released into the atmosphere in 1993.

While carbon dioxide is the major contributor to the greenhouse effect, it is a less effective absorber of infrared radiation than other greenhouse gases which are less abundant in the atmosphere, and another uncertainty lies in what will happen with these as a result of human activity. Trends in concentration levels of the four major greenhouse gases are shown in Figure 4.1. At the moment, carbon dioxide accounts for just under half of the absorption of radiation in the atmosphere, methane a further 20% or so, nitrous oxide (N_2O) 6%, chlorofluorocarbons (CFCs) 14% and low-level ozone (O_3) 12%.

The rate of increase of carbon dioxide concentration in the atmosphere during the last three decades has been 0.2–0.7% (average 0.4%) per annum. Concentrations of methane, which is four times more effective than carbon dioxide as an absorber of long-wave radiation, have risen at a rate of 1–2% (average 1.3%) per annum, with current levels about 1.7 ppm. About one-fifth of all methane emissions come from pipeline leaks. Another source is seepage from landfill sites, where it is a product of decomposition. It is also a by-product of many agricultural activities, especially from crops such as rice and ruminant livestock such as cattle and sheep (Figure 4.2). It is also a waste product of termite activity, as is carbon dioxide. Global emissions of methane and carbon dioxide by termites have been estimated at 19.7 ± 1.5 Mt year^{-1} and 3500 ± 700 Mt year^{-1}, respectively (1 Mt $= 10^9$ kg), equivalent to

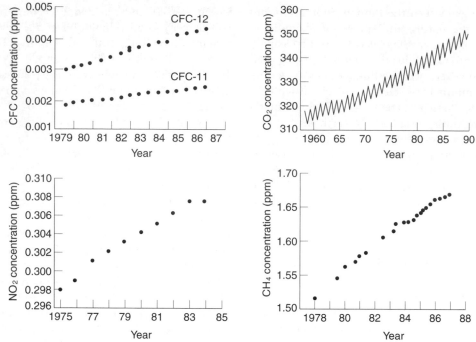

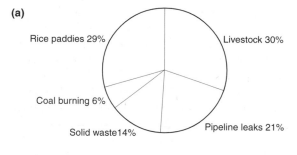

Figure 4.1 Changes in concentrations of some 'greenhouse' gases in the atmosphere (adapted from Ashmore, 1990).

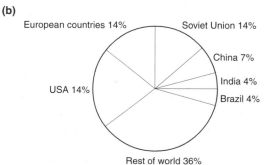

Figure 4.2 Global sources of methane from human activities. The most important sources are livestock, rice paddies and pipeline leaks (a), and the USA contributes about a fifth of the global total (b).

about 4% and 2% of the global cycling of these gases (Sanderson, 1996). Given that, for example, the world's cattle population has doubled since 1950, and that termites are associated with tropical grassland, which has extended in area following forest clearance, it is not surprising that methane concentrations in the atmosphere are increasing rapidly, and indeed are doing so at a rate more than double that of carbon dioxide.

Nitrous oxide is a natural outcome of microbial activity in the soil, but recent increases (at rates of 0.2–0.3% per year) reflect emission following application of nitrogen-based fertilisers, together with the burning of fossil fuels, forests and crop stubble. It is currently found in the atmosphere at a concentration of about 0.31 ppm.

Chlorofluorocarbons (CFCs) are entirely anthropogenic, their use in refrigerators, fire extinguishers, aerosol propellants and air conditioners having been curtailed during the last decade as their pollutant nature has been realised. Atmospheric concentrations are nevertheless still increasing, although no longer at the rates of over 5% for CFC-11 and CFC-12, 10% for CFC-13, or 11% for CFC-22 witnessed during the 1980s. Current levels of CFC-12 are about 0.00045 ppm and of CFC-11 0.00026 ppm, but CFCs are disproportionately important as greenhouse gases because they are very efficient absorbers of long-wave radiation and they are very long-lived, persisting in the atmosphere for 50 to 100 years, so even rapid reduction in their use will not be effective until after many years.

Heat pollution resulting from human activity may contribute only 5–10% of the total warming caused by greenhouse gases (Fischer, 1990), but this is enough to drive global temperatures and other climatic factors beyond thresholds that are critical for ecosystem functioning, and as a consequence the nature and distribution of both species and ecosystems may well change in the near future.

4.2.2.2 Changes in temperature and precipitation

If concentrations of greenhouse gases in the atmosphere continue to increase at current rates, it is anticipated by GISS and other model builders that, compared with the 1960s, global mean annual surface temperatures will have increased by 0.5 °C by 2005, 1.5 °C by 2015–2050 and 3 °C by 2050–2100, although some models have suggested a 5.5 °C rise by 2100 (Boer and de Groot, 1990). Greater increases are predicted for higher latitudes than nearer the Equator, but even within similar latitudinal belts some regions will probably demonstrate rapid, pronounced warming while others will actually have lower mean annual temperatures than today.

At a global level, the greenhouse effects will almost certainly lead to higher levels of precipitation, but again there are great uncertainties about particular regional patterns. Higher mean temperatures will also increase potential evapotranspiration, so plants may suffer water stress even where precipitation remains the same (Bazzaz, 1990).

More critical, perhaps, than changes in annual mean figures for temperature and precipitation are likely seasonal changes. Northern latitudes, for example, are expected to have shorter cold seasons and longer warm seasons; increased temperatures would be proportionately greater in colder periods; and wetter autumns and winters, drier springs and summers, would probably prevail. Tropical regions would, in general, probably witness greater amounts of rainfall, while subtropical areas would become drier. The late 1990s have seen a greater number of extreme climatic events such as floods, droughts, hurricanes and typhoons: this might be due to just chance or natural climatic changes, including a greater frequency and intensity of El Niño (see Section 1.2) (Michener et al., 1997)

4.2.2.3 Changes in fresh waters and soils

Climatic change will affect stream flow and water quality, this being especially pronounced in semi-arid and sub-humid regions (Falkenmark, 1990). Indirect effects will be seen on groundwater (for example raising or lowering the water table) and soil moisture (for example capillary action 'pulling' water to the surface, evaporating and leaving a film of salt). Direct effects on soils will probably include changes in soil temperature, soil moisture and soil biota. In northern parts of North America and Eurasia, soil productivity will almost certainly increase, together with temperature, as a result of enhanced microbial activity, but so too will soil acidification and the effects of toxic chemicals such as heavy metals (Stigliani, 1990; Szaboles, 1990). Also, elevated temperatures in high latitudes will lead to permafrost thawing out, with flooding one of the consequences.

Climatic warming will affect lakes as well as streams. Glacial retreat and rising snowlines, for example, will alter the volume of spring melt-water. Schindler et al. (1990) reported that during the 1970s and 1980s lake temperatures in the experimental lakes area of north-west Ontario had risen by 2 °C, and the length of the ice-free season had extended by three weeks. Rates of water renewal had decreased, and many chemicals in the lake had increased in concentration. Species that had a preference for colder water, such as lake trout (*Salvelinus namaycush*) and the opossum shrimp (*Mysis relicta*), had declined. Some models predict deep water temperatures increasing by 8 °C in this part of Canada and have projected a northward shift in geographical boundaries for cold-preference fish species of 500–600 km (Magnuson *et al.*, 1997).

Similarly, doubling carbon dioxide concentration and a projected commensurate increase in annual temperatures of 3–5 °C has been predicted to cause a 21% reduction in annual stream flow in the mid-Atlantic region of the USA and a 31% reduction in New England waters as a result of greater evaporative water loss. Also, most of the bog ecosystems of these regions could disappear (Moore *et al.*, 1997).

Using the same carbon dioxide scenario, summer increases in temperature of 4 °C and winter increases of 9 °C are expected in Arctic and sub-Arctic North America, but there is less agreement about parallel changes in precipitation, which will almost certainly increase overall in these high latitudes. Exactly where, with what regional variations and to what extent, however, are all uncertainties, yet these amounts and distributions will be critical for every aspect of hydrology and limnology (lakes) in the far north. Spring flooding of ice-jammed north-flowing rivers such as the Mackenzie crucially renews the water supply of many lakes, especially in the delta regions, and provides a particular habitat for aquatic organisms: whole communities will be affected by changes in water quality (including nutrients) and quantity. Lengthening of the growing/breeding season and increasing water temperatures, especially in spring, will again affect water life and probably have deleterious overall effects on the food chain. And finally, the extensive wetlands and peatlands of these regions are an important component of the global carbon budget: if conditions are warmer and less water is actually available (because of diversions or increased evaporation), these habitats will shrink and they will become a source of atmospheric carbon (as more is emitted, less is absorbed) rather than, as currently, a storage compartment or sink. There is evidence that this is already happening (Rouse, *et al.*, 1997).

4.2.2.4 Changes in sea level

Most scenarios also predict rises in sea levels: as ocean water becomes warmer it will expand. Glaciers are also demonstrably melting, and polar ice is also very vulnerable. In March 1998, such warming was responsible for the destruction of 180 km² of the Larsen B ice shelf, which extends from Antarctica towards Tierra del Fuego. Current estimates are of sea levels rising by 2.4 mm a year, and by 2050 rises of 24–34 cm have been predicted. If nothing is done to curb global warming, however, rises of 60 cm by 2050, of 1 m by 2100 and even several metres by 2200 have been predicted using some models (Pirazolli, 1989).

Just as importantly, rises in mean sea levels will be accompanied by changes in tidal regimes, especially increasing tidal amplitude, with mean high waters in particular rising to a greater extent; in current patterns, with changes in sediment transport affecting shoreline environments and ecosystems (Reed, 1990); and in wave action (Boorman, 1990). Climatic change and the ocean carbon cycle are also closely linked: warmer water is less able to hold carbon dioxide, so global warming may lead to reduced carbon dioxide uptake by marine waters, exacerbating problems of the atmospheric increase in greenhouse gases (Williamson and Holligan, 1990).

The obvious implication of rising sea levels is that floods and severe coastal erosion will lead to the loss of beaches, mudflats, dunes and coral reefs and atolls in most low-lying parts of the world. Many of these areas contain already rare, endangered and functionally important ecosystems. Many such areas, too, support dense human populations, and often also consist of agricultural land critical to the well-being of the national economy. Indeed, some entire nation-states are vulnerable, particularly islands in the Pacific such as Tuvalu, or large parts of other low-lying countries bordering the sea, such as Bangladesh. Parts of Europe such as eastern England and the coastal Netherlands will also almost certainly see major flooding, however effective further investment in coastal defences might be.

4.2.2.5 Plant species and community responses to carbon dioxide enrichment and global warming

Changes in carbon dioxide concentration are inextricably linked with changes in temperature and water availability. While current global warming largely reflects human activity in increasing the emission of greenhouse gases, it must not be forgotten that, globally, the largest CO_2 fluxes are not anthropogenic: photosynthesis is the largest user of carbon dioxide, respiration the greatest emitter of CO_2 back into the atmosphere. If plant growth is stimulated by both greater carbon dioxide concentrations and higher temperatures, then one might expect a greater removal of (anthropogenically increased) carbon dioxide because of the increased photosynthesis: plants store more carbon – they become a more substantial *carbon sink*. However, any such change in the carbon flux could be at least partially offset by higher temperatures increasing the rate of respiration, thereby releasing greater amounts of carbon dioxide.

Changes in carbon dioxide concentrations will affect the responses of plants to changes in climatic factors (temperature, precipitation and evapotranspiration, especially where seasonal changes also occur), and *vice versa*. In turn, there will be knock-on and reciprocal effects on animals and microbial communities.

The physiological effects of increased carbon dioxide concentrations on plants depend on the particular physiological pathway that has been adopted. Photosynthesis is most likely to be affected in plants using C_3 *metabolism* (see Ecology Box 4.2). An increase in CO_2 will effect an increase in photosynthesis and hence growth, although generally not in a directly proportional manner. The photosynthetic reponse is likely to be greater in nutrient-rich than in nutrient-poor environments. Water availability is also important, and this is often the limiting factor on growth. As plants take up water from the soil they commensurately lose water from their leaves. A typical C_3 plant will use 170 g of water to fix a single gram of carbon dioxide, so even brief periods of water shortage can lead to water stress as the soil dries out, and plant growth will be reduced or temporarily cease. Carbon dioxide enrichment, however, increases the water-use efficiency of the plant: in C_3 plants, doubling ambient CO_2, for example, could lead to a reduction in water use by 30% and a 75% increase in the amount of dry matter fixed per unit of water used (Graves and Reavey, 1996).

Temperature is also critical in regulating photosynthesis rates. Conditions that are too warm or too cold will reduce photosynthetic efficiency and, like water, temperature can act as a limiting factor (see Section 4.3).

Species can only survive and function within particular environmental limits. There will be an absolute range of temperatures, for example, outside of which species cannot survive, whether on a day-to-day basis in terms of living or over a longer period, for example where the growing season is too short (see Section 4.3). Species will also have preferred ranges of temperature and other environmental variables. Clearly, if temperatures increase there will be a general shift in the geographical distribution of species: in very general terms, species with a preference for cooler conditions will tend to retreat polewards or to contract their geographical range to higher altitudes or to regions with more continental climates, while species preferring warmer conditions will tend to expand their range. There will be equivalent responses to changes in precipitation and evapotranspiration regimes.

There is a danger, however, in adopting too mechanistic an approach to predicting species responses to changing climates (Hengeveld, 1990). Some species are more adaptable or have greater potential for adaptation than others. Some species find it easier to disperse or migrate than others. Species do not exist in isolation, and therefore their ability to shift geographical distribution will depend on what shifts are evident in the whole community of which they are a part.

Climatic change is nothing new, but it is the rapidity with which change is taking place that causes most concern for the survival of many species and communities today. The Pleistocene glacial and interglacial periods reflect climatic shifts that took thousands of years, not decades or even centuries. Even so, fossil and other evidence indicates that global warming following the end of the last glacial advance caused individual species distributions to change along environmental gradients in different directions, over different periods and at different rates. During the post-glacial period, or Holocene, the maximum rate of movement of tree species in

ECOLOGY BOX 4.2

Photosynthetic pathways

(See also Ecology Box 1.4)

Photosynthesis occurs in two stages. The first, *light reaction*, involves the conversion of light energy (as protons) into forms of energy usable by the plant to fuel chemical synthesis. The second stage, *dark reaction*, actually does the synthesis, producing the energy-rich sugar compounds that can be used or stored by the plant. The first product of the most common process of carbon fixation consists of two three-carbon sugars, so this is called the C_3 *pathway*.

Under some conditions, however, high risks of water stress attach to the C_3 pathway. In hot, dry environments, for example, plants would lose dangerously large amounts of water as they open their stomata to absorb CO_2. Similar problems of 'physiological drought' occur in salt marshes and other salt-stressed environments. Some plants have therefore acquired a particular photosynthetic pathway that reduces water loss, and in so doing produces a four-carbon compound during its dark reaction, hence C_4 *pathway*. The enzyme responsible for building the four-carbon compound has the ability to scavenge CO_2 at very small concentrations yet use it with great efficiency. The four-carbon compounds are subsequently converted to a different form (pyruvate) and release CO_2, which then enters the normal C_3 pathway. Only about 5% of the world's plant species are C_4 species, but they include some of the most important crops, e.g. sugar cane (in which the system was first identified), maize, millet and sorghum.

Some plants, especially those of very hot and arid conditions, take this a stage further: they possess the leaf anatomy of a C_4 plant but only open their stomata at night when conditions are cool and water loss will be minimal. Carbon is stored as four-carbon compounds until daylight, when the plant can use them for photosynthesis but without having to open its stomata. As with the C_4 pathway, the compounds can then undergo conversion and lose CO_2 to the C_3 pathway. While storing and moving the carbon uses up energy, the reduction in water loss is more critical under such stressful conditions, and so there are net benefits. This particular system uses a *crassulacean acid metabolism* (CAM), so called because it was first discovered in desert succulents of the family Crassulaceae, but it is used by many other families as well: 10% of the world's plant species use CAM. Succulent plants of hot deserts, however, are certainly characteristic examples of CAM species, their water-retaining leaves possessing features that can store the C_4 compounds.

A few plants can switch between C_3 and CAM pathways: inducible CAM plants. An example is *Mesembryanthemum crystallinum*, a salt-tolerant plant found in California and Israel. In the rainy season, it grows rapidly using a C_3 mechanism, but in the dry season it changes to CAM.

Because of their particular photosynthetic mechanisms, C_4 and CAM plants will not demonstrate the same high growth responses to CO_2 enrichment as C_3 plants, although the prickly pear cactus (*Opuntia ficus-indica*) has been found to increase in dry weight by 23% when grown at 650 ppm CO_2 (Nobel, 1991).

Europe has been estimated as equivalent to 300 m a year for beech (*Fagus sylvatica*), 500 m for oaks (*Quercus* spp.), limes (*Tilia* spp.) and ash (*Fraxinus excelsior*), 1000 m for elms (*Ulmus* spp.), and perhaps 1500 m for hazel (*Corylus avellana*) (Wilkinson, 1999). These differences have thus created new community structures and community dynamics (Graham and Grimm, 1990). If the rate of warming caused by current climatic changes is greater than ever before, as appears to be the case, then the responses of individual species are likely to be unpredictable either on the basis of their current community dynamics or by analogy with what has happened previously.

Nevertheless, attempts are being made to model species and community responses, especially to plants, including those of agricultural importance. Physiological responses of plants to raised levels of carbon dioxide in particular have been incorporated into ecosystem models (Shugart, 1990; Woodward, 1990). The effect of carbon dioxide enrichment on gas exchange and transpiration will probably be an increase in the sensitivity of forests and other plant communities to other aspects of climatic change (Peters, 1990). However, small differences in initial conditions or in the driving variables of a model can lead to major differences in how a community will respond to climatic change, and Cohen and Pastor (1991) warn that our ability to predict ecosystem responses to such environmental changes may be limited.

Soil nutrients are one set of initial conditions that can vary greatly. Kirschbaum et al. (1998) concluded that growth is likely to be highly stimulated by increasing carbon dioxide concentration in forests with high intrinsic fertility, for example with an abundance of nitrogen-fixing plants, or which are prone to fire or removal of wood-stored nitrogen such as through logging. Forest systems that are more open with respect to nutrient gains and losses are likely to be more responsive to increases in carbon dioxide. However, this research also suggested that the effects of increasing carbon dioxide can differ substantially between forests as a result of inter-action between a large range of factors that affect nutrient supply.

Similarly, from their work on temperate grass-land, Tate and Ross (1997) suggest that increases in below-ground net primary productivity and increases in the rate at which carbon is cycled in the soil are both likely consequences of carbon dioxide enrichment. Changes were also noted in the structure and functional relationships of the soil fauna. Soils of moderate nutrient status, moderate to high clay content and low to moderate soil moisture are most likely to be effective sinks for the storage of carbon in a future where carbon dioxide concentrations have increased.

The speed at which climatic change seems to be taking place is probably too great for some plant species, which will not be able to spread rapidly enough to ensure continued success, at least through part of their geographical range

(Kullman, 1991). The same is true of many plant communities, which will be unable to maintain equilibrial development. In other words, there will often, perhaps usually, be a time lag between changed climatic conditions and the development of a plant community in equilibrium with these changes. Chapin and Starfield (1997), for example, modelled possible advances of the North American Arctic treeline in response to different scenarios of changes in temperature, precipitation and fire regimes. With a gradual change in annual mean temperature of 3 °C during the twenty-first century, they estimated a 150–250-year time lag in the forestation of Alaskan tundra and concluded that with rapid warming under drier conditions there would be widespread development of a type of grassland/steppe that currently is found south of the coniferous forest in interior parts of the continent.

Climatic change is effective in three dimensions. Mountain areas, for example, would not necessarily simply witness a vertical shift in altitudinal vegetation zones, since temperature changes may not parallel those in precipitation. Kienast et al. (1997), for instance, predict a change in the submontane Swiss Alps from beech-dominated forest to oak–hornbeam communities if mean annual temperatures were to rise by 2.0–2.8 °C without a simultaneous increase in precipitation, and the montane coniferous belt would be invaded by deciduous species. Warmer and drier conditions (due to increased evapotranspiration) would also lead to an increase in species richness, and some assemblages would have no present-day equivalents (Fischlin and Gyalistras, 1997).

While some species will be able to change in abundance or distribution as a response to global warming, others might become extinct. Risks of extinction are greatest where species have already limited geographical distributions, small and perhaps scattered populations, a slow rate of reproduction, problems in dispersing, and low genetic variability. High genetic variability might be able to buffer climatic change to some extent where a fraction of a population may be more tolerant of climatic shifts and indeed may thrive under warmer conditions, drier conditions, or whatever. However, climatic change itself can affect certain components of micro-evolution, including the rate of gene flow within a population and the susceptibility of a population to mutations, some of which might favour new climatic conditions (Holt, 1990).

Experiments using annual meadow grass (*Poa annua*) have indicated the possibility of cumulative inter-generation changes in response to climatic change: second-generation plants grown, like their parents, under elevated carbon dioxide showed a biomass increase of 50% over their parents at the end of the growth stage (Bezemer *et al.*, 1998).

Some plants may adjust their carbon dioxide uptake by effecting morphological changes. The evergreen Mediterranean holm oak (*Quercus ilex*), for example, increases stem biomass production in response to elevated CO_2 but has significantly lower branch biomass, decreased branching and lower leaf area per unit branch biomass, the overall effect being to reduce photosynthesis by the canopy, an important response where water shortage is a common environmental stress (Hattenschwiler *et al.*, 1997).

Under non-stressed conditions, however, Rey and Jarvis (1997) found that young birch (*Betula pendula*) exposed to 700 ppm (2 × ambient levels) of carbon dioxide for four and a half years (one of the longest studies to date on a deciduous tree species) had a 58% increase in biomass at the end of the experiment. It was only the carbon dioxide enrichment of the first three years that were important, however, and the relative growth rate during the fourth year had little to do with exposure to elevated CO_2 concentrations. Trees grown in CO_2-enriched air invested more carbon in fine roots: fine root density probably helped the trees to meet higher nutrient demands. These trees also had less leaf area per unit of growth compared with trees grown under ambient conditions, probably reflecting greater photosynthetic efficiency in the CO_2-enriched atmosphere.

A similar study using loblolly pine (*Pinus taeda*) found that seedlings grown at elevated CO_2 levels produced 90% more biomass than those grown at ambient concentrations after four growing seasons, primarily due to a 217% increase in leaf area in the first growing season; a 'compound interest effect' then followed, with the increased leaf area of one year producing an

even greater leaf area (and biomass) the following year (Tissue *et al.*, 1997). Increasing temperatures, however, may lead to water stress in loblolly pine and similar species. For example McNulty *et al.* (1996) have demonstrated a strong probability that the natural range of loblolly pine would be severely reduced across the southern USA were mean annual temperatures to rise by 7 °C.

On balance, however, coniferous forests – like forests generally – are expected to be a major storage compartment (sink) for future increases in atmospheric carbon. Extrapolating results from a variety of research undertaken on coniferous species suggests that growth enhancement due to greater atmospheric carbon could lead to coniferous forests as a whole being a greater sink for the fossil carbon emitted to the atmosphere through industrial activity, and in this way providing an even more significant negative feedback in the atmospheric part of the global carbon cycle.

Grassland, too, is projected in many cases to act as a carbon sink. Thornley and Cannell (1997) conclude that, in humid temperate grassland at least, increasing carbon dioxide alone will produce a carbon sink while it continues to increase photosynthesis and therefore net primary productivity (NPP). Increasing temperature alone, however, would actually produce a carbon source, because soil respiration would be accelerated more than would be offset by gains in NPP. Putting the two together, the net effect of increases in both CO_2 and temperature is likely to be a carbon sink of 5–15 gC m^{-2} year^{-1} for at least several decades. A similar conclusion is drawn for tropical grasslands by Scurlock and Hall (1998). However, a note of caution is sounded by Hungate *et al.* (1997), who noted that while, overall, CO_2 enrichment increased grassland ecosystem uptake, this was somewhat offset by a greatly increased rapidity with which carbon was cycled in the below-ground part of the grassland.

Projected benefits of vegetation acting as sinks for carbon are, however, only likely up to a point, and if global warming continues at the present rate a massive dieback of vegetation in the tropics may ensue (Ecology Box 4.3).

ECOLOGY BOX 4.3

Carbon uptake by global terrestrial vegetation: impacts on the tropics

At the climate summit conference at Kyoto in December 1997, Melvin Cannell and his colleagues from the UK Institute of Terrestrial Ecology at Edinburgh revealed the results of their simulations of the effects of various climate change scenarios on the carbon, nitrogen and water cycles involving terrestrial vegetation.

As is generally acknowledged, the initial consequence of an increase in atmospheric carbon will be for much of the vegetation to act as a carbon sink, storing the carbon and responding by increased growth and biomass. The amount of carbon dioxide pollution absorbed by global terrestrial vegetation will initially rise from the 2 billion tonnes a year being produced in the 1990s (about a third of all emissions from burning fossil fuels) to about 2.6 billion tonnes by 2050. After the middle of the twenty-first century, however, warming by up to 8 °C in parts of the tropics would almost certainly lead to higher rates of evapotranspiration in the context of a climate that would actually have less rainfall. This in turn would lead to the deterioration and disappearance of present-day ecosystems. 'Tropical grasslands will shrink from 8% to 1% of the global land area ... Tropical forests will change to savanna, grassland or even desert.'

The decline in vegetation biomass means that less carbon will be stored or sequestered, and Cannell anticipates that by around 2080, carbon dioxide uptake will be negative, with decomposing plant material emitting more carbon than the remaining vegetation can absorb.

Yet in temperate forests in Eurasia and North America, such warming would lead to an increase in forest biomass by 70% between the 1990s and the 2080s (Pearce, 1997c).

Vegetation and climate possess a number of reciprocating feedback mechanisms. Disentangling the different feedback loops and attempting to predict their consequences are major tasks for eco-environmental modelling (Cao and Woodward, 1998). Woodward *et al.* (1998), for example, point out that global warming and CO_2 enrichment lead to greater amounts of heat actually being produced via the heat-transfer functions of leaf stomata, so that there is a further local 'top-up' warming effect over and above the larger-scale warming, i.e. a positive feedback. This (accentuated) warming, however, leads to changes in vegetation structure, and at the global scale these provide a negative feedback as the vegetation 'adjusts' to the new prevailing climatic conditions. At high latitudes, increases in the *leaf area index* (leaf areas as a proportion of the ground area it covers, a measure of how much leaf area is available for photosynthesis) and vegetation height cause a positive feedback. At lower latitudes, where vegetation becomes sparser because of global warming, the underlying soil, now more exposed, is likely to reflect

greater amounts of solar radiation, leading to a general cooling effect. Negative feedbacks are also likely to be caused by increased evaporative cooling with increasing leaf area index.

4.2.2.6 Animal species and community responses to carbon dioxide enrichment and global warming

Like plants, animals can also tolerate only certain environmental conditions, and again there will be a number of direct and indirect effects of such climatic changes as increasing carbon dioxide concentrations and rising temperatures.

Carbon dioxide enrichment itself will be less significant. Carbon dioxide is a waste product of metabolic activity in animals and must be removed from the body, for example by the exhalation of CO_2-rich air from the lungs, to allow the animal to respire. Excessive CO_2 in the animal's immediate atmosphere can cause damage, symptoms of which, for example in mammals, include a constriction of the pulmonary arteries (bringing oxygenated blood to the lungs), breathing more heavily (increased ventilation), reduced contraction of heart muscles, and a fall in blood pressure. 'Hypercapnia' is the general term used for these symptoms.

While the atmosphere as a whole comprises 0.036% CO_2 (360 ppm), some environments habitually used by certain animals contain much greater amounts: concentrations inside beehives are 0.2–6.0%; in warm, moist soils, 3–5%; and in the burrows of ground-dwelling mammals can be 0.5–4.8%, being higher after active digging and consequent increases in metabolic activity and heavier breathing. Figure 4.3 shows the responses of six mammal species to different atmospheric CO_2 concentrations, illustrating differences in the amount of air inhaled per minute (Darden, 1972). Animals such as pocket gophers (*Thomomys bottae*) may tolerate enhanced CO_2 levels by possessing a series of distinctive physiological characteristics such as a slow heart beat, low metabolic rate (reducing the amount of gas exchange necessary) and low breathing rate. If CO_2 levels are high, oxygen levels are almost certainly low, and this in itself

will lead to decreased physiological efficiency, distress and possibly death.

But this is not going to be a problem with climatic change. If humans, for instance in a submarine, can tolerate 0.9% CO_2 (i.e. 9000 ppm), and other animals can tolerate the levels noted in the previous paragraph, a rise in atmospheric CO_2 concentration from 360 to around 700 ppm will have no significant direct effect. More critical will be indirect consequences, where animals have to respond to changes in plant activity as a result of CO_2 enrichment – plants that serve as food, hosts and so on. Often, the effects of changes in CO_2 concentration and temperature need to be considered together.

The nutritional quality of leaves of pedunculate oak (*Quercus robur*), for example, was reduced by a rise in temperature of 3 °C, which in particular reduced leaf nitrogen concentration and increased the content of tannin, an anti-herbivore chemical produced by the tree. Doubling atmospheric carbon dioxide reduced leaf toughness but increased total phenolics in the second leaf flush. Phenolics are secondary plant compounds or metabolites (those not needed for primary functions such as photosynthesis and growth), used for example as antimicrobial agents and for pigmentation, and making the plant less palatable and less nutritional. The development of larval defoliators such as caterpillars, and hence adult fertility, will in turn be adversely affected by such changes in leaf quality (Dury *et al.*, 1998). Such responses by phenolics and tannin are probably general phenomena, ones that will certainly have important short-term effects on herbivores (though not decomposers), but there is currently no consistent evidence of any longer-term effects at the complex ecosystem level (Penuelas and Estiarte, 1998).

In many plants, elevated levels of carbon dioxide will affect the timing of flowering events (flowering phenology) as well as the number of flowers produced and nectar quality and quantity. This may adversely affect the activities of pollinating insects, which feed on the nectar. Fewer plants will then be pollinated and then even fewer plants will be available to flower the following season (Erhardt and Rusterholz, 1997; Rusterholz and Erhardt, 1998).

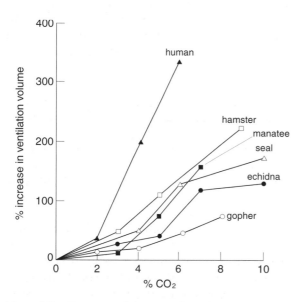

Figure 4.3 Responses of six mammal species to different CO_2 concentrations in the air. The seal and manatee are aquatic species. The echidna is a terrestrial species that spends much of its time burrowing for food. The gopher is sealed in subterranean burrows for most of its lifetime.

It might be anticipated that global warming by itself would be critical to animals, with the various effects of rising temperatures on metabolism, physiology, behaviour, autecology and community ecology integrating into changes in geographical distribution. Current distributions, however, bear only very general relationships to maximum and minimum temperature tolerance thresholds because so many other environmental factors combine to resolve themselves into particular distributions (Hoffmann and Blows, 1994).

These environmental factors interact. Rainfall is another climatic factor that will change as global warming proceeds and will combine in a number of ways with changes in temperature to produce differences in seasonal climate. For example, black-throated blue warblers (*Dendroica caerulescens*) in forest habitat in the White Mountains, New Hampshire, have been predicted to benefit from higher temperatures in their summer quarters both by an increase in the abundance of their insect food and through a lengthening of their breeding season (Rodenhouse, 1992). If rainfall were to increase at the same time as temperature, however, egg and nestling mortality would be greater, and reproductive success would decline. Indeed, if rainfall were to increase by 20% over present-day amounts, the numbers of birds fledging could decline by 26%. If rainfall were to increase by 10%, the negative consequences would approximately balance the benfits of higher temperatures. If rainfall were to decrease by 10% – as in parts of the species' range is quite likely – then reproductive success could be 25% better than today. The effects of climatic change in different parts of the birds' range could therefore vary considerably.

Four possible general responses of species to climatic change are (1) changes in distribution; (2) tolerance of change; (3) evolutionary change; and (4) extinction (Graves and Reavey, 1996).

Moss (1998) has identified a number of long-term effects of global warming on habitats and ecosystems as they might affect birds in the United Kingdom:

- There will be changes in the start and end of the growing season, which as a consequence will be longer, with knock-on effects on birds in terms of habitat and food.

- There will also be shifts in the geographical distribution of plants, with adverse effects on upland ecosystems such as the Scottish moorlands and arctic–alpine locations. Woodland with species such as beech may replace oak-dominated mixed woodland, scrub and carr (low tree and shrub vegetation bordering freshwater sites) will replace reed swamp and marsh, and heather (*Calluna vulgaris*) may well replace areas of heath (*Erica* spp:).

- Global warming will allow insects to extend their ranges and increase their populations as winter mortality is reduced, which will affect the breeding range and reproductive success of insectivorous birds.

- The current balance between predators and prey will be affected.

- Farmers will be able to grow new crops, for example sunflowers (*Helianthus annuus*) and maize (*Zea mays*), which in turn may have an impact on farmland birds.

- Disruption of long-established relationships between species will occur by changing the timing of specific events in their life cycles.

Specific effects of global warming on birds are likely to be:

- A more regular influx of birds characteristic of southern Europe, with an increase both in the number of such species and in their population sizes. Examples are likely to include hoopoe (*Upupa epops*), black kite (*Milvus migrans*) and cattle egret (*Bubulcus ibis*).

- Changes in temperatures and rainfall during spring and summer are already permitting many species to begin laying earlier and with larger clutch sizes, with more young actually fledging.

- Resident species will benefit from warmer winters.

- Rises in mean summer temperatures will result in changes in breeding range, some birds benefiting, others losing out, and wintering ranges will also be affected by higher winter temperatures.

- Sea-level rises will affect both resident and migrant wading birds, which rely on tidal habitats for food.

- Changes in wind patterns will affect migration patterns to and from the UK, including the presence or otherwise of birds arriving by chance.

Birds that will benefit from climatic change will be those with already large populations; that can adapt rapidly to change; that are able to breed across a wide range of temperatures; that can tolerate habitats radically altered by human activity; for which Britain is on the northern edge of their range (such as firecrest (*Regulus ignicapillus*) and golden oriole (*Oriolus oriolus*)); or that are introductions, especially from warmer climates, with no competitors in the UK, for example the Egyptian goose (*Alopochen aegyptiacus*) and rose-ringed parakeet (*Psittacula krameri*). Species likely to suffer include those with an already declining population as a result of land-use changes, such as the tree sparrow (*Passer montanus*) and the corn bunting (*Miliaria calandra*); species such as the bittern (*Botaurus stellaris*), which depend on fragile, limited habitat such as reedbeds; those with already highly restricted breeding ranges; and those for which Britain is on the southern edge of their range.

Indeed, generally, where climate provides a distributional constraint, species at the edge of their geographical range will be particularly susceptible to climate changes, especially where they have very specific physical environmental, food or habitat requirements. Taylor and Wilson (1990), for example, noted that population changes in Adelie penguins (*Pygoscelis adeliae*) in the Ross Sea during the 1980s were correlated with climatic changes. Lloyd Peak of the British Antarctic Survey has reported that over 90% of all penguin chicks and seal pups born in the Antarctic spring of 1999 could perish (and he had already noted chick deaths of 99%) as a result of food shortage, in turn a consequence of the interaction between El Niño and global warming (*The Guardian*, 27 March 1999: 12).

Brown (1991) has predicted northerly shifts in the ranges of marine bird species off Nova Scotia and Newfoundland, caused as much by climatic change-induced alterations of the distribution of prey fish species as by any direct effects of warming on the birds themselves. Botkin *et al.*

(1991) suggest that Kirtland's warbler (*Dendroica kirtlandii*) could be a subtle indicator species of global warming: jack pine (*Pinus banksiana*) forests in central Michigan, the primary nesting habitat of this endangered species, will respond to warming by growing at a slower rate and may therefore become unsuitable for the warbler within 30 to 60 years. Environmentally sensitive species may indeed have important roles as indicators and monitors of climatic change (Jarvis, 1994).

Given the anticipated rate of climatic change, only species that can disperse rapidly will be able to respond to global warming at the margins of their geographical range. This will not be a problem with the majority of animals, but there could be difficulties if host and food plants cannot spread with equal rapidity. However, it would be appropriate for few species simply to map current distribution in relation to particular climatic parameters then superimpose an equivalent distribution on a map of predicted future climate. This is because species tend not to be found absolutely everywhere they can be in terms of climatic preferences or requirements: other factors, often to do with community interactions, affect distribution (see Chapter 8), and not all components of a community are likely to respond to climatic change in the same way or with the same speed, if indeed they can survive at all.

This in turn means that some biotic constraints might be lifted (if a predator dies out regionally, for example) or may be added (as new predators enter the community, facilitated by the change in climatic conditions). Tolerance levels and limits are therefore another variable, very difficult to predict.

Major evolutionary changes are unlikely as a response to climatic change in such a short time scale, but smaller micro-evolutionary changes might be found. Here, rather than the appearance of new species, changes in gene frequencies or genetic recombinations might occur. These can happen in the space of a few generations and has been seen for example in the rapidity with which many weeds and pests have developed resistance to chemicals. In some cases, fractions of a population may already have been naturally resistant, and these elements (together with their built-in genetic resistance) can reproduce successfully under the new conditions, which are stressful to the majority of the population. But in other cases, actual genetic changes (for example, mutation and recombination) will have taken place. There is no reason to suppose that responses to the stresses of climatic change would be any different. Some species, however, will not be able to tolerate change and will be unable to disperse, or at least disperse quickly enough: local extinction will then occur, and in some cases total extinction.

4.2.2.7 Climatic change and agriculture

Temperature and the amount, seasonality and reliability of precipitation are key decision factors in what crops to grow and livestock to raise. With climatic change, there will inevitably be shifts in where particular crops and pasture species can grow and livestock raised profitably. The extent to which carbon dioxide enrichment will contribute to this remains debatable, although the growth of most crops will be stimulated, especially where nutrients are readily available. Higher temperatures will in general push the limits of a particular agricultural enterprise polewards. Changes in precipitation, however, will in places offset such changes, especially where drier conditions prevail, and may be the most critical climatic shift. Global climatic change may well particularly affect parts of the developing world that are already struggling to produce consistent yields (see Chapter 2), especially with seasonal shifts in such critical features as the monsoon rains, in terms of both amount and timing. Climatic change will also affect the range and effects of agricultural weeds, pests and diseases. In other words, some regions will benefit, others suffer possibly serious disadvantages, and many places may well witness changes in agricultural systems.

Carbon dioxide enrichment will predominantly affect C_3 crops such as wheat, rice and soya beans but have less impact on C_4 species such as maize, sorghum, millet and many pasture and forage grasses. Although crop species vary in their response to elevated CO_2, there is a tendency for most C_3 species to show a 1%

increase in growth for every 10 ppm increase in CO_2 concentration. The response is unlikely to be linear, however, and for some species there is experimental evidence to suggest that greatest stimulation to growth occurs between 500 and 600 ppm CO_2. Much experimental work has been undertaken at concentrations between 600 and 700 ppm CO_2 (i.e. using a 2 × ambient scenario), at which levels plants may show less sensitive reponses. Even under experimental conditions there is great variation in the responses of different crop species (Figure 4.4), and in the field there are many other environmental variables to confuse the picture.

A typical example of an experimental single-crop study is that by Hakala (1998), who examined the effects of elevated CO_2 and temperature on the growth, yield and nitrogen content of spring wheat. Leaf canopies were exposed to CO_2 concentrations of 700 ppm and temperatures 3 °C higher than ambient throughout the growing season, although to simulate conditions predicted for a future warmer climate the experimental crop was sown up to three weeks earlier than the control (present-day

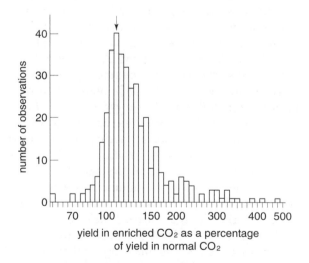

Figure 4.4 This diagram collects together a large number of observations on how growing in enriched atmospheric CO_2 affects crop yield. The most common observation (indicated by the arrow) is that yield is enhanced by 30%, but in many cases the yield increase was higher. It is also interesting to note that in a very few cases there was a decrease in yield.

conditions). Biomass and grain yield both increased in CO_2-enriched conditions by 5–60%, the increase in yield mainly reflecting an increase in the density of ear-bearing shoots. There was a small (7%) but significant decrease in the nitrogen content of the grain with CO_2 enrichment at ambient temperatures. Temperature did increase the development rate of the wheat in one of three study years, but it was clearly CO_2 enrichment that had the greater effects on the crop. This was expected, since photosynthesis in plants like wheat is CO_2-limited in the present-day atmosphere.

Using the same values for elevated CO_2 and temperatures, Nonhebel (1996) has modelled likely consequences for wheat yields in Europe. With initially sufficient water, a 3 °C rise led to a decline in yield as a result of increased water demand in the face of greater rates of evapotranspiration. Doubling CO_2 caused an increase in yield of 40% because of higher assimilation rates. When water was currently limiting, however, a rise in temperature led to a smaller reduction in yield, and elevated CO_2 increased yield even more. This was because both changes altered the water requirements of wheat. Combining the two, modelling predicted a net increase in wheat yield of 3 tonnes ha^{-1} compared with that of today.

Looking at an example of forage plants, Schenk et al. (1997) showed that white clover (*Trifolium repens*) monocultures showed an increase in yield of 16–38% under 670 ppm rather than 380 ppm CO_2; rye grass (*Lolium*) showed a 5–9% increase; and mixed swards, a 12–29% increase. However, declines in the nutritive value of the plants were also observed under high CO_2: potassium and sodium levels fell, although not to below minimum requirements for ruminants, but crude fibre content did at times fall below the minimum acceptable level.

Water is a key variable driving the productivity of grazing lands. Higher atmospheric CO_2 concentrations will almost certainly alter water relations within plants and have knock-on effects in terms of ecosystem function, carbon storage and nutrient cycling. Predictions of such consequences, however, are made more complicated because another key variable is what the pastoralist does with the grassland: what happens to the pasture or rangeland thus reflects economics-based decision making as well as environmental changes in response to climatic change (Campbell et al., 1997).

The greater water-use efficiency of plants under CO_2 enrichment (see Section 4.2.2.5) implies that yields of many crops could increase in semi-arid or seasonally dry parts of the world, or that the distribution of such crops could extend into drier regions than at present. Gifford (1979), for example, has estimated that yields of wheat in Australia are increasing by 5–13% kg ha^{-1} yr^{-1} (total yields approximating 1.2 tonnes ha^{-1} yr^{-1}). Nitrogen-use efficiency is also higher under higher CO_2 concentrations, although effects are highly variable, but in general the implication of a reduced need for fertilisers for equivalent yields will be a boon for farmers in the developing world and for subsistence farmers everywhere.

Low-temperature constraints on crop production will be lifted in many regions, but there is a risk at high temperatures that photosynthetic CO_2 assimilation will drop dramatically. Also, some autumn-sown crops such as barley and oats require cold to initiate germination and in some cases to stimulate flowering, and hence grain production.

Global warming will inevitably also affect livestock production and distribution, again more a reflection of changes in pasture plant communities than direct effects on the animals. It has been estimated, for example, that for every 1 °C increase in mean temperature the northernmost boundary of sheep production in Australia will shift to the south by 167 km (Russell, 1991).

While it remains generally difficult to predict changes in regional climate with any great confidence, it is clear that the Northern Hemisphere will see some degree of above-average warming. This in turn should see a poleward extension of the northern boundaries of most crops. While in theory a 1 °C increase in mean annual temperature will move northern boundaries 150–200 km further north (Graves and Reavey, 1996), in practice this will be modified by other climatic factors, such as the continued occurrence of frosts, and by non-climatic factors such as soil fertility.

ECOLOGY BOX 4.4

Day degrees

Day degrees (d.d.) are a measure that multiplies the number of days with a temperature at or above a base temperature with the number of degree units at or above that base. Thus, with a base temperature of $10\,°C$, 1 day at $10\,°C = 1$ d.d.; 30 days at $10\,°C = 30$ d.d.; 30 days at $11\,°C = 60$ d.d.; and 60 days at $12\,°C = 180$ d.d. The base temperature is generally the temperature at which growth of a particular species is possible ($10\,°C$ in the case of maize). This is a particularly valuable measurement in agriculture, since it allows the determination of the length of the growing season for a particular crop, together with a quantification of warmth, and hence (other factors being equal) the crop's distribution.

In Europe, for example, the northern limit of grain maize should in theory move northward by around 300 km for every $1\,°C$ rise in mean annual temperature, but more critical to this crop is the number of day degrees (d.d.) (see Ecology Box 4.4). Grain maize is very susceptible to cold and needs a great deal of summer warmth to grow sufficiently, and the northern limit to the cultivation of this crop is around 850 d.d. using a base temperature of $10\,°C$. Predicted changes in the distribution of four crops in Europe, including maize, are shown in Figure 4.5. In North America, maize again appears to be limited in the north by the number of frost-free days and the length of the growing season, but to the west it is soil moisture that is more critical. If, as predicted, the climate in continental North America becomes warmer and drier, it is anticipated that the corn belt will move in a north-easterly direction by about 175 km for every increase of $1\,°C$ (Parry, 1990; Graves and Reavey, 1996).

Parry (1990) suggests that by the middle of the twenty-first century Scandinavia and Canada will, in general, witness an increase in agricultural productivity of 10–20%, but drier, mediterranean areas and the American South and South-west will probably see a decline, although estimates vary from 5 to over 35%. In Australia, the predicted 40% increase in rainfall will lead to an increase in cereal yield of over 20%, but this will vary considerably region by region.

While the improved water use efficiency of crops under elevated CO_2 will tend to improve yields in dry tropical areas, it is likely that in the humid tropics climatic change will adversely affect crop production, but to what extent and where remain difficult to predict, and there will be many exceptions. Evapotranspiration will increase, even though rises in mean annual temperature will not be as great as in temperate latitudes, but in places this may be offset by increases in rainfall.

4.2.3 Other climatic changes: aerosols and the ozone layer

The amount of dust, smoke and other particulates entering the lower atmosphere is increasing as a consequence of urbanisation, industrialisation and the burning of vegetation. These aerosol particles scatter and absorb solar radiation and therefore might influence temperatures, but there is great uncertainty about climatic and environmental consequences.

Another set of climatic changes is associated with the depletion of the ozone layer. This is a layer of relatively high concentration of ozone in the stratosphere 16–18 km above the Earth's surface near the poles, increasing to a height of about 25 km in the tropics, which absorbs incoming ultraviolet radiation, thereby warming the stratosphere and creating a steep temperature inversion at altitudes between 15 and 50 km. This in turn affects convective processes and circulation in the troposphere is affected by this layer, so changes in ozone thickness ultimately affect the global climate. Human activities have indeed led to such changes, in particular emission of *chlorofluorocarbons* (CFCs) from refrigerant

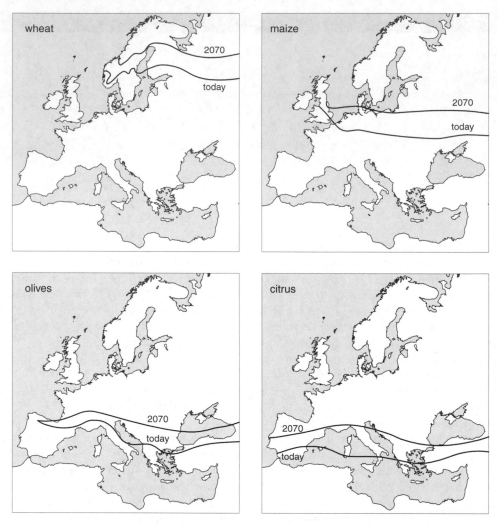

Figure 4.5   Predicted changes in the northern cropping boundary of four selected crops in Europe.

systems, aerosols and foam food containers, but also *nitrogen oxides* (largely products of internal combustion engines and nitrogenous chemical fertilisers) and a variety of combustion products (jet aircraft being a major source). Appreciation of the damage caused to the atmosphere by these chemicals has led to reduced production and, in the case of CFCs, the development of substitutes, so emission of such pollutants has certainly declined in recent years (Issues Box 4.1).

The problem was first noted in 1984, when a 50% decrease in the ozone column was recorded over Antarctica, and alerted by this climatologists have subsequently observed pronounced if variable ozone depletion at all latitudes. Thinning is particularly evident in September and October. These 'holes' in the ozone layer represent reductions in ozone concentration of up to 67%. Levels of stratospheric ozone have probably been decreasing at an accelerating rate for several decades, with concentrations over Europe and North America dropping by almost 10% since the 1950s (Raven *et al.*, 1998). By the mid-1990s, the hole covered 23.3 million km². In October 1998, the World Meteorological Organisation reported that the surface area of the ozone layer was still increasing, being 15% more than the previous year and exposing a global area two and

ISSUES BOX 4.1

Phasing out CFCs

The main chemicals responsible for ozone depletion in the stratosphere are the group of compounds known as *chlorofluorocarbons* (CFCs), which have been used as solvents, as coolants in refrigerators and air-conditioning plants, as propellants for aerosol cans, and as foam-blowing agents for insulation and in packaging material such as Styrofoam.

Other agents attacking ozone include the nitrogen oxides and combustion products mentioned in the text, together with halons (present in a number of fire extinguishers), methyl bromide (a fumigant pesticide), methyl chloroform (an industrial solvent), and carbon tetrachloride (found in some pesticide and dye manufacture as well as other industrial processes).

In 1978 the USA – the world's largest user of CFCs – banned the use of these compounds in domestic aerosol products. More significantly, in 1987 there was agreement by signatory countries to the Montreal Protocol to reduce CFC production by 50% by 1998, and since then over 150 nations have agreed to phase out all use of CFCs by the end of the century.

There was also a response from manufacturing industries, with non-damaging compounds being developed and substituted, for example *hydrofluorocarbons* (HFCs), which do not harm the ozone layer (although ironically they are greenhouse gases) and *hydrochlorofluorocarbons* (HCFCs), which are less destructive to ozone than CFCs. HCFC-123 is currently the best CFC alternative, with a lifespan of only 1.4 years. It is anticipated that, eventually, a set of non-fluorocarbon compounds will be commercially available.

CFCs, methyl chloroform and carbon tetrachloride were essentially banned in the USA, the European Union and other developed parts of the world by 1996. In the developing world, CFCs are due to be phased out by 2006. Methyl bromide is currently scheduled to be phased out in 2010, HCFCs by 2030. Despite the end of the production of these chemicals, their persistence will ensure a major impact on the ozone layer well into the twenty-second century (Raven *et al.*, 1998).

a half times the size of Europe to potentially damaging radiation. While ozone depletion is expected to reach its maximum severity by the early years of the new millennium, conditions are not predicted to return to those of the 1970s until the middle of the twenty-first century.

The ozone layer, by controlling the amount of ultraviolet radiation reaching the Earth's surface, affects the rate of photosynthesis. Oceanic phytoplankton are particularly susceptible to increases in ultraviolet-B radiation (Ecology Box 4.5). Any reduction in planktonic primary production will have serious implications for the entire oceanic food chain. Increasing susceptibility to carcinogenic reactions as a result of increased amounts of ultraviolet radiation will also affect unprotected mammalian skin, and the increased risk of skin cancers and cataracts in humans has certainly been an issue during the last two decades (Jarvis, 1994).

4.3 Ecological concepts

- Environmental gradients, ranges of tolerance and limiting factors
- Regulatory environmental factors and environmental rhythms
- Geographical distributions

4.3.1 Environmental gradients, ranges of tolerance and limiting factors

It was emphasised in Section 4.2.2.5 that plants can only survive within particular environmental limits. The same is true for animals and microbial organisms. Temperatures, for example, can be too high or too low for a particular species to survive. There will also be preferred temperatures, where individuals may, for example, grow

ECOLOGY BOX 4.5

Ultraviolet radiation

This is subdivided by wavelengths into:

- UV-A (320–400 nm)   most damaging to organisms in terms of disrupting DNA, causing cell death and mutation.
- UV-B (290–320 nm)   the wavelength most likely to increase with ozone thinning. Causes mutagenesis, slow organic growth, eye damage. Damage to construction materials like rubber or PVC.
- UV-C (<290 nm)   almost totally filtered out by normal ozone levels. Less damaging to organisms.

Ozone concentration units: a frequently used unit of measurement is the *Dobson unit* (DU). The DU has been developed from spectroscopic measurement techniques and can best be comprehended by making the following hypothetical assumption: all ozone dispersed overhead is somehow brought down to sea-level pressure and a temperature of 0 °C so the thickness can be measured – one DU would be equivalent to one-thousandth of a cm of ozone measured in that manner. Between the 1950s and 1970s typical austral winter-time Antarctic readings would have been *c*. 300 DU).

Note: Ozone absorbs shorter wavelengths best. The angle of the Sun, altitude and clarity of the atmosphere affect exposure: high Sun, high altitude and clean, cloud-free air is the worst scenario: low Sun, low altitude and polluted, misty air means reduced UV receipts.

most rapidly or function most efficiently in conditions where thermal stress is absent. Species will thus have minimum and maximum temperature thresholds, below and above which they cannot survive at all, and close to which they will find stressful, and there will also be an optimal range of temperatures where, other things being equal, they can best survive and function. The full range of temperatures in an environment can be thought of as an *environmental gradient*. The same responses by organisms will be found whatever the species and whatever the environmental factor. Other environmental gradients would be water availability (along a gradient from drought to free water), salinity and oxygen. Species possess a range of tolerance for each of these environmental factors. The maximum and minimum points of tolerance along the environmental gradient represent the *limits* of tolerance for that species (Figure 4.6).

Species also have ranges of tolerance for environmental resources such as nutrients. Indeed, it was in connection with nutrition that scientific understanding of these ideas began. Justus Liebig was an agricultural chemist active in the mid-nineteenth century who ascertained that crop

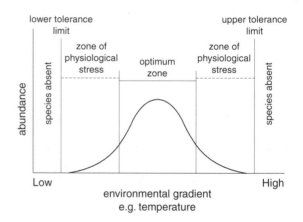

Figure 4.6   A plot of abundance of a species against some environmental parameter, in this case temperature. This shows the range to which a species is best adapted, and the same sort of pattern would be found for any important parameter, such as water availability, nutrient level, salinity and so on. Outside the optimum range, numbers decline rapidly because individuals have to expend energy or other resources to adapt physiologically to the poor conditions. At extreme temperatures, conditions are too harsh and the species is not found. We could make the same sort of plot for any other measure of a species' performance, such as reproductive success or growth rate.

growth and yield were rarely limited by soil nutrients present in large quantities, even if these were also needed in large quantities – the macronutrients nitrogen, phosophorus and potassium, for example. Rather, it was often the requirement for trace elements such as boron or cobalt that was critical: although only needed in minute quantities only small amounts were present in the soil, so even minor fluctuations in availability would be critical to the crop – or indeed any plant. The key point is that, even when all other nutrients are available in sufficient amounts to allow a plant to grow, if a single essential nutrient falls below the minimum limit of tolerance then the plant cannot thrive, and indeed if the situation persists it will not be able to survive. That nutrient has, in those circumstances, become the *limiting factor* for that plant. Liebig's observation that 'Growth of a plant is dependent on the amount of foodstuff [= nutrients] which is presented to it in minimum quantity' has become known as Liebig's law of the minimum (Liebig, 1840).

This 'law' can only be expressed under steady-state conditions, that is when inflows of energy and materials balance outflows. Under transient-state conditions, where such a balance is absent, the amounts – and therefore effects – of many inputs are changing rapidly. For example, with *cultural eutrophication* – excessive nutrient enrichment of a water body by the input of, for example, sewage or fertiliser runoff – the algal response is generally a rapid population growth (an 'algal bloom'), which then dies off, the subsequent decomposition by aerobic bacteria consuming vast amounts of oxygen, which may lead to animal deaths. Continued nutrient input will trigger another bloom, and the cycle continues. At different stages, i.e. under different transient states, different chemical elements or compounds may replace each other as the limiting factor: carbon dioxide, phosphorus and nitrogen, for example, have all been implicated as limiting factors in such oscillating circumstances.

Another complicating factor is that high concentrations or ready availability of some substance may modify the amount of the potentially limiting substance that is required. Some plants, for instance, need less zinc when growing in shade compared with full sunlight, so a particular amount of zinc in the soil may be limiting in light but not in shade. We have also seen how CO_2 enrichment increases both the water-use efficiency (WUE) of a plant (Section 4.2.2.5) as well as the nitrogen-use efficiency (Section 4.2.2.7), i.e. under elevated CO_2 low availability of water or nitrogen becomes less likely to be limiting. Higher nitrogen amounts themselves improve WUE, so wilting is less likely in nitrogen-rich soil. These are all examples of *factor interaction*.

While it has been argued that the law of the minimum should relate only to chemical elements and compounds, it is useful to view other environmental factors in terms of minimal thresholds (Taylor, 1934), and there is no reason why temperature could not be the limiting factor when there is a sufficiency of nutrients, water and carbon dioxide (plants) or oxygen (animals) but when it is too cold for the organism to survive.

However, an organism, can also have too much of something as well as too little – conditions can be too hot, too dry, too exposed to sunlight, for example, or with too much copper or zinc, which in effect turns a nutrient into a pollutant heavy metal. The idea of the limiting effects of maximum as well as minimum quantities was first fully proposed and exemplified by Shelford (1913), hence Shelford's law of tolerance.

An individual or population will have different limiting factors at different places and/or at different times. A species will possess limits of tolerance for a number of environmental factors, but not for every single one. Terrestrial animals, for example, will have minimum but not maximum thresholds of tolerance for oxygen. Species may have a wide range of tolerance for one factor but a narrow range of tolerance for another. To distinguish the degree of tolerance to each factor the prefixes 'steno-' (from the Greek meaning narrow) or 'eury-' (broad) can be used, so a *stenothermal* species has a narrow range of tolerance for temperature, while a *eurythermal* species can tolerate a wide range of temperatures. Similarly, *stenohydrous/euryhydrous* refers to water, *stenohaline/euryhaline* to salinity, *stenophagous/euryphagous* to diet breadth, and *stenoecious/euryecious* to habitat specialists/generalists

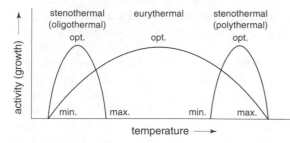

Figure 4.7 Comparison of the relative limits of tolerance of stenothermal and eurythermal organisms. Minimum, optimum and maximum lie close together for a stenothermal species, so that a small difference in temperature, which might have little effect on a eurythermal species, is often critical. Note that stenothermal organisms may be either low temperature tolerant (oligothermal), high-temperature tolerant (polythermal), or in between.

(Figure 4.7). Examples of soil moisture tolerance ranges for some North American tree species are shown in Figure 4.8.

Species with wide ranges of tolerance for all environmental factors (*eurytopic*) will tend to be the most geographically widespread, provided that there are not other constraints such as physical barriers or pronounced biological competition.

Organisms are rarely able to live under optimal conditions. A common reason for this is competition (see Chapter 8). For example, it has been shown experimentally that some plant species associated with salt marshes actually grow better under non-saline conditions, where, however, in nature they are generally outcompeted by more vigorous species. They are not true saltwater-adapted plant species (*halophytes*) but are nevertheless tolerant of often high levels of salinity (*miohalophytes*). They therefore grow in what are for them suboptimal conditions but where, nevertheless, they can at least survive, for example by increasing water uptake in order to dilute the salt (Glenn and O'Leary, 1984).

Sometimes organisms thrive in suboptimal conditions for one environmental factor because of constraints imposed by another such factor. Some tropical orchids, for example, photosynthesise more efficiently in full sunlight than in shade, but direct sunlight is associated with temperatures

that are too high, so in nature they grow in cooler shady conditions.

Ranges of tolerance also shift at different stages in an organisms's life. Very young and old mammals are often more susceptible to temperature extremes than are adults (humans are an example here), and different environmental requirements may be found when plants and animals are in reproductive mode. The North American swamp cypress (*Taxodium distichum*), for instance, can grow under dry or flooded conditions but requires moist unflooded ground for seedling development.

Individual organisms will tend to have minor differences in tolerance for different environmental factors, but in aggregate it is possible to distinguish characteristic ranges of tolerance for different species. Species with wide geographical distributions, however, may well have developed locally adapted populations, or *ecotypes*, which have evolved to adjust to the particular conditions of the different parts of their range, with optima and limits of tolerance rather different between ecotypes (Figure 4.9).

4.3.2 Regulatory environmental factors and environmental rhythms

The three most important environmental factors on land that might act as limiting to plants and animals are light, temperature and (quantity and quality of) water. In the sea they are light, temperature and salinity; with deep-sea organisms, pressure must be added. In freshwater systems, other factors such as oxygen become of major significance. Availability of nutrients may also be a common constraint. All these factors are not only potentially limiting factors to particular species but at appropriate levels they are also beneficial and necessary *regulatory factors*: organisms that are adapted to a particular suite of environmental conditions will thrive, and community homeostasis will be high.

The community will indeed have evolved to become 'programmed' to particular diurnal, monthly or seasonal changes. Day and night provide cues for particular behaviours in animals

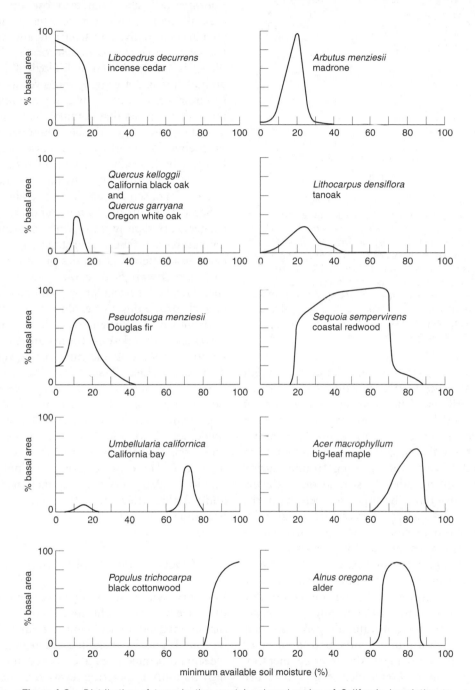

Figure 4.8   Distribution of trees in the coastal redwood region of California in relation to minimum available soil moisture during the year. Each soil has a certain potential water-storage capacity, and the minimum available moisture is the lowest value to which soil moisture falls.

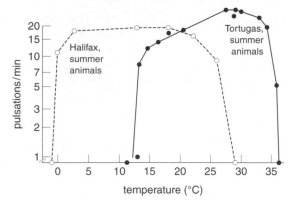

Figure 4.9 Temperature compensation at the species and community levels. The relation of temperature to swimming movement in northern (Halifax) and southern (Tortugas) individuals of the same species of jellyfish, *Aurelia aurita*. The habitat temperatures were 14 and 29 °C, respectively. Note that each population is acclimated to swim at a maximum rate at the temperature of its local environment. The cold-adapted form shows an especially high degree of temperature independence.

(for example a switch from a cohort of night hunters to day hunters) and plants (such as onset of photosynthesis). The quasi-diurnal rhythm of tidal highs and lows (24 hours 50 minutes for a complete cycle) are critical for intertidal communities, but tides also have a monthly rhythm, with highest and lowest waters being fround during the monthly spring tides, least tidal range during neap tides. Annual rhythms are seen with the onset of reproductive behaviour, migration, hibernation (and its hot-season equivalent, aestivation), and so on as the seasons progress.

Plants and animals anticipate these rhythms. For example, many vertebrates mate in late winter or early spring to anticipate favourable conditions for raising young during late spring and summer. Hibernating animals stoke up their fat deposits in autumn in anticipation of their period of torpor and markedly reduced metabolism during winter. Long-lived plants that are deciduous by definition drop their leaves and reduce their metabolsim, in some cases altogether, 'closing down' to anticipate then to avoid the rigours of winter.

A major cue by which organisms in temperate latitudes time their activities is day length, or *photoperiod*, since unlike most other environmental factors – for instance, temperature – that change seasonally, day length is always the same for a given time at a particular locality. Photoperiodicity is linked with the biological clock of an animal (acting through the eye as a sensory receptor) or a plant (acting, for example, through pigment receptors that stimulate particular enzyme activities). At a particular photoperiod, certain biochemical–physiological processes automatically kick in, be it seedling growth in some plants, for instance, or hormonal changes in animals that initiate the onset of reproductive readiness.

Some regulatory factors and environmental triggers vary slightly from year to year, for example temperature. Spring, for instance, is a predictable event in temperate latitudes but it can be later or earlier, and warmer or cooler than average. Other such factors are irregular and unpredictable yet are crucial for the onset of ecological events in certain environments, particularly those of climatic extremes. In hot deserts, for instance, rainfall is the key trigger for a whole range of especially reproductive activities. The seeds of ephemeral plant species, for instance, germinate, grow rapidly, flower and seed in the space of a few weeks. An equivalent example of an animal response is the spadefoot toad (*Scaphiopus*), which aestivates under the desert surface to emerge with the rains, mate and lay eggs, emergent tadpoles growing rapidly, a few surviving to metamorphose into adults, which then bury themselves to await the next rains (Figure 4.10).

4.3.3 Geographical distributions

In theory, with a knowledge of the limiting factors of a species we ought to be able to define the maximum geographical limits within which it could be found, and by including the regulatory factors we should be able to predict its actual geographical distribution. In practice, however, there are too many other factors that affect distribution for this to be done with any degree of accuracy or consistency. For example, the predicted and actual distribution of the moss *Tetraphis pellucida* are shown in Figure 4.11, predictions having been based on what is known, experimentally, about the species'

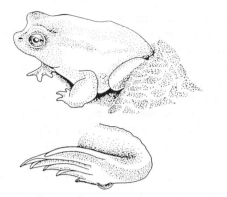

Figure 4.10   The spadefoot toad of the Sonoran Desert can escape to depths as great as 90 cm below the surface during unfavourable climatic conditions. Digging is facilitated by the presence of a horny projection on the foot.

temperature and relative humidity requirements. Not all of the potential range has been colonised, but more surprisingly there are locations beyond the predicted northern and southern limits of distri-

bution, which might reflect relict populations of Pleistocene interglacial or pre-Pleistocene origin (Forman, 1964).

Some of the confounding factors in the spread and geographical distribution of species are:

- **Evolutionary history** – species that are evolutionarily 'young' will have had less chance to extend their range. Willis (1922) proposed a strong relationship between age and area size, but this would only hold for expanding, evolutionarily young taxa with identical ecological requirements and uniform habitats. Older groups have the widest dispersal, all other factors being equal, but all other factors are seldom equal.
- **Population size** – species that produce large numbers of viable spores, seeds, eggs or offspring may have a spatial as well as numerical advantage over those with constrasting features, although quantity is often at the expense of quality (see *r* and *K* selection in Section 5.3.5).

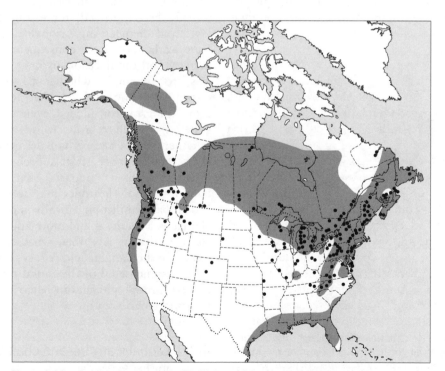

Figure 4.11   Predicted and actual distributions of the moss *Tetraphis pellucida* in North America. The shaded area is the theoretical distribution based on temperature and relative humidity. The dots represent the actual distribution (after Forman 1964).

- **Dispersal ability** – species with effective dispersal mechanisms will tend to be more widespread. Wind dispersal of seeds, for instance, will be more efficacious than vegetative spread by suckering.
- **Geographical barriers** – spread may be halted by geographical barriers such as mountains, deserts, ice or seas, or by biological barriers such as a vegetation type inimical to a particular species, for example a grassland herb at the forest–savanna boundary.
- **Geological history** – barriers emerge or disappear with events that take place over geological time scales. Thus continental drift will separate land masses, leading to *disjunct distributions*, or join them, allowing further dispersal along new corridors (Figure 4.12). Glaciation has also affected the distribution of many species, some of which now exist as *relicts* of a previous range. Other climatic changes have taken place over geological time.
- **Competition** – if a species enters the geographical range and habitat of a superior competitor it may not be able to survive there at all. In effect, this presents a *biological barrier*.
- **Predation, parasitism and disease** – these, too, can provide biological barriers in the same sense as extreme competition.
- **Human activity** – this has effected major changes in the distribution of many species, whether through accidental or deliberate introductions or by habitat alteration. Introduced species, in turn, may be competitors, predators, parasites or pathogens on native (and other introduced) species, so once again there can be major consequences in terms of range contractions, local extinctions and even total extinctions (see Chapter 8).

4.4 Issues in environmental management

Some of the consequences of current global warming on the physical environment have already been outlined, for example rises in sea level and changes in seasonality. In turn, these have rather obvious consequences for human activity and the decision–making associated with this, for example whether to try to prevent coastal flooding and whether to change what crops to grow or indeed even the agricultural system by which to grow crops.

Other effects are perhaps less obvious at first sight. For instance, it has been suggested that diseases such as malaria that are currently confined to low latitudes may spread polewards. If global anthropogenically–induced climatic change is a reality – and more and more evidence suggests that it is – then what can be done to minimise the dangers and reduce, if not stop altogether, some or all of the causal factors, whether this be through changes in behaviour or developments in technology?

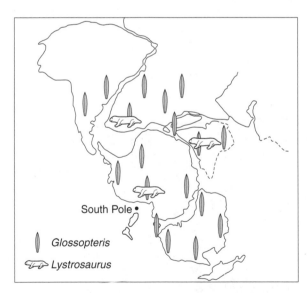

Figure 4.12 Map of Gondwana showing the distribution of Permian fossil leaves of *Glossopteris* and the Triassic reptile *Lystrosaurus*. The outlines of the present continents are shown in their position in the supercontinent of Gondwana in the late Permian–early Triassic (from Colbert, 1973; Chaloner and Lacey, 1973).

South Pole

Glossopteris

Lystrosaurus

4.4.1 Global warming and changing patterns in disease

It is a real fear that global warming will encourage the spread of malaria, yellow fever, dengue fever, viral encephalitis and schistosomiasis (see Issues Box 4.2), as well as other tropical human diseases, out of the Third World and into Europe, North America and Australia. Livestock and crop diseases, too, will undoubtedly spread under the warmer and more humid conditions predicted for temperate latitudes, for example trypanosomiasis (sleeping sickness), which affects humans as well as cattle and is spread by the tsetse fly. Quite small climatic changes would be enough to trigger an acceleration in the spread of disease carriers (*vectors*) such as the *Anopheles* mosquito, which transmits the malaria parasite (Pearce, 1992).

Malaria is arguably the most worrying disease threat, since it is becoming increasingly resistant to drugs and indeed is now essentially spreading out of control in many parts of Asia and South America (Collins and Paskewitz, 1995). Malaria is caused by four species of protozoan parasite of the genus *Plasmodium*. The most widespread species, *P. vivax*, has been wiped out from parts of Europe and the USA only in the postwar period. The last outbreak of malaria in the UK caused by *P. vivax* occurred in the Kent marshes in the early 1950s. The mosquito vectors lived in the brackish marsh waters, hence the local name of 'marsh fever'. The most virulent species is *P. falciparum*, which is climatically restricted by its need for constantly high temperatures and high humidity; it also needs standing water for the aquatic larvae of its mosquito vectors to develop.

Both *Plasmodium falciparum* and *Anopheles* mosquitoes, however, are sensitive to small changes in climate. An increase in mean temperature from 16 to 20 °C would halve the time the parasite takes to develop and increase its population within its mosquito host. The optimum temperature for development is 26 °C, a figure likely to be common in southern Europe by the early twenty-first century.

Where malaria is currently found, human populations have generally acquired some immunity, but were the disease to emerge in the countries of the Mediterranean basin, for example, where there is no natural immunity, especially if it does so in a drug-resistant form, major loss of life is to be expected. Massive mortality from malaria was indeed seen in upland Madagascar during the late 1980s: the region had not suffered from this disease for so long that any immunity had disappeared, and in some areas half of those infected died. The total death toll was 20 000.

As a pessimistic but not unrealistic scenario, Pearce (1992) suggests that a warmer UK some time not too far into the twenty-first century could see malaria invading just as sea waters rise sufficiently, also through global warming, to increase the extent of brackish coastal waters. He reports the words of David Wadhust of the London School of Hygiene and Tropical Medicine: 'The mosquitoes are still here ... And with 2000 people returning to Britain from abroad each year with malaria, the risk of local outbreak is always there. Global warming could greatly increase that risk.'

4.4.2 Responsibilities and risk reduction: political will and technological change

It is possible to ignore global warming, but it will not go away, and indeed it would then get worse. Other options are to adapt to it, counter it, mitigate it, remedy it or avoid it (Barrow, 1995). Counter-measures demand an understanding of the processes involved, the rate of change and likely consequences. They also require the establishment of just who is emitting what and in what amounts. There will be a need for an agreed control strategy and for decisions to be made on how to fund, monitor and exert control. Costs will almost certainly be high – but not as high as the costs that will occur if no action is taken.

It is difficult to assess accurately which countries and which enterprises are the major emitters of anthropogenic greenhouse gases, but the major 'players' are evident (Figure 4.13). Most developed countries and most industries have adopted what they view as a 'precautionary principle', whereby they have needed 'proof' of global warming before forgoing profit or investing in measures of mitigation or reduction. This in itself is sensible, but many organisations continue to deny the evidence of links

ISSUES BOX 4.2

Flukes and schistosomiasis

Flukes belong to the Class Trematoda and occur as either external or internal parasites on other animals. Externally parasitic (*ectoparasitic*) flukes possess a sucker at their anterior end surrounding the mouth, used to cling to their host. Many have a second sucker at the posterior end or underneath the body near the centre. All flukes that parasitise humans are internal (*endoparasites*). Endoparasitic flukes embed themselves into the tissues of the host or cling to the lining of cavities far from the surface of the skin, again using suckers or sometimes small hooks. A major problem of internal parasites is to establish offspring in new hosts. The most important fluke parasites of humans are *blood flukes*, species of *Schistosoma*. These are slender, elongated trematodes that – uncharacteristically for this group – occur as two sexes rather than as hermaphrodites.

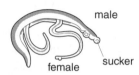

Blood flukes live in blood vessels of the intestine or urinary tract, clinging to the walls and feeding on the blood. The female lays her eggs in the walls of small blood vessels. As the vessels become congested with eggs the walls rupture and the eggs are discharged into the intestinal cavity, enter the excretory system and emerge from the host in the faeces. If the faeces find fresh water they hatch into a larval form, the *miracidium*, which can swim by beating small thread-like appendages (*cilia*). The miracidium needs to find an *intermediate host* – in this case a particular species of freshwater snail – within about 24 hours or it dies, but if it does encounter an appropriate animal it burrows into its body and feeds on the tissues. The miracidium transforms into a membrane-encased sac (*sporocyst*), which produces asexual buds inside its body. These buds (*cercaria*) break out of the sac then burrow their way out of the snail host itself. They look like miniature versions of the adults but with tails that allow them to swim freely in water, where they may come into contact with a human (or indeed may be drunk). The cercaria attach themselves to the skin and eat their way into a blood vessel, from where they are transported by the blood stream to the blood vessels of the intestine or urinary tract. There the young fluke feeds and grows into an adult, to mate with other flukes at the same site. The life cycle is now complete.

Schistosomiasis (often called *bilharzia* in Africa) is caused by species of *Schistosoma* which damage the human lung, liver, urinary tract and nervous suystem. Symptoms are body pains, rashes and heavy coughing, followed by blood in the urine, diarrhoea, general weakness, lack of energy and repeated abdominal pains. Victims may live for many years but gradually become emaciated and weak, and may eventually die from exhaustion or succumb to other diseases to which their weakened state has made them more susceptible.

The spread of this disease will almost certainly follow on from global warming, but it is important to stress that other human activities in increasing the extent of freshwater bodies have already been crucial in spreading schistosomiasis. Irrigation ditches and dams have particularly contributed to this. Many inhabitants of Egypt, for example, currently suffer from schistosomiasis, in large part following the construction of the Aswan Dam, built on the Nile in 1902 to control flooding, but since 1960 also used for hydroelectric power. Present-day estimates are that about half the population possess the parasite, but prewar figures may have been as high as three-quarters (Buschbaum, 1948; Barrow, 1995).

Other tropical water-borne diseases whose spread may be facilitated by global warming include cholera, dysentery, amoebic dysentery and typhoid.

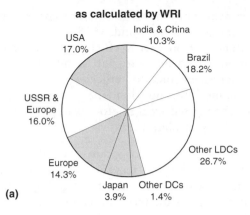

(a)

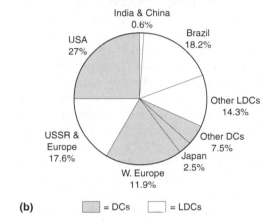

(b)   ▨ = DCs   ☐ = LDCs

Figure 4.13 Percentage responsibility for net emissions of 'greenhouse gases': (a) as assessed by the World Resources Institute, Washington, DC; (b) as assessed by the Centre for Science and Environment, New Delhi. (*Source:* Agarwal and Narain 1991: 15).

between carbon emissions and climatic change. Members of the Global Climate Coalition such as Ford Motors, General Motors and Exxon, for example, have maintained this position. The *true* precautionary approach when dealing with unpredictable environmental problems is to pre-empt possible dangers and take relatively inexpensive action to forgo possibly greater costs and perhaps irreversible situations later on. Barrow (*ibid.*) argues that 'the most sensible response would be to adopt a "no regrets" approach: counter-measures offer benefits even if warming fails to materialize, for example, carbon-sink afforestation still yields timber and amenity value.'

Despite the inherent technical difficulties and political problems of doing so, it is possible to calculate indices of the emissions of greenhouse gases on a country-by-country basis. For example, UNEP (1991) has published a 'greenhouse index' (carbon heating equivalents per capita, based on 1988 data) for all countries but, even given uncertainties in the raw data, estimates based on per capita emission may be viewed as favouring countries with sizeable, young and rapidly growing populations.

One of the agreements at the 1992 Rio Conference was the Convention on Climate Change, (Issues Box 4.3) whereby signatory countries agreed to provide cogent estimates of their own emissions (Brown and Adger, 1993). Calculation of emission indices should be followed by agreed amounts of taxation, emission quotas or emission reductions.

ISSUES BOX 4.3

United Nations Framework Convention on Climate Change

This was one of the agreements signed at the United Nations Conference on Environment and Development held in June 1992. At the Rio Conference, this agreement established broad principles and outlined ethical and legal obligations of nations to reduce the emission of greenhouse gases. It perhaps over-optimistically suggested stabilising such emissions at 1990 levels by the year 2000, for example.

The agreement is effectively non-binding, but it provided a basis for further discussion at national and international levels. Signatories were required to conduct national inventories of greenhouse gas emissions and to submit plans for reducing these emissions.

Measures to control emissions had been discussed before Rio. In 1988, for instance, the Toronto Conference on the Changing Atmosphere called for a 20% reduction in global carbon dioxide emissions by 2005. The policy leading to the Rio agreement was first thrashed out in Geneva in 1990 at the Second World Climate Conference. An agreed policy is hard enough to achieve: monitoring and the imposition of sanctions are even harder. Part of the problem lies with the fact that developed countries have a vested interest in maintaining the *status quo*, while developing nations seek economic development under the demands of expanding populations and, commonly, a dependence on energy based on hydrocarbons. Another part of the problem is that the atmosphere into which the greenhouse gases are being emitted can be viewed as a 'free resource' and as such is subject to the problem of the 'tragedy of the commons' (Hardin, 1968) – here with countries using the atmosphere with little regard for either the issue of pollution or of the rights of other nations (Issues Box 4.4).

Barrow (1995) has indicated a number of ways in which such issues can be addressed. Measures to control emissions by agreement could use:

- **Fuel use tax** – this should discourage hydrocarbon fuel use and consequent carbon emissions. It might encourage energy-efficient and sustainable technology as well as a reduction in the emission of greenhouse gases.
- **Carbon emissions tax** – the carbon content of various fuels could be calculated, and pollution released by power stations, motor vehicles, etc. assessed, followed by a tax on the import, production or processing of such fuels. This accords with the 'polluter pays' principle.
- **Tradeable emissions quota** – this would give each country quotas or permits which if unused could be sold, but if exceeded would have to be paid for with high charges (see Issues Box 4.5). Such quotas were a major part of the Kyoto Agreement in December 1997, and the fact that this has introduced a 'market-based instrument' has been seen by many as a way to safeguard the practical

implementation of greenhouse gas reduction (Grayson, 1998; Brand, 1998).
- **Standards on energy efficiency** – national (or even agreed international) standards could be established on the efficiency of industrial, commercial and domestic usage of hydrocarbon-based energy, for example regarding building insulation.

These options incorporate general ideas on energy conservation, recycling and technological advances, which are part of mitigating, counteracting and avoidance measures. These also include:

- **Control of biomass burning** – burning of vegetation is responsible for around 40% of the annual release of CO_2, 32% of carbon monoxide, 21% of nitrogen oxides and 38% of tropospheric ozone (Levine, 1991).
- **Sequestration of carbon by vegetation** – enhancing carbon sinks by afforestation, agroforestry and the use of carbon-storing crops. Much recent research has confirmed the CO_2 storage capacity of large forested areas such as the Amazon basin, strengthening arguments about the high environmental value of unlogged forest (but see Ecology Box 4.3).
- **Carbon extraction and sequestration** – it is technologically feasible, although perhaps not yet economically viable, to extract CO_2 from the atmosphere, liquefy or solidify it, and store it in underground reservoirs or the deep ocean.

There is a need for debate about the development of alternatives to fossil fuels such as energy derived from wind, tides, the Sun and nuclear power.

Much that can be done is in our own hands. Greater efficiency in the use of energy would be the speediest, cheapest and most effective way of reducing greenhouse gas emissions. The US National Academy of Sciences has argued that this alone could lower such emissions in the USA by 10–40% at no net cost to the economy (Miller, 2000). There is also, however, a need for technological innovation (for example, recent advances in trapping CO_2 before its emission from stacks) and shifts towards renewable, non-polluting forms of energy. There is also a need for the poli-

ISSUES BOX 4.4

The tragedy of the commons

Some natural resources are essentially incapable of being owned and are freely available. Examples include air, sea water, sea life (including fish) and migratory birds. These are called *common property resources*.

While such a resource is freely available to be used, its very use may diminish its quality or value. Air, for instance, is a compartment into which pollutants are deliberately or inadvertently released. While the atmosphere can accommodate, disperse and dilute a certain amount of waste material, if a critical threshold of particulate or gaseous concentration is exceeded then air pollution occurs. Similarly, if fish stocks are freely available there is a risk of uncontrolled overexploitation: yields will fall, preferred species will dwindle in numbers, and inappropriately small mesh sizes will trap young fish, which, were they to be left for a few years more, would grow (an increase in biomass) and reproduce (an increase in numbers).

Garrett Hardin has described an imaginary scenario as an allegory of the problems associated with common property resources (Hardin, 1968). In mediaeval times in much of Western Europe, villagers had the right to graze their livestock on common land. In economic terms, each livestock owner received all the benefits of grazing from each unit of stock that he owned, but the costs of grazing (the consumption of grass) were borne by all the stock owners. If one of the owners put an extra animal on to the common land he got all the benefits from doing so (for example, wool and meat in the case of a sheep), but the additional costs of that extra animal – a deterioration of the grazing land, however slight – were shared between all the villagers. For one extra sheep, the additional costs for every owner would be few and might be tolerated. But if one sheep owner did this it would make sense for other villagers to do the same, or the first villager might add a second sheep. Incrementally, then, a situation would eventually arise where the added profits per villager would be overtaken by the added losses – the common land would be overgrazed and everyone would suffer. Eventually, no one benefits. Hardin called this 'the tragedy of the commons'. The tragedy occurs when short-term individual gain is placed before the long-term welfare of society as a whole.

Parallels with today are obvious. This is why we now have legislation to restrict the nature and quantity of pollutants dumped into air and water. This is why countries have exclusive fishing zones, so that exploitation of national coastal waters, at least, is regulated. The atmosphere and the oceans are *global commons*.

For the wise and sustainable use of a common property resource it is necessary for all the users to agree on some kind of regulation of that use. There must therefore be agreement on who should be responsible for that regulation, how to establish limits on use (and who, indeed, the users should be), how to monitor use, and how to impose restraints and sanctions. It makes good environmental and long-term economic sense to use such resources at rates no higher than their self-sustaining yields or self-regulating quality. There are major difficulties, however, in determining what such thresholds might be, and in any case many individual companies and countries still retain a philosophy of short-term economic gain regardless of future economic or environmental consequences.

Central to environmental management, therefore, are issues relating to *common property rights*: societies must manage their own environments for the benefit of the whole community, whether at the global scale or in the context of an individual community (Ostrom, 1990; Bromley, 1992).

tical will to transfer efficient forms of energy production and waste reduction technology from the developed to the developing world.

Modelling suggests that carbon dioxide emissions should be reduced by 80% to slow predicted global warming to an acceptable rate, yet so far countries have had problems agreeing even to a 20% reduction. The problems and perhaps loss of nerve seen at the Rio+5 Conference (i.e. five years after the 1992 conference) in Kyoto, Japan, in December 1997, and its follow-up in Buenos Aires, Argentina, in November 1998, are evidence

ISSUES BOX 4.5

The Climate Change Summit at Kyoto, Japan: December 1997

The Third Conference of the Parties of the Climate Convention was held in Kyoto in December 1998, where political problems in agreeing on how to curtail the emission of greenhouse gases were evident. Well into the conference, the European Union had twice refused to agree to the proposed rate of reduction (8% of the 1990 emission of greenhouse gases) to be reached by 2010 on the grounds that the USA had only agreed, first to 2% then to 5%. On the very last day, however, the USA announced the results of a behind-the-scenes liaison – the establishment of a 'Carbon Club' comprising itself, Canada, Japan and Russia, which would trade 'permits' between themselves. This meant that the USA would now be willing to raise its rate of greenhouse gas reduction, but only if it were allowed to buy additional 'rights to pollute' from Russia. Russia's carbon dioxide emissions are currently 30% below 1990 levels and will reach only two-thirds of that before the year 2008, when trading will start.

Russia then demanded that its targets be reduced yet further from the proposed 5%, giving it yet more in the way of tradeable emission credits to sell to the USA. With this additional buffer, the USA was then prepared to raise its target to a 7% reduction, i.e. just 1% less than that of the EU. At the same time their fellow club members indicated their willingness to raise their agreed rates from 5 to 6% in the case of Canada, and Japan from 4.5 to 6%. The EU delegates were forced to accept this deal, otherwise nothing positive would have come out of the conference, yet economists versed in energy analysis predict that the agreement would allow the USA and Japan to *raise* their true domestic emission by 12–16% above the actual national targets of, respectively, a 7% and a 6% *reduction*. Hardly in the spirit of Rio, and in any case virtually impossible to police (Pearce, 1997c, 1997d).

Greenhouse gas reduction targets agreed at Kyoto: changes to 1990 levels by 2010

	Target	Country
Increases:	10%	Iceland
	8%	Australia
	1%	Norway
No change:		New Zealand, Russia, Ukraine
Reductions:	−5%	Croatia
	−6%	Japan, Canada, Hungary, Poland
	−7%	USA
	−8%	EU (as a whole), Bulgaria, Czech Republic, Estonia, Latvia, Liechtenstein, Lithuania, Monaco, Romania, Slovakia, Slovenia, Switzerland.

The overall effect would be to reduce the output of greenhouse gases by industrial nations by around 5%. The UK in fact anticipated a 12.5% reduction, which would allow it 'credit' over the EU figure of 8%, which it could then trade (Pearce, 1997a). The March 1999 budget in the UK indeed introduced a 'climate change levy' – a tax on the energy used by industry. Combined with increases on duty for transport fuel (which led to lorry drivers blockading town centres in protest), this 'long-term signal to industry to change its ways' (Greenpeace) should alone reduce the UK's carbon emissions by up to 6.5 M tonnes by 2010, more than 4% below 1999 emissions.

By March 1999, over 80 countries had signed the Kyoto protocol, but Iceland had failed to sign the agreement by its 15 March deadline, having demanded renegotiations for a 25% increase (rather than the agreed 10%), partly to accommodate the high fuel demands of a new aluminium smelter.

ISSUES BOX 4.6

Wind power in the UK: the Climate Change conference at Buenos Aires, Argentina: November 1998

Ways of implementing agreed reductions in greenhouse gas emissions continued to be sought nearly twelve months after the Kyoto summit. At Buenos Aires, Michael Meacher, the UK's environment minister, promised a fivefold increase in renewable energy by 2010, which would mean that around 10% of energy would be of this nature. Half of the renewable energy would come from wind. By 1998, 700 wind turbines were generating a total of 330 megawatts of power in the UK, mostly sited in otherwise scenically attractive hill areas. By 2010, it was anticipated that 2000 or so wind turbines would be in operation, many of them in less controversial locations offshore.

By way of comparison, Denmark in 1998 had around 4000 wind-driven turbines, and over 10 000 people had a share in the profits of nearby wind farms so not unnaturally were rather in favour of this method of generating power.

of the difficulties of agreeing on and implementing rational policies to reduce the risks of global climatic change (Issues Boxes 4.5 and 4.6).

4.5 Conclusions

The debate about whether there is, or is not, climatic change, and whether any such change is a consequence of human activity, has essentially ended. The Intergovernmental Panel on Climate Change is clear in its judgement on this, although understandably cautious in its predictions. The voices of a few lone climatologists and atmospheric physicists, whose work is often sponsored by vested interests such as the oil industry and motor manufacturers, fade in the changing wind.

Nevertheless, there is still a long way to go before consensual global political action is taken on identifying how climatic changes, in particular global warming, can be reduced or offset; in exercising coordinated mechanisms of control; and on implementing sanctions that genuinely bite. Even were the most rigorous controls exercised today, the climatic effects and environmental consequences resulting from the actions of the late twentieth century would reverberate well into the twenty-second century, and probably beyond.

Further reading

Department of the Environment (1994) *Global climate change* (third edition) (London: HMSO).

Department of the Environment/Meteorological Office (1997) *Climate change and its impacts: a global perspective* (London: HMSO).

Good, R. (1964) *The geography of the flowering plants* (third edition) (London: Longman). Part II – The factors of distribution: 332–414.

Houghton, J. (1994) *Global warming: the complete briefing* (Oxford: Lion Publishing).

Krause, F., Bach, W. and Kooney, J. (1990) *Energy policy in the greenhouse: from warming fate to warming limit* (London: Earthscan).

Krebs, C.J. (1972) *Ecology: the experimental analysis of distribution and abundance* (New York: Harper & Row). Part Two – The problem of distribution: populations: 17–135.

Pearman, G.I. (ed.) (1991) *Limiting greenhouse effects: controlling carbon dioxide emissions* (Chichester: Wiley).

Udvardy, M.D.F. (1969) *Dynamic zoogeography: with special reference to land animals* (New York: Van Nostrand Reinhold).

Vernberg, F.J. and Vernberg, W.B. (1970) *The animal and the environment* (New York: Holt, Rinehart & Winston). Chapter 3 – The zone of resistance: 65–102.

Woodward, F.I. (1987). *Climate and plant distribution* (Cambridge: Cambridge University Press).

QUESTIONS BASED ON CHAPTER 4

Q1. Why would an increase in the atmospheric concentration of carbon dioxide not necessarily result in a corresponding increase in photosynthesis in a particular plant species?

Q2. What is the single most important difference between global warming today and the warming that took place after the last glacial period? Why is this so important to species, communities and ecosystems?

Q3. Outline some of the possible consequences of global warming to mountain environments and their communities.

Q4. Identify actual or potential limiting factors in each of the following ecosystems:
Hot desert
Coral reef
The floor of a tropical moist forest
Salt marsh
Ephemeral (seasonal) pond

Q5. Many small nocturnal mammals demonstrate a characteristic rhythm in the intensity of feeding activity that is correlated with the phases of the moon. To what might this rhythm be a response?

ANSWERS

A1. Because other factors can limit photosynthesis and carbon fixation, e.g. availability of appropriate levels of water, nutrients and photosynthetically active radiation. Thinning of the ozone layer might also increase deleterious ultraviolet-B radiation. NB: there will also be different reponses to carbon dioxide enrichment by plants using C_3, C_4 or CAM photosynthetic pathways.

A2. The rapidity of the change. Some species may be unable to disperse *to* regions with appropriate climatic conditions, or to move *from* conditions which in some way extend beyond their limit of tolerance. Differential dispersal abilities will lead to different community compositions (different species, different abundance patterns) and different interactions. Some ecosystems will be particularly vulnerable to the consequences of global warming, for example the effects of rising sea levels on coral reefs, estuaries and salt marshes, and the geographical restriction or regional disappearance of alpine and sub-alpine ecosystems.

A3. Retreat of glaciers, less snow and earlier snowmelt, with generally less stable upper slopes and greater frequency of avalanches. The treeline would reach a greater altitude, and there would be a general shift up-mountain of all vegetation zones, with commensurate shifts in associated animals. Agricultural limits may also shift upwards, with some movement therefore of arable and pasture weed communities.

A4. Hot desert – water availability is the main one, although nutrient deficiency may be limiting at times. Temperature is *not* likely to be a limiting factor.
Coral reef – changes in temperature, UV-B radiation and sea level (light) – all possible consequences of global warming; sedimentation and excessive nutrients, possibly associated with human activities.
The floor of a tropical moist forest – light, mineral nutrients below ground.
Salt marsh – fresh water influx, excessive salinity (as found in salt pans), changes in tidal patterns.
Ephemeral (seasonal) pond – water availability.

A5. Activity is often greatest around the time of the new moon, least with a full moon. The most probable explanation, for which there is some experimental as well as observational evidence, is that small mammals are most vulnerable to visually hunting predators during the greater light of the full moon, least vulnerable during the dark new moon phase.

Discussion topics

D1. What are the arguments for allowing coastal lowlands to be flooded as sea levels rise following global warming, rather than paying for expensive engineering solutions?

D2. Why might developing countries be more reluctant than developed nations to cut down their use of fossil fuels in order to reduce global warming? Why will adaptation to the consequences of global warming be more difficult for developing than for developed countries?

D3. Identify examples of common property resources not examined at length in this chapter and discuss the extent to which their use exemplifies the 'Tragedy of the commons'.

EXERCISES

E1. At the next national budget, or with reference to the last one, identify the components that you feel are measures that will in some way help environmental health and sustainability, and those that you feel are the opposite. Where do you think the balance lies? Look at a copy of the government's election manifesto (public libraries will have a copy, or send for a copy from the party headquarters). Do you feel, on the basis of budget measures and laws that have been enacted since the previous election, that the government is doing what it promised for the environment?

E2. In your day-to-day activities, what are the greatest risks of injury that you take? Why do you take them? Other than ceasing to perform these activities, how might you reduce these risks? What behaviour do you undertake that in some way puts the environment at risk? Compare your answers to these questions with those of friends and colleagues, and examine why there are any differences.

Chapter 5

Population growth and control

Summary

Populations of all species change in size, make-up and distribution, a function of reproductive success and survival, which in turn affects reproductive strategies that take place within the opportunities and constraints of the environment. The concepts of the individual, population and metapopulation are examined, modes of reproduction are outlined, and ideas concerning density, population structure and population growth are developed. The last requires a study of fertility, natality, mortality, growth rates and growth forms. The exponential growth model is distinguished from the logistic growth model, and the ideas of carrying capacity and population regulation are introduced. Discussion of life history strategies focuses on the distinction between r selection and K selection. Low population sizes have implications for population survival that reflect population structure and genetic characteristics, in particular the degree of heterozygosity, with risks including inbreeding depression. There therefore exist threshold population sizes, or minimum viable population sizes and minimum viable areas. Population growth also reflects the nature of species interactions, and the difference between functional responses (largely behavioural) and numerical responses (changes in population size) is highlighted. Factors underlying population cycles are mooted and exemplified. An understanding of populations is important in the human exploitation of resources, as shown by examination of marine fisheries and the risks of overfishing. Problems of fisheries management focus on the use of surplus yield models and the idea of maximum sustainable yield. International regulatory measures to reduce the risk of overfishing are outlined. The issue of overfishing shows the need to understand minimum thresholds of population size. Maximum thresholds are a useful way of studying why some organisms are perceived as weeds or pests, although other factors are also important, for example biological attributes and economic enterprise. Control of weeds and pests depends in part on what options (physical, chemical and biological) are available, but it also requires a knowledge of the biology and ecology of target organisms, as well as differing needs and judgements concerning the level of control required.

5.1 Populations

Chapter 2 discussed the crucial importance to humans of feeding a global population that is growing at a geometric rate. Populations of all animals, plants and microbial organisms are more or less constantly changing in size, make-up and distribution. This is a function of reproductive success and survival, which in turn reflect particular reproductive strategies and the opportunities and constraints of particular biological, chemical and physical components of the environment. Populations thus grow or decline, sometimes in a regular manner in the form of population cycles. These population dynamics are the focus of this chapter, in which some of the relevance of understanding populations to environmental and economic issues such as fisheries and pest control are also reviewed.

5.2 Key environmental issues: marine fisheries; weeds, pests and their control

5.2.1 Marine fisheries and overfishing

The oceans contain vast numbers of fish and shellfish, which play a crucial part in our food supply. Nearly 90% of the global marine catch is of fish. Molluscs such as clams, oysters, scallops, squid and octopus count for a further 6%, while crustaceans such as crabs, lobsters, shrimp and krill make up about 3%. The remaining 1% or so consists largely of various kinds of marine algae such as carageenan.

Seafood is highly nutritious, in particular as a source of protein. Globally, as much as 5% of protein in our diet comes from seafood, and a billion people, most in the developing world, actually rely on fish and shellfish as their only source of protein. Local fisheries are crucial for the survival of many small coastal settlements around the world, but the bulk of the world's total catch comes from large fleets of sizeable fishing vessels using huge nets or lines. The demand for fish has grown so rapidly, from 21 million tonnes in 1950 to a peak of 109 million tonnes in 1994, that many species and many stocks have clearly been overfished and are now endangered (Table 5.1). There has therefore been a need to enforce fishing limits of various kinds, for example by target species, via limits on mesh size (which regulates the minimum size of fish caught) and using exclusive economic zones (see Section 5.4.1.2).

The open ocean, however, is a common property resource and is susceptible to over-utilisation, another example of 'the tragedy of the commons' (see Issues Box 4.4). The UN Food and Agricultural Organisation (FAO) has estimated that 70% of the world's oceanic fish stocks are

Table 5.1 Examples of fish species whose stocks are endangered through overfishing (after Raven et al., 1998)

Fish	Peak year catch in tonnes (year of peak catch)	1993 catch in tonnes
Haddock	914 300 (1970)	249 712
Atlantic cod	3 106 400 (1970)	1 134 147
Peruvian anchovy	13 059 900 (1970)	8 299 944
Cape hake	1 122 000 (1972)	199 252
Southern bluefin tuna	55 487 (1972)	14 355
Capelin	4 008 745 (1977)	1 742 149
Chub mackerel	3 412 602 (1978)	1 462 117
Japanese pilchard	5 428 922 (1988)	1 796 132

either fully or overexploited. Part of the reason for the increase in exploitation and the depletion of many stocks is simply because the human population is increasing and needs feeding. However, the *means* to feed more mouths has also altered, and technological advances, especially in fishing vessels and fishing gear, have made it possible to extract great numbers of fish from the sea on any one trip.

Fish schools themselves can now be spotted by sonar, radar and satellite tracking. Enormous *long lines*, some over 100 km in length with 35 000 baited hooks, are trailed behind fishing vessels, attracting large numbers of open-ocean (*pelagic*) fish, while 60 km *drift nets* – huge ribbons of plastic webbing – are so effective that they have now been banned by most countries. Funnel-shaped *trawl nets*, however, remain in use, pulled along the sea floor to catch bottom-dwelling (*benthic*) fish, with 25 tonnes often being caught in a single trawl. *Purse-seine nets* are enormous nets which are set out to surround large shoals of fish; when encirclement is complete the net is drawn together and the fish are trapped.

A major concern of environmentalists is the amount of *bycatch* – the collective term for unwanted catch, comprising not only fish that are caught but subsequently discarded as being of no commercial value but also animals such as dolphins and turtles that get trapped in the nets. The FAO has reported that 21% of all marine animals caught are thrown back into the sea. Most of the bycatch dies. Many diving seabirds also die, having ingested the hook as well as the fish already caught on a long line. In February 1999, the FAO's Committee on Fisheries ratifed an agreement by eighty nations to reduce the incidental catch of birds from long-line fisheries by such methods as weighting the hooks (so they lie deeper in the water), night setting, avoiding discharge of offal, and using bird-scaring methods during line setting.

Fish are in general highly mobile and some, such as salmon and tuna, migrate over great distances, but it is evident that discrete stocks (semi-isolated populations) can be distinguished in many species, and some parts of the world's oceans contain more fish than others. This latter reflects the food chain: nutrient availability in the oceans varies regionally, and this is reflected in the biomass and productivity of plankton and, in turn, of plankton-eating organisms, which include fish, and of course the fish that eat other fish (*piscivores*). The picture is made more complex by shifts in the circulation of oceanic waters, especially in areas of cold upwelling water, which brings nutrients from the ocean floor into near-surface waters.

Such upwelling areas are especially associated with the western edge of continental masses, and the availability of nutrient-rich waters of this sort has been the basis of some important fisheries. Only 0.1% of the oceans consists of upwelling waters, yet these contribute about half of the world's fish catch.

5.2.1.1 The Peruvian anchovy fishery

One of the richest marine ecosystems is associated with the Humboldt Current upwelling system off the coast of Peru and Chile. During the 1960s and 1970s, this part of the South-east Pacific provided just under 20% of the total world fish landings (McCredie, 1994).

One of the most important fish species off the coast of Peru has been anchovy (*Engraulis* sp.), which, before 1953, had been caught only for local consumption, and the fishery was relatively small. In 1953, however, the first processing plants were constructed to produce oil and fish meal for export, based on the anchovy harvest.

During the rest of the decade and the 1960s this venture was so successful that Peru became the top fishing nation in the world by volume, with anchovies representing 94% of the total catch. During the seven-month fishing season in 1969–70, Peru's 1700 purse-seiners landed 11 million tonnes of anchovies, in contrast to the 100 fishing vessels in 1953 catching around 85 000 tonnes.

More and more fish-processing plants were built, and more and more pressure was placed on the anchovy fishery. During the late 1960s, fisheries scientists had estimated that no more than 9.5 million tonnes of anchovy could be caught each year if the population was to be able to sustain itself, yet the need to earn foreign currency through exports and the political and economic dangers of declining employment drove the Peruvian government to permit harvests much beyond this figure: 12.4 million tonnes in 1970, for example, and 10.5 million tonnes in 1971.

In March 1972, the scientists seemed to have been proved very wrong indeed, for nearshore anchovies were present in abundance, and a record 170 000 tonnes was caught each day. These fish, however, had been forced inshore by uncharacteristically warm waters and had represented a large proportion of the stock. By the end of the season, despite the early fisheries frenzy, the annual catch was only 2.5 million tonnes.

The warm waters had been caused by El Niño (see Section 1.2). Substitution of nutrient-rich cold upwelling waters by warm nutrient-poor waters led to a collapse of biomass along the entire food chain, including anchovy. Only 1.8 million tonnes was landed in 1973, 3.6 million tonnes in 1974, 3.1 million tonnes in 1975 and 3.9 million tonnes in 1976. In 1976–77 and 1986–87, El Niño struck again with similar consequences, and from 1977 to 1987 annual landings of anchovy averaged around 1.2 million tonnes (Figure 5.1).

It was not El Niño, however, that caused the collapse of the Peruvian anchovy fishery. El Niño merely accentuated the effects of the real culprit, overfishing. The level of exploitation made the fishery unsustainable. Numbers of fish caught exceeded numbers of fish being born, and with fewer and fewer fish of reproductive age in the fishery the smaller and smaller the chance of

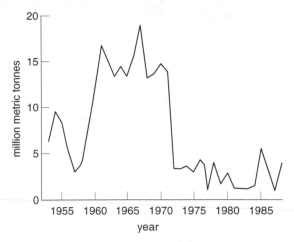

Figure 5.1   Estimated anchovy biomass in the Peruvian upwelling system, 1953–88.

stocks being replenished. Any sensible fisheries policy has to include some notion of the minimum population size and appropriate age structure that will permit at least year-by-year replacement, and indeed it must also take into account unpredictable fluctuations in environmental conditions that will affect the rate of reproduction and population growth (see Section 5.4.1.1).

The Peruvian example has been echoed in other parts of the world. The Alaskan salmon fishery collapsed during the 1960s and 1970s. The Newfoundland cod fishery essentially ended in the early 1990s. And in 1994, the National Marine Fisheries Service of the US Commerce Department placed a moratorium on fishing on Georges Bank in the North-west Atlantic, previously another of the world's richest fisheries. Catches of the main commercial species – cod, haddock and yellowtail flounder – had been declining there more or less steadily since a peak in the mid-1960s (Figure 5.2). In all these cases, the main reason for the decline was overfishing until numbers of commercial fish became so low that they were no longer profitable to catch. Globally, the sustainable yield of marine fish has been estimated to lie between 62 million and 87 million tonnes (McCredie, 1994). That overfishing is a general global trend is suggested by Figure 5.3, which shows that since the mid-1980s the total world marine fish catch has consistently

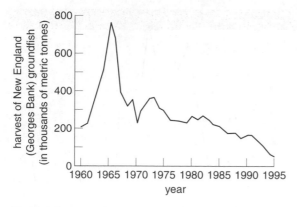

Figure 5.2 Harvest of ground fishes (cod, haddock and yellowtail flounder) from the Georges Bank, 1960–95.

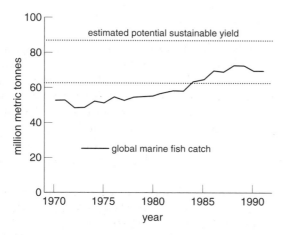

Figure 5.3 Global marine fish catch and potential sustainable yield (upper and lower estimates), 1970–91.

and substantially exceeded the lower (safe) estimate of the numbers required for replacement.

5.2.2 Weeds, pests and diseases

The fisheries examples show the need to understand minimum thresholds of population size, below which a desirable enterprise will be unable to continue. The study of weeds, pests and to some extent diseases shows the need to understand maximum thresholds of population size, above which (in general terms) a desirable enterprise will become non-viable.

Some plants are given the status of weeds because even small numbers cause damage, for example ragwort (*Senecio jacobaea*), which contains the alkaloid toxins senecionin and senecin as chemical defences (see Ecology Box 5.1), and is poisonous to some livestock. Similarly, some animals are pests because even one is dangerous, for example a malaria-transmitting mosquito. But most weeds and pests are essentially given such a status by virtue of their numbers: it is not so much what they do in the environment as how many of them are doing it.

What is also important is that the damage caused by weeds and pests affects human enterprises such as growing crops or pasturing livestock. Weeds and pests are therefore not biological phenomena so much as cultural ones. Weeds and pests nevertheless tend to possess certain biological attributes that predispose then towards such cultural status, and many of these attributes are to do with population size or the persistence of high numbers in the face of attempts at control.

Weeds, for example, often possess a high capacity to reproduce and spread. Groundsel (*Senecio vulgaris*), for instance, can produce 1000–2000 seeds per plant, and shepherd's purse (*Capsella bursa-pastoris*) 3500–4000 seeds per plant. Many are persistent in the seed bank and can emerge many years after the parent plant's death. Persistence is also seen in the deep tap root that plants such as dandelion (*Taraxacum officinale*) and broadleaved dock (*Rumex obtusifolius*) possess, making them difficult to extract. These are also plants that spread by growing from root fragments that become dispersed in the soil. A similarly persistent weed is coltsfoot (*Tussilago farfara*), whose maze of roots is very easily broken up, each piece capable of growing into a new plant. These are indeed plants, known as *ruderals*, that thrive in disturbed soil.

With such traits, it is not surprising that, given a chance, these plants form large populations, often with rank, extensive growth habits. They are plants that are not only disturbance-tolerant but are often also highly competitive, outcompeting other plants for resources such as light, water, soil nutrients and space. They may exude chemicals (*auxins*) from their roots that

ECOLOGY BOX 5.1

Physical, chemical and behavioural defences in plants and animals

Plants and animals do not want to get eaten or injured, and evolution has allowed the development of a number of means of defence, which very broadly may be divided into physical, chemical and behavioural. Many of these mechanisms, however, can be circumvented by often specialist predators and grazers, some of which adopt the same kinds of strategy as their food species. Indeed, there is an evolutionary 'arms race' in which both predator and prey strive to maintain an advantage over each other. Such species are, in a sense, constantly evolving simply to keep up with other species in their community. This is rather like the situation commented on by the Red Queen in Lewis Carroll's *Alice through the looking glass*, where 'it takes all the running you can do, to keep in the same place', and ideas supporting the 'antagonistic co-evolution' of such an arms race have become known as the *Red Queen hypothesis* (Van Vale, 1973).

Physical

- *Shells* protect many animals against predators as well as the physical environment. Crustaceans such as crabs and lobsters, and molluscs, especially snails and bivalves such as mussels, oysters and clams, are good examples. Shore birds such as oystercatchers (*Haematopus ostralegus*), however, have developed different ways of opening bivalve prey (prising, hammering and chiselling), modifying both behaviour and bill shape to do this. Thrushes hammer snail shells on a stone 'anvil' to get to the flesh inside, while some species of crow drop shellfish from a height to break them. Similar defence is achieved through *armoured scales*, such as with armadillos and pangolins, which in turn requires the behavioural response of a curled posture. Equivalent protection is afforded to plants by, for example, nut shells and seed husks.
- The above forms of protection can be enhanced by the production of *spines*, as is evident in hedgehogs and porcupines, and the aptly named porcupine fish (*Diodon hystrix*). Some zooplanktonic taxa are normally unspined but as an *induced response* can develop spines or crests when predators are present. Examples are the rotifer *Keratella cochlearis* (which can develop a basal spine) and the water flea *Daphnia pulex* (which can develop a head crest). Many plants also produce spines and thorns, such as cacti, hawthorn, gorse and rose. Plants can also develop prickly leaves, such as with holly, which will deter larger browsers. Hairy leaves or stems, such as on tomato (*Lycopersicon esculentum*), can deter leaf-feeding insects.
- Physical defences include shape and colour, and therefore include *mimicry*, where a plant (such as a stone plant (*Lithops*)) or an animal (such as a stick insect) mimics something it is not, usually something inedible. Caterpillars of the viceroy butterfly (*Limenitis archippus*) resemble bird droppings in form, colour and apparent moistness.
- Allied to mimicry is *crypsis*, where the plant or animal 'hides' in its environment. Stone plants are hidden when they grow among real stones. *Camouflage* is a form of crypsis, as is *disruptive patterning*, seen for example in zebras.
- Mimicry also occurs when a palatable or harmless animal mimics an unpalatable or dangerous one. This form of defence is *Batesian mimicry*, which relies on there being more 'models' than mimics in the environment and that predators learn to avoid unpalatable prey. The blue jay (*Cyanocitta cristata*), for example, learns to avoid the distasteful monarch butterfly (*Danaus plexippus*; see below) but in doing so also avoids the perfectly edible viceroy butterfly, which mimics the monarch. *Müllerian mimicry* occurs where a group of distasteful or dangerous animals have evolved similar warning signals, often as bright, conspicuous patterns so that predators only have to learn a few such signals. The black and yellow/orange/red stripes of many stinging insects such as bees and wasps are an example. Again, these warning signals may be mimicked by harmless species.
- *Startle displays* include bright colour spots on animals, exposed only in flight, and can confuse predators, which fixate on where the spot *was* rather than where the prey has moved to, as is seen in some frogs and insects. *False eyespots* on insect wings and fish may deflect the blow of a predator to a less vulnerable part of the body. Some caterpillars, such as those of the puss moth, have large false eyes on the heads (or indeed tails), which, when the animal rears up, looks like a(n admittedly small) snake, which again deters predators. One anti-predator response by the armadillo is to leap vertically into the air – another startle display.

ECOLOGY BOX 5.1 (cont)

Chemical

- *Toxins* or *unpalatable compounds* can be produced by plants to deter grazers. Unripe seeds of animal-dispersed plants may be protected by bitter-tasting pulp and advertised as such by a warning colour. When ripe, however, sugars develop in the pulp and the fruit changes colour, for example to red, orange or black, to indicate to potential dispersers that it is now edible. Specialists may be able to detoxify such compounds, however, and indeed use them themselves as defence. Monarch caterpillars, mentioned earlier, sequester the cardiac glycosides from its food plant, milkweed (*Asclepias*), which the plant has produced to make it generally inedible, but which now makes the caterpillar similarly emetic. Stinging nettles (*Urtica*) produce urtic acid. Ants secrete formic acid.
- The bombardier beetle (*Brachinus crepitans*) has a reservoir in its abdomen filled with hydrogen peroxide and hydroquinose: when threatened the chemicals are mixed with a peroxidase enzyme in a special chamber, which transforms the mixture into quinone, a noxious material explosively sprayed at its opponent through the anus by a simultaneous release of oxygen.
- Chemicals can be harmless but possess a noxious smell, for example with striped skunks (*Mephitis mephitis*) and stink badgers (*Mydaus javanensis*), which both possess anal gland secretions with this effect.

Behavioural

- *Avoidance* and *escape behaviour* can be seen in animals that hide in holes or indeed actively burrow, or that flee from predators where there is a premium on speed. Many predators, too, have evolved ways of running, flying or swimming rapidly. Predators, however, are merely hunting for a meal; potential prey are running for their lives. Plants, too, can 'hide', for example succeeding more in habitats or surrounding vegetation where they are less conspicuous, and they may grow in a prostrate rather than erect form.
- A few animals can increase their size, such as the puffer fish (*Tetraodon cutcutia*), which can inflate its body with water until it is almost globular, or at least the appearance of size, as happens when some mammals adopt a more erect posture and make their body hair stand up.
- Behaviour must reflect form, as was evident with cryptic species and mimics, which must behave in a way appropriate to their background or model. Leaf insects, for instance, not only look like leaves but remain on branches for much of the time, not moving around, but possibly swaying slightly as if in a breeze. Similarly, spikes and scales are little protection if there is a vulnerable underbelly, so hedgehogs and armadillos roll into a ball when threatened.
- By pretending to be dead (*thanatosis*) animals may not elicit a killing or eating response, as is evident with possums playing . . . possum.
- Grouping can provide safety in numbers, whether as defence or simply by reducing the chances of being eaten (a dilution effect). Predators may be identified sooner if there are many eyes on the look-out, or sentinels may be posted, as is the case of meerkats (*Suricata suricatta*). In either case, more time is available for feeding, etc. by the group.
- Some trees produce exceptionally large numbers of seeds (*masting*), too many for seed-eaters to consume them all (seed-predator satiation), so some seed will escape and have a chance to germinate. This is particularly effective after a year or more of low seed production, which will have had the effect of keeping seed-predator numbers low before the masting year. Trees may also produce seed at times when alternative food is abundant, thereby reducing the per capita rate of seed predation.
- A few plants can defend themselves against grazers by using the behaviour of other animals. This is seen in some acacias, for example, which are defended by aggressive stinging ants, which repel intruders. The ants live in large hollow thorns and feed on nectar produced by the plant as a reward, not via flowers as usual, but in special organs called *extra-floral nectaries*. Plants thus provide home and food for their protectors.

suppress the growth of surrounding would-be competitors, an effect known as *allelopathy*. Such plants are better termed competitive ruderals. Many weeds are also resistant to attempts at controlling their presence or number (see Section 5.4.2.2).

Weeds can also occur in aquatic systems. A characteristic example is the water hyacinth (*Eichhornia crassipes*), whose rapid growth rate has resulted in it taking over many freshwater habitats in the world (see Issues Box 5.1). It is also evident that algae can become problem plants, with high and rapidly increasing numbers leading to algal blooms, which can dominate ponds, lakes and streams, reducing light infiltration and, following their death, leading to anaerobic conditions as oxygen consumption by decomposer bacteria increases. The term 'weed', however, is generally used in connection with large plants (*macrophytes*) rather than microscopic ones.

In many ways, pests are animal weeds (or indeed weeds are botanical pests). Rats and mice, for example, are clearly pests in the context of human activity, in the home or field, and in conservation terms on oceanic islands where they have been introduced with devastating consequences for native fauna. They breed prolifically and are difficult to control. The same is true of grain-eating birds such as the quelea in Africa, or consumers of young cereal shoots such as many geese species in the temperate world. Locusts are an obvious example of a devastating insect pest in a general agricultural context, as is the Colorado beetle (*Leptinotarsa decemlineata*) on a specific crop (potatoes). Forestry insect pests such as the gypsy moth (*Lymantria dispar*), spruce budworm (*Choristoneura fumiferana*) and bark beetles (*Dendroctonus* spp.) have a similarly damaging effect on both natural and plantation forests during outbreaks, when numbers increase rapidly to exceed a threshold of environmental or economic tolerance (see Section 5.4.2.1).

If weeds and pests are culturally subjective attributes, then so too, in some ways, are diseases. Disease organisms, or *pathogens*, usually microbial, often only cause disease when – as with weeds and pests – their numbers build up to exceed a critical threshold of health. A healthy plant or animal can be readily distinguished from a diseased organism that is weakened or even moribund (although that is by no means always the case). The threshold at which we can say that an organism is showing physical or behavioural evidence of disease, however, is often like the definition of when a plant or an animal becomes a weed or a pest – one of perception. Unlike weeds and pests, however, diseases are found in the wild and can weaken populations (making them more susceptible to other environmental stresses such as cold or drought) and can themselves kill.

Disease can be *endemic*, constantly present in a reservoir population at generally low (chronic) levels but with occasional outbreaks (acute levels) during which symptoms become more evident and pronounced, and illness and death may result. Allied to the number of disease organisms is the resistance of the host. In some cases, rather than attempting to get rid of an endemic disease it is more effective (and certainly often cheaper) to breed resistant strains of the host, for example tsetse-resistant cattle.

Diseases that become acute and widespread are known as *epidemics*. Five factors are critical to the development of every epidemic:

- the population of hosts must be susceptible, preferably as uniformly as possible;
- the hosts should be clustered or crowded together;
- a virulent pathogen must be present and have the potential to increase in abundance – the faster the better;
- the weather and other environmental factors should be favourable for disseminating the pathogen and for the development of the disease; and
- the timing of favourable conditions should be sufficient to sustain the epidemic.

ISSUES BOX 5.1

Water hyacinth as a weed

Water hyacinth (see figure) has been declared the most significant aquatic nuisance plant in the world, it being a particular problem where it is an introduced species. It has now spread from South America to many parts of the tropical and semi-tropical world, where it dominates many freshwater habitats, in particular those which are nutrient-rich. It has a very high rate of vegetative growth, demonstrates a wide ecological amplitude and exhibits great phenotypic plasticity, i.e. adjusting its growth form and behaviour to local environmental conditions.

Water hyacinth, *Eichhornia crassipes*.

It has interfered with the use of water by causing obstruction to navigation and recreational uses, by reducing water flow in irrigation and drainage channels, and by degrading water quality for domestic use. It has also drastically effected changes in the plant and animal communities of the freshwater environment, and as huge amounts of dead material decompose so the uptake of oxygen by aerobic bacteria becomes excessive, the water becomes oxygen-deficient and many animals die in what have become near-anaerobic conditions. Fish kills, for example, are not uncommonly associated with water hyacinth invasion.

Water flow can be reduced by 40–95% in irrigation channels, and this can cause flooding, as has frequently been the case in Malaysia and Guyana. In the Mississippi delta, impediment to flow has resulted in annual losses in excess of $40 million. Vast sums of money have been spent keeping the Panama Canal free of this weed. Rice paddy fields in

ISSUES BOX 5.1 (cont)

the Indian subcontinent and the Far East have been smothered. Water hyacinth also carries pathogens such as *Attractomorpha crenulata* and *Rhizoctonia solani*, which affect crops such as tobacco, brinjal and jute.

Most countries in which water hyacinth has been invasive have introduced some kind of legislation to reduce its spread and impact. Attempts at control, however, have been of little use in the long term, whether using manual/mechanical removal or chemical methods such as 2,4-D, diquat, paraquat, amitrole or glyphosate. Biological control using herbivorous fish, especially Chinese grass carp (*Ctenopharyngodon idella*), has perhaps been of greater effect, and some value has been found in the weevils *Neochetina bruchi* and *N. eichhorniae*, a couple of pyralid moths, *Acigona infusella* and *Sameodes albiguttalis*, and the water hyacinth mite (*Orthoglumna terebrantis*), all of which are specific to this weed species, or are strongly preferential towards it for feeding. Virulent pathogens have also been used to try to control this nuisance plant, but only the fungus *Cercospora rodmanii* has been found suitable for large-scale field treatment.

Elimination of the weed on a long-term basis almost certainly requires some kind of integrated control. Insect-damaged and chemically treated plants are more susceptible to disease, for example, and various combinations of biological and chemical control might be the way forward. One other option, however, must be mentioned – actually *using* water hyacinth as a resource, and this has been done in different places as a source of protein for humans; as green fodder for livestock; as mulch or compost; as bedding material for mushroom cultivation; for conversion to paper and board; as a biomass fuel (biogas); and as a means of filtering out nutrients and heavy metals from water (see figures).

Source: Gopal, 1987

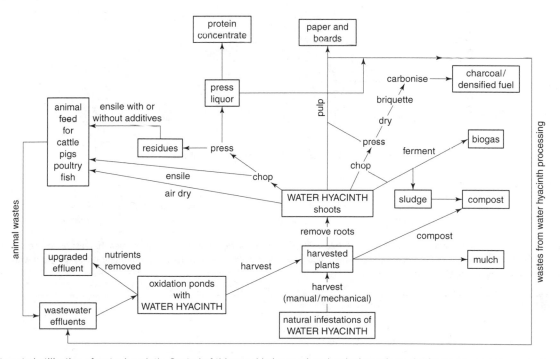

Integrated utilisation of water hyacinth. Control of this weed below noxious levels depends on the frequency and biomass of harvest.

ISSUES BOX 5.1 (cont)

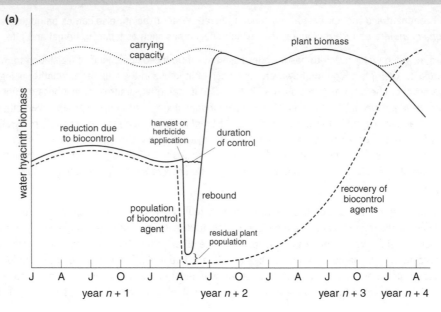

(a)

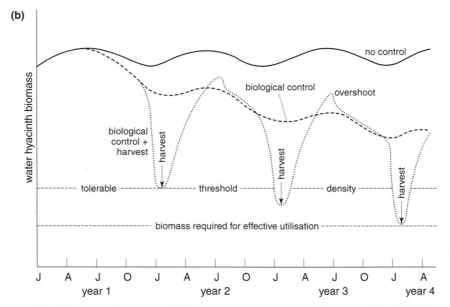

(b)

(a) Model illustrating the effect of drastic control measures such as herbicide application or mechanical harvest on the population of a biocontrol agent and water hyacinth. (b) A theoretical scheme of water hyacinth management integrating biocontrol with utilisation by regulating the harvest.

5.3 Ecological concepts

- Individuals, reproduction, populations and metapopulations
- Density, population structure and population growth
- Population growth rates
- Population growth forms
- Life history strategies: *r* and *K* selection
- Threshold population sizes
- Species interactions
- Functional and numerical responses
- Population cycles: extrinsic and intrinsic factors

5.3.1 Individuals, reproduction, populations and metapopulations

Many organisms consist of a number of *individuals*, many or some of which reproduce *sexually* to produce discrete offspring, many or some of which mature and in turn reproduce. The idea of the individual is here a clear one. Each offspring contains the genes of its parents yet is genetically distinct. Other organisms, however, increase their numbers by *asexual reproduction*. The result may again be a set of discrete individuals, but here they would be genetically identical to each other and to their parent.

Bacteria, fungi and other microbial organisms, however, may challenge the whole idea of the individual, not least because it is unclear where one individual ends and another begins. Rayner (1997) argues that, rather than being discrete bounded entities, microbial organisms have the dynamic characteristics of a network. An individual toadstool is in fact the tip of a huge biological iceberg consisting of an integrated mass of underground mycelia. One mammoth fungus has spread across 15 ha of forest in Montana; it is probably well over a thousand years old and weighs more than 100 tonnes. Should we really view this as an individual? But if it is a collection of genetically identical individuals, how do we separate them?

Yet other organisms reproduce asexually, but the offspring remain attached in some way to the parent for at least a part of their life. An example of this is a strawberry plant that produces runners on which develop daughter plants; these will send down their own roots and their own leaves will photosynthesise, yet they will, initially at least, still be attached to their parent. That for a while the daughter plant receives nutrients from the parent plant is a sound reproductive strategy, increasing the chances of success and survival. At what stage does the daughter plant become an individual rather than just a growth from the parent plant? Physically, perhaps, only when the connecting runner is severed, but in practice it is when the daughter is capable of undertaking some physiological processes by itself, however reliant it might still be on the parent.

Many plants can reproduce both sexually (mixing genetic material from both sexes) and asexually (forming genetically identical modules – *clones* – which subsequently separate); some plants are either male or female, while others contain characteristics of both; and some can self-fertilise, while others require at least one other plant. Animals also show a range of options, both of sexual reproduction (one or more males mating with one or more females) and of asexual reproduction (where fertilisation occurs in the absence of a male the process being known as *parthenogenesis*). Asexual reproduction can be undertaken by individuals, for example the common or laboratory stick insect (*Carausius morosus*), or as part of a colonial grouping such as with corals. Some animals are simultaneous or sequential *hermaphrodites*: snails, for example, can behave as male or female (or both) at any one time, while oysters change sex annually. In the absence of a male, females of some wrasse species (a kind of fish) can be hormonally prompted to change into fully fertile males. Aphids are an example of an insect group that alternates reproducing parthenogenetically (an all-female cohort) with generations that contain both sexes and in which reproduction is sexual.

Reproductive modes, then, can be complex, and it is necessary to distinguish between individuals that are genetically distinct from their parents (*genets*) and those that are genetically identical (*ramets*), bearing in mind that some offspring might includes examples of each, for example in many bulbous or tuberous plants such as crocuses, bluebells and potatoes, which produce both genets (seedlings) and ramets (where the bulb or tuber splits).

A *population* is a group of individuals of the same species present in a particular area at a particular time. The area under consideration may be large or small, and clearly or fuzzily defined. Population boundaries are more often a convenience than a reality, and in the case of mobile species the notion of a specific area becomes rather less useful. There may be geographical limits to a population, for example because of a physical or ecological barrier. Population characteristics change through both space and time.

Where populations are more or less discrete but between which there is some level of dispersal or interbreeding, we have a *metapopulation* – a sort of population of populations. The dynamics of metapopulations have become important to understand in the context of the conservation, indeed the survival, of many endangered species.

5.3.2 Density, population structure and population growth

Populations possess a number of inherent characteristics or qualities. The number of individuals per unit area is that population's *density*, averaged (usually from a sample) for the entire area occupied by the population, or showing differences in density between different parts of an area. Differences in density can reflect a number of circumstances to do with environmental quality, a social factor such as territoriality, or – often – a combination of the two. The individuals in a population can be all of the same age and sex, but much more usually they present a more complex picture. Populations with overlapping generations will possess an *age structure* that reflects reproductive strategy and environmental contraints (Figure 5.4). The critical features leading to a particular age structure are birth rate, death rate, longevity, fertility and dispersal.

In animals, the *birth rate* (or *natality*) is the total number of live births in the population

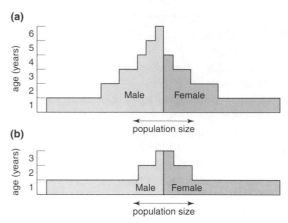

Figure 5.4 Age–sex pyramids. (a) Equal sex ratio at birth; high infant mortality; steady decline in male numbers; disproportionate female mortality, suggesting greater susceptibility to environmental stress, perinatal mortality, etc. (b) High birth rate but also very high infant mortality; no sex differences in mortality, but longevity is low, suggestive of *r* selection (see Section 5.3.5).

within a breeding cycle or within a set period such as a year. In a general sense, *fertility* is simply the ability of an organism to produce offspring, but it is a term often more specifically used (although sometimes distinguished as *fecundity*) in relation to the number of eggs produced by an individual that develop into living young. While age of sexual maturity in males is therefore an important attribute of populations, even more so is the age of sexual maturity in females (onset of fertility, or *menarche*) and, in long-lived animals, the decline and cessation of fertility (*menopause*). The period between menarche and menopause defines the reproductive window of a female. Some animals, of course, can only breed once. Other variables are the length of the *gestation period*, that is the time between fertilization and egg laying (*oviposition*) or live birth (*vivipary*), and the time it takes for females to come into reproductive condition after egg laying or birth. Age-specific natality is thus important in examining population dynamics and is usually considered in terms of the number of female offspring per reproductive female.

The *death rate* (or *mortality*) includes all deaths. Mortality is often highest in the period soon after birth, and in many species the birth rate is high precisely because it is usual for newborn or juvenile mortality to be massive. High mortality in the reproductive part of a population obviously can put the population at risk. Following the infant mortality peak, the likelihood of death becomes greater as individuals age, whether by an accumulation of risk and environmental stress or simply through the ageing process itself. The average *longevity* of a population is therefore another important component of population structure, and age-specific mortality becomes a key feature in looking at how a population behaves.

Animals generally disperse, or at least a component of the population disperses. Many terrestrial vertebrate populations, for example, see a post-juvenile dispersal of at least a fraction of the newly or soon-to-be-mature individuals. This is frequently the case with young males. Populations may thus include *in-migrants* (or immigrants) and lose some of their numbers as *out-migrants*. Among other benefits, this kind of dispersal reduces the risk of inbreeding (see Section 5.3.6).

Another crucial characteristic in examining population change is the rate of reproduction. *Reproductive rate* (R_o) can be expressed as

$$R_o = N_g/N_o$$

where
N_o = initial number of reproductive adults, and
N_g = number of offspring reaching reproductive age in the next generation.

R_o is the average reproductive rate per breeding individual in the population, and in this simple form makes what is often a quite unrealistic assumption, that generations do not overlap: parents die before offspring themselves reproduce. In nature, however, many species have females that reproduce again and again (a feature known as *iteroparity*, in contrast to *semelparity*, in which each reproductive individual has a single reproductive event in its life, after which it dies). More useful, therefore, is the calculation of the net reproductive rate (R_N), where

$$R_N = N_t/N_o$$

i.e. where, after a specified period of time (t) the number of individuals remaining (N_t) is divided by the initial number (N_o). R_N includes both births and deaths over the sampling period, so where numbers of survivors and their offspring at the end of the time interval have increased, $R_N > 1$; where numbers are lower (more individuals have died than have been born), $R_N < 1$. Life tables can be drawn up to identify R_o and R_N, using age-specific survival rates, age-specific death rates and age-specific natality rates for each age cohort.

The essence of what has been written concerning animals is also true of plants. They too have rates of germination, equivalent to birth rates; they die, and do so at different ages, young plants being particularly vulnerable; they grow to different ages; they have periods of fertility that reflect age and habit, from an annual that dies after a single flowering and seeding event to a long-lived perennial that flowers for many years. Most germinated plants do not disperse (North American desert tumbleweeds being an exception), but seeds may be carried over long distances, and many plants can reproduce vegetatively by the rooting and subsequent development of fragments that have been transported.

A population may therefore vary from having a simple structure to demonstrating the complexities of many overlapping age cohorts. It may reflect population growth from one or a few founder members or it may be a chance aggregation of individuals that just happened to have arrived in that location.

Populations generally change in size. If there is an excess of births over deaths, an excess of in-migrants over out-migrants, or a combination of these (for example, more deaths than births but a high number of in-migrants that more than compensates for the deaths), then the population grows. The reverse leads to population decline. Some populations, at least for a while, remain essentially static. Metapopulations may be important where some members of a *source population* disperse to maintain the viability of otherwise declining *sink populations*.

5.3.3 Population growth rates

Populations changing in size will show a *growth rate* or a rate of decline which can be viewed as a negative growth rate. Growth rate is measured over time so that

$$N_t + 1 = N_t + (B - D) - (I - E)$$

where N = number

t = base time

$t + 1$ = one unit of time (e.g. one year) after the base time

B = number of births in the unit of time being considered

D = number of deaths in the unit of time being considered

I = number of in-migrants in the unit of time being considered

E = number of out-migrants in the unit of time being considered.

To take a simplified example, for the moment ignoring in- and out-migration, let us look at a population of bacteria in which all members are reproducing by division. If the initial population size is 100 individuals and after an hour it has grown to 300 individuals, the following observations can be made and expressed in a simple mathematical form:

N	(initial number)	=	100
ΔN	(change in number, the Greek capital letter Δ – delta or 'd' – being the mathematical term for change of this sort)	=	200
$\dfrac{\Delta N}{\Delta t}$ (or $\Delta N / \Delta t$)	(growth rate, i.e. average rate of change per unit time, here 1 hour)	=	200/ hour

It is often useful to identify the average rate of change per unit time per individual, i.e. dividing the growth rate by the initial population number, so that

$$\frac{\Delta N}{N.\Delta t} \text{ (or } \Delta N / N\Delta t) = 2/\text{hour/individual}$$

(i.e. a 200% increase per hour)

This last notation is known as the *specific growth rate*. As well as the average growth rate over a

period of time, it is often useful to consider a theoretical instantaneous rate of growth at a particular time – the rate of change, as it were, when Δt is close to zero. In calculus, the Greek letter δ (lower case delta) is used in place of Δ when instantaneous rates of change are being considered. Doing so, the above notations become

$$\delta N / \delta t = \text{rate of change in number per unit time } at\ a\ particular\ instant$$

and

$$\delta N / N\delta t = \text{rate of change in number per unit time per individual } at\ a\ particular\ instant.$$

This last notation thus becomes the *instantaneous growth rate*, which is designated by r. While this can only be an abstract, theoretical notation it becomes a useful one when examining certain kinds of growth curve. The notation r is the exponent in the equation for population growth in an unlimited environment, i.e.

$$r = \delta N / N\delta t$$

This being so, then

$$rN = \frac{N.\delta N}{N.\delta t} = \frac{\not{N}.\delta N}{\not{N}.\delta t} = \frac{\delta N}{\delta t}$$

The parameter r is, in effect, an instantaneous coefficient of population growth.

Were the environment to exert no constraints on the growth of a population – where space, physical environment, food, competition and predation/herbivory did not limit population growth in any way, i.e. an ecological 'vacuum' – the specific growth rate would be constant and would occur at the maximum possible rate for any particular population with any particular initial age structure. This maximum (theoretical) instantaneous growth rate is designated as r_{max}. Here, birth rate is maximal and mortality rate is minimal. Even so, there will be differences in r_{max} between species that, on the one hand, take a long time to reach sexual maturity and produce few offspring either at any one time or measured throughout their lifetime, and on the other hand those that reach sexual maturity rapidly and produce many offspring.

African elephants (*Loxodonta africana*), for instance, live for 30–40 years, reaching maturity at 12–14 years. The mother produces one baby at a time, with a gestation period of 22 months. Averaging all this out gives an r_{max} of only 0.06 per year. Many small rodents, in contrast, live for only a few months but come into reproductive condition in a few weeks. They have an 18–25-day gestation period and produce sizeable litters. In such cases, r_{max} may be 0.3–8.0 per year. That r_{max} is rarely achieved in nature, however, reflects constraints imposed by the environment, interspecific competition, variable nutrition, predation, diseases, and failure to find a mate or pollinator. For example, while it is unclear what the average life expectancy of leatherback turtles (*Dermochelys coriacea*) might be, females many decades old are known to breed. While 60–100 eggs are lain in excavations on the beach, however, a sizeable number are dug up by predators and many hatchlings are also lost to predation as they shuffle down the shore to the sea, so each breeding event for each female produces perhaps just one or two survivors, and r_{max} is never achieved.

5.3.4 Population growth forms

Growth rate can be plotted using an *x*-axis (horizontal axis, abscissa) for time and a *y*-axis (vertical axis, ordinate) for population size. The importance of rN becomes evident when considering two contrasting population growth forms, which, when graphed using arithmetically scaled axes, produce J-shaped and S-shaped (sigmoid) growth forms (Figure 5.5).

In the J-shaped form, the birth rate is high and mortality is low, so population size (and therefore density) increases rapidly and (in the same way as compound interest) exponentially. Clearly, no population can maintain such a rate of growth indefinitely, for it would otherwise overwhelm the world. What happens is that the environment imposes a limit or constraint such that massive mortality takes place. The population, for example, could run out of food or space, or maximum growth might occur in warm con-

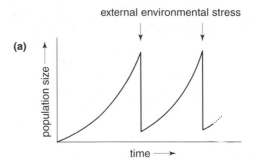

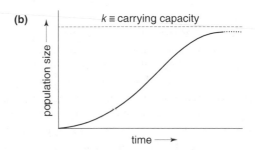

Figure 5.5 The exponential and logistic population growth curves.

ditions but a cold spell then kills off most of the population, and the growth curve would begin again from this newly established low size base (Figure 5.8a). This latter event is what happens in temperate latitudes with many annual plants and many insects, the numbers of which increase dramatically over a number of generations during summer then crash with the onset of cold conditions in late autumn and winter. This growth form may be represented by a model based on the exponential equation given earlier: $\delta N / \delta t = rN$, but with a definite limit on N. Population size is *controlled externally* by the environment.

With the sigmoid curve, the population also begins to increase relatively slowly then accelerates, but accelerating only to a particular point; the rate of growth subsequently decreases and the growth curve eventually flattens out, hence the characteristic S shape (Figure 5.8b). Here the population is *responding* to the environment rather than being controlled by it, as was the case with the J-shaped growth form. What the population responds to is the *carrying capacity* of the environment, which is the maximum population size that the environment can sustain without degradation of that environment through overuse. The population controls itself: as the carrying capacity is approached, environmental 'resistance' increases, and *internal control*, or *population regulation*, begins to operate. This growth form is generally associated with longer-lived species, and regulation can be achieved in a number of ways. Fewer individuals may (be allowed to) reproduce, for example; sexual maturity might be deferred; seed/egg productivity per individual may decline; or seedling/juvenile mortality might increase.

Once a more-or-less equilibrium level is reached at (or more commonly, to give a safety margin, somewhat below) the maximum density that does not exceed the carrying capacity, the population size is maintained. Changes in population size will still take place, whether by chance increases in mortality, for example through disease, or as the carrying capacity itself fluctuates according to long-term weather and climatic changes, flooding, geotectonic events, and so on.

The sigmoid growth form is characterised by a simple logistic model:

$$\frac{\delta N}{\delta t} = rN.\left(\frac{K - N}{K}\right)$$

where K is a constant representing the upper asymptote of the sigmoid curve (Figure 5.8b), i.e. the carrying capacity or equilibrium level.

The sigmoid curve of the logistic model is, in a sense, conditioned by density, i.e. it is *density-dependent*. This contrasts with the J-shaped curve, which is *density-independent*. This contrast, in turn, has been used to distinguish between two life history strategies.

5.3.5 Life history strategies: *r* and *K* selection

Some organisms look very similar from birth to adult form, superficially changing only in size. Grasshoppers, for example, hatch as *nymphs*, which have a morphology that resembles the adult except for size and a lack of reproductive organs. Apart from growth there is little visible change as the various nymphal stages proceed,

each stage (*instar*) moving to the next via a moult, which sheds the external chitin-based skeleton (*exoskeleton*) until the adult form is reached and the internal organs have developed to include those associated with reproduction (Figure 5.6a). The young stages not only look like the adults, they also live in the same habitat and eat similar food. Such insects, which include some primitive wingless orders and some secondarily wingless parasitic taxa as well as more advanced groups such as the Orthoptera (grasshoppers and crickets), are known as *exopterygote* insects, the term reflecting that the development of wings takes place outside the body.

In contrast, *endopterygote* insects have young (in which the wing buds develop internally) that differ in appearance and often in habitat and environmental requirements compared with the adult form. Eggs hatch into *larvae*, which again may go through a number of instars but then enter a resting (*diapause*) phase in a protective case as a *pupa* or *chrysalis*, during which the body is essentially rebuilt, the adult (imago) emerging in a completely different shape and with equally different internal organs: *metamorphosis* has taken place (Figure 5.6b). A familiar example is the change from caterpillar through pupa to adult butterfly or moth.

The nymphal or larval stages of insects may live in completely different environments to the adults. Young mayflies, stoneflies, dragonflies, caddis flies and alder flies, for example, live in water and have feeding and breathing apparatus (gills) appropriate to such a medium. The final

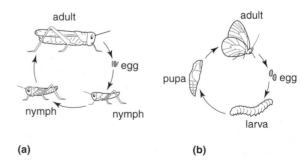

(a)   **(b)**

Figure 5.6   Life history of (a) a grasshopper (an exopterygote insect); and (b) a butterfly (an endopterygote insect).

juvenile stage eventually emerges from the water, the nymphal skin splits and the adult emerges into a terrestrial/aerial environment. Adults then move away to feed (although short-lived mayflies do not feed and have no mouthparts) and reproduce. Eggs laid, the cycle recommences.

Such intraspecific age-dependent differences in life history are seen in other animal groups. Amphibians, for example, demonstrate similar tactics, for example the eggs of frogs and toads laid in water to hatch as tadpoles, which eventually metamorphose into adults, which, possessing lungs, require a terrestrial environment (although they can hibernate beneath the water surface). Plants, too, show some degree of developmental differentiation between the seedling, the pre-reproductive plant and the sexually mature specimen: contrast the relatively soft-stemmed newly germinated oak, horse chestnut or pine with the woody juvenile phase, where emphasis is on rapid growth, and with the more slowly growing, flowering and seeding mature specimen.

Other differences in life history link reproductive strategy with population dynamics. The previous section, for example, contrasted the exponential curve resulting from density-independent population growth and the logistic curve representative of density-dependent growth. Populations demonstrating traits characteristic of the former may be said to be r-selected; those reflecting the latter are called K-selected.

The idea of r and K selection has been extended to incorporate a number of features associated with life history, the origin of this approach lying in the observation by Dobzhansky (1950) that natural selection in the tropics appears to operate in a rather different manner to that in temperate regions. Dobzhansky noted that much of the mortality under temperate conditions is independent of population size, mass winter kills in particular being characteristic of many animals. (While Dobzhansky focused on animals, the same is largely true of plants). In the tropics, however, where climatic conditions are relatively constant, mortality tends to be associated with individuals with poorer competitive abilities that therefore do not acquire resources appropriate in

quantity or quality that would enhance their chances of survival. Selection in temperate zones thus often favours quantity of offspring at the expense of quality, massive egg or infant mortality, rapid growth and massive more-or-less simultaneous mortality of adults. In the tropics, however, lower fecundity and slower growth serve to increase competitive ability, with parents producing lower numbers of higher-quality offspring and putting more investment (especially time and energy) into them to increase their chances of survival.

McArthur and Wilson (1967) first used r and K selection to distinguish the underlying nature of such differences. It is important to emphasise that the temperate versus tropical distinction is oversimple, for there are very many examples of r selection in the tropics, and *vice versa*. It is equally important to stress that 'pure' r selection does not exist, since this would assume no competition, no density effects and no environmental constraints (until the 'kill' factor is introduced); nor does pure K selection exist. Indeed, it is more useful to consider organisms as being placed along a sort of r–K continuum rather than in one of two discrete groups.

Nevertheless, it is instructive to generalise and simplify some of the characteristics of the r and K ends of the continuum (Table 5.2; Pianka, 1970). Pianka suggests that terrestrial vertebrates appear to be relatively K-selected, while most insects, and perhaps terrestrial invertebrates in general, are relatively r-selected. It is probably more useful, however, to make comparisons within rather than between major groups such as these. In mammals, for example, bats, primates (including humans) and ungulates (including horses, pigs, deer and cattle) are K-selected, and rodents are r-selected. Within the arthropod phylum, which includes the insects, one might contrast the usual short life of many species with the longer and more competitive lives of such taxa as the periodic cicadas (with their 13- or 17-year life cycle) and part-aquatic species such as dragonflies, where nymphs might live for a number of years before emerging as adults.

The notion of r and K selection can be extended to plants. A constrast is evident between the rapid growth and massive production of

Table 5.2   Some correlates of *r* and *K* selection (after Pianka, 1970)

	r selection	*K* selection
Climate	Variable and/or unpredictable	Fairly constant and/or predictable
Habitat	Often temporary or disturbed	Permanent, undisturbed
Mortality	Often catastrophic, density-independent	Density-dependent
Population size	Variable in time, non-equilibrium. Usually well below the carrying capacity of the environment. Unsaturated communities. Re-establishment each year	Fairly constant in time, equilibrial. At or approaching the carrying capacity of the environment. Saturated communities. Recolonisation unnecessary
Intra- and interspecific competition	Variable, often weak	Usually strong
Selection favouring	1. Rapid development 2. High r_{max} 3. Early reproduction 4. Small body size 5. Semelparity 6. Weakly competitive	1. Slower development 2. Lower reproductive threshold 3. Delayed reproduction 4. Larger body size 5. Iteroparity 6. Competitive
Longevity	Short, usually <1 year	Longer, usually >1 year
Leads to	Productivity	Efficiency

small, low-quality seed by many so-called weed species (groundsel, for example, producing 1000–2000 seeds per plant, shepherd's purse 3500–4000 seeds per plant – see Section 5.2.2) and the lower number of high-quality, protected seeds of, say, a horse chestnut (*Aesculus hippocastanum*) or coconut (*Cocos nucifera*).

Life history characteristics may also be linked to those of habitat. In temporary or disturbed habitats such as fields or small shallow water bodies, plants and animals that have short life cycles with early reproduction and high fecundity will succeed, while organisms possessing the opposite traits would find it difficult to do so. In the former case, the ability to disperse and colonise transient habitats, grow and reproduce in a short period of time, and produce vast numbers of spores, seeds, eggs or live young is an adaptive trait. Never mind that the quality of the propagule is not high: the important thing in order to survive is to pump as many potential offspring into the world as possible in the hope that even chance dispersal will permit some to survive in another perhaps short-lived habitat

patch. Such *r*-selected organisms are also usually eurytopic – possessing a built-in tolerance of a wide range of environmental conditions, which reflects either *genotypic breadth* (genetic breadth and mutability), *phenotypic adaptability* (in which the individual or population can adjust its morphology or behaviour to adapt to particular circumstances within constraints set by the genotype), or both.

K-selected organisms gear their life history to environments that possess (relatively) scarce resources. Maximum population size reflects carrying capacity and competition, and reproduction can be deferred or the reproductive rate reduced when times are harsh and competition pronounced. Even in favourable conditions, success is density-dependent. Once carrying capacity is approached, births – or at least the production of new reproductive individuals – cannot be allowed to exceed deaths. Mortality rates can still be high among the young (although not as high as with *r*-selected species, even proportionally), and not all adults may be able to breed.

5.3.6 Threshold population sizes

The ideas behind r and K selection have practical implications for human activities. It is important, for example, to know about the life history strategies of commercial fish in order not to overharvest. Many rare and endangered species of conservation interest are K strategists, which has serious implications for both *in situ* protection and captive breeding programmes when numbers (and genetic variability) are low. And many weeds and pests are problematic not so much because of what they do as by how many of them are doing it – the fact that population size is so great and/or rate of reproduction is so high. Plants and animals are often perceived as being weeds or pests only when a threshold population size has been exceeded. This is examined in Section 5.4.2.

The smaller the population the greater the risk of its extinction. If the population is dispersed, there may be a problem of actually finding a mate. Marsupial moles (*Notoryctes typhlops*) for example, live in the Australian desert. Resources are scarce, and each mole tends to have a large home range. Encounters between males and reproductively receptive females are therefore unpredictable and not especially common. Living in a precarious environment as they do, anyway, survival of a population of this species is therefore made all the more difficult. (Life gets even more difficult for the male: on completion of mating a rush of hormones places so much pressure on his body that he has a heart attack and he dies, but this reduces competition within the local area for its scarce resources, so his offspring have a greater chance of using them and therefore his genes have a stronger chance of surviving in the next generation.)

With dispersed populations, the sex ratio becomes very important since if, unlike the marsupial mole, males can mate on a number of occasions during a breeding cycle it is the number of females, each of which by definition can breed only once during that cycle, that will determine the opportunities for population replacement or even growth. In turn, the number and proportion of young that are themselves female become critical for long-term survival of the population. The capacity of a population to survive is thus tied in with number, time to sexual maturity, age structure and sex ratio. The proportion of a population that is capable of reproduction is called the *effective population size*.

Other risks to a small population come from dangers inherent in a small gene pool. The smaller the range of genetic material the more likely it is to be eroded (lost as it is transmitted from one generation to the next) without the influx of new genetic material via in-migrating organisms, or by a high rate of mutation. With a reduced gene pool, the greater the chances of a female being fertilised by a closely related male sharing a high proportion of the same genetic code. In such circumstances, it is all the more likely that *recessive genes* will be contributed by both parents and be expressed in the genotype and phenotype of the offspring. Recessive characteristics are often deleterious and maladaptive, thereby reducing the fitness of the offspring, i.e. their ability to survive and to reproduce successfully. In this way, an already low population number is reduced yet further and the problem becomes even more acute. This consequence of a limited gene pool is called *inbreeding depression*. It is particularly a risk in variable environments, since genetic uniformity (*homozygosity*) or, more likely, strongly reduced genetic variability (low *heterozygosity*) will lead to fewer phenotypes (the physical expression of the genotype, as outlined in the previous section) and therefore a lower chance of individuals succeeding by adapting to a changed environmental situation.

Genetic isolation can also lead to locally adapted races or *ecotypes*, which may be unable to breed with neighbouring ecotypes. Such reproductive isolation may indeed be the initial stage of *speciation*.

If these are dangers associated with low population sizes and low heterozygosity, then it follows that there must be a minimum size above which, other things being equal, the viability of the population is secure. Establishing the size and structure of such minimum viable populations has been the concern of many of those working with rare and endangered plant and animals, and this is complemented by the concern to establish minimum viable areas in which organisms can live and reproduce successfully.

There are a number of successes in conservation, however, based on breeding from a relict population of very few individuals. Numbers of the Chatham Island black robin (*Petroica traversi*), for example, had plunged to a mere five individuals by 1980, when conservation managers began a rescue programme, removing robin eggs to be incubated by species of tit and in this way raising up to three clutches from a single pair each season rather than just one. Today, there are around 200 robins on two islands in the Chatham Island group, 850 km east of New Zealand, all actually descended from a single pair of birds. The population is extremely inbred, yet it is clearly thriving, and indeed just over 70% of young survive to the fledgling stage, compared with 42% for their mainland congenerics, the bush robin (*P. australis*).

Density and size are clearly key features in the success or otherwise of populations. As well as overall density, so too is the degree of *aggregation*, i.e. the extent to which organisms 'clump' together in response to local differences in habitat, as a consequence of daily or seasonal changes in weather, as a result of reproductive requirements, or (in animals) as a result of social attraction. Aggregation may increase competition for resources, but this may be outweighed by increased survival of the group. The level of aggregation that results in optimum population growth and survival varies with species and environmental conditions. A lack of aggregation as well as overcrowding can be deleterious and limiting to the population. This is known as Allee's principle (Allee, 1931).

5.3.7 Species interactions

The Allee effect, on the other hand, occurs where an animal population has a disproportionately low rate of increase or recruitment when its density is low, or certainly below a critical threshold. This may reflect the situation described above, where mates become difficult to find. In some circumstances, it might be that a resource can only be exploited by a population at or above a critical number. Often numbers are kept low because of interspecific competition or predation.

A parallel effect is seen with plants.

Both competition and predation can be intraspecific, the latter being *cannibalism*. They also commonly occur as interspecific interactions. Odum (1971) neatly encapsulates a range of two-species population interactions by using combinations of the signs:

0   where there is no significant interaction;
+   where growth, survival or other population attributes benefit; and
−   where growth, survival, etc. are inhibited.

Table 5.3 summarises most of the key interactions.

One must take care in using and interpreting this schema, however. For example, in the case of predation the table is misleading for density-dependently regulated populations. Clearly, an individual predator benefits from eating a prey (+), and the individual prey does not (−), since it dies and loses the opportunity to transmit its genes. However, numbers of some prey populations are suppressed by predation. Removal of predation thus leads to a population explosion in the (former) prey population, which then runs the risk of overexploiting its own environmental requirements, particularly food, leading to a population crash. In practice, such events are rare (see Section 5.3.8), but where they occur then clearly Odum's signs are inappropriate: for density-dependent populations *at the population level*, it is beneficial for both predator and prey that predation takes place (+ +) and is mutually disadvantageous (− −) where it does not.

Another exception to Odum's use of (+ −) for predation comes from organisms that *need* to be eaten. The blood flukes discussed in Issues Box 4.1, for instance, need to be eaten by their intermediate host, freshwater snails. Similarly, *parts* of organisms may need to be eaten for that organism's success: nectar is produced by plants as a reward for their pollinators, and seeds may be dispersed having been excreted by animals that have consumed the surrounding fruit.

5.3.8 Functional and numerical responses

In the short term, an animal coming across a rich source of food can adjust its behaviour to eat the

Table 5.3   Two-species population interactions (after Odum, 1970)

Type of interaction	Species 1	Species 2	Nature of interaction
1. Neutralism	0	0	Neither population affects the other
2. Interference competition	–	–	Direct inhibition of each species by the other
3. Exploitation competition	–	–	Indirect inhibition when common resources are in short supply
4. Amensalism	–	0	Population 1 inhibited, 2 not affected
5. Parasitism	+	–	Population 1 (parasite) generally larger than 2 (host)
6. Predation	+	–	Population 1 (predator) generally smaller than 2 (prey)
7. Commensalism	+	0	Population 1 (commensal) benefits while 2 (host) is not affected
8. Protocooperation	+	+	Interaction favourable to both, but Is not obligatory
9. Mutualism	+	+	Interaction favourable to both and is obligatory

same amount as before but at a faster rate and therefore in a shorter time, or it can eat at the same rate but eat for longer and therefore eat more, or adopt a combination of the two. Given a range of prey items it might demonstrate selectivity, for example preferentially eating the larger items, more nutritious items, items present at greater density, or items easier to find and handle. Generally, less time and effort will need to be spent in feeding than in times of fewer riches, saving energy, decreasing the time the animal may be exposed to environmental risks (including the risk of itself becoming a food item), and increasing time available for other behaviours such as mating.

The relationship between an organism's feeding rate and food density reflects the consumer's *functional response*. Holling (1959) classified these reponses into three types:

1. **Type 1 functional response** (Figure 5.7a) – feeding rate increases to a maximum level in a linear manner in response to an increase in food density, then remains at this maximum even where food density continues to increase.

This is not a particularly common response. Rigler (1961) experimentally demonstrated that water fleas (*Daphnia magna*) consumed yeast cells in a Type 1 fashion, the animals

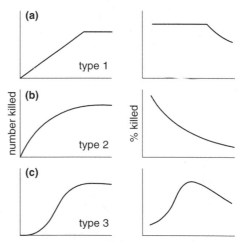

Figure 5.7   Types 1, 2 and 3 functional responses: the number and percentage of prey killed per unit time by a single predator are graphed against density of prey.

filtering out the cells at a rate directly proportional to the concentration presented to them via a constant flow of water, up to 10^5 cells ml^{-1}. Above this concentration, however, the water fleas were simply unable to consume any more food, so the rate of feeding remained constant and maximal.

A somewhat more common version of the Type 1 functional response is one in which, once again, feeding rate responds in a linear manner to increased food concentration, but the maximum rate is never achieved. This is found in a number of herbivores, for instance, where – as the biomass (i.e. availability) of food increases – the animal simply eats more rapidly, usually via larger mouthfuls rather than as an increase in the number of mouthfuls per unit time (Figure 5.8). In such situations in nature, the amount of food

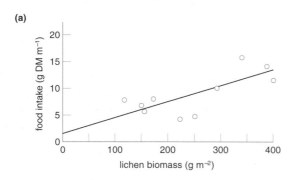

(a)

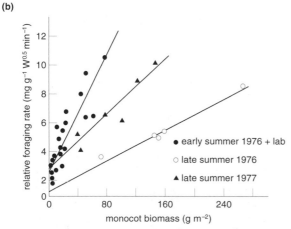

(b)

Figure 5.8 Type 1 linear functional responses of two herbivores: (a) reindeer feeding on lichen; (b) brown lemmings feeding in cotton grass/sedge communities.

is never so high that a ceiling on feeding rate is reached.

2. **Type 2 functional response** (Figure 5.7b) – feeding rate increases with food density but gradually decelerates until a ceiling is reached at which rate of consumption essentially remains constant even if food density continues to increase. This is the most commonly found response.

This response reflects a combination of the *search time* of feeding organisms, which is the time taken by predators in finding and pursuing a prey, and *handling time*, which is the time taken in capturing and consuming a prey item. Handling time might also incorporate digestion, which releases space in the gut for further ingestion of food. The greater the density of prey the easier it is to find and so search time decreases. Handling time for each prey item, however, remains the same, so handling takes up an increasing proportion of the total feeding time of the predator. At very high prey densities, the predator spends minimal time (effectively, perhaps, no time) in search and spends essentially all its time handling the prey, so consumption rate becomes maximal: the animal simply cannot handle any more prey.

3. **Type 3 functional response** (Figure 5.7c) – this is similar in operation to the Type 2 response, but the response to increasing availability of food at lower densities initially shows a geometric increase, i.e. there is an accelerating phase in the rate of consumption. Consumption rate then slows down to become linear and finally, as with Type 2, becomes constant and maximal. The resulting curve is sigmoidal. Type 3 functional responses occur when an increase in prey density leads either to an increase in the predator's search efficiency or a decrease in its handling time.

One common explanation for the early accelerating phase is that the predator is in the process of switching from one food type to a preferred type, for example as the population of one prey type is depleted and that of another is perceived as being energetically or

ECOLOGY BOX 5.2

Predator–prey cycles: snowshoe hare and lynx

One well-studied example of a cyclic population is that of the North American snowshoe hare (*Lepus americanus*). Quantitative evidence of this goes back to 1821, when the Hudson Bay Company of Canada began keeping records of skins (pelts) of fur-bearing animals brought in by trappers. These records indicate that the number of hare skins reached maximum figures every 8 to 11 years, the average being 9.6 years, with minimum values showing a similar periodicity. Assuming that trapping success reflected population size, this species thus appears to have a regular population cycle: over about 10 years population peaks are followed by rapid declines to a trough followed by subsequent build-up of numbers to another peak.

Moreover, a similar population cycle was shown by the lynx (*Lynx canadensis*), its peak abundance generally occurring a year or two after that of the snowshoe hare (see figure). Snowshoe hares are a key component of the lynx diet. It is tempting to argue a case for cause and effect, linking the population size of both species as density-dependent numerical responses in the form of coupled oscillations. Thus large hare populations will support a large lynx population, with a year or two delay while the lynx population adjusts to the abundance of food. But increased lynx numbers place greater predation pressure on the hare population to the extent that the hare population crashes. Lynx starve, and they too see a population crash. With predation pressure released the hare numbers begin to increase again, and so the cycle persists. The two populations thus provide negative feedbacks to each other in a density-dependent manner, and a mutually-dependent oscillation in population numbers ensues.

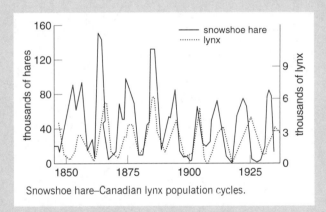

Snowshoe hare–Canadian lynx population cycles.

Except that this is not the explanation. For a start, the cycles cannot present a simple cause–effect pattern, since hare populations also cycle in parts of North America where there are no lynx. Also, while the hare is indeed the lynx's main source of food where both are present and the hare is abundant, the hare is also preyed upon by other predators, and the lynx, too, has other sources of food, so we are not looking at a simple two-species predator–prey interaction. All we can say is that lynx numbers track those of the hare.

Moreover, the decline phase in the hare cycle is associated with low birth rates, low juvenile survival, low growth rates and pronounced loss of body weight in adults. These are characteristics that are associated with food shortages, and there is evidence of less forage being available during periods of peak hare abundance, especially during winter, suggesting a degree of overgrazing. Furthermore, heavy grazing triggers an *induced response* by the plants whereby they produce higher levels of *secondary compounds* (see Ecology Box 5.1) as chemical defences, which make the herbage and browse unpalatable if not actually toxic to the hares. This is probably the most critical part of the story, all the more so given that the high levels of secondary compounds remain in the plant for two or three years after being triggered by the heavy grazing. This leads to a time lag of around 2.5 years between the decline in the hare population and the recovery of the food supply when the secondary compounds return to low levels. Such a time lag being about a quarter of a 10-year cycle is what would be predicted using simple models of delayed density-dependence.

Linking population dynamics with food chains, we have therefore moved from the suggestion that the predator (lynx) population drives the prey (hare) population, which in turn affects the extent to which vegetation would be grazed, an attribute of community dynamics known as *top-down control*, to the idea that the decline and recovery of the hare population is driven by vegetation, and the predators (not just lynx) simply track the hare cycle, a process known as *bottom-up control*. This is shown in the figure below, where yet another interacting species is shown: ruffed grouse (*Bonasa umbellus*) are particularly preyed upon when the predator-to-hare population ratio is high and other sources of food are sought.

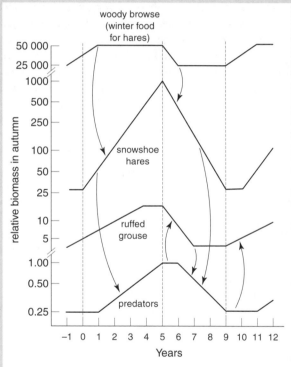

Fluctuations in the relative biomass of woody browse, snowshoe hares, ruffed grouse and predators during a 10-year cycle in Alberta, Canada. Arrows indicate major causative influences.

nutritionally more profitable to pursue or as being easier to find and capture. Switching is a behavioural response to the perception of changes in *relative* density of more than one prey type, while functional responses reflect responses to *absolute* density. Nevertheless, in nature, the two are often closely associated.

Functional responses are readily examined using single predator–prey associations. Most predators, however, are polyphagous, consuming more than one species of prey, although at any one moment there may well be such a preference that only one prey type is sought. Likewise, most prey species are consumed by more than one predator. Functional responses may therefore be less clear-cut in nature.

Herbivores and omnivores also demonstrate functional responses. Cattle and sheep in lush pasture will have a low search time, although in mixed sward they do show food preferences and avoidances, but on the whole they need only lower their heads to graze. Nor do the forage plants require much handling in terms of 'capture', although the digestion process in ruminants – chewing the cud, where the food is regurgitated internally and redigested to extract as much energy and nutrients as possible from the cellulose – does consume time and needs to be incorporated into handling time. Search time for such animals, however, increases in open rangeland, and their non-domesticated equivalents on prairie and savanna grassland may have to roam considerable distances to find appropriate grazing, so search time can be substantial. Dietary specialist herbivores, for example fruit and nectar eaters, will certainly have to travel and search. Handling time, too, can be substantial for some herbivores, for example in breaking through the physical defences of plants that produce spines, rind and shells as protection for their fruit or seed.

The different kinds of functional response affect population dynamics. Where consumption rate accelerates as prey density increases, as happens at low density levels in Type 3 responses, then feeding response is density-dependent: prey individuals at higher densities are more likely to be consumed than those found at lower densities. Such a negative feedback will tend to stabilise the population dynamics of both components of the predator–prey interaction. The reverse is also true, so if the feeding rate declines as food density increases (Type 1 as the ceiling is reached, all Type 2, and Type 3 at higher densities) we find inverse density-dependence, which will tend to destabilise the population dynamics.

Functional responses thus reflect adjustment of feeding behaviour in relation to the availability of food, but changes in food availability can also have longer-term impacts on population size and growth rate. For example, if food is more readily available breeding animals become, in one sense, fitter, more offspring may be produced, and the chances of offspring surviving – other things being equal – become greater. Population size increases. These longer-term impacts on populations are known as *numerical responses*.

5.3.9 Population cycles: extrinsic and intrinsic factors

Population levels fluctuate in response to changing environmental conditions. Favourable conditions lead to a higher carrying capacity and allow an adjustment of population size through higher rates of survival: the population grows. Less favourable environmental conditions have the opposite effect. This is density-independent population regulation, driven by *extrinsic* factors. Some environmental conditions, for instance weather, fluctuate seasonally, and the population also exhibits a cyclic pattern as a response, but this pattern is not controlled by density, and it remains a density-independent phenomenon.

Some oscillations in population size, however, are driven by *intrinsic* factors characteristic of the population itself, including density. Populations do not live in an environmental vacuum, so in practice they respond to both extrinsic factors such as weather, food and availability of safe sites, and intrinsic factors such as density, nutritional state and genetic structure. The interaction of extrinsic and intrinsic factors is shown for brown lemmings (*Lemmus sibiricus*) in Figure 5.9. Oscillations may exhibit such regularity that the term 'population cycle' seems appropriate. Population cycles of two or more species can interact as coupled oscillations, although the mechanisms by which this is achieved may not be as simple as might first appear (see Ecology Box 5.2).

Population cycles are evident in several mammal species, including microtine rodents

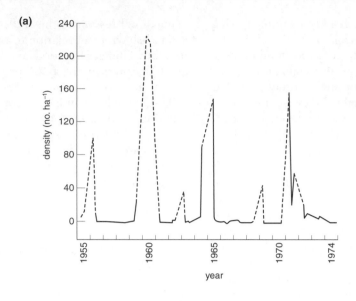

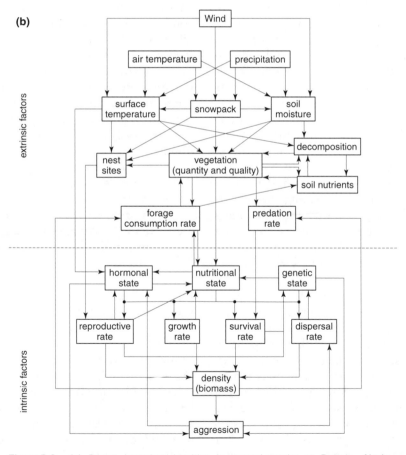

Figure 5.9 (a) Brown lemming densities in coastal tundra at Barrow, Alaska, 1955–74; (b) interaction of factors influencing population dynamics of lemmings.

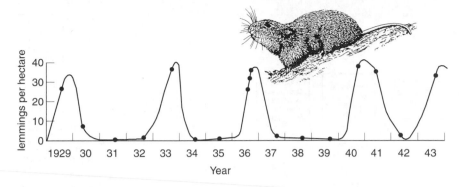

Figure 5.10   Changes in the number of collared lemmings (*Dicrostonyx*) in northern Manitoba, Canada, from field estimates and trapping data (from Shelford, 1943; 1945).

(those belonging to the subfamily Microtinae) such as voles and lemmings. Every three or four years, in the tundra of both North America and Eurasia, lemming species reach high population levels only for numbers to crash after a short period. Figure 5.10 shows this for Richardson's collared lemmings (*Dicrostonyx groenlandicus* var. *richardsoni*) in Manitoba and Figure 5.9 for brown lemmings in Alaska. Brown lemming populations peak and crash within a year. Numbers build up rapidly during late winter and early spring and reach a peak in May, when breeding ceases. Lemmings are herbivores, and huge amounts of grass and sedge are consumed. In spring and summer, however, many lemmings are themselves consumed as prey. Numbers thus fall dramatically, and the population indeed remains low for a further two or three years before, once again, it rises rapidly to a new peak. The cycle is therefore not symmetrical in terms of changing numbers.

It is difficult to disentangle the various factors contributing to such pulses in number, and indeed any one species is not necessarily cyclic throughout its distributional range; nor are different cyclic species in a region necessarily cyclic at the same rate or time as each other. The amplitude of a cycle (the difference between maximum and minumum numbers) can vary over two or three orders of magnitude, but the periodicity tends to be fairly regular. Other characteristics include the fact that, during periods of early populaton increase, most individuals have both a high reproductive rate and a high rate of dispersal, while during periods of high but declining numbers most individuals have a low reproductive rate and dispersal is limited (Warkowska-Dratnal and Stenseth, 1985).

One driving force behind microtine cycles could be food, in terms of quantity (biomass) and/or quality (nutritional value). If grazing pressure increases, recovery of plant tissue cannot keep pace with consumption. Plant nutrients and energy resources can also be exhausted by bouts of flowering, fruiting and seed production, so small mammals find dwindling supplies of poorer-quality food. Induced responses can add to these problems by making herbage unpalatable or even toxic. Nutritionally deficient animals become prone to parasites and disease and are even more readily caught by predators. The population thus crashes, but this then allows the vegetation to recover. This is certainly a plausible explanation for population cycling (Figure 5.11). One criticism is that experimental food supplementation has failed to prevent the population decline phase, but this could simply be the result of predators being attracted to the better-fed populations from neighbouring non-supplemented prey populations.

The idea of nutrient quality lies behind another possible explanation. Schulz (1964) proposed that shortage of phosphate and other mineral nutrients could adversely affect the reproductive success of microtines. But plants, too, become nutrient-depleted and could be nutrient-limited and, after eating, the lemmings release nutrients back into the soil via urine and faeces. Thus, while intensive

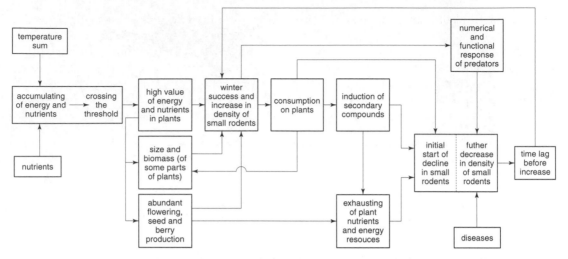

Figure 5.11 A conceptual model of the generation of microtine population cycles in northern Fennoscandia.

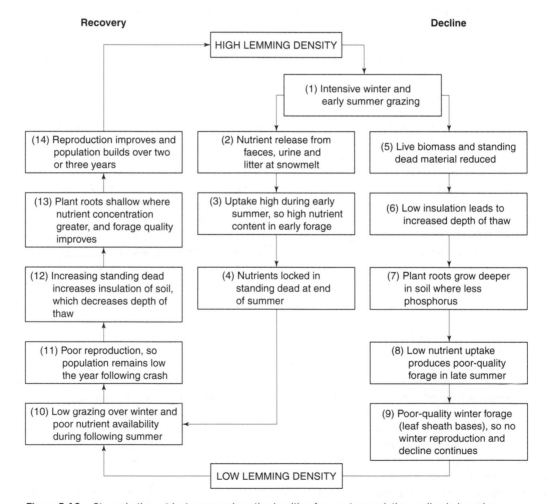

Figure 5.12 Stages in the nutrient recovery hypothesis with reference to population cycling in lemmings.

grazing would lower plant biomass it also provides nutrient supplementation via excreta. The low biomass would contribute to lowered lemming numbers via starvation or debilitation, but the nutrients added to the soil when lemming numbers were high would be stored in the uneaten plant tissue (standing crop). These nutrients would then help in the renewed growth of the plants, which after a while would allow lemming numbers to increase once again. Possible interactions and consequences are shown in Figure 5.12, which illustrates what has become known as the *nutrient-recovery hypothesis*, which goes some way towards explaining cyclic increases and declines in populations of such rodents.

Another set of arguments focuses on intrinsic factors: population cycles might be driven by changes in the proportion of aggressive and non-aggressive individuals, strong dispersers and weak dispersers, and high- and low-reproductive individuals in any one population. Such changes affect density. It might be that individuals are non-aggressive to close relatives but aggressive to unrelated individuals; aggression is thus commonest when numbers are high and there are high rates of dispersal and a consequently greater number of interactions between non-related animals.

Dispersal is an integral part of lemming population dynamics and can often involve large numbers. These irruptions, however, are *not* of hunger-crazed animals blindly seeking new sources of food, pausing at no obstacle and suicidally jumping over cliffs: this is myth (Ecology Box 5.3).

Recent work along the northern coast of Siberia has drawn together many of these ideas focusing on the population dynamics of Arctic foxes (*Alopex lagopus*) and their main prey, lemmings – chiefly Siberian lemming (*Lemmus sibiricus*), with collared lemming (*Dicrostonyx torquatus*) next in importance (Angerbjörn *et al.*, 1999). The numerical responses of foxes to changing *Lemmus* densities showed a lag of one year, but litter size in foxes showed no such lag, with a relatively simple linear relationship – more lemmings, larger litter size. There was no evidence of a numerical response to change in *Dicrostonyx* density. The functional (dietary) response of Arctic foxes followed a Type 2 curve for *Lemmus* but a Type 3 curve for *Dicrostonyx* (Figure 5.13). The authors conclude that, as *Lemmus* specialists, Arctic foxes probably increase the amplitude and frequency of the lemming population cycles, but for *Dicrostonyx* the foxes behave as generalist predators, which dampen but do not drive population oscillations.

5.4 Issues in environmental management

5.4.1 Fisheries management

5.4.1.1 Surplus yield and maximum sustainable yield

Fish are a renewable resource. Successful fisheries management lies in finding an answer to the question of how many fish can be taken without destroying the stock. More precisely, how can the harvest of fish biomass be maximised without impairing the option of exploiting the fishery again in the future? How can one most efficiently harvest the surplus yield?

Every ecosystem has a carrying capacity – the number or biomass of organisms with their particular resource requirements, usually of food, that the system can support. Seas, lakes and rivers are no exception, and there will therefore be an upper limit on how much biomass of fish they can support. Figure 5.14 indicates some of the responses of this biomass to particular harvesting events, where the carrying capacity is the upper limit of biomass, B_∞.

Starting from maximum biomass (although in reality the fish stock would be unlikely to have reached this level) we can imagine a situation where the fish would be heavily harvested (point *A*) but allowed to recover, and after a while the harvested biomass is replaced through growth of the remaining fish, natural increase, and perhaps also in-migration. The recovery curve is often sigmoidal, but it need not be. At *B*, the fish are harvested once more, in this instance not as heavily as before, which is less profitable:

ECOLOGY BOX 5.3

The Norway lemming

Scandinavian legend tells of armies of lemmings descending every few years from the hills to invade farmland, consuming entire pastures and destroying crops. Blind to obstacles they fall into wells, contaminating the water. Many die. Their decomposing bodies cause giddiness and disease among the farming community. Driven by a terrible compulsion they march unstoppably onwards, across rivers and ravines, over cliff faces and, should they survive all this, suicidally swim out to sea.

Other stories (for that is all they are) tell of the spontaneous generation of lemmings from 'foul matter' in the clouds, falling to earth in thunderstorms and heavy rain. Similar tales come from North America. Many Inuit, for example, considered that lemmings were extraterrestrial: their name for one species translates as 'creatures from outer space'.

It is easy to see how such stories came about. In most years, lemmings are little seen. During winter and early spring they tunnel and build nests under the snow, living as individuals or small family groups off underground parts of plants where they can and emerging as little as possible. With snowmelt many tunnels risk flooding and the animals come to the surface, but again they tend to spend time in shallow tunnels on higher ground or at the base of dense vegetation. In peak years, however (see text), the high density of animals means that clustering inevitably occurs, and groups are forced to come together by virtue of limited food resources and local topography. Although lemmings are aggressive towards non-related individuals, the continued accumulation of animals becomes so great that they do sometimes form swarms, which move rapidly from site to site. In such high numbers and with such great activity lemmings inevitably come to the attention of the local human inhabitats. The relatively sudden appearance of large numbers of dispersing animals gives rise to the stories of spontaneous birth, descent from the heavens and suicidal migration.

The first known representation of lemmings, from Olaus Magnus, *Historia de gentibus septentrionalibus* (1555).

The earliest known illustration of lemming swarms is shown in the figure. This is a woodcut in *Historia de gentibus septentrionalibus* (*History of the northern people*), written by Olaus Magnus in 1555. The illustration shows lemmings falling from the sky, indicates a migration inland and alludes to the high predation suffered by the rodents by cats and other predators.

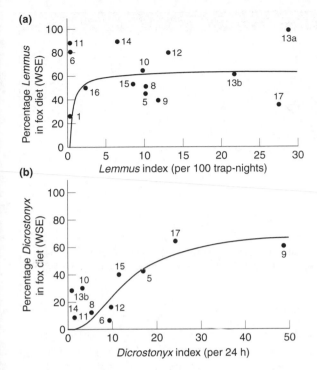

Figure 5.13   Functional response of Arctic foxes to different population densities of (a) *Lemmus* and (b) *Dicrostonyx*. A Type 2 curve is fitted for (a), Type 3 for (b).

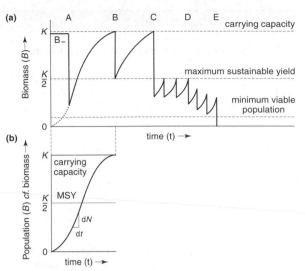

Figure 5.14   (a) Theoretical scenario of biomass/population change with different harvesting strategies. For explanation of A–E, see text; (b) the logistic curve to show that MSY is at $\frac{K}{2}$. After harvest, point A, the curve representing biomass recovery, is equivalent to the upper two-thirds of this logistic curve.

if recovery time is much the same following a heavy harvest (A) as a lighter one (B) it makes some sense to fish heavily.

From point C, the diagram shows a series of regular, frequent harvests. Biomass fluctuates between the indicated levels, and the fish population is not allowed to approach the carrying capacity. However, this is sound fisheries management, since the fishery is exploiting that part of the S curve that shows the maximum rate of biomass regeneration, the point at which one gains the *maximum sustainable yield* (MSY) (Issues Box 5.2). However, at *D* the harvests become too frequent and are at levels too high for the fish stock to recover, until the minimum viable population threshold is exceeded: numbers are too low to sustain the population, which therefore crashes.

From the biological and ecological point of view, the best fishery strategy is one that provides the maximum sustainable yield – the biomass should not exceed the MSY shown on Figure 5.14. MSY will vary spatially and through time, as well as for fish stocks of different species and age structures, because the growth rate of the fish population and the carrying capacity of the environment will vary depending on seasonal and inter-annual environmental variations.

Up to a point, older fish tend to be more fecund. Also, as fish get older they get bigger, and continue to do so. This is why age structure is important in understanding how biomass changes through time. One could harvest the same biomass by catching many small (or young) fish or fewer large (old) fish. By capturing young fish, however, one would be depleting part, at least, of the future potential breeding stock. Generally, therefore, only larger fish should be caught, and this means using wider-meshed nets.

Fisheries management must take into account economic as well as ecological and biological factors. Fisheries incur costs as well as earn revenues. Also, revenue and yield do not have a linear relationship, since

- low fish stocks will be costly to catch therefore expensive to sell; sales are unlikely to be high

ISSUES BOX 5.2

Surplus yield and dynamic pool models

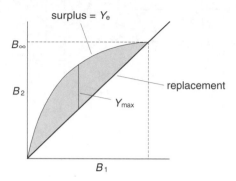

Biomass at two successive time units plotted against each other to show the basis of the surplus yield model. The system is in equilibrium when the quantity of biomass harvested equals the surplus. At some level of growth between 0 and B_∞, the rate of production of surplus biomass becomes maximal (i.e. Y_{max}).

Two main kinds of model can be constructed to predict maximum sustainable yield:

- **Surplus yield models**, where population *processes* are ignored, and changes in *population size* are critical. The figure shows a standard surplus yield model. B_1 and B_2 represent fish biomass at two different times, for example B_2 may be the biomass one year after B_1. The replacement curve is the line representing an exact replacement of biomass, i.e. the amount gained equals the amount harvested. Any surplus lies 'above' this line (i.e. surplus of B_2 over B_1), shown by stippling on the diagram. When the quantity of biomass harvested equals the surplus, then the system is in equilibrium, because at the end of year 2 (B_2) the same biomass remains as at the start of that year (or end of year 1). However, at some level of growth between 0 and B_∞, the *rate* of production of surplus biomass becomes maximal (Y_{max}), shown on the figure by the line of greatest 'distance' between the replacement curve and the curve showing the excess of B_2 over B_1. This is equivalent to the steepest slope on the sigmoid curve in Figure 5.14.

- **Dynamic pool models**, in contrast, consider the different components of growth and population dynamics leading to changes in fish biomass production. Fish biomass can increase by there being more fish of the same size (i.e. an increase in numbers), or the same number of fish of greater size (i.e. an increase in growth or growth rate), or – as is usual – a combination of the two. In simple terms,

$$B_2 = B_1 + (R + G) - (M + F)$$

where

B_1 and B_2 = biomass of the stock at the start of two successive time periods
$\quad R$ = recruitment of new individuals $\Big\}$ adds to stock biomass
$\quad G$ = tissue growth
$\quad M$ = natural mortality $\Big\}$ reduces stock biomass
$\quad F$ = mortality from fishing

because of the high price, so the fish becomes unprofitable to harvest; and

- high fish stocks can be a glut on the market, with prices so low that, in a different way, the fish again become unprofitable to harvest.

Fisheries management thus has to take current and predicted prices, the number of fishing vessels in rival fleets, and the location and fishing effort of such competition into account. Fish have been viewed in the past as common property resources (see Issues Box 4.4), hence the use of quotas, and the need for international regulatory measures on species, stocks, methods of fishing, mesh size and location.

5.4.1.2 The Law of the Sea and international regulatory measures

Certainly by the late 1950s and early 1960s, many fleets were competing in the open seas, especially in the Pacific, where American, Japanese and Soviet trawlers often covered the same waters. Most national claims on coastal waters had previously been more than 4 nautical miles (n.m.). It was Iceland that first declared an Exclusive Economic Zone of 12 n.m., leading to the 'cod wars' with the UK, the latter eventually conceding Iceland's rights (which were extended to 50 n.m. in 1972), and indeed the UK subsequently using the same arguments itself. In the 1960s, too, it became important to divide the North Sea into areas over which particular countries had economic rights as oil and gas exploitation indicated a new source of wealth from the ocean floors.

To regulate fisheries and other oceanic resources, including minerals, the *UN Convention on the Law of the Sea* was signed by 159 nations in 1982. This gave all coastal countries the right to control exploitation of marine resources within 364 km (200 n.m.) of their coasts. By the 1990s, over seventy nations had claimed such rights for fishing. A number of major fishing countries, however, including the USA, UK, Germany and the former USSR did not ratify the treaty, preferring to set wider oceanic limits (Coull, 1993; FAO, 1992; Mather and Chapman, 1995).

5.4.2 Weed and pest control

5.4.2.1 Perception, satisfaction and decision making

The idea of environmental tolerance to potential weed and pest species, introduced in Section 5.2.2, ties in with the notion of ecosystem stability examined in Section 3.3.1. Numbers of a particular species may become so high that they alter and perhaps destabilise an ecosystem, but if

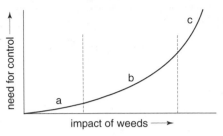

Figure 5.15   Decision making on weed control. In zone (a), weeds are present but it is not worthwhile taking control measures. In zone (c), the need for weed control is high, whatever the economic cost. Zone (b) represents where at some point the farmer will probably decide to effect control measures; the closer to zone (c) the greater the need and the more expensive control probably becomes.

no damage is done to human enterprises then they cannot be thought of as being weeds or pests. Economic tolerance is a rather different situation that can be illustrated by considering the decisions that, say, a farmer would have to make as uncontrolled weed numbers increased. Figure 5.15 shows how at low plant numbers (zone a) the farmer may not even view it as a weed, and certainly it would not be worth the farmer's while to incur costs in order to control the low numbers. As numbers of the plant increase, however, there comes a point (zone b) where some control is needed if the farmer's crop is to have an acceptable yield or show an acceptable profit. As weed numbers increase, and the adverse impact on the crop increases (zone c), so it becomes imperative for the farmer to do something. The point at which the farmer decides to exercise control measures depends not only on what options are available, their cost and their effectiveness but also on the farmer's perception, knowledge, judgement, profit orientation and level of satisfaction (since maximising profits might require more time or input costs than the farmer is prepared to spend). Thus we have *zones* b and c rather than *points* b and c.

Figure 5.15 shows that as weed numbers increase the (potential) damage increases at a geometric rate. Plotting the *effectiveness* of a control measure in relation to costs leads to a sigmoid curve. Purchase of labour, equipment and materials will lead to initial costs, even before these are applied to

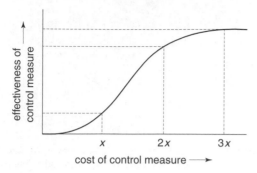

Figure 5.16 Effectiveness of weed control in relation to costs.

the field. Application is then increasingly effective until a point when diminishing returns begin to operate and eventually a plateau of effectiveness may be reached: however much money or effort is thrown at the problem the effectiveness of the control measure has reached a maximum level (Figure 5.16). In practice, therefore, weed (and pest) control lies in reducing *numbers* to below the threshold of acceptable damage. Figure 5.16 shows that the farmer may decide to spend less on control (£x) and merely reduce the weed pressure to gain a satisfactory return, or he/she may wish to spend more (e.g. £2x) in order to get near-maximum returns by suppressing all or most of the weed growth. With diminishing returns on the investment into control measures, however, increasing costs of control (e.g. £3x) are not offset by gains and it is not worth the farmer's while to invest so much. The farmer's decision is thus based on perception and economic goals.

5.4.2.2 *Pest control options – chemical, biological and integrated*

It is important to distinguish between what is feasible and what is practical in the control of weeds, pests and, to an extent, diseases. An appropriate technology might exist, for instance, but be far too expensive to implement, or a chemical might be available but with undesirable side-effects. It is also important to understand what the goals might be of any control programme, from elimination to suppression below what is perceived to be a critical environmental or economic threshold.

Weeds, pests and diseases can often be controlled through:

- *Sanitation*, for example cleaning farm equipment and using weed-free seed.
- Crop or land-use *rotation*, preventing the build-up of nuisance organisms or pathogens.
- Pest insects, in particular, might literally be side-tracked by the use of *trap crops*, which are of preferred but non-economic species planted alongside field crops. An analogous technique with pest insects is to use sexual-attractant scents (*pheromones*) to draw them away from crops or, more usually, towards sites where they can be trapped or chemically controlled.
- *Interference with reproduction* in insect pests can be achieved chemically but can also be undertaken by swamping the environment with artificial pheromones, to confuse or habituate the males so that mating does not occur when a receptive female, pumping out natural pheromones, appears on the scene. Another method is through chemo-sterilisation or sterilisation through irradiation. Many female insects will mate only once. By sterilising males in massive numbers and releasing them into the environment, they mate with females but do not fertilise them. The female will then lay only non-fertile eggs. This method was used successfully, for example, against the screwfly – a major pest of livestock – in southeastern parts of the USA in 1958.
- *Genetic engineering*, through which genes conferring resistance to disease or pests can be incorporated (see Section 6.4.3.2). An example of the latter is where normally smooth leaves and stems of crops are modified to become hairy, and this deters a number of small insect pests, which find movement impaired because of this.
- *Physical control*, which, while often crude and labour-intensive, is nevertheless often highly effective. Pulling up weeds or hoeing are clearly options for weed control, especially against annual plants; perennials with long tap roots tend to be resistant to this kind of disturbance, however, and indeed plant fragments might be spread in this way and the weed problem exacerbated. In some circumstances, flooding, burning and smothering can be used. For pests, trapping and shooting come into

this category, as do such means of moving the problem elsewhere as placing webbing or a gel on ledges of buildings to discourage roosting by birds in towns.

- *Chemical control* was formerly crude and non-target specific, using arsenical compounds for example. There remains a risk that a chemical can accumulate in soil or water or biomagnify through the food chain to become a pollutant (see Section 3.3.2). Increasingly, however, chemicals have been developed that are selective (target-specific) and that break down rapidly in the environment to assume non-toxic forms or remain at non-toxic concentrations. Even so, only about 1% of the chemical hits its target.

  For weeds, advantages include reduction in labour costs (although the chemicals themselves will almost certainly be a major capital investment), non-physical disturbance of the soil or pasture, the possibility of application as a pre-emergent method of control (killing off weeds before the economic plant emerges), and the fact that many perennial weeds are only susceptible to chemical control.

  In both pests and weeds, one major problem is the risk of the development of pesticide resistance on the part of the target organism. The temptation is to increase pesticide dosage and increase frequency of application, but in the long term this becomes self-defeating (resistance can continue to develop), costly and liable to pollute the environment – the 'pesticide treadmill'.

  For pests, chemical control can include poisons, sterilants and taste aversion compounds. Some diseases are also susceptible to chemical control, for example carbon disulphide has been used against *Phylloxera*, which causes the death of grape vines, since 1869.

- *Biological control* is the action of parasites, predators and pathogens in maintaining another organism's density at a lower average than would occur in their absence. This is a density-dependent approach: if the population of the target organism increases so too does that of the control organism, but the aim is to use the control species to maintain a low density of target organisms, i.e. at numbers below the threshold of nuisance value.

Agents of biological control must be target-specific, which essentially means using only the target species – and no other species – for food (monophagy) or as a host. The risk, otherwise, would be for the putative control agent to begin to control non-pest or non-weed species, interfering perhaps disastrously with the environment. One such case is that of the cane toad (*Bufo marinus*), which was introduced to Queensland to control pest slugs in sugar cane plantations. This toad, however, has proved to have a much wider diet than anticipated and has caused major problems in many places in eastern Australia, not least because it produces a toxic secretion that has killed native fauna and domestic pets. A classic example of successful biological control, however, also comes from Australia – the introduction of the moth *Cactoblastis* in order to control prickly pear cactus.

Diseases have sometimes been used as a means of control, for example the myxoma virus, which causes myxomatosis, transmitted by the rabbit flea and introduced to control rabbits.

Predicting the consequences of biocontrol organisms before their release in the field is very difficult. Indeed, fewer than 40% of such introductions against weeds and pest insects result in effective control. With risks to non-target species and the ecosystem as a whole, it is right that great caution is exercised but wrong to lose sight of the initial need for control. Thomas and Willis (1998) suggest some guidelines for increasing the likelihood of success:

- Evaluation studies before control: quantification of the extent to which weeds and pests cause economic damage or threaten biodiversity, which in turn leads to the determination of control priorities and the provision of baseline data.
- Compliance with the FAO Code of Conduct for the Import and Release of Biological Control Agents.
- Improved non-target testing, extending the range of species tested for adverse interactions with the putative control organisms, and

ISSUES BOX 5.3

Some examples of integrated pest management

Rice in Asia

Despite applications of a variety of chemicals, rice production in most parts of Asia suffered as a result of upsurges in diseases and insect pest numbers during the late 1960s. Chemically based strategies were increasingly viewed as ineffective and costly, in particular through outbreaks of insect pests that were actually induced by pesticide application (reduction in numbers of targeted pests leading to release of competitor pressure on other insect species, which then surged in numbers), together with the evolution of insecticide resistance. From the early 1970s, the International Rice Research Institute in the Philippines, in particular, has worked on a number of interlocking strategies for reducing damage and increasing yield. One major approach has been to develop host plant natural resistance, early success coming from resistance to rice brown planthopper and green leafhopper vectors (transmitters) of rice tungro virus. By the late 1970s, research also focused on regulating pest insect population densities by manipulating natural enemies (Kenmore, 1996). Not all Asian countries followed these practices, however. In Indonesia, for example, introduction of dwarf rice varieties in the 1970s (as part of the green revolution) was accompanied by *increased* use of pesticides, a trend that only ended in the late 1980s. Similar trends were also seen in Thailand and Japan (Whitten *et al.*, 1996).

Cassava in Africa

The need for pest management for cassava (*Manihot esculenta*), an important crop introduced to tropical Africa from South America, became apparent during the 1980s as the cassava mealybug (*Phenacoccus manihoti*; also introduced) began to spread rapidly and in huge numbers. A search was made for natural predators of this insect in its region of origin, and a population of cassava mealybug was found in the Paraguay River basin with low numbers and erratic distribution, together with a range of natural enemies, including the very effective parasitic wasp *Epidinocarsis lopezi*, which has now successfully been introduced into Africa. Simultaneously, improvements in cassava cultivation have incorporated plant health management techniques that enhance plant vigour and – partly by the use of disease-resistant strains – reduce the chances of disease. The main form of pest control is thus classical biological control, but cultural and sanitation methods are also important supplementary methods (Herren, 1996).

Bananas in Costa Rica

Monocultural plantations of banana were established on cleared rain forest land in the 1940s and 1950s, and mass application of dieldrin began in 1950 to control the two major pests, the banana rust thrips (*Chaetanaphotrips orchidii*) and the banana weevil (*Cosmopolites sordidus*). By 1960, six species of moth pests had become problematical, despite increased insecticide use, because these pesticides incidentally reduced numbers of many natural predators of these new pests. In 1973, therefore, all insecticide spraying was halted, and within two years most of the pest insects had disappeared because their natural enemies had re-established themselves. The thrips remained a pest, but damage was reduced by covering the fruits with plastic bags. While no further insecticide spraying has taken place, bananas remain susceptible to black sigatoka disease, and (perhaps excessive) use is made of fungicides. Bananas are thus protected by biological control (natural predators), physical control (plastic bags) and chemical control (fungicides).

Cotton in the Canete Valley of Peru

A wide range of insecticides were introduced in 1949, including DDT, BHC and toxaphene, with aldrin, dieldrin, endrin and parathion following soon after. By 1955, many pests of cotton had developed pesticide resistance, requiring heavier and more frequent applications, yet six new species had acquired pest status. There were now at least thirteen serious insect pests of cotton, and yields were actually declining. In 1956, the government banned all synthetic pesticides and reintroduced beneficial insects, which serve as natural predators. Farming practices were also improved, with early-maturing varieties planted and crop residues (which might serve as residues for pests) destroyed. Pest impact was greatly reduced, as indeed were control costs, and cotton yields began breaking records. Substitution of biological and cultural control methods for chemical control was thus efficacious.

quantifying results in the context of the population dynamics of both the biocontrol agent and its target.

- Post-release evaluation, looking at the effectiveness of control; the rate and direction of the spread of the biocontrol organism, and what factors influence this; variation in host selection; interactions with native species; and community consequences, especially in terms of food web interactions.
- Identification of priority control areas and examination of the means of integrating biocontrol with other control methods (see integrated pest control, below).

Target-specificity is a major advantage of this method, therefore, but so too is the fact that the beneficial organisms already exist and will themselves, having been placed in the general environment, seek out the targets. The agents, too, have self-perpetuating populations that adjust in size and distribution according to what is happening to the target organisms. Disadvantages are that initial control might be slow and that it has not always been possible to predict environmental consequences even with rigorous pre-field testing.

One way around the problems of initial slow control is to reduce the weed or pest population rapidly using chemical control and then introduce agents of biological control to maintain low numbers. This introduces the idea of integrated pest control or integrated pest management (phrases that in practice also incorporate weed and disease control), which is based on knowledge of the natural ecosystem and of overall production systems. Losses are reduced by integrating a number of monitoring and control techniques, which tend to minimise use of chemical methods and maximise use of biological and cultural means. Some examples are given in Issues Box 5.3.

5.5 Conclusions

Living renewable resources can only be managed effectively with some knowledge of the biology of the species, an understanding of their population dynamics and an appreciation of their interactions with the environment, yet management decisions can usually only be made on the basis of partial information and a weak ability to predict any outcome. Resource management therefore comes to rely on perception, experience and judgement. Even so, as is evident even with a cursory examination of the problems of ocean fisheries, short-term economics and, not infrequently, politics dictate that precaution is a luxury unappreciated in the marketplace.

Similar conclusions can be drawn in an examination of the control of weeds and pests: however robust the population growth models, however accurate the predictions of the extent to which weeds and pests might affect economic or cultural enterprises, and however full the knowledge is of control options and their likely outcomes, we can never really be certain of the outcome of any strategy, and decisions are inevitably subjectively based.

It is right that certain decisions are taken out of the hands of the user population by law, for example the use of too small a mesh size in ocean fishing and the use of certain chemicals for weed control when the knock-on effects damage the environment. A worrying trend in recent years, however, has been the control exercised by companies that have come to dominate particular enterprises, for example the contractual obligation by some farmers in the USA to buy certain genetically modified crop seeds that contain cross-gene material that inhibits pest activity (see Section 6.4.3.2 and Issues Box 6.3). That the option exists to grow such crops is fine; an obligation to do so, however, is not.

Further reading

Jennings, S. and Kaiser, M.J. (1998) The effects of fishing on marine ecosystems. *Advances in Marine Biology,* **34**: 201–352.
Meadows, D.H., Meadows, D.L. and Randers, J. (1992) *Beyond the limits* (Post Mills, Vt: Chelsea Green Publishers).

QUESTIONS BASED ON CHAPTER 5

Q1. Why is a declining birth rate in itself an unreliable indicator of future trends in population growth?

Q2. How might an animal population reduce its birth rate via internal population controls?

Q3. How might an absence of fishing, a moderate level of fishing and overfishing of a lake affect the species diversity of fish in that lake?

Q4. Give examples of circumstances where a single plant is almost certain to be considered a weed.

Q5. What are the risks of introducing an organism that is a food generalist for the purpose of biological control?

ANSWERS

A1. Because population growth rate also depends on death rate, including child mortality, which reduces the number of future potential fertile members of the population. Other factors that could affect growth rate, although usually much less significant, include the extent of any delay in the onset of fertility (which may be tied in with health and nutrition), any deferral of childbirth (which in humans may be cultural), and changes in the sex ratio (fewer females between menarche and menopause mean fewer births).

A2. Fewer individuals may breed or be allowed to breed, for example limiting reproduction to high-status animals in a hierarchical society with a distinct pecking order. Sexual maturity might be deferred, i.e. males and/or females begin breeding or come into reproductive condition at a later age. Productivity per individual breeder might decline, for example female rabbits and badgers embed the egg in the womb but fertilisation is delayed, so if population pressures are too high fertilisation does not occur at all. Juvenile mortality might increase, for example some parent birds will reduce brood size by ceasing to feed one or more chicks: it is better that one or a few offspring have a good chance of survival than all offspring have a poor if equal chance of doing so.

A3. In the absence of fishing, species diversity will reflect opportunities for arrival, water quality and species interactions. Larger, more nutrient-rich (but not eutrophic) lakes associated with a large watershed will tend to support more fish. If species tend to coexist, species diversity will be higher than if one or a few fish species dominate the waters. Overfishing will at first tend to exploit the larger, more readily caught fish rather than smaller fish with refuge behaviours. Overall, though, and with increasing fishing effort, fish species diversity will tend to drop dramatically, perhaps to zero. Moderate levels of fishing will not overexploit any one species and will tend to retain a balanced age structure so that all species are able to regenerate. If overall moderate fishing effort nevertheless captures large numbers of dominant fish, competitive release might encourage greater species diversity.

A4. Remembering that the status of 'weed' is context-dependent, examples will be appropriate along the lines of a single non-grass species (whether dandelion or daffodil) in a prize lawn, a single non-moss specimen in a moss garden, or a stray unplanted tree in a forest monoculture plantation. Another situation is where the weed species is toxic or dangerous, for example poison ivy or deadly nightshade, but again this is context-dependent.

A5. A food generalist is not target-specific and will therefore almost certainly consume non-target species. It may actually prefer non-target species if these are more abundant, more palatable, easier to find and (in the case of prey) easier to catch. The target species may indeed be avoided altogether. The biocontrol organism may in these ways itself become a pest.

Discussion topics

D1. How have the characteristics of the human population been affected by twentieth-century advances in medicine, agriculture, industry and transport?

D2. In terms of methods of population control, why is it ethically dangerous to view options for humans as being the same as for other animals?

D3. Consider a common species of animal that is not at present perceived to be a pest. What circumstances might change that perception?

D3. Phenotypic adaptability is where the individual or population adjusts its morphology or behaviour to adapt to particular environmental circumstances, within constraints set by the genotype. What examples of phenotypic plasticity are or have been evident in humans?

EXERCISES

E1. Examine the environmental and other factors that favour the outbreak of epidemic diseases. Illustrate this exercise by reference to one human, one animal and one plant disease. What differences and similarities are there between your three examples?

E2. Your local public or institutional library should have copies of census returns going back many years. (In the UK, the records should go back to the first national census of 1801). Collect data for your town or local area that will allow you to construct age–sex pyramids for different periods from the earliest records you can find to the most recent. Describe changes in total population size and in the shape of the age–sex pyramids. Explain these changes in terms of natural growth and migration. How do these population trends for a human population differ from those of other K-selected mammals?

Chapter **6**

Biodiversity and species richness

Summary

Biodiversity is both a political and an ecological buzzword in the post-Rio world, encompassing genetic diversity and habitat diversity as well as taxonomic diversity. Species diversity is closely connected with but distinct from species richness, and in understanding the community characteristics of species assemblages, as well as possible conservation value, it is important to incorporate ideas of relative abundance, in particular characteristics of evenness (equitability). For conservation purposes it is often valuable to identify indicator species and endemic species. Parts of the world of high species richness and high levels of endemism, i.e. biodiversity hotspots, are under threat of habitat destruction or modification and commensurate species impoverishment, and it is here that particular conservation efforts should be made. Conservation has benefited from frameworks established by the World Conservation Strategy (1980) and the Convention on Biological Diversity (1992), among others, although entering the political arena has brought difficulties as well as benefits. Biodiversity action plans are one way in which conservation needs can be identified and goal-oriented programmes initiated and monitored. If the species is the key taxonomic level for most conservation work, then it is important to define just what is meant by a species (the biological species concept), how they evolve (speciation) and the extent to which extinction is a natural process. A number of latitudinal gradients appear to exist in species richness. Climate is a key factor in explaining species richness, but it is not the only one. Different notions of diversity are introduced and the value to conservation of biodiversity indices, biological monitoring and critical fauna analysis (incorporating ideas on complementarity) is exemplified. The importance of genetic resources to conservation, as well as to economic enterprises such as agriculture, is stressed, and some implications of genetic engineering are explored.

6.1 Biodiversity and species richness

This chapter examines different ways of approaching one of the political as well as ecological buzzwords of the post-Rio world, 'biodiversity', and explores some of the implications of this concept to conservation. In doing so, ideas relating to species richness and geographical distribution are also considered, and comments are made on one way in which genetic diversity has been increased, via genetic modification.

Biodiversity, a contraction of 'biological diversity', is often thought of as equivalent to *species richness*, which is the total number of species present in a defined area. Biodiversity, however, encompasses much more than this. First, it is a term that can be used to reflect not only species diversity but diversity at higher taxonomic levels such as families and orders, so *taxonomic diversity* is a better phrase. It also encompasses *genetic diversity* within a species. And it is also used in the context of *habitat diversity*. It is a convenient if often misused tool in wildlife and environmental conservation, and it has a political resonance following the 1992 Rio Conference, where the Convention on Biological Diversity was one of the major agreements signed by 153 countries.

Even when being used in the context of species diversity, biodiversity can reflect a number of attributes of ecological and conservation importance (Gaston, 1996). Even allowing for problems in identifying just what represents a species (a taxonomic issue) the total number of species present in an area can never be fully known, not least because one would have to include all microorganisms, where taxonomy is often little understood and where problems of finding and identifying all taxa within even a small group would be intractable. In practice, biodiversity measures are usually of readily distinguishable and rather better understood taxonomic groups.

However, even if two areas had an identical number of species in a particular taxonomic group, for example birds or vascular plants, they would be unlikely to have identical faunas or floras. Most obviously the species themselves would probably be different, although there might be considerable overlap, but even were the species to be identical it is likely that they would be present in different proportions, and it becomes useful to introduce the idea of *evenness* or *equitability*. These ideas are important in ecology because different proportions of different species with different environmental requirements will have different impacts on community and ecosystem functioning. They are also important to conservation, because some species may be endangered, or may be endangering other components of the community. Also, some individual species may be critical to the survival of a particular community – *keystone species*, which are discussed more fully in the next chapter. Not all species, therefore, are of equal significance in a community – whether in terms of number or function – although it may not be appropriate to adopt the view that any species is redundant.

For conservation purposes, many ecologists have been trying to identify *bio-indicator species* – species whose fate reflects that of their community and ecosystem and which may be viewed as barometers of environmental health (see Section 6.3.3) – environmental health rather than environmental change, because not all environmental change is unnatural or undesirable. Nevertheless, it is clear that much environmental change resulting from human activity is deleterious, and bio-indicators provide a means of monitoring such an impact.

Also, communities can remain more or less identical, yet the species content can vary from year to year, as shown in Figure 6.1. where the bird communities of urban open spaces change in species content within such a time scale, or over longer periods, as evidenced on many islands. This phenomenon is known as *species turnover* (see Section 8.3.5.3).

Two other phenomena are explored in this chapter: the extent to which latitudinal and other environmental gradients exist in species richness; and the notion of *endemism*, a term used to describe the limited geographical distribution of a taxonomic group, usually at family, genus or species level. Endemic taxa may have very specific ecological requirements that are found in only a few places; they could be evolutionarily 'young' and not yet have had the time or opportunity to spread out geographically; they could be

relict species, whose range has contracted over geological time from a formerly much wider distribution; or they might have been adversely affected by human activity, so that their current distribution does not reflect their natural range. Their limited geographical range and often small populations mean that endemic species are often endangered and therefore of great conservation interest. And conservation value is often enhanced by the fact that a high number of endemic taxa often – although by no means always – coincides with a region of high taxonomic richness.

6.2 Key environmental issue: the conservation of biodiversity

6.2.1 Priorities in protecting biodiversity and the importance of endemics

Despite the caution just urged about distinguishing between biodiversity and species richness, the latter being just one expression of biodiversity, the fact remains that at regional and global scales it is to species richness that we have to turn for analysis and comparisons because this is the only indicator of diversity for which – at least for some taxonomic groups – adequate data are available. The first thing to stress is that species diversity is not evenly distributed.

As a very general rule, species richness increases with decreasing latitude, i.e. there tends to be more species in a given area in the tropics than in temperate regions, which in turn are more species-rich than polar regions. As another generalisation, more species are found per unit area at lower than at higher altitudes. These trends do not always hold for individual taxonomic groups. Latitudinal, altitudinal and other environmental gradients are examined more critically in Section 6.3.2.

Areas of high species richness *and* a high level of endemism are clearly areas of high conservation value, and they are often referred to as *biodiversity hotspots* (Reid, 1998). Many such

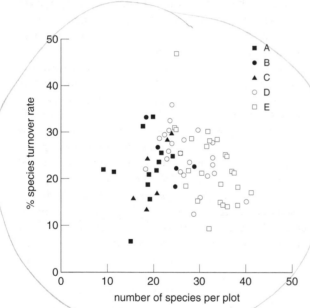

Figure 6.1 Bird species annual turnover rates of plots in relation to number of species per plot and to habitat type in Berlin. A: block buildings; B: highrise buildings; C: industrial zone; D: residential zone; E: parks and cemeteries. Thus block buildings tend to have few species but with various rates of turnover. Parks and cemeteries have more species, again with a variable turnover rate, one park with 24 species having a turnover rate of nearly 50% i.e. nearly half of the bird species seen one year would be replaced by other species the next.

Table 6.1   Numbers of endemic species in eighteen hotspots

Region	Higher plants	Mammals	Reptiles	Amphibians
Cape Region (South Africa)*	6300	15	43	23
Upland western Amazonia	5000	n/a	n/a	70
Atlantic coastal Brazil	5000	40	92	168
Madagascar	4900	86	234	142
Philippines	3700	98	120	41
Borneo (northern)	3500	42	69	47
Eastern Himalaya	3500	n/a	20	25
SW Australia*	2830	10	25	22
Western Ecuador	2500	9	n/a	n/a
Colombian Chocó	2500	8	137	111
Peninsular Malaysia	2400	4	25	7
Californian floristic province*	2140	15	15	16
Western Ghats (India)	1600	7	91	84
Central Chile*	1450	n/a	n/a	n/a
New Caledonia	1400	2	21	0
Eastern Arc Mts (Tanzania)	535	20	n/a	49
SW Sri Lanka	500	4	n/a	n/a
SW Côte d'Ivoire	200	3	n/a	2
Total	50255	375	892	737

Note: all regions are classified floristically as tropical forest except (*), which are of mediterranean climate floras.
Sources: Myers (1988; 1990); World Conservation Monitoring Centre (WCMC) (1992).

hotspots are experiencing pronounced levels of habitat alteration or modification, making their conservation value even greater. Myers (1988; 1990) has identified eighteen such hotspots, fourteen in tropical moist forest and four in mediterranean climate regions. Together, these hotspots contain over 50 000 endemic vascular plant species, or around 20% of the world's total plant species (Table 6.1).

By concentrating on these hotspots, conservation effort would be put into areas where the needs are arguably greatest and where the pay-off from safeguarding these sites would also be greatest. This is particularly important given that resources, including money and personnel, are never going to be sufficient to put equal effort into all threatened regions, and it is a way of prioritising effort and maximising effectiveness (Vane-Wright *et al.*, 1992).

If endemism follows similar geographical patterns for different taxonomic groups, then conservation measures in areas of high endemism will have even greater effectiveness for any given input of effort or resources. Table 6.1 shows that, using Myers' eighteen hotspots, there may be some broad similarities between different vertebrate and plant taxa, but there are also a number of differences. For example, the Colombian Chocó region has high numbers of endemic plant species (*c.* 2500), reptiles (137) and amphibians (111) but only eight endemic mammal species. Similarly, the Cape of Good Hope region has the highest number of endemic plant species (6300) but only fifteen endemic mammals.

Statistically, however, countries with high numbers of endemics in one vertebrate group tend to have high numbers of endemics in other vertebrate groups, with especially high correlations between numbers of endemic mammals and birds, and of mammals and reptiles (Table 6.2).

Table 6.2   Rank order of countries richest in endemic land vertebrates

Country rank order	Mammals		Birds		Reptiles		Amphibians	
					Numbers of endemic taxa			
1	Australia	210	Indonesia	356	Australia	605	Brazil	293
2	Indonesia	165	Australia	349	Mexico	368	Mexico	169
3	Mexico	136	Brazil	176	Madagascar	231	Australia	160
4	USA	93	Philippines	172	Brazil	178	Madagascar	142
5	Philippines	90	Peru	106	India	156	Ecuador	136
6	Brazil	70	Madagascar	97	Indonesia	150	Colombia	130
7	Madagascar	67	Mexico	88	Philippines	131	India	110
8	China	62	New Zealand	74	Colombia	106	Indonesia	100
9	former USSR	55	Solomon Is.	72	Ecuador	100	Peru	87
10	Papua NG	49	India	69	Peru	95	Venezuela	76
11	Argentina	47	Colombia	58	Cuba	79	Cameroon	65
12	Peru	46	Venezuela	45	South Africa	76	Zaire	53

Source: WCMC (1992).

However, by considering countries rather than the smaller geographical regions of Table 6.1, an area effect becomes an important variable, since larger countries such as the former USSR, China and the USA tend to have larger numbers of species and indeed larger numbers of endemic species in each taxonomic group. The taxonomic richness of Brazil owes a great deal to its tropical moist forest, but the area effect must also be a factor here as well. Similarly, Australia's large endemic fauna owes much to its long geological isolation, but once again its very size must contribute to its species richness.

Prendergast *et al.* (1993) analysed data from the UK mapped on a 10 km × 10 km grid to examine the extent to which species-rich areas for different taxa coincided, and whether species-rich areas contained proportionately greater numbers of rare species. No strong support was found for either proposition, with the greatest overlap in hotspots among five taxonomic groups being 34%. Even so, if it were possible to protect every species-richness hotspot designated for birds in the UK (the 5% of grid cells with greatest species richness), then 87% of birds, 100% of butterfly species and over 90% of dragonflies, aquatic plants and liverworts would be included (Williams *et al.*, 1996).

6.2.2 The World Conservation Strategy and the Convention on Biological Diversity

The need to conserve the world's biological diversity was explicit in the World Conservation Strategy of 1980 (see Section 2.4.2), which had three main objectives: to maintain essential ecological processes and life-support systems; to preserve genetic diversity; and to ensure the sustainable utilisation of species and ecosystems. The second of these thus anticipates the concern for biodiversity that has so dominated conservation a decade later. The strategy included a map of the priority terrestrial biogeographical provinces for the establishment of protected areas, although criteria were largely those of threat and lack of the then current provision rather than species richness (Figure 6.2).

The need to conserve genetic diversity was made again in 1992 in the context of the Convention on Biological Diversity signed at Rio. The 153 signatories indicated a commitment to protecting diversity and using it in a sustainable manner. Protection, in other words, was combined with an acceptance that opportunities could still be sought for exploitation, an outcome that could be viewed either as rational

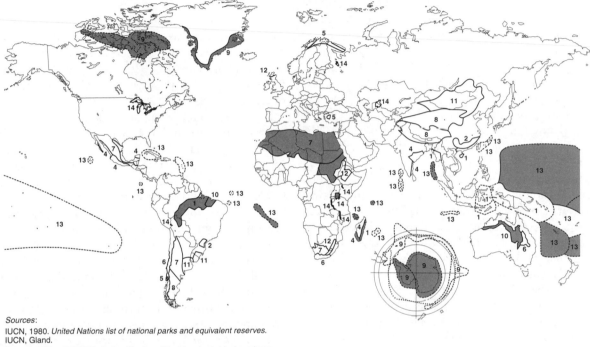

High priority: biogeographical provinces with no national parks or equivalent reserves.

Priority: biogeographical provinces in which national parks or equivalent reserves protect a total area smaller than 1000 km² (or smaller than 100 km² in the case of oceanic island provinces).

1. Tropical humid (rain) forests.
2. Subtropical and temperate rain forests.
3. Temperate needle-leaf forests.
4. Tropical dry or deciduous forests (including monsoon forests).
5. Temperate broadleaf forests (including subpolar deciduous thickets).
6. Evergreen sclerophyllous (mediterranean-type) forests.
7. Warm deserts and semideserts.
8. Cold-winter deserts and semideserts.
9. Tundra and barren arctic desert.
10. Tropical grasslands and savannas.
11. Temperate grasslands.
12. Mixed mountain and highland systems.
13. Mixed island systems.
14. Lake systems.

Sources:
IUCN, 1980. *United Nations list of national parks and equivalent reserves.* IUCN, Gland.
Udvardy, Miklos D.F. 1975. *A classification of the biogeographical provinces of the world.* IUCN, Gland.

Figure 6.2   Priority biogeographical provinces of the land for the establishment of protected areas.

and pragmatic or as compromise and expedient. Even so, the USA did not sign at the time, largely because it did not want any conflict with patent rights for the commercial exploitation of biodiversity (especially genetic diversity) for biotechnology.

Specifically, Article 1 stated that the objective of the convention was

the conservation of biological diversity, the sustainable use of its components and the fair and equitable sharing of the benefits arising out of the utilisation of genetic resources, including by appropriate access to genetic resources and by

appropriate transfer of relevant technologies, taking into account all rights over those resources and to technologies, and by appropriate funding.

National autonomy was guaranteed. Article 3 stated that

States have, in accordance with the Charter of the United Nations and the principles of international law, the sovereign right to exploit their own resources pursuant to their own environmental policies, and the responsibility to ensure that activities within their jurisdiction or control do not cause damage to the environment of other States or areas beyond the limits of national jurisdiction.

6.2.3 Biodiversity action plans

The convention itself is perhaps bland and open to different interpretations: for example, there is no consensus on any distinction between 'principle' and 'obligations and rights'. Like Agenda 21, which has been devolved to national and local levels (LA21 – see Section 2.4.2), the Convention on Biological Diversity has of necessity (given the need for national autonomy) been adopted to a greater or lesser extent by the signatory countries and, again, encouragement has been given for the production of county, borough or local biodiversity action plans (BAPs), sometimes explicitly within the context of LA21, often in their own right.

There thus exists a comprehensive strategy for the United Kingdom – *Biodiversity: the UK Action Plan* (Department of the Environment, 1994). This was produced following consultation between wildlife experts and government officers. For example, in December 1993 the Royal Society for the Protection of Birds, Worldwide Fund for Nature, Wildlife Trusts, Friends of the Earth, Plantlife and Butterfly Conservation together published a major discussion document (*Biodiversity challenge: an agenda for conservation in the UK*) as an *input* to the final UK action plan, with a much enlarged second edition emerging as a *response* to the UK action plan in 1995 (Wynne *et al.*, 1995).

Subsequent publications have focused on assessment and issues of implementation, for example, *Biodiversity assessment: a guide to good practice* (Jermy *et al.*, 1995), Volume 1 of which is *UK resources as a contribution to global biodiversity assessment*, while Volumes 2 (plants and fungi) and 3 (animals) are practical manuals aimed at field use.

The 1994 UK action plan emphasised the need for an integrated policy reflecting a variety of interests, which were brought together in a steering group that, in 1995, identified the need for around 400 action plans for the UK's most threatened species and 40 plans for the country's most vulnerable habitats. These action plans have been published in three volumes. An example of the standard layout is shown for the nightjar (*Caprimulgus europaeus*) in Issues Box 6.1.

Together, the action plans will be the core response by the UK for a national BAP.

The underlying hypothesis is that, if minimum standards for the provision and appropriate management of particular habitats are introduced, then the 'health' of the UK environment will be ensured: there will be a rich and sustained mixture of habitats, which in turn will hold a rich and varied set of species, and protection measures aimed at endangered species should, incidentally but importantly, also protect the commoner species. In other words, the UK's biodiversity – habitats and species – will be at least maintained and probably enhanced. It is also important that procedures are put in place to monitor the success of any measures.

At the regional level, one example is the BAP for Birmingham and the Black Country, which emphasises that even conurbations contain species and sites of value to wildlife that make an important contribution to regional and national biodiversity. Predominantly built-up areas, however, do have characteristics and problems perhaps not evident in predominantly rural areas. The approach is hierarchical, the overall BAP comprising BAPs for 'classic habitats' such as woodland, heathland and wetland and for characteristically 'urban habitats' such as public open space and wasteland. In turn, individual BAPs are presented for indicator species, for example bluebells (*Hyacinthoides non-scripta*) for woodland, orchids (*Dactylorhiza* spp.) for urban wasteland, and the black redstart (*Phoenicurus ochruros*) for the built environment. Interestingly, the regional plan also contains BAPs for 'issues' such as site and species protection, species and habitat management, biological records and environmental education. The framework for both the local species and the local habitat action plans closely follows that of the national scheme indicated in Issues Box 6.1.

6.3 Ecological concepts

- Taxonomy, speciation and extinction
- Species richness and latitudinal gradients
- Diversity, abundance and evenness

ISSUES BOX 6.1

Action plan for the nightjar, *Caprimulgus europaeus*, in the UK

1   Current status

The nightjar, *Caprimulgus europaeus*.

1.1   The nightjar (see figure) is a summer migrant insectivorous bird whose numbers and geographical range have been in decline during much of the twentieth century. Between 1968–72 and 1992 there was a 52% decline in its range, although by 1992 the population had increased from the low of 1981 (2100 males recorded) to 3400 males. Breeding mainly in southern England, scattered populations exist as far north as central Scotland (see figure). The most important habitats are lowland heath and young forestry plantations. An increase in forestry clear-cuts, together with extensive tree damage associated with strong winds, has aided recent population growth, with >50% of the total population found in this habitat in 1992. In Europe, the species has been declining in numbers and range since at least 1950, particularly in north and north-west parts.

ISSUES BOX 6.1 (cont)

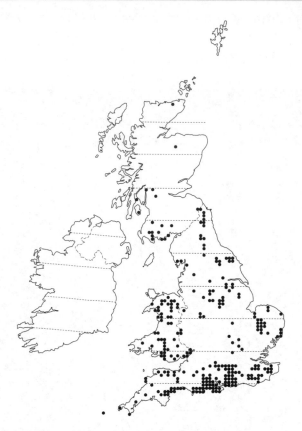

Breeding distribution of nightjars in Britain and Ireland (by 10 km square) (*source:* RSPB, 1992 nightjar survey).

1.2   The nightjar is protected under the Wildlife and Countryside Act 1981 and Schedule 1 of the Wildlife (Northern Ireland) Order 1985, and is listed in Annex 1 of the EC Birds Directive and Appendix II of the Bern Convention.

2   Current factors causing loss and decline

2.1   This century has witnessed a dramatic reduction in the area of heathland in the UK. Some 40% of England's lowland heath has been lost since the 1950s. Where heathland lacks appropriate management it will become unsuitable as nesting habitat due to invasion by shrubs and trees. Nightjars require extensive areas of suitable feeding habitat, especially uncultivated land: loss of such habitats within a few kilometres of the nesting area may result in a decline in numbers.

2.2   A decline in the availability of large insects caused by changes in agriculture and/or climatic change may have affected nightjar populations.

2.3   In commercial forests, nightjars nest on bare ground. If no other suitable habitat becomes available in other new or young stands, local population declines could occur as young plantations mature.

3   Current action

3.1   Detailed research into nightjar ecology has been carried out by the RSPB in Thetford Forest, where Forestry Commission practice now aims at maintaining a constant area of young plantation as nightjar breeding habitat.

ISSUES BOX 6.1 (cont)

3.2   Nightjar have benefited from specific management on some nature reserves and on various heathland management projects.

4   Action plan objectives and targets

4.1   Maintain a population of at least 3400 singing males.

4.2   Halt the decline in range. (There were 268 occupied 10 km squares in 1992.)

4.3   Increase the numbers and range to 4000 singing males in at least 280 10 km squares by 2003 (an 18% population increase and 5% range increase in 10 years).

4.4   In the next 20 years, restore the nightjar to parts of its former range, e.g. south-west England, west Midlands, north-west England, south-west Scotland and Northern Ireland.

5   Proposed action with lead agencies

Objectives and targets to be achieved through protecting, maintaining, restoring and re-establishing lowland heathland and associated foraging habitats; adopting sympathetic forestry management practices; and promoting extensive agricultural systems. Monitoring of population numbers and range.

5.1   **Policy and legislation**: specific targets and appropriate management on Forest Enterprise and Ministry of Defence land. Extension of the Wildlife Enhancement Scheme. Support for extensive farming practices.

5.2   **Site safeguarding and management**: to consider important nesting and feeding sites as Sites of Special Scientific Interest (Areas of Special Scientific Interest in Northern Ireland). Designation of areas of national importance for breeding populations as Special Protection Areas.

5.3   **Further research and monitoring**: national surveys every 10 years. Investigation of availability of food. Evaluate the condition of heathland in the former range, and potential for remedial management.

Source: UK Biodiversity Group (1998)

6.3.1 Taxonomy, speciation and extinction

The *species* is the most commonly used taxonomic level in ecology, but it is important to remember that the species represents just one of a hierarchy of taxonomic units, or *taxa* (see Ecology Box 1.3). It is thus often important to consider both 'higher' levels such as genus, family, order and class, and 'lower' levels such as subspecies, variety and (for domesticated plants) cultivar. *Taxonomy* is a classification system and the study of taxonomic relationships is called *systematics*. The basis of systematics lies in evolution, so that – even if at times we have to go back to the early millennia of life on Earth – there is an evolutionary connectedness between all lifeforms. The evolutionary relatedness of taxonomic units

(*phylogeny*) thus also involves genetics, since it is through genetic material (DNA, chromosomes and genes) that the form of any organism persists from one generation to the next.

Taxonomic classifications have traditionally been based on morphology. In flowering plants, for example, the morphological characteristics of the flower have been the key to distinguishing species, genera and families. Recently, however, other tools and analytical methods have been introduced that suggest alternative evolutionary relationships between taxa. Chemotaxonomy, for example, looks beyond morphology to consider the closeness, or otherwise, of the chemical make-up of organisms. Molecular phylogeny, using DNA sequences, has recently suggested some perhaps counter-intuitive degrees of relatedness, such as in

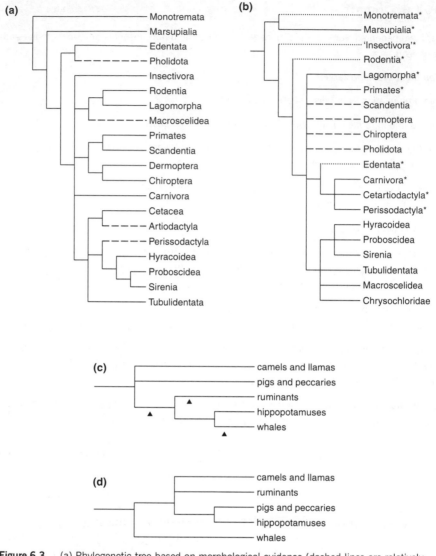

Figure 6.3   (a) Phylogenetic tree based on morphological evidence (dashed lines are relatively ambiguous relationships). (b) Recent developments in mammalian molecular phylogeny. Solid lines are supported by independent, and combined nuclear and mitochondrial sequence data. Dotted lines represent proposals based on concatenated sequences of 12 of the 13 mitochondrial-encoded proteins. Asterisks indicate orders for which complete mitochondrial genome sequences have been published. Dashed lines represent orders where data do not allow firm conclusions. (c) Nesting of whales in the cetacean–artiodactyl clade. (d) DNA sequences from the mitochondrial cytochrome *b* gene strongly support a whale–hippo clade.

mammals where, for example, hippos and whales appear to be more closely related evolutionarily than was previously suspected (Figure 6.3) (de Jong, 1998). *Cladistics* treats the process of evolutionary change as a series of branching events, at each of which a single group divides into two daughter groups. At each dichotomy, one or more of the characteristics of the group (usually morphological) changes from the initial (primitive) state into a derived state. The evolutionary history of the group can then be illustrated using a branching 'cladogram' (Figure 6.4).

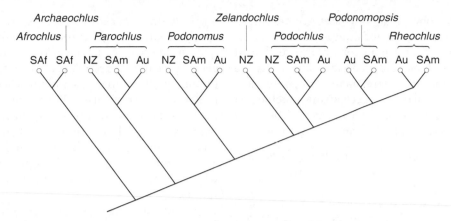

Figure 6.4 Simplified taxon–area cladogram of some of the Gondwana genera of non-biting midges (Chironomidae; Podonominae). The names in italics are those of the genera involved, while the circles represent individual species. The initials indicate the continent in which each species is found: Au, Australia; NZ, New Zealand; SAf, South Africa; SAm, South America. The African genera appear to have diverged first. In each of the other genera, the divergence of the New Zealand species preceded the divergence between the South American and the Australian species.

6.3.1.1 The species and speciation

The biological concept of 'species' relies on the notion that species maintain their identity and genetic integrity because they do not interbreed. This is certainly the norm, but equally clearly there are many exceptions.

Crosses between species (and sometimes between genera) do exist. Many such *hybrids* are infertile, but some are able to reproduce and maintain the hybrid form, and a few are particularly successful in nature. An example is common cordgrass (*Spartina anglica*), a hybrid of the native British small cordgrass (*S. maritima*) and the North American introduction smooth cordgrass (*S. alterniflora*), both plants of salt marshes. The first hybrids were sterile, although they spread vegetatively by the dispersal of small fragments via tidal currents, but the cross underwent an internal doubling of its chromosomes, which had the effect of allowing it to reproduce sexually. This 'new' plant is now by far the commonest cordgrass in the UK and has been successfully introduced in many other parts of the world, especially as a means of stabilising estuarine mud in harbours.

'New' organisms, however, normally evolve through the differentiation or mutation of genetic material, a process known as *speciation*. Most mutations do not persist. Even if they are fertile they are often poorly adapted to the environment and either die without breeding or produce offspring that have a poorer chance of surviving and themselves breeding, so again the mutation will die out, having a lower level of fitness than the original form. Selection leads to the survival of the fittest, *fitness* here being defined in terms of ability to produce viable offspring that will in turn be able to reproduce successfully. The idea behind *natural selection* is that individuals that have favourable genetically derived traits will have more offspring surviving into the next generation, with a similar genetic package that gave the higher fitness in their parents, so this package tends to persist. Fit individuals will thus contribute a disproportionately high number of offspring to future generations compared with their less fit contemporaries, and the genetic make-up of subsequent generations will shift towards the successful genetic package. Natural selection caused by ecological changes or the colonisation of new habitats (often of human origin) plays an important part in adaptive divergence and speciation (Orr and Smith, 1998).

There may come a point where genetic differentiation between different groups leads to *reproductive isolation*, and it might be argued that at this stage we have two species rather than a single one, since they are unable to interbreed. Reproductive isolation mechanisms include a number of situations where gene flow is prevented between species living in proximity:

- **Ecological or habitat isolation** – where taxa are found in the same general area but in different habitats.
- **Seasonal or temporal isolation** – where the mating season, flowering period, etc. takes place at different times of the year.
- **Gametic isolation** – where male gametes (sperm) and female gametes (eggs) are not attracted to each other, or are non-viable.
- **Sexual isolation** – where there is no attraction between different taxa, often because species-specific recognition factors are different (see below).
- **Mechanical isolation** – where there are morphological differences in reproductive parts, e.g. between male and female genitalia, or between pollen and *stigmata* (pollen receptors at the tip of the female sexual organ).
- **Pollinator isolation** – where related plant species have different specialist pollinators.
- **Post-mating isolation** – where hybrids are sterile or have greatly reduced fertility.

Some intraspecific fertilisation occurs by chance, as with wind pollination, where grass pollen drifts across a prairie or pine pollen through the canopy of a coniferous forest, a few grains of which blow on to the stigmata of the appropriate species. Some is directed fertilisation, such as with a bee attempting to mate with a bee orchid (*Ophrys apifera*), which, as its name indicates, mimics the shape of a bee, the insect receiving pollen on its body then transmitting this to another bee orchid. And some fertilisation in animals relies on a specific mate recognition system, which can involve combinations of colour, display, vocalisation and, by the production of sex pheromones, scent. Male courtship in many vertebrates, for example, is often to confirm that a member of the appropriate species is involved as well as to convince a female of the fitness of that particular male.

Allopatric speciation occurs when a new species evolves in geographical isolation from its 'parent' species. If members of a species become geographically separated, it is likely that they will gradually differentiate to a point where reproductive isolation takes place. Put succinctly, extrinsic physical barriers will lead to intrinsic genetic barriers. Natural selection may favour different sets of genotypes in each group, and genetic drift and mutations are also likely to contribute to what will have become a distinct taxon – a new species.

In contrast, *parapatric speciation* is seen when speciating populations share a distributional boundary. This is often the case where a species is found over a wide geographical range in which environmental conditions, for example climate, differs substantially, and where ecotypic differentiation leads not just to differences in tolerance but to reproductive isolation and genetic incompatibility.

Finally, *sympatric speciation* takes place following the evolution of intrinsic barriers to gene flow in the absence of extrinsic barriers, i.e. where there is no geographical separation between the speciating populations. A shift in habitat, host or food preference, however, may lead to reproductive isolation. A particular form of sympatric speciation is seen with *polyploidy*, where there is a mutational multiplication (often doubling) of the number of chromosomes. Such a genetic change is usually fatal in animals, although it is occasionally viable in amphibians, but it is common in plants. In the example given earlier, this is what happened in *Spartina anglica*, which doubled its chromosome number to $2n = 122$ from the parental hybrid, where $2n = 61$. (The $2n$ refers to the fact that sexually reproducing organisms contain two sets of chromosomes, one from each parent, and are therefore diploid; n = number of chromosomes in one set; $2n$ = number in both sets).

6.3.1.2 Extinction

Extinction is (as it were) a fact of life and is a normal part of the changing pattern of life on Earth through geological time. There have been periods when the rate of extinction has increased.

The massive extinctions at the end of the Cretaceous Period, for example, which witnessed the demise of the dinosaurs, may well have been triggered by massive environmental changes resulting from the impact of a large meteor on what is now the Yucatán Peninsula of Mexico. The extinction of many large mammals in the Pleistocene may have been a consequence of the last ice ages and their aftermath, but it has also been suggested that the disappearance of so many animals was the result of overkill by early human hunters.

What is undoubtedly the case is that human activity has been the crucial factor behind the huge numbers of extinctions seen in the last 500 years or so, a global rate of extinction that has almost certainly never been witnessed before. This has been the consequence of direct killing, habitat alteration, inappropriate introduction of species and a whole series of environmental changes, including climatic changes. Estimates vary between ten and 140 species becoming extinct *every day* because of human activities.

Rare species are particularly at risk. By definition, they do not have the population size, rate of reproduction, geographical range or habitat generality to withstand accentuated pressures. Many such species might well be expected to become extinct anyway, without the clumsy hand of humans, but that does not take away our responsibility or blame. But even once common species have been made extinct in recent years through human action. Examples include the passenger pigeon and the heath hen (see Issues Box 6.2).

Reducing the rate of extinction and protecting rare and endangered species have together thus become the key global conservation issue. Local extinctions, too, where a species disappears from a particular region, are important to prevent and have become components of many national plans and legislation.

6.3.2 Species richness and latitudinal gradients

Latitudinal variations in light and temperature are a function of the Earth's tilt and its changing orientation to the Sun in the planet's annual orbit (see Section 1.3.2). In Section 6.2.1, it was noted that, as generalisations, species richness decreases with increasing latitude and altitude, i.e. the closer to the poles and at greater heights the fewer species one tends to find per unit area. Light affects photosynthesis and therefore plant growth, and more plant material can support more animal life. Higher temperatures are also associated with rapid plant growth, although only where there is sufficient moisture. Low latitudes, high temperatures and high rainfall are thus associated with high biomass, but they are also associated with high species diversity and complex community interactions. High latitudes, low temperatures and low availability of water are conditions associated with low biomass, low species diversity and relatively simple communities.

That the tropics are the most species-rich regions on Earth (and this is true of both oceanic and terrestrial ecosystems) is exemplified by the tropical moist forest biome, which covers 6% of the Earth's land surface yet possesses an estimated 70% of all non-microbial land species. It may be that not only are such tropical regions warm and moist but that environmental conditions are also constant, which has allowed the evolution of a greater number of specialist species, including a greater number of co-evolved mutualistic interactions. For example, different species of tree in the tropical forest may flower and fruit at different times of the year, but conditions are such that at any one time animals can find flowers and fruit available. This has allowed the evolution of specialist nectar- and fruit-eating birds and mammals. Such specialist *nectarivores* and *frugivores* cannot exist in seasonal temperate regions, because for part of the year their single source of food would not be available.

It is important to appreciate, however, that species diversity in the tropics (as indeed in any biome, and in any habitat) reflects a number of interacting trends. Species diversity of trees in tropical forests, for example, tends to

- increase with rainfall and decrease with seasonality in mature lowland sites;
- increase with soil fertility in the neotropics (Central and South America), allowing for the

ISSUES BOX 6.2

Passenger pigeons (from millions to Martha) and heath hens (from millions to Martha's Vineyard)

The passenger pigeon (*Ectopistes migratoria*; see figure) was a North American bird that once numbered billions. In the early 1800s, ornithologist Alexander Wilson reported on a flock of over 2 billion individuals migrating in a swathe 386 km (240 miles) long and 1.6 km (1 mile) wide. By 1914, the last passenger pigeon had died.

The passenger pigeon, now extinct. (From J. J. Audubon (1939) *Birds of America* (Royal Octavo edition): Plate 285).

Three related factors led to the extinction of this species. As people moved west into the prairies, natural habitat was destroyed. Equally important was what replaced it: farmland, in particular the cultivation of cereals, meant an abundance of alternative food for this granivorous pigeon, and it was soon perceived to be a pest. Finally, it was good to eat. Sometimes the pigeons would be blasted out of the sky. An alternative was to catch one pigeon alive, sew up its eyes, then tie it to a perch, or stool. Its calling would then attract other birds, which would land beside the 'stool pigeon' – hence the origin of this phrase. In a flocking species such as this, hundreds more birds would land, to be shot or snared.

By 1860, passenger pigeon hunting had become a major commercial enterprise. In 1878, one professional made $60,000 by slaughtering 3 million birds at their nesting grounds near Petoskey in Michigan. Live birds were even used as targets in fairground shooting galleries. Whole roosts were asphyxiated by burning sulphur and other choking material under them.

ISSUES BOX 6.2 (cont)

So great was this persecution that by the 1880s only a few thousand birds remained. This was below a viable population size (see Section 5.3.6) for a species where the female laid only one egg per nest. On 24 March 1900, the last known passenger pigeon in the wild was shot. The last passenger pigeon in the world, Martha, died in Cincinnati Zoo in 1914.

Halliday (1980) argues that the final stages in the decline of this species were too rapid to be accounted for entirely by human persecution and suggests that social factors – colony size and reproductive success – were related in such a way that, even when the species was still relatively common, its breeding rate was insufficient to offset mortality.

A similar tale is seen with the heath hen. Once abundant in the eastern United States, numbers and range declined, as with the passenger pigeon, through habitat alteration and hunting. By the end of the nineteenth century, it had become restricted to Martha's Vineyard in Massachusetts. Although part of this island was made a reserve in 1907, numbers had by then declined to around 100. Nevertheless, protection allowed population growth and by 1916 there were some 800 birds in the reserve. In 1916, however, fire destroyed most of the birds' nesting habitat, and the following winter unusually high numbers of goshawks arrived on the island, preying heavily on the heath hens, whose population crashed to 200. The species became extinct in 1932, probably as a consequence of deleterious genetic effects.

Sources: Miller (2000); Botkin and Keller (1995)

effects of rainfall. In Indonesia, however, it tends to decline at high levels of soil phosphorus and magnesium;

- increase with forest stature but decrease as average tree growth becomes greater;
- increase with rate of tree turnover (or tree replacement rate), and with time since catastrophic disturbance.

Climate is thus a key factor, perhaps the predominant one, in explaining species richness, but it is not the only one. The tropics contain the greatest actual land mass on the planet, and one might simply expect more species in a larger area, but Givnish (1999) proposes that four principal factors interact to determine tree species richness in tropical forests along local gradients of rainfall, seasonality and soil fertility (Figure 6.5). These are:

1. natural enemies – damage by host-specific herbivores or pathogens maintaining plant diversity (Janzen, 1970).
2. forest structure, especially where this affects the degree of shading.
3. seed dispersal, especially by animals, as a form of mutualism (see Section 7.3.2.1).
4. intensity of competition and in rates of competitive exclusion (see Section 8.3.2).

The soils of many tropical areas are nutrient-poor and can actually be nutrient-deficient. The presence of particular plant species in part reflects the availability or otherwise of a particular nutrient or suite of nutrients. Low fertility and nutrient deficiency may prevent any one plant species becoming abundant and dominant, and this diversity in turn might encourage diversity in animal species. Species-rich communities possess many interactions, which in turn provide more opportunities for organisms to find a 'place', or to fill an available niche (see Section 8.3.2). Undisturbed, nutrient-rich soils tend to encourage competitive plants, which possess the ability to acquire environmental resources rapidly and effectively, out-competing less competitive species (see Section 5.2.2). Vegetation therefore becomes dominated by competitive species and as a result tends to be species-poor. The reverse is true: in less fertile soils no one plant or group of plants can dominate, so species richness is greater.

Disturbance is another factor affecting plant species richness. A disturbance factor is one that

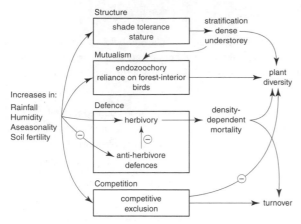

Figure 6.5 Proposed effects of variation in rainfall or effective site fertility on the creation and/or maintenance of woody plant diversity in tropical forests. Arrows indicate positive effects over ecological or evolutionary time, unless marked with a minus sign. The pathway involving defence against natural enemies should play an especially important role in tropical forests; 'herbivory' in this figure refers to the activities of both traditional herbivores (e.g. leaf- or seed-eating insects) and pathogens (e.g. fungi). The pathway involving competition between plants should become more important outside the tropics, favouring maximum plant diversity at intermediate levels of site productivity.

damages plant tissue. An absence of disturbance may allow competitors to dominate. Too much disturbance and species cannot survive, or turnover is very high, and species richness at any one time is again reduced. At intermediate levels of disturbance, however, species richness may be greatest: competitive species are suppressed, yet there is enough environmental stability for species-rich communities to become established. A rich diversity in animal life tends to follow a rich diversity in plant species. High species richness in variable or disturbed environments can therefore be explained by the *intermediate disturbance hypothesis*, but disturbance is unlikely to lead to a latitudinal gradient. One kind of disturbance is fire, which can affect temperate forest, warm temperate (mediterranean) scrub and semi-arid grassland: in all cases species diversity is promoted. Similarly, treefall gaps in *all* forest types are critical for forest regeneration, and in these gaps a number of light-

demanding plant species will grow as well as the regenerating trees, so again species richness is enhanced by disturbance.

Greater community structural complexity means a greater opportunity for specialism, for example in food or habitat, but it also allows a greater number of functional linkages. Plants and animals thus have a constant battle to escape from grazers and predators, parasites and pathogens. There is an arms race in which eater and the potentially eaten evolve characters and character-istics that might give them that extra chance of surviving (see the Red Queen hypothesis, Ecology Box 5.1). This in turn implies sex, because sexual reproduction means a greater mixing of genes and therefore genetic variability, and a greater chance that a particular genetic combination of greater survival value might result. Sexual reproduction does seem to be more commonly found in the tropics, compared with proportionately more asexual reproduction in many taxa of temperate latitudes. More genetic variability, as indicated in Section 6.3.1.1, means greater opportunities for speciation, and in this way species richness might again be enhanced in the tropics.

Currie (1991) argues that regional species richness may be limited by environmentally avail-able energy. Using 336 quadrats covering all of North America (following lines of latitude and longitude $2\frac{1}{2}° \times 2\frac{1}{2}°$ south of $50°$ N and $5°$ ([latitude] $\times 2\frac{1}{2}°$ [longitude] north of $50°$ N), he examined patterns of species richness of mammals, birds, reptiles, amphibians and trees in relation to 21 environmental descriptors. For the vertebrate groups, 80–93% of the variability in species richness was explained statistically by a single variable, annual potential evapotranspira-tion. Tree species richness was more closely related to actual evapotranspiration. Both aspects of evapotranspiration appear to be measures of available energy. Results (Figures 6.6a–d) show broadly latitudinal trends, but Figure 6.7 shows that for birds, mammals and amphibians (but not reptiles) maximum species diversity does not lie at the most southerly latitudes, a result that might be analogous to the intermediate disturbance hypothesis.

Beeby and Brennan (1997: 244) neatly encap-sulate the possibility that

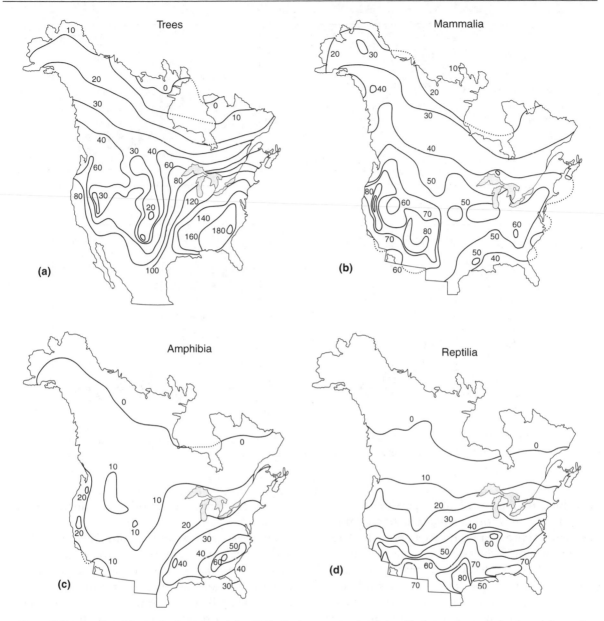

Figure 6.6   Species richness in Canada and the USA. Contours connect points with the same approximate numbers of species per quadrat.

two or three abiotic factors set off a chain of biotic reactions that accentuate the differences between latitudes ... As the community builds, so it serves to amplify the number of opportunities for other species. The contrast between latitudes perhaps follows from this potential for positive feedback, so that adding more species promotes further complexity, supported in the tropics by higher productivity.

6.3.3 Diversity, abundance and evenness

Species richness is simply the number of species present in a community, in some respects a useful value to know but in other respects misleading. One problem is that of taxonomy – being able to distinguish and identify the species in whatever taxonomic group is being studied. Another is

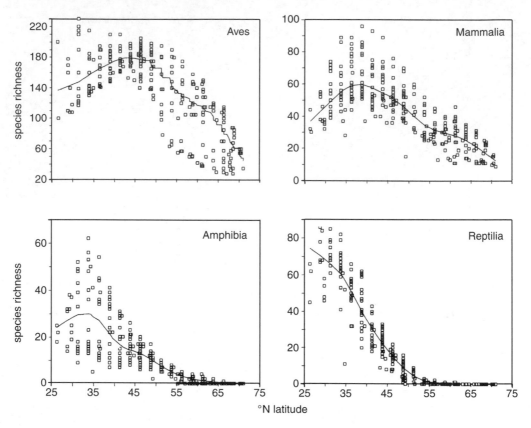

Figure 6.7   Species richness of birds, mammals, amphibians and reptiles in relation to latitude. Birds, mammals and amphibia show a mid-latitude peak in richness.

sampling, because it is rarely possible to explore even a relatively small area and be certain that one has 'captured' all the species present. Another is that species richness can change through time, whether daily, seasonally or interannually. Most importantly, perhaps, species richness alone tells us little about the relative abundance and likely ecological importance of the constituent species.

It is therefore necessary to introduce the idea of *evenness* (or *equitability*) by using the notion of *abundance*. A contrast can be drawn, for example, between two communities, each containing 100 individuals and ten species, but where in one community each species is represented by ten individuals, while in the other one species has 91 individuals and each of the others just one (Figure 6.8). The structure of the two communities is clearly different, one where all ten species are equally represented (showing a high degree of evenness), the other dominated by one species.

Diversity incorporates both species richness and individual species abundance, and a number of *diversity indices* have been used in order to characterise and compare different communities (see Ecology Box 6.1). A useful visual representation of the distribution of species abundance in a community is to rank each species according to its abundance, i.e. the most abundant being ranked 1, the next most abundant ranked 2, and so on, then to plot the proportion of its abundance within the whole community (P_i) against that rank (Figure 6.9). The P_i for the most abundant species is plotted first along the x-axis, followed by the next most abundant and so on until the least abundant species is reached. This produces a *rank–abundance diagram*. In practice, P_i can be the proportional value of each species

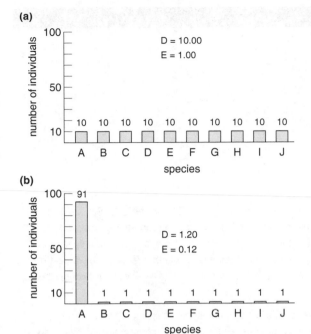

Figure 6.8   Two communities with the same ten species (A–J) but with different indices of diversity (D) and equitability (E), because of differences in abundance.

for number (abundance), cover (for example in the case of plants) or biomass. P_i values are generally plotted along the y-axis using a logarithmic scale. Figure 6.9 shows relative cover values for plant species in abandoned fields of different ages in Illinois. Here, species richness increases with time, i.e. more species will have colonised older fields. Evenness also increases with time: one species is clearly dominant after 40 years, but this curve flattens in the middle parts, showing that there are many species with more or less the same cover values (Bazzaz, 1975).

It is important to distinguish between measures of diversity over different spatial scales:

- **Alpha diversity** (α diversity) is the diversity of species within a habitat or community (local scale).
- **Beta diversity** (β diversity) measures the rate of change in species composition along an environmental gradient (regional scale).
- **Gamma diversity** (γ diversity) measures species diversity across a number of communities (regional or inter-regional scale).

6.4 Issues in environmental management

6.4.1 Biodiversity indicators and biomonitoring

The use of biological indicators (bio-indicators) in ecology and conservation is in its infancy. There is a need to identify features of the environment, usually species or habitat characteristics, that serve as barometers of environmental change. In this way, changes in the population size or geographical range of species, for example, will reflect improvements or declines in environmental quality. Like indices, indicators can be used to characterise communities, but it is important to stress that these are two quite different concepts.

Biodiversity indicators are valuable in monitoring environmental change, although many environmental changes can be monitored using abiotic indicators (Goldsmith, 1991). Monitoring requires the assessment of environmental changes against some standard, target or base level and involves surveillance and measurement of data in such a way that the nature of any change is identified and quantified, and the reasons for any change iluminated (Furness *et al.*, 1993; Greenwood *et al.*, 1995; Hellawell, 1991; Spellerberg, 1991; Usher, 1991).

In order to draw conclusions about the impact of human impact, we need to know what natural variations might be expected, for example in population size or in mean annual temperature. Furthermore, monitoring needs to be undertaken with a clear understanding of its objectives and the selection of key indicators that can be measured appropriately so that, by cutting through 'environmental noise', we finish up with a clear indication of what environmental changes are taking place, why they are occurrring and, ideally, what the management options are for remedial action. Ecosystem management in turn implies knowledge and understanding of the ecological science underpinning the environment.

ECOLOGY BOX 6.1

Indices of diversity and equitability

The simplest diversity index is *Simpson's diversity index*:

$$D = \frac{1}{\sum\limits_{i=1}^{S} P_i^2}$$

where D = Simpson's diversity index
  S = total number of species
  P_i = proportion of total individuals in the ith species

In other words, the index first calculates the proportion of total individuals in Species 1, Species 2 ... Species S. In Figure 6.8a there are ten species, each with the same number of individuals (ten), so the proportion of total individuals in each species is 0.10 (i.e. 10%). In Figure 6.8b, the values are 0.91 for the most abundant species and 0.01 for each of the remaining nine. Each of these values is squared and then added together. D is the reciprocal of this value. For Figure 6.8a, $D = 10.00$ and for Figure 6.8b, $D = 1.20$, the former much greater value reflecting the high degree of evenness or equitability.

Thus for a given species richness, D increases with evenness. Similarly, it can be shown that for a given evenness, D increases with richness. It is possible, however, for a species-rich but uneven (inequitable) community to have a lower diversity index than one that is species-poor but very even.

Equitability itself can be calculated by expressing D as a proportion of the maximum possible value of D were all individuals to be equally abundant (evenly distributed) among the species, as in Figure 6.8a.

Thus equitability,

$$E = \frac{D}{D_{max}}$$

D_{max} is the same values as S; E always has a value between 0 and 1.

Another commonly used index is the *Shannon diversity index*, H, where

$$H = \sum_{i=1}^{S} P_i \ln P_i \quad \text{(where } \ln P_i \text{ is the natural logarithm of } P_i)$$

from which follows: equitability, $J = \dfrac{H}{H_{max}}$

Holdgate (1979) distinguishes between *target monitoring programmes*, which measure actual or potential targets (anything that might be expected to demonstrate change in numbers, distribution or performance) and *factor monitoring programmes*, which measure anything that might cause changes in the environment. Target monitoring can involve abiotic components or biological ones at different scales, i.e. ecosystems, communities, species, populations or individuals. Factor monitoring can also use physical, chemical or biological variables.

For a biomonitor to be useful it must respond in a sensitive way to change in the variable for which it is a proxy, or indirect, measure. The responses must be predictable and easy to measure and monitor, and it should also provide a high signal-to-noise ratio, so that any response is readily distinguishable from natural background variations. The importance of biomoni-

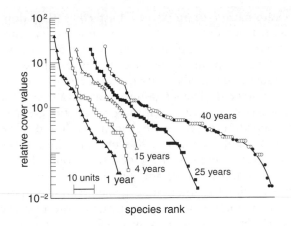

Figure 6.9 Relative abundance data (in terms of cover) for plant species in abandoned fields of different ages in southern Illinois.

toring lies in the use of organisms to establish the integrated, collective impact of environmental changes on components of the ecosystem and the wider environment (Furness *et al.*, 1993).

Species may be used as bio-indicators when their tolerance ranges and environmental preferences indicate that they represent particular environmental conditions. Their presence, absence, abundance and population dynamics indicate the extent of environmental change. Indicator species are particularly valuable if they are representative of and unique to a particular group of sites or habitats (high specificity) as well as being abundant and widely distributed within that group (high fidelity). Such species have a high information content about what is being monitored, and at the same time have a high probability of being sampled (Dufrêne and Legendre, 1997). The taxonomic level of study need not be the species, for in many cases almost as much information may be acquired by using diversity and other indicators at the genus or family level, an important conclusion where rapid survey is needed or where the taxonomic group is difficult or little studied (Williams and Gaston, 1994).

Noss (1990) suggests a hierarchical approach to monitoring biodiversity, placing the primary attributes of biodiversity (community composition, structure and function) into a nested hierarchy that incorporates elements of each attribute at four scales – landscape (regional), ecosystem/

community, population/species and genetic. Indicators can then be identified as monitors at each level of organisation. However, caution needs to be exercised. Niemi *et al.* (1997), for example, looked at 'management indicator and sensitive species' in northern Wisconsin to conclude that a lack of consistency in habitat preference cast doubt on the legitimacy of using a few species as indicators for the well-being of other species, especially rare ones.

Organisms can be used as indicators of an unexpected environmental problem. This was the case, for example, with the damaging effects of pesticides on wildlife following their biomagnification through the food chain, which was identified when it was observed that birds of prey were declining in numbers (see Section 3.2.2). Birds of prey were a specific means of identifying a wider environmental insult and were thus biomonitors of pollution. Specific indicators were not only population numbers and geographical distribution but also the eggshell thinning, which could be measured and which directly reflected a physiological effect of the pollutants.

It has been argued that, in general, animals are more useful than plants as biomonitors because they respond more rapidly to most environmental changes, whether in terms of population or (because of their mobility) range. It has also been suggested that animals at the top of a food chain are of potentially greatest use as bio-indicator species, using the argument that if the status of the top carnivore is 'healthy' this indicates general ecosystem health, which in turn implies general environmental health.

An example of this is that of birds of prey and pesticides. One has to be cautious, however, in accepting the suggestion as dogma. The red fox (*Vulpes vulpes*), for example, is a predator usually found at the top of a food chain, but its population size tells us little about what is happening to other components of the environment. During the 1950s, when the population of a major prey item, the rabbit (*Oryctolagus cuniculus*), crashed following the introduction of myxomatosis, fox numbers in Western Europe did not show a commensurate fall, since it was able to switch to alternative prey (Lloyd, 1980). Also, in rural parts of the UK, fox numbers may be affected by hunting, and in towns it has changed its feeding habits from predation to that of scavenging.

The use of threatened species as bio-indicators in biodiversity action plans is doubly valuable. Monitoring allows us to identify what is happening to such species in terms of their status, and therefore specific management plans and conservation practices can be implemented to reduce the threats and improve the environmental circumstances that will allow population recovery. But, more widely, appropriate indicators can tell us something about particular habitats, and sometimes about the environment as a whole, and are therefore valuable tools in biodiversity monitoring and the implementation of BAPs.

It is important to stress, however, that non-threatened species are also valuable in biodiversity monitoring. Indeed, it might be argued that changes in the status of rare species can occur through chance environmental fluctuations and therefore they are of less value as biomonitors and bio-indicators than common species. This is why, for example, the current status of farmland birds in the UK is causing so much concern, for numbers of most species are declining dramatically (Figure 6.10). These declines reflect changes, among other things, in cropping patterns, intensification of farming practice and the continued use of pesticides (Jarvis, 1993; Greenwood et al., 1995).

6.4.2 Assessment of biodiversity and implications for conservation

The biological importance of countries and regions can be gauged using a number of approaches, including consideration of rarity, endangerment, endemism and species richness. One idea that has been found of value in the objective determination of conservation prioritisation is that of complementarity and its use in critical faunas analysis.

6.4.2.1 Critical faunas analysis

The concept of 'complementarity' was devised by Ackery and Vane-Wright (1984) in their

examination of milkweed butterflies (Lepidoptera: Danainae), but it soon became evident that it had wider application. The entire set of taxa within the group being studied, for example the endemic mammals of a particular country, is the *complement*. The single most important site for conservation is assumed to be where the greatest proportion of the complement is found. The species not included in this primary site are the *residual complement*, and selection of the second most important site is determined by identifying the site that adds the greatest proportion of the residual complement to the primary site. This process can proceed in a step-wise manner until all sites have been ranked according to their importance. Ackery and Vane-Wright (*ibid.*) found that in order to conserve all 158 species of milkweed butterfly, 31 sites (or *critical faunas*) would need protection, the island of Sulawesi being the most important. In fact, 24 sites would be sufficient to protect all the narrow endemics.

Using a similar approach, Collins and Morris (1985) examined endemism in another butterfly group, the swallowtails (Lepidoptera: Papilionidae). They found that if the five countries with the greatest number of *endemic* species were to implement successful conservation plans, then 54% of the world's *total* number of swallowtails would be protected. Adding a further five countries would raise this figure to 68%. Protection enacted by the 45 most 'critical' countries would include 99% of the world's swallowtail species.

Critical faunas analysis has also been used to identify the priority sequence of protected areas for the conservation of antelopes in Africa. The Serengeti National Park in Tanzania is the most species-rich site, with breeding populations of 24% of all African antelope species. By adding Kafue National Park in Zambia, the two parks combined hold 38% of Africa's antelope species (some species being found in both, but Kafue possessing an additional 14%), and with Haut Dodo Faunal Reserve (Côte d'Ivoire) and Ouadi Rimé-Ouadi Achim Faunal Reserve (Chad), 56% of Africa's antelope species are represented.

Critical faunas analysis maximises the represen-

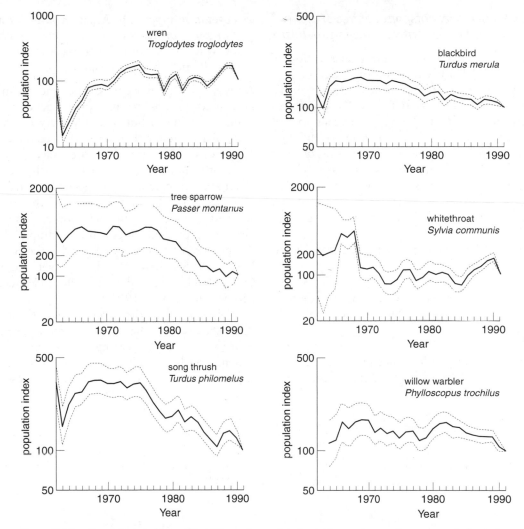

Figure 6.10 Population changes of six bird species on farmland. The continuous line represents the index calculated using the Mountford moving windows technique, the pecked lines bootstrapped 95% confidence limits. Vertical scales are logarithmic and have different population index ranges.

tation of the floral or faunal group under consideration in particular areas that, if protection is effective, might maximise conservation effort. It benefits from an objective analytical approach, but this is also its weakness, for it considers all species as being of equal importance to conservation. The fact is that some species are more at risk than others. Similarly, some species are more critical to ecosystem functioning. Bibby *et al.* (1992) assigned taxonomic uniqueness values to endemic species based on the diversity of the

genus and family to which a particular species belongs. It might therefore be argued that a species such as the giant panda (*Ailuropoda melanoleuca*) in a monotypic genus (i.e. where a genus contains one species only) should be given higher priority than a polytypic genus. And there may well be other reasons for giving a species such as the giant panda priority, given its endangered status and its resonance with the general public. These are ideas that are developed in the next chapter.

6.4.2.2 Biodiversity hotspots: centres of plant diversity and centres of avian endemism

The International Union for the Conservation of Nature (IUCN) Plant Conservation Programme is currently attempting to identify the world's centres of plant diversity (CPD). CPDs are places especially rich in plant life, which are therefore of biogeographical and ecological interest, bearing in mind comments made earlier in this chapter about distribution and speciation, as well as being important for conservation, because if such areas can be protected, a sizeable proportion of the wild plants on this planet might be safeguarded.

The IUCN has distinguished three interrelated types of CPD site:

- *botanically rich sites* that can be defined geographically, e.g. Mount Kinabalu in Borneo;
- *geographically defined regions* with high species diversity and/or endemism, e.g. Cordillera Bética in Spain, and the Atlas Mountains;

- *vegetation types* (e.g. Amazon rain forest) and *floristic provinces* (e.g. the south-west province of Western Australia) that are exceptionally rich in plant species.

As well as species richness and endemism, sites also tend to possess important gene pools of plants of value to humans, a variety of habitats, and plants adapted to specific edaphic (soil) conditions. Sites are therefore selected on the basis of botanical importance, but they are also often areas threatened by large-scale destruction.

Figure 6.11 shows that most of the 241 sites selected so far are in the tropics. Many are already protected sites, for example Bwindi ('impenetrable') Forest in Uganda, the Sinharaja Forest of Sri Lanka and the wet tropics of Queensland, Australia (World Conservation Monitoring Centre, 1992).

In similar vein, the International Council for Bird Preservation has undertaken a project to identify areas supporting large numbers of endemic birds. Locality records were collected for species with breeding ranges of less than

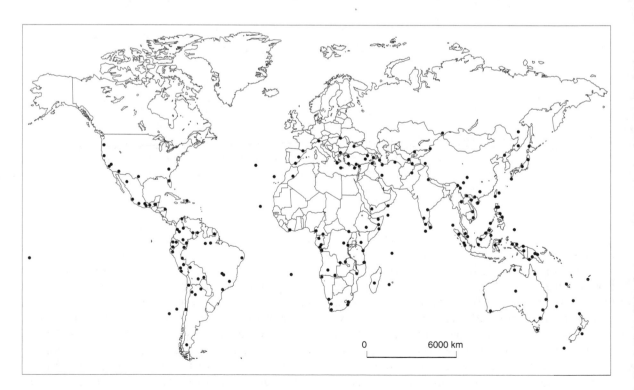

Figure 6.11   Centres of plant diversity: the world.

50 000 km² (about the size of Denmark, Costa Rica or Sri Lanka). Some 2608 species (or 27%) of the world's birds are found within such small ranges, and moreover endemics tend to aggregate together, for example on islands and mountains. A total of 221 endemic bird areas (EBAs) were identified (Figure 6.12), which together account for 2480 of the 2608 endemic species. Once again, the significance of the tropics emerges clearly, possessing 76% of all EBAs. Indonesia is the most important country, with 411 restricted-range species, 339 of which are confined to this country. Venezuela, Colombia, Peru, Ecuador, Brazil, Mexico, Papua New Guinea, the Philippines and the Solomon Islands each contain over 100 endemic bird species.

The conservation value of these sites is evident when it emerges that 757 (27%) of restricted-range birds are threatened in some way; indeed, they comprise 77% of all threatened birds in the world. The main habitat used by endemic birds is forest (69%), followed by scrub (12%), habitats in general most under threat from human activities such as forestry (Bibby *et al.*, 1992).

Areas of importance for endemic birds also tend to be important for mammals, reptiles, amphibians, insects and molluscs, as well as for plants. The ecological and biogeographical factors leading to centres of endemism and species richness are thus probably similar, and the conservation importance of such sites becomes all the more pronounced.

6.4.3 Access to genetic resources and genetically modified organisms

6.4.3.1 Genetic resources

Before the 1992 Convention on Biological Diversity, the principle of free access to genetic resources was recognised by the FAO Undertaking on Plant Genetic Resources of 1983. However, under Article 15 of the convention there is now a recognition that the authority to determine access to new genetic resources lies with a nation's government, and is subject to national legislation.

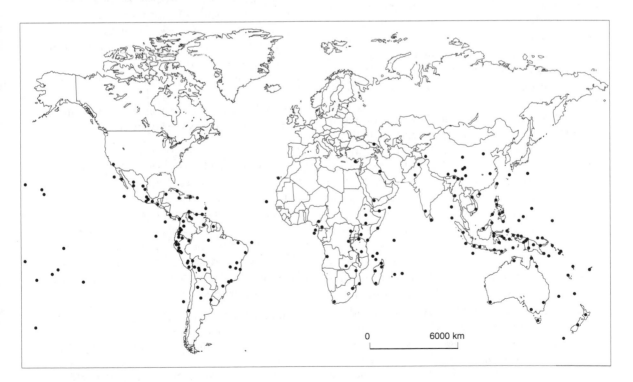

Figure 6.12   Endemic bird areas: the world.

This means that a country can retain exclusive rights, including commercial rights, on genetic material, whether a newly discovered (or newly distinguished) species, or genes newly identified or previously not exploited in a previously known species. New drugs, for example, are continually being discovered from analysis of plant material from the world's rain forests. These rain forests are found in developing countries. Why, such countries ask, should pharmaceutical companies from the developed world get all the benefit from such a resource at the expense of generating income in the country where the resource is found? Genetic material is now in part subject to patent laws. Yet the big companies still exert a major influence on the commercial exploitation of genetic material, and this is particularly evident in the development and use of genetically modified material, including food.

6.4.3.2 Genetically modifed organisms

Genetic engineering has been an important tool in a number of ways in applied ecology, for example in agriculture, pest control and bioremediation (see Issues Box 6.3). Recent concern has been expressed about the use of genetically modified (GM) material in human food, and a major contrast is evident between the USA and Europe in responses by both government and the general public.

In the USA, the Food and Drug Administration (FDA) does not require food labels to indicate the presence of GM material, and a survey by the International Food Information Council in February 1999 indicated that 62% of those questioned claimed that they would actually be more likely to buy vegetables that had been genetically engineered to taste better or fresher. Such a situation has therefore encouraged farmers: in 1994 no GM crops were grown, but in 1998 20.5 million ha was sown with GM crops, mostly soya beans, corn, cotton and potatoes. Over half the soya bean products now sold in the USA are GM, as are around 75% of all processed foods. Dependency by farmers on GM crops may be exacerbated if they are obliged to use developments such as 'the terminator' – a GM seed that self-destructs after one crop, forcing farmers to buy new seed stock each season.

It has been argued that the reason for the widespread use and acceptance of GM foods lies in carefully cultivated links between the GM industry and the US government (Borger and Bates, 1999). The dominant GM food corporation is Monsanto, which successfully lobbied the Reagan administration in 1986 to persuade it that new legislation to regulate GM foods was unnecessary. The corporation has since made substantial financial contributions to both the Republican and Democratic parties, and there have been major personnel links between Monsanto and all post-1986 administrations. FDA rulings include:

- Presence of GM food in a product is not a material fact: information does not have to be on a label on the grounds that a consumer *might* want to know it.
- Any GM labelling would not refer to the nature of the product itself, since this has 'substantial equivalence' in natural produce, but rather to the *process* of production, and therefore labelling is not required.
- Information on risk assessment acquired through testing can be withheld as 'confidential business information'.
- Even companies labelling their products as *not* containing GM material can, in some states, be subject to prosecution for libel, since such labelling implies superiority to GM products.

In a late 1990s Britain still suspicious of even non-GM methods of food production after, among other scares, the BSE crisis and the banning of beef on the bone (bovine spongiform encephalitis being implicated in deaths from Creutzfeld–Jakob disease) it is perhaps unsurprising that public opinion has not strongly accepted GM products. This involves a suspicion not only of the food itself but also of the motives behind its introduction.

> Monsanto takes for itself exclusive patent rights over plants and organisms ... Small farmers and producers everywhere in the world could be forced to buy their 'terminator' seeds, herbicides and fertilizers. For what? Not to feed the world; not to make food cheaper, safer or more equitably

ISSUES BOX 6.3

Genetic engineering – knowledge versus wisdom

DNA (deoxyribose nucleic acid) is the basic building material of life. Genes are blocks of DNA that contain the genetic code needed to produce a specific protein. *Genetic engineering* involves the splicing of genes in order to recombine sequences of DNA molecules to produce DNA with new genetic characteristics (*recombinant DNA*). Genetic material could in theory come from any living source or be synthesised but in practice most transgenes (the controlling sequences) are from bacteria or viruses because the small genome size makes the isolation of genes easier (Giddings, 1998).

By introducing new and desirable traits from one species to another in this way we are thus in a position to develop, for example, crops that are resistant to particular diseases or pests, that can withstand drier or colder conditions, that can grow at a faster rate, or that can produce higher yields. Genetically engineered microorganisms can be induced to degrade toxic waste, consume spilled oil or serve as pharmacological 'factories'.

In some ways, genetic engineering is an extension of what has been going on for thousands of years: breeding crops and stock to enhance desirable traits, with recent advances in understanding leading to a more systematic use of, for example, cross-pollination in improving crop, horticultural and forestry plants. Hybridisation has been common in, but not limited to, economic plants. Genetic engineering, however, goes a couple of important steps beyond. First of all, geneticists are now able to *splice* genetic material, introducing specific, desirable characteristics from one organism to another. Second, it is now possible to transfer genetic material from one species to a very different one – *transgenic engineering*. Thus genes responsible for producing toxins have been transferred from bacteria to plants in order to increase resistance to insect pests. It is transgenic engineering that in particular has raised a number of ethical issues in the minds of scientists, politicians and the public.

There are also commercial implications. In 1980, the US Supreme Court ruled that genetically engineered organisms could be patented. Large companies were quick to identify major commercial opportunities. Recent concern has been expressed in many countries about field trials of genetically modifed (GM) crops, with the risk of pollen from such plants entering non-GM crop areas, and indeed entering plants in non-agricultural areas, before trials have been completed, with literally unpredictable consequences for agriculture and (semi)natural plant communities.

Indeed, many products already contain GM soya and maize (corn), and labelling of such products is often patchy and inappropriate. The public is rightly concerned that it should have a choice in purchasing such products, but it is easy to influence opinion and misguide judgement by selective or partial information, and to use scare tactics by referring to GM-modified products as 'Frankenstein foods'.

The rhetoric of much public opinion is often based on analogy with the green revolution, pointing out that the promotion of would-be wonder crops benefited the rich and made many poorer farmers bankrupt, and that this is also happening with GM products. A call is made (quite rightly) for an end to world hunger by reducing inefficient or inappropiate use of land, by fairer allocation of wealth and power, by a reduction in bureaucracy and corrupt practices, and by more effective methods of storage and distribution. All these things are desirable, but it is a *non sequitur* then to claim that GM foods cannot be part of this package. GM food by itself will not cause world hunger to disappear, but it can help.

Concern, however, has also been expressed by scientists. The consequences of deliberate or accidental introduction of GM organisms into the environment remain largely unknown. There is a risk of mutation, with changes in form, behaviour or ecological impact, and unlike manufactured products GM organisms cannot be recalled. Such risks are no doubt small, but potential profits from this kind of biotechnology are tremendously high, and greed tends to prevail. In many ways, GM organisms are indeed equivalent to introduced taxa, and experience has shown that, while the vast majority of introductions have no impact on the environment, a few nevertheless do, and wreak havoc on ecosystem and environmental functioning (see Chapter 8).

ISSUES BOX 6.3 (cont)

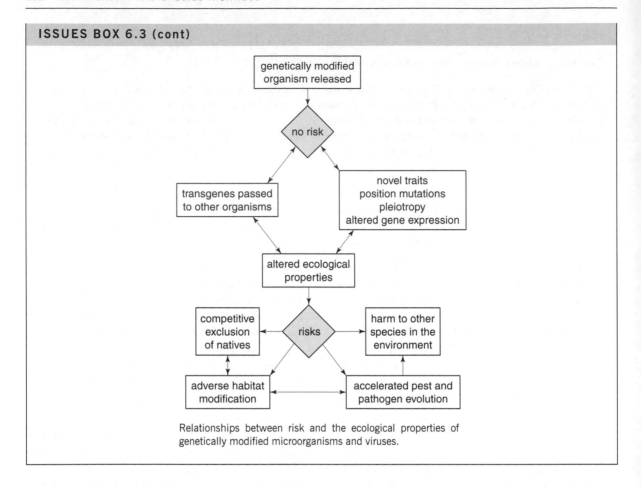

Relationships between risk and the ecological properties of genetically modified microorganisms and viruses.

distributed, but for their own corporate profit. This is an international smash and grab on the world's food future.

(Hilda Bernstein, letter to *The Guardian*, 20 February 1999)

In fact, the debate over GM foods has been going on in continental Europe for some time. Even so, the European Commission has been unable to reconcile its commitment to free trade and its obligations under world trade agreements to import GM products from the USA, which earns £900 million in such trade.

The EU has authorised eighteen GM organisms for experimental growth. However, a difference between trade agreements and permissive cultivation on the one hand and practice on the other is evident. Austria and Luxembourg, for example, have been threatened with prosecution for refusing permission to grow an authorised modified maize

in their countries, but the EU has not actually enforced compliance. In summer 1998, France announced a moratorium on the cultivation of a GM oilseed rape. In 1998, global production of GM crops was 27.8 million ha in the USA and less than 1% in the whole of Europe (Figure 6.13).

Delegates from 170 countries met in Cartagena, Colombia, in February 1999 to devise a Biosafety Protocol aimed at the production of guidelines for trade in GM food. However, the meeting was sabotaged by the United States, fearful of its business and trade interests, which refused to allow soya beans and corn (which account for 90% of the world trade in GM food products) to be included in any agreement. 'The US is willing to threaten biodiversity in the name of short-term profits. It wants a biotrade, not a biosafety, protocol,' argued Louise Gale, a political adviser to Greenpeace, according to a report in *The Guardian* (Lennard, 1999).

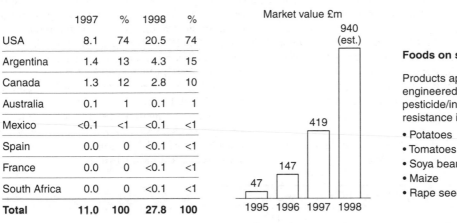

The GM food mountain
Hectares (m) and % of world total

	1997	%	1998	%
USA	8.1	74	20.5	74
Argentina	1.4	13	4.3	15
Canada	1.3	12	2.8	10
Australia	0.1	1	0.1	1
Mexico	<0.1	<1	<0.1	<1
Spain	0.0	0	<0.1	<1
France	0.0	0	<0.1	<1
South Africa	0.0	0	<0.1	<1
Total	**11.0**	**100**	**27.8**	**100**

Market value £m

940 (est.)

419

147

47

1995 1996 1997 1998

Foods on sale in the USA

Products approved and engineered for insect or pesticide/insecticide resistance include:

- Potatoes
- Tomatoes
- Soya beans
- Maize
- Rape seed

Source: International Service for the Acquisition of Agri-biotech

Figure 6.13 The GM food mountain: amount of land under GM crops in 1997 and 1998 for the eight leading producer countries, and global market value of GM crops, 1995–98.

6.5 Conclusions

Although conservationists had been concerned about the erosion of biological diversity for at least three decades before Rio, the Earth Summit brought the situation to a more public eye and into the political arena. It also led to the allocation of funding aimed at increasing the knowledge base. This in turn helped in a rediscovery of the importance of taxonomy and field survey, and appreciation of the need to know something about the conservation status of species and their habitats so that predictions could be made with some degree of confidence about the environmental consequences of no change, some change or lots of change in terms of protection measures.

Buzzwords are fashionable words, and things go out of fashion. 'Biodiversity' has been a buzzword for the 1990s, and it is important that, fashionable or not in the future, the efforts that have been made in the 1990s to retain and enhance biodiversity are continued. There has also emerged a public as well as scientific appreciation that it is not just rare and endangered species and habitats that need protection but common ones as well. The conser-

vation momentum must continue, and the sense of urgency not lost.

Another public sentiment that gathered momentum as the millennium approached concerned genetic modification. It is absolutely right that tests on GM crops, for example, are undertaken rigorously and safely, and that any conclusions are guarded and conservative. It is perfectly legitimate to view monopolistic diktats from big business with concern. It is important to discuss ethical stances on issues such as transgenic engineering and cloning. But there is a risk in all this of adopting a neo-Luddite attitude to new technology. GM crops, for example, will not by themselves save the world from hunger but, provided that safeguards are in place, they could make a major contribution.

Further reading

Ehrlich, P.R. and Wilson, E.O. (eds) (1988) *Biodiversity* (Washington DC: National Academic Press).

Gaston, K.J. (ed.) (1996) *Biodiversity: a biology of numbers and difference* (Oxford: Blackwell Science).

Given, D.R. (1994) *Principles and practice of plant conservation* (London: Chapman & Hall).

Ho, M.-W. (1998) *Genetic engineering: dream or nightmare* (London: Gateway Books).

Jeffries, M. (1997) *Biodiversity and conservation* (London: Routledge).

Raeburn, P. (1995) *The last harvest: the genetic gamble that threatens to destroy American agriculture* (New York: Simon & Schuster).

Ricklefs, R.E. and Schluter, D. (eds) (1993) *Species diversity in ecological communities: historical and geographical perspectives* (Chicago: University of Chicago Press).

Skelton, P. *et al.* (1993) *Evolution: an interdisciplinary introduction* (Harlow: Addison Wesley).

Soulé, M. (ed.) (1987) *Viable populations for conservation* (Cambridge: Cambridge University Press).

Swanson, T.M. (1998) *The economics and ecology of biodiversity decline: the forces driving global change* (Cambridge: Cambridge University Press).

Wilson, E.O. (1992) *The diversity of life* (Cambridge, Mass.: Belknap Press of Harvard University Press).

Wolf, E.C. (1987) *On the brink of extinction: conserving the diversity of life* (Washington DC: WorldWatch Institute).

World Resources Institute (1992) *Global biodiversity strategy: guidelines for action to save, study, and use Earth's biotic wealth sustainably and equitably* (New York: World Resources Institute).

QUESTIONS BASED ON CHAPTER 6

Q1. Is a species a renewable or a non-renewable ecological resource?

Q2. Why is the house mouse unlikely ever to become an endangered species?

Q3. What species of mammal shows the greatest degree of intraspecific morphological variation? (Clue: not through natural selection.)

Q4. Identify three examples of hybrid plants (other than common cordgrass) and/or animals that have proved to be ecologically successful.

Q5. Why are local extinctions important to prevent, given that the species can be reintroduced from another source?

ANSWERS

A1. Both. It is renewable because breeding or regeneration allows population renewal, and the species survives, provided that any population loss does not fall below a replacement threshold (minimum viable population level). If a species becomes extinct, however, it is gone for ever, and that resource has then become non-renewable.

A2. House mice are commensal, opportunistic, eurytopic, *r*-selected animals, characteristics that together allow them to survive and reproduce rapidly in a variety of habitats and environments.

A3. Almost certainly this has to be the domestic dog, *Canis familiaris*.

A4. There is clearly no definitive list here. If you have thought of three hybrid taxa and are genuinely confident of their status, well done!

A5. The reasons for a species becoming locally extinct will still be present unless measures have been taken to prevent this happening again. The species as a whole may be rare, so taking members of other populations, which might also be at risk of local extinction or which might bring numbers below a minimum viable size, does not make good conservation sense. Local populations will often be genetically quite distinct from populations elsewhere, and it is important to retain that distinctiveness, especially since the population may well have adapted to the particular ecological conditions that obtain in that area. Remember that biodiversity conservation includes the preservation of genetic diversity.

Discussion topics

D1. Why is the species commonly viewed as the basic taxonomic unit in ecology and biological conservation? What are the problems and disadvantages of using the species in this way?

D2. What single most important measure, if fully implemented, would do the most good in maintaining global biodiversity?

D3. Captive breeding of rare animals is often undertaken with the view to returning them to the wild. What measures must you take before such a reintroduction programme is appropriate? Think of what you must ensure with the species itself and its natural environment.

EXERCISES

E1. Look at the biodiversity action plan (BAP) for the nightjar in the UK (see Issues Box 6.1). Construct a BAP for a plant or animal that you are familiar with in your local environment.

E2. Select two bird and two mammal species in which males perform courtship rituals in front of the female, and find out more about these displays. What senses are used in these displays? How complicated are they, and why? What similarities can you find between the displays of your four species?

Chapter 7

Conservation and wildlife management

Summary

Biological conservation is defined as the goal-oriented management of biological resources – from the genetic through species and communities to whole landscapes – in such a way as to maintain, restore or enhance desirable characteristics. The importance of wilderness is indicated, and different approaches to conserving such wild landscapes, including legislation, are exemplified in the contexts of Antarctica, the USA and the UK. The value of designating areas of particular importance to nature conservation as national parks and biosphere reserves is shown. Rarity is an important criterion in both species and habitat conservation, but not all rare species are endangered, threatened or vulnerable. Species also vary in their ecological significance to community functioning, as shown by the notions of keystone species and umbrella species. Movement of species is examined by consideration of different modes of dispersal, migration and colonisation. Relating species and communities to environmental gradients (externally controlled by allogenic or exogenous factors) introduces the idea of zonation, and community changes through time (internally controlled by autogenic or endogenous factors) are related to succession and climax. Explanations of succession involve ideas of facilitation, tolerance and inhibition. Dynamic community processes such as succession often pose problems for conservation managers, and clearly defined goals are essential in any management programme. Amenity, recreation and tourism also often need to be integrated into conservation programmes, and strategies to accommodate conflicts of interest are indicated. Particular problems of poaching and illegal trade are noted, and the success of the Convention on International Trade in Endangered Species is evaluated. Finally, some isses of reclamation, restoration, revegetation and habitat creation are highlighted, and the advantages and disadvantages of *in situ* and *ex situ* conservation are suggested.

7.1 Conservation and wildlife management

Chapter 6 highlighted the importance of biodiversity and indicated the need to protect the living resources of the world. This chapter looks more closely at how and why some plants and animals have become endangered and considers ways in which such protection might be implemented. The key word here is *conservation*, which is the goal-oriented management of resources in such a way as to maintain, restore or enhance desirable characteristics and some kind of natural balance. Biological conservation, by definition, focuses on the wise management of biological resources, from the genetic, through species and communities, to habitats, whole ecosystems and landscapes. Ultimately, we are concerned with safeguarding the living resources of the whole planet. There are clear links between the ideas of conservation and sustainability.

That so many species are under threat and that so many habitats and landscapes are rapidly being degraded and destroyed is our own fault. This is not to argue that we should not use landscapes and living resources, but it is a reflection of the fact that we have often not used these resources wisely. We have not, for example, taken care to ensure that renewable resources are in fact renewed, nor have we been much concerned about our responsibilities to take precautions against the impoverishment of the richness of life.

Care and concern are key attributes to bear in mind. There is the *anthropocentric* and short-term economics-based view that because we are now so much the dominant species on Earth we have the right and authority to use all resources expediently, with no thought for the future because technology will always find solutions for any resource shortage. Anything that is not perceived as a resource is expendable. The *ecocentric* view, however, is that to survive in the longer term we need to adopt the idea that we are part of a functioning global system that is in danger of being destabilised and perhaps destroyed by profligate use and careless activity. It is actually very much in our own interests to maintain global homeostasis and to retain a diversity that might include species of future value. With power comes responsibility, and another argument for conservation is an ethical one: it is inherently wrong to hasten the extinction of any species.

The conservation of species is therefore important. Whole landscapes and ecosystems are, by the same arguments, worthy of conservation. The two ideas are linked by the fact that individual species (particularly plants) are components of landscapes and, by definition, all species belong to ecosystems; and by the fact that the most effective way of conserving an endangered species is to protect its environment. Conservation measures therefore include species-targeted protection and the management of whole landscapes. Many kinds of protected area are also of value to humans for a wide range of recreational activities, and it is important wherever possible to rationalise land use and management to allow such activities. At times, management for wildlife and recreation are incompatible, but often they can complement each other. These are themes explored in this chapter.

7.2 Key environmental issue: wilderness and the protection of landscapes

7.2.1 Wilderness

'Wilderness' was defined by the US Wilderness Act of 1964 as areas 'where the Earth and its community of life are untrammeled by man [*sic*], where man himself is a visitor who does not remain.' In 1987, the Sierra Club – a powerful US conservation group – estimated that 34% of the planet's land surface can be called true wilderness, wild areas of at least 400 000 ha. Wilderness as a percentage of total land area is shown in Figure 7.1. Antarctica and Greenland, together

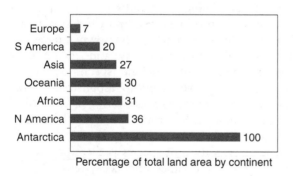

Percentage of total land area by continent

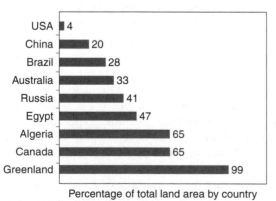

Percentage of total land area by country

Figure 7.1 Wilderness as a percentage of the total land area by continent and country.

with much of Canada, Alaska and northern Asia, are ice-dominated wildernesses. Hot desert wilderness is found in North and South America, Africa, Asia and Australia. Wilderness in South America largely comprises the rain forest of Brazil and bordering countries, although this continent also includes the Andes, and other mountain wildernesses are seen in the Rockies and in the Himalaya–Central Asian ranges. Only about 20% of these areas are in some way protected.

Wilderness areas are important in providing undisturbed habitats for wildlife and plants. 'Undisturbed', however, does not mean unvisited by people – the 'visitors who do not remain' of the Wilderness Act. They provide recreation in the broadest of senses, from the purely aesthetic through walking and camping to outdoor pursuits commensurate with maintaining the integrity of the landscape and its components.

7.2.1.1 Antarctica

The 11.65 million km^2 (and 10% of the world's land mass) that is Antarctica comprises the coldest, windiest, driest and iciest of the seven continents. Ice covers 98% of the surface, dry valleys the remaining 2%. Antarctica contains 90% of the Earth's ice and stores 70% of the planet's fresh water. The ice and surrounding seas contain 88 million penguins, 80 million seabirds, half the world's population of seals, twelve species of whale and over 200 species of fish. It is essentially an unspoiled wilderness on which the only permanent settlements are the 69 scientific research stations, where great care is taken to keep even the local environment pristine.

Nobody owns Antarctica, although the UK, Norway, France, Australia, New Zealand, Chile and Argentina all possess territorial claims covering 85% of the continent (and those of the UK, Argentina and Chile overlap), but under the terms of the Antarctic Treaty of 1959 these claims are held in abeyance. The treaty, which came into effect in 1961, and which involves 26 voting members, includes the agreement that Antarctica south of 60° S should be used only for peaceful purposes, and that no commercial or military bases are permitted. Nevertheless, during the 1980s, negotiations involving 33 nations resulted in the 1988 Convention on the Regulation of Antarctic Mineral Resource Activities. This would have allowed exploitation of Antarctica's minerals, but it required a unanimity to be ratified, and in 1989 several countries, including France and Australia, refused to do this on the grounds that even careful mineral extraction would cause irreparable damage to the environment. As a result, the Protocol to the Antarctic Treaty on Environmental Protection (often referred to as the Madrid Protocol) was agreed in 1991, one of the terms being a moratorium on mineral exploitation for at least 50 years. A two-thirds majority of the voting nations will be needed to lift this ban. Even so, the protocol will not become law until all 26 voting members of the Treaty have ratified it. President Clinton did not sign until 1996, and Japan and Russia have (as of mid-1999) yet to do so. Other agreements include the 1972 Convention for the Conservation of Antarctic Seals and the 1980 Convention on the Conservation of Antarctic Marine Living Resources.

Maintaining Antarctica as a pristine wilderness is important for the integrity not only of its environment but also that of the world, for the immense mass of ice and the surrounding cold waters regulate many aspects of the global climate and oceanic systems. Many environmentalists want Antarcica to be designated a permanent world park or international wilderness reserve. Even today, 4000 visitors a year are allowed to come to Antarctica, under strictly controlled conditions – an example of ecotourism (see Section 7.4.2.3).

7.2.1.2 Wilderness, national parks and conservation legislation in the USA

Wilderness, parks and wildlife refuges make up about 9% of the 9 363 130 km^2 that is the USA. It is interesting to see how and why such a land use has emerged over so much of this country.

When European settlement of North America began in earnest in the early seventeenth century, the pioneers found a huge continent with apparently unlimited resources. Settlers saw a hostile wilderness that needed to be tamed to allow

settlement, farming and trade. Resources were often squandered because one just had to move west to find more. This 'frontier attitude' led to the destruction of much that is now regretted, not just of landscapes but of people – many of the Native Americans. A contrast is evident, with hindsight, between the literally resourceful, sustainable Native Americans, who had no concept of land ownership, and the often non-sustainable colonists, who brought the cultural values of Europe with them, including the notion of ownership of land.

By 1850, around 80% of the total land area of the USA was owned by the government. Much of the eastern forest had been cleared, and the grasslands of the Mid-west had been degraded. In 1865, Congress legislated against fencing in public land for private use, but cattle ranchers on the prairies ignored the law with impunity, and cattle – having replaced the by then nearly extinct bison – overgrazed the rangeland. By 1890, over half the public land had been sold cheaply to homesteaders, land speculators, timber and mining companies, the railways, and an array of private and public institutions. The low prices served to emphasise the apparently unlimited resources available.

During the mid-nineteenth century, however, there were some who became concerned at the disappearance of the natural landscape and the profligate use of resources, and calls were made – at first unheeded or indeed opposed – for the protection of some of the wild areas remaining in government hands. With the eventual realisation that natural forests, in particular, were disappearing rapidly the government at long last began to act. Yosemite, in California, was designated a park in 1864, although the term 'national park' was first used in 1872 with the establishment of Yellowstone National Park, an area of nearly 810 000 ha largely of forest, in north-west Wyoming, edging into Montana and Idaho.

These were the first national parks in the world and were the beginning of a whole series of actions that were aimed in one way or another at protecting and conserving land and its wildlife. National parks were formally established in 1912, although it was later that the National Park System Organic Act was passed, declaring the aim of such areas to be to 'preserve scenery, wildlife, and natural and historical objects for the use, viewing, health and pleasure of people.' By 1950, the USA had just under 12 million ha of land under national or state parks. By 1990, this had risen to 32 million ha, largely by the incorporation into the system of land in Alaska. The most recent additions to the national park system are Death Valley National Park, Joshua Tree National Park and Mojave National Preserve (all in 1994) and the Grand Staircase Escalante National Monument, Utah, in 1996.

Subsequent legislation, such as the 1891 Forest Reserve Act, paved the way for more federal lands to be set aside for sustainable use, for example to ensure the protection of timber and water resources. Public pressure on government was itself sustained by the establishment of the conservation-oriented Sierra Club in 1892, its founder the naturalist John Muir.

Even greater protection of wilderness and wildlife came with the presidency of Theodore Roosevelt in 1901–09. Roosevelt was an ardent supporter of the conservation movement and introduced the notion of federal wildife refuges, the first on Pelican Island off the east coast of Florida in 1903. Roosevelt also tripled the size of the country's forest reserves and, in 1905, was the driving force behind Congress's creation of the US Forest Service, the role of which was to protect and manage the forest reserves. In 1907, these forest reserves were renamed national forests.

Another President Roosevelt, Franklin D. Roosevelt, promoted further legislative changes associated with conservation over the period 1933 to 1945, for example the Taylor Grazing Act of 1934, which regulated grazing of livestock on public lands; the Migratory Bird Hunting Stamp Act of 1934, which required waterfowl hunters to buy a licence; and the creation of the Soil Conservation Service in 1945.

During the twentieth century, a split has been evident in the United States between preservationists, who believe that wilderness areas should be left completely alone, and the 'wise-use school', who feel that wilderness and other public lands should be open to wise management to provide resources for people. An early example of this

division was in 1913, when the Tuolumne River was dammed in the Hetch Hetchy Valley in California to provide drinking water for San Francisco, a development supported by the head of the US Forest Service, Gifford Pinchot, but opposed by preservationists led by John Muir. Even today there are calls for the removal of the dam.

From the 1960s to today three main strands have come together in the environment movement:

1. A range of issues-related concerns, for example an increasing resistance to activities leading to pollution, especially following the publication of Rachel Carson's *Silent Spring* in 1962 (see Section 3.4.2), and present concerns over the potential environmental and health impact of genetically modified organisms (see Section 6.4.3.2).
2. Species protection, which has become enshrined by law through the Endangered Species Act (ESA) of 1973 (see Issues Box 7.1) and the Convention on International Trade in Endangered Species (see Issues Box 7.4).
3. A number of contentious issues related to particular protected areas, or areas where protection perhaps ought to exist.

An example of how the conservation of species and the protection of land come together is seen with the debate over the threatened northern spotted owl (Issues Box 7.2).

The 1964 Wilderness Act authorised the protection of undeveloped public land as part of the National Wilderness System (NWS), although Congress could later revoke any such agreement on the grounds of 'need for the national good'. Land protected under the Act could be used only for non-destructive forms of recreation such as hiking, camping and boating, with permanent camp sites forbidden and hunting restricted by area, season and permit. The amount of land under the NWS was tripled in 1977 by President Carter, most of this increase being located in Alaska.

1968 saw the Wild and Scenic Rivers Act, which aims to protect rivers with exceptional scenic attractiveness, recreational value or impor-

ISSUES BOX 7.1

The Endangered Species Act of 1973

The ESA was enacted to 'provide a means whereby the ecosystems upon which endangered species and threatened species depend may be conserved [and] to provide a program for the conservation of such species.' To qualify for ESA protection, a species must appear on the official list of *endangered species*, defined by law as those likely to become extinct within all or a significant portion of their range; or on the list of *threatened species* – those likely to become endangered in the forseeable future.

The Secretary of the Interior, via the US Fish and Wildlife Service (FWS), and the Secretary for Commerce, via the National Marine Fisheries Service (NMFS), have authority to add to or delete from these lists, based on whether or not a species faces extinction due to any natural or human-caused factors. The Secretaries must also draw up 'recovery plans' for each listed species, setting out conservation goals and specifying actions necessary to achieve these goals. In 1991, the list included over 600 species that occur in the USA, with another 500 or so that occur elsewhere.

Under Section 7 of the ESA, federal land managers and other federal agencies are directed to ensure that their activities do not jeopardise the continued existence of protected species, or adversely modify habitat critical to such species. Managers and agencies must acquire a written 'biological opinion' from the FWS or NMFS, which details

- the likely effect of any proposed activity on a protected species;
- alternatives or modifications that would avoid or lessen adverse effects; and
- the biological information upon which opinions are based (biological determinations).

Under Section 9, private individuals, corporations and state and local governments are forbidden to 'take' any endangered species, or to alter the habitat of an endangered species so as to increase its vulnerability.

Between 1987 and 1991, only nineteen of the >7000 projects evaluated by the FWS/NMFS were blocked or withdrawn as a result of the ESA. Criticisms of the ESA partly lie in its cumbersome administration and the slowness with which species are listed, by which time their threatened status might well have declined further. Ecologically oriented criticisms also include the opinions that

- The Act protects only high-profile individual species rather than serving to protect and enhance overall biodiversity. If species are endangered through habitat loss and fragmentation and reduction in habitat quality, then ecosystem conservation is preferable to species conservation and would serve broader conservation aims.
- The Act lacks clearly defined thresholds to identify endangered, threatened or indeed recovered species or populations.
- Many biological determinations are inadequately documented, preventing informed, meaningful scrutiny of decisions, or participation in the conservation process by the public or the scientific community
- The Act does not protect existing habitat reserves sufficiently to sustain populations if and when they recover.
- The Act reflects an approach that is reactive rather than pre-emptive.

tance to wildlife. Another important piece of legislation was the Federal Land Policy and Management Act of 1976, which authorised the Bureau of Land Management to manage the public lands under its control, most of which lie in the western states. As a result, however, the so-called sagebrush rebellion – a coalition of farmers, ranchers, loggers, developers and miners – protested at extended restrictions on the use of such land and campaigned for a removal of most western lands from public to state ownership. This response was met with sympathy and support from President Reagan, who between 1981 and 1989 generally attacked most of the conservation and environmental laws of the previous 80 years. Despite strong opposition from Congress, public opinion and the courts, the Reagan administration certainly slowed down the

ISSUES BOX 7.2

The northern spotted owl

The northern spotted owl (*Strix occidentalis caurina*) is essentially restricted to old-growth Douglas fir forest in the Pacific North-west, in particular western Oregon. Its range includes twelve national forests. Each pair requires 900–1800 ha of prime forest land in which to breed and hunt. Only 2000–3500 individuals remain, and the species is vulnerable because of threats to its habitat from logging and because of its low rate of reproduction added to a low juvenile survival rate. In 1990, it was added to the federal list of threatened species, which means that any human activity that could decrease its chances of survival are forbidden. This includes logging, which is a crucial industry in this part of North America in terms of commerce and employment.

During the late 1980s and early 1990s, this situation inevitably crystallised into an issue of owls versus jobs, especially since 1991, when the courts ordered suspension of all logging in owl habitat. But the owl's habitat is important for resources other than timber. There are 40 other species listed as endangered or threatened, including the economically important Pacific yew (*Taxus brevifolia*), source of a drug of value in treating cancer, and the forests contain streams that are vital in maintaining salmon and other economically, as well as ecologically, important fish. The northern spotted owl is in many respects an indicator species: its continued survival reflects the survival of a diverse, ancient forest ecosystem.

Yet much of the old-growth forest has already been felled, and while some has been replanted it does not have the structure, species or species diversity of the original. The ESA is the main weapon in the environmentalists' armoury: by insisting on the protection of the owl they are protecting the national forests and other similar areas in the region.

Furthermore, while one can find sympathy for the loggers and mill workers whose jobs are at risk, employment was already declining. Between 1977 and 1987, while logging in Oregon's national forests had increased by over 15% employment had dropped by 15% (representing 12 000 jobs), a consequence of automation. For most workers, cutting down the remaining old-growth trees would not have postponed unemployment for long, since if the rate of logging in the 1980s had continued most of the remaining old-growth forest would have disappeared 20 years later.

The way through the impasse between conservationists and big business is sustainable use of the forest, a combination of limited, selective logging, appropriate replanting, economic diversification and tourism. The result of a Timber Summit in Oregon convened in 1993 by President Clinton has indeed been a revitalisation of Oregon's economy and employment, many loggers having been retrained for other careers. A compromise has been reached: logging has resumed in the Pacific North-west, but at a fifth of the 1980s level, and 75% of federal timber land has been afforded protection.

In a sense, the problem reflects an even wider issue, the low price of timber, which makes sustainable logging unprofitable. The real costs of degrading and destroying such old-growth forest are not met, because the market economy does not include the full environmental and social costs. And this is a broader issue alluded to in Chapter 2: until we amend the market system to include *all* costs, we will continue to overexploit the world's resources and, in the long term, perhaps finish with greater and less readily recoverable unemployment.

Sources: Miller (2000); Raven *et al.* (1998)

momentum of the environmental movement, although ironically – as a response to this political intervention – membership of environmental organisations soared.

George Bush promised to be more environmentally understanding, but his presidency (1989–1993) had little concrete to show in this respect. Bill Clinton's vice president, Al Gore, however, is knowledgeable about and sympathetic towards environmental matters, although towards the end of Clinton's presidency it had become apparent that rather less had been achieved for the environment than had been hoped for.

7.2.1.3 'Wilderness', national parks and conservation legislation in the UK

The USA, with an area of 9 363 130 km², includes vast tracts of remote, wild landscapes, in contrast with the 244 100 km² of the UK, where nowhere on the mainland is further than 16 km from a public road, and where a map of 'remote areas' shows that very few places exist, even in the Scottish Highlands, more than 3.2 km (2 miles) from a tarred road (Figure 7.2) (Huxley, 1974).

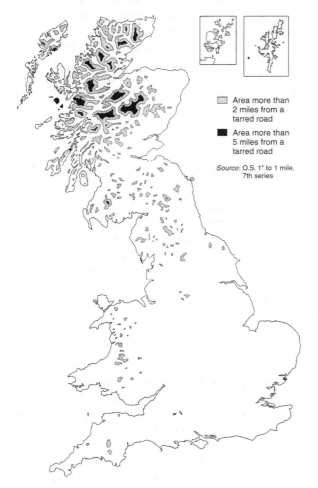

Area more than 2 miles from a tarred road

Area more than 5 miles from a tarred road

Source: O.S. 1" to 1 mile, 7th series

Figure 7.2   Remote areas in Great Britain.

This leads to rather different notions of 'wilderness'. This is one reason why there are major differences between the USA and the UK in both the way land is protected and managed for scenic value and conservation and the way the conservation movement has evolved.

Another contrast lies with the ownership of the land. About 35% of land in the USA is owned by the federal government (mostly in Alaska and the western states), and a further 7% by state and local governments. This allows public governance of how wild areas are managed. In the UK, most land is in private ownership, which in many ways limits what can be enforced in the way of conservation measures. Institutional ownership tends to be in areas of commercial forestry (the Forest Enterprise arm of the Forestry Commission), Ministry of Defence land, and other tracts where land use is also prescribed, although some of these are of value to nature conservation (Table 7.1). 'In Britain, conservation means intervention and active manipulation of the environment. In North America, conservation management is rooted in assumptions about the purity and inviolability of wilderness' (Henderson, 1992).

The first key piece of legislation in the UK to identify areas where certain conservation-oriented land uses and management procedures were prescribed (or, more accurately, where certain activities were forbidden) was the National Parks and Access to the Countryside Act of 1949. This Act confirmed the status and extended the brief

Table 7.1   Top ten institutional land owners in the UK, 1994

		ha
1	Forestry Commission	840 000
2	Ministry of Defence	24 000
3	National Trust	22 000
4	Public utilities	21 000
5	Pension funds, insurance companies, etc.	20 000
6	County farms (local authority-owned)	14 000
7	Crown estate	12 000
8	Oxford and Cambridge colleges	10 000
9	Church of England	8 000
10	Cooperative Wholesale Society Agriculture Ltd	7 200

of the Nature Conservancy (the world's first statutory, non-voluntary conservation body), created the previous year; it designated areas of outstanding natural beauty (AONBs), which would receive no special treatment but the naming of which was aimed at promoting public enjoyment of the landscape; and it designated, established and provided the framework for maintenance of national parks (Table 7.2), where public access was granted over wide areas of great natural attractiveness. National parks, with their Scottish equivalents, National Scenic Areas, form the basis of a patchwork of protected areas in the UK (Figure 7.3).

From the 1970s onwards the UK has, to an extent, fulfilled the requirements of a number of international and European agreements or directives that related to the conservation of particular kinds of site. Key European examples are the Convention on Wetlands of International Importance, especially as Wildfowl Habitat (the Ramsar Convention) of 1971; the Berne Convention (1982) on the Conservation of European Wildlife and Natural Habitats; the Directive on the Conservation of Wild Birds (1979) which initiated the identification of Special Protection Areas (SPAs); and the very important Directive on the Conservation of Natural Habitats and of Wild Fauna and Flora (Habitats Directive) of 1992, which set up Special Areas of Conservation to integrate with SPAs to provide a network of key sites of importance for conservation throughout Europe, known as Natura 2000.

The UK has a hierarchy of sites or areas in one way or another identified as being of value to conservation, from National Nature Reserves through Sites of Special Scientific Interest (SSSIs) to Local Nature Reserves and Sites of Importance/Sites of Local Importance to Nature Conservation (SINCs/SLINCs) (Table 7.3). The Wildlife and Countryside Act (1981) had three main sections, on species protection, habitat conservation and access to the countryside. Habitat conservation focused on SSSIs, with an emphasis on the formal notification of such sites to landowners, a requirement for a period of consultation before any changes in land use, and compensation for profits forgone by retaining the original land use at the expense of agricultural improvement. The scheme was weakened by its voluntary nature rather than legally enforceable requirements, to which can be added the insufficient funding for compensation, and a relatively few but not inconsequential landowners who abused the system, and many SSSIs continued to be damaged or destroyed (Table 7.4).

7.2.2 National parks and biosphere reserves

National parks in the USA and the UK are evidently different in origin, goals and management. Indeed, UK national parks do not conform to the definition of national parks used by the International Union for the Conservation of Nature (IUCN). Nevertheless, in both cases there is a concern for measures that will maintain both physical and living components of the landscape, and do so for wildlife and wildlife habitat on the one hand, and appropriate human use on the other.

In 1975, the IUCN defined a national park as a 'relatively large area where (a) one or several ecosystems are not materially altered by human exploitation and occupation, where plants and animal species ... and habitats are of special scientific, educative and recreational value, or which contain landscape of great beauty, and (b) where the highest competent authority of the

Table 7.2 National parks in England and Wales

Year	National park	Area (km²)
1951	Peak District	1404
	Dartmoor	945
	Lake District	2243
	Snowdonia	2189
1952	North York Moors	1432
	Pembrokeshire Coast	583
1954	Exmoor	686
	Yorkshire Dales	1761
1956	Northumberland	1031
1957	Brecon Beacons	1344

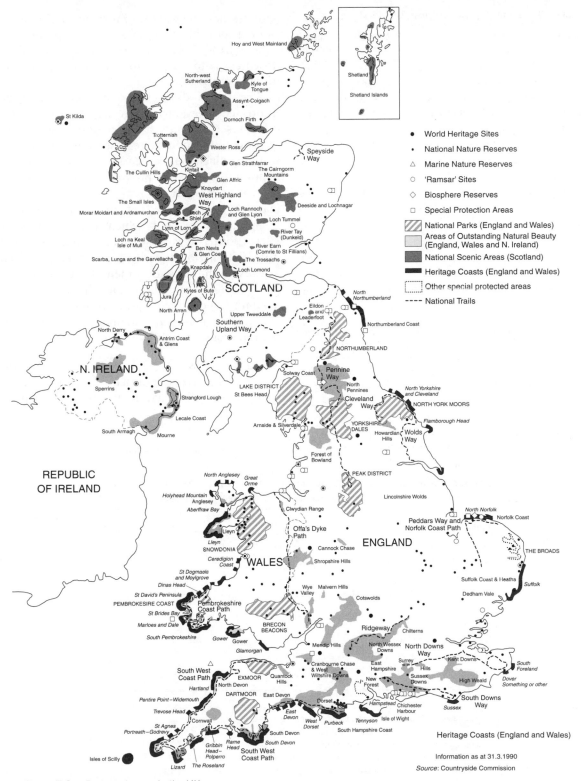

Figure 7.3   Protected areas in the UK.

Table 7.3   Statutory protected areas, UK, 1991

Status[1]	Number	Area (000s ha)
National Nature Reserves	286	172.5
Local Nature Reserves[2]	241	17.1
Sites of Special Scientific Interest (SSSIs)[2]	5 671	1 778.5
notified under 1981 Act	5 576	1 721.5
subject to S15 management agreements	(a)	98.5
Areas of Scientific Interest[3]	46	63.4
Areas of Special Scientific Interest[3]	26	6.9
Special Protection Areas	40	134.4
Biosphere Reserves	13	44.3
'Ramsar' wetland sites	44	133.7
Environmentally Sensitive Areas	19	785.6

(a) = 2032 agreements

Notes:

[1] Some areas may be included in more than one category. For example in Great Britain NNRs, SPAs, Biosphere Reserves and Ramsar sites are all SSSIs.

[2] Great Britain only.

[3] Northern Ireland only.

Source: NCC, DOE (NI), MAFF

country has taken steps to prevent or eliminate as soon as possible exploitation or occupation of the whole area ... and (c) where visitors are allowed to enter ... for inspirational, cultural and recreational purposes.'

The IUCN distinguishes between Category I protected areas, which are large tracts of scientific reserves and strict nature reserves that possess outstanding, representative ecosystems, and to which public access is generally limited. National parks and provincial parks come into Category II – large areas of national or international significance not materially altered by human activity, but which may be used for recreation. This is why such a definition excludes the UK's national parks, since a range of land uses is permitted within them. Category III areas are natural monuments and similar areas that contain unique geological formations, unusual habitats or plants and animals of special ecological or conservation importance.

- Africa possesses 260 Category I–III sites, covering 91.2 million ha; 34 of these sites are over 1 million ha. Kenya has 31 such sites

Table 7.4   Sites of Special Scientific Interest reported as damaged, Great Britain 1990–91

Damage[1] caused by	Short-term damage[2]	Long-term damage[3]	Partial or full loss[4]	Total
Agricultural activities	102	6	3	111
Forestry activities	3	2	–	5
Activities given planning permission	1	9	2	12
Activities of statutory undertakers and other public bodies not included above	13	5	1	19
Recreational activities	38	5	1	44
Miscellaneous activities[5]	60	6	3	69
Insufficient management	16	–	–	16

Notes:

[1] Some cases of damage are caused by more than one activity.

[2] Damage from which the special interest could recover.

[3] Damage causing a lasting reduction in the special interest.

[4] Damage which will result in denotification of the special interest.

[5] Including pollution, unauthorised tipping and burning.

Source: EN, CCW, SNH

covering 3.4 million ha, South Africa twenty (3.3 million ha) and Zambia also twenty (6.4 million ha). Madagascar, a major biodiversity hotspot, has sixteen category I–III sites (0.7 million ha).

- In Asia there are 422 Category I–III sites covering 36.1 million ha; eighteen of these sites are over 1 million ha. Indonesia possesses 108 such sites (13.9 million ha), Thailand 66 (3.4 million ha) and India 60 (3.7 million ha).

- Equivalent figures for North and Central America are 606 sites and 170.4 million ha; 37 sites are over 1 million ha. The USA has 290 Category I–III sites (38.7 million ha), Canada 132 sites (26.8 million ha) and Mexico 42 (2.0 million ha).

- In South America, the 314 Category I–III areas (65.8 million ha) include 25 sites over 1 million ha. Brazil has 112 sites (18.4 million ha), Venezuela 49 (13.8 million ha), Colombia 35 (9.0 million ha) and Chile 31 (8.4 million ha).

- In Europe there are 298 such sites (8.5 million ha), although they tend to be smaller than elsewhere in the world. Norway has 52 sites (1.3 million ha), Finland 36 (0.5 million ha), Bulgaria 28 (0.2 million ha) and the Netherlands 26 (0.2 million ha). Because of its permissive approach to public access, the UK has no sites in categories I–III. The former USSR totals 164 such sites (23.8 million ha), four being over 1 million ha. The Russian Federation possesses 74 such sites (20.0 million ha), Georgia fifteen (0.2 million ha), the Ukraine thirteen (0.3 million ha) and Azerbaijan eleven (0.2 million ha) (data from Table 20.1 in World Resources Institute, 1994).

National parks (Category II) are an important part of this network, but a variety of models of national park are found throughout the world. The earliest national parks in the USA were created to preserve wild landscapes. Increasingly throughout the world, however, emphasis has shifted to include what might broadly be called nature conservation, with the safeguarding of areas of high biodiversity, endemism and threatened habitat a priority. Costa Rica, for example, introduced a system of national parks in the 1970s that now gives protection to 12% of its land, and that are a focus for both scientific research and the tourism which in the 1990s has become the country's second largest source of outside income. The two main national parks are La Selva, largely a tropical rain forest area, and Guanacaste National Park. The latter comprises former and remnant seasonal tropical forest subject to a major restoration programme and designated an International Biosphere Reserve.

Sengwa National Park in Zimbabwe was created solely for research purposes. Most African national parks, however, are explicitly geared to ecotourism. An example is Kenya, where tourism – largely safari-based ecotourism – has been the nation's greatest source of foreign income (currently over US$250 million per annum) since 1988. Seventeen national parks and wildlife reserves cover 7.5% of the land area, generating income and employment, and conserving soil, vegetation and wildlife. Tourism is estimated to be 50 times more valuable to Amboseli National Park, for example, than agriculture would be. The annual value to the tourist industry of one lion in Amboseli has been estimated at $27 000 and one herd of elephants, $610 000 (Raven et al., 1998).

The need to protect representative natural areas is also seen by some countries as being important. In New Zealand, for instance, a major conservation goal is to include at least one area in the suite of national parks that represents each major ecosystem found in that country. Even small countries can provide this kind of protection: Taiwan, for example, has four national parks, all created since 1980.

Another approach to protecting areas and their constituent species is through *biosphere reserves*. In 1981, UNESCO proposed that at least one, and preferably five or more, such reserves should be established in each of the world's 193 biogeographical regions. By the late 1990s, over 300 biosphere reserves had been created in 76 nations. Biosphere reserves must be large enough to avoid the risk of species loss from extrinsic factors such as disturbance and intrinsic factors such as inbreeding depression. Indeed, such reserves are generally large enough to incorporate three different kinds of use and management: a legally protected *core area*, which is used as a strict nature reserve; a *buffer zone*, which serves to protect the core but in which certain prescribed activities may take place, for example sustainable forestry and recreation; and a *transition zone*, where local economic development is integrated with conservation, for example agroforestry and silvopastoralism.

7.3 Ecological concepts

- The status of individual species in the ecosystem: rarity and ecological significance
- Dispersal and migration
- Colonisation
- Zonation
- Succession

7.3.1 The status of individual species in the ecosystem: rarity and ecological significance

While the structural integrity and functional efficiency of an ecosystem depend on the interaction of its component species (community interactions), not all species are necessarily of equal importance. It is dangerous to argue that any particular species is redundant, but loss of a species is often apparently accompanied by no essential change in any community characteristics. The extent to which a species is merely a constituent part, important or crucial to a community and its ecosystem may reflect its abundance and its functional role.

It might be expected that rare species would have less impact on a community than common ones. There are different kinds of rarity, however, with different kinds of importance to the community. Rarity is a relative concept, and we have to ask, rare in relation to what? Small geographical range, food or habitat specialisms, and low population size all potentially interlink. Thus many predators have a wide geographical and habitat range but occur at low densities and are therefore uncommon at any particular location, for

example golden eagles (*Aquila chrysaëtos*). The bee orchid (*Ophrys apifera*) has sizeable self-sustaining populations in Western Europe but is limited to a particular habitat of limited occurrence, chalk downland.

Thus *geographical scale* is important, and we need to distinguish between species that are

- rare in a particular locale but common elsewhere in their range, e.g. ling (*Calluna vulgaris*), rare in the West Midlands region of the UK but common elsewhere in the country.
- nationally or globally rare, with low populations at any one location, for example the giant panda (*Ailuropoda melanoleuca*).
- nationally or globally rare, but with high populations at some or all locations, for example marine iguanas (*Amblyrhynchus cristatus*), unique to the Galapagos Islands.

Similarly, the *evolutionary and palaeogeographical history* of a species is important, distinguishing between species that are

- evolutionarily young (recent speciation) and, other things being equal, yet to expand, common with microspecies such as are found in dandelions (*Taraxacum*).
- evolutionarily old and contracting in range, for example the plant genus *Jovellana*, today found only in New Zealand and parts of Chile (the disjunct distribution reflecting continental drift).
- relict species, for instance those that 'migrated' upslope as ice advanced during the Pleistocene glaciations, surviving on nunataks (mountain tops extending above the ice) then stranded there when the ice retreated, for example the alpine plant *Koenigia islandica*, restricted in the UK to high altitudes in the Scottish islands of Skye and Mull.

Ecological requirements are also crucial, for instance regarding species that have

- specific food or habitat requirements, in this way restricted to where their particular requirements are found, for example the bee orchid mentioned above, or the osprey (*Pandion haliaeetus*), which has a wide geographical range but is limited by its dietary specialisation on fish.

- populations that are suppressed by predators, disease, etc., but which would expand in numbers and range were this constraint to be lifted.
- a high trophic position: top predators, especially large ones, tend to be few in number because of the loss of energy at each transfer of energy from one trophic level to the next (see Section 2.3.7) and therefore the number of animals at the 'end' of a food chain that can be supported by the available energy at that stage.

Rare species may be at risk of extinction, whether from instrinsic factors such as inbreeding depression or extrinsic ones such as human activities. Nevertheless, rarity in itself does not necessarily mean that the status or indeed continuation of a species is at risk. Many rare species have survived for long geological periods, for example the coelacanth (*Latimeria chalumnae*), a primitive fish limited to the Indian Ocean off the Comoro Islands, which until 1938 had been known only as 90-million-year-old fossils.

All the same, species that are in some way endangered tend to be rare species. In the context of plant conservation (although equally applicable to animals) the IUCN has made the following distinctions:

- *endangered species* are those in danger of extinction within all or a significant part of their range in the near future, and whose

survival is unlikely if the causal factors continue to operate (also see Issues Box 7.1). An example is *Echium pininana*, reduced to a single population in the cloud zone of La Palma, Canary Islands, threatened by goats and by collecting for horticulture.

- *threatened* and *vulnerable species* are those likely to become endangered in the foreseeable future if the causal factors (threats) continue to operate, or if such threats are introduced. An example is American yellowweed (*Cladrastis lutea*), a small tree with a sporadic distribution in ten states of the eastern USA, always rare in its few localities but the threat of extinction accentuated by flooding following dam construction.
- *rare species* are those with a small total population size or restricted to a small geographical area, and by virtue of this are at risk. An example is *Saxifraga biternata*, known only from two small, mountainous localities in Spain, at slight risk in one of these from picnickers but reported to be abundant at both sites, and with no evidence of any population decline (Synge, 1981).

The *1988 IUCN red list of threatened animals* (Wilcox, 1988) identified 1672 animal species in these four categories, but some less studied invertebrate groups are certain to be greatly under-represented (Tables 7.5 and 7.6). Estimates for

Table 7.5 Status of animals worldwide

Group	E	T	V	R	Total
Mammals	167	1	143	39	350
Birds	111	0	69	122	302
Reptiles	36	4	39	41	120
Amphibians	8	0	9	20	37
Fish	79	3	135	83	300
Molluscs	67	0	22	20	109
Annelids	2	0	8	1	11
Spiders	1	0	1	1	3
Crustacea	1	0	3	9	16
Insects	117	2	150	155	424
Totals	592	10	579	491	1672

Key: E = endangered; T = threatened; V = vulnerable; R = rare

Table 7.6   Threatened species as a percentage of species known, late 1980s

Country	Mammals	Birds	Fish	Reptiles	Amphibians	Vascular plants
Australia	13.4	3.3	–	1.6	4.0	12.3
Austria	29.4	28.4	36.2	46.2	10.5	15.9
Belgium	21.5	29.0	–	75.0	100.0	24.0
Canada	7.3	3.8	1.2	2.4	2.4	0.8
Denmark	28.6	17.4	7.8	0.0	21.4	13.7
Finland	11.3	6.0	12.1	20.0	20.0	5.6
France	52.2	39.8	18.6	38.9	62.1	8.4
Ireland	16.1	23.7	–	0.0	33.3	–
Italy	13.4	14.3	13.9	52.2	46.4	10.0
Japan	7.4	8.1	10.6	3.5	6.3	10.2
Netherlands	48.3	33.1	22.4	85.7	66.7	–
New Zealand	20.3	5.7	0.4	17.9	–	4.8
Norway	7.4	10.2	1.2	20.0	40.0	4.5
Portugal	51.2	39.6	28.2	37.1	23.5	–
Spain	14.8	14.5	18.2	14.1	4.2	2.5
Sweden	15.4	6.8	4.6	0.0	38.5	8.2
Switzerland	46.3	50.9	–	80.0	78.9	25.8
Turkey	30.5	16.9	18.7	50.5	72.2	–
United Kingdom	31.2	15.0	3.4	45.5	33.3	9.6
United States	10.5	7.2	2.4	7.1	3.6	0.5
West Germany	46.8	32.1	70.0	75.0	57.9	28.2

Source: OECD Environmental Indicators, 1991. *The State of the Environment*, Paris, France. OECD Publications Office

vascular plants are that 20 000–25 000 come into these four categories, with 15 780 actually listed as endangered or threatened (Davis *et al.*, 1986; Lucas and Synge, 1978).

Discussion of community indicators and of top-down or bottom-up control (see Section 5.3.9 and Ecology Box 5.2) indicated that in many communities there is one species (or sometimes group of species) that controls community dynamics. Other species depend on or are at least greatly affected by such a species. This critical component of the system is known as a *keystone species*: like the keystone in the centre of an arch its disappearance would mean the collapse of the structure, in this case the community and perhaps even the whole ecosystem. Keystone species in systems with top-down control are, by definition, top predators, and equally by definition they are unlikely to be abundant. They may even be considered to be rare, yet they exert a profound influence.

Keystone species are thus critical for conservation biologists to maintain, because the decline or disappearance of a keystone species would probably also lead to the disappearance of many other species. Hunting large carnivores such as wolves and big cats to (local) extinction may allow grazing animals to increase dramatically in numbers, to overgraze their pastures or range, in turn leading to a population crash (see Sections 5.3.7 and 5.3.8). This appears to have happened with the grey wolf (*Canis lupus*) in Yellowstone National Park. Wolves were shot and trapped to extinction there in the 1930s under a federal programme of extermination, but deer (*Odocoileus*) and elk (*Alces alces*) numbers then shot up, over-browsing much of their forage and starving to death in their thousands during harsh winters. With much of the vegetation damaged herbivorous insects also declined, and many insectivorous birds disappeared.

Off the coast of California, from Monterey Bay

to Point Conception, and in the Aleutian Islands of Alaska, are remnant populations of sea otters (*Enhydra lutris*). These animals feed on crustaceans, molluscs and sea urchins. Sea urchins in particular are important grazers on giant kelp (*Macrocystis*), a large brown seaweed that forms dense swards on the sea bed and provides important habitat for a number of other species. Where sea otters are abundant (as at Amchitka Island, Aleutians) they keep numbers of urchins low, so there is little grazing pressure on the kelp, which also thrives. Where sea otters are absent (as at Shemya Island), urchin numbers expand and consume large quantities of kelp, and the whole system is impoverished (Figure 7.4). Sea otters thus have a key community

effect: this is indeed a keystone species and an example of top-down control (Estes and Duggins, 1995). However, it could be argued that the kelp is also a keystone species: it is the critical basis of the whole food web, and without it there would be fewer shellfish and perhaps no sea otters, an example of bottom-up control. Take away the otters and the system *changes*; take away the kelp and the system *disappears*.

By concentrating effort and perhaps ensuring the survival of one keystone species, conservation biologists thus go a long way to ensure survival of a whole community in a cost-effective manner. Other species may not be crucial to the integrity or species richness of a community, but their survival nevertheless enhances the chances of the survival of other species. Examples are fig (*Ficus*) trees in tropical moist forests, the fruit of which provides a dependable, year-round resource for many vertebrates, and baobab (*Adansonia digitata*) trees in the African savannas, which serve as mini-oases of shade and safety for a large and varied animal community. By focusing attention on such *umbrella species* (i.e. species affording protection to a range of organisms) conservation again becomes cost-effective (Issues Box 7.3).

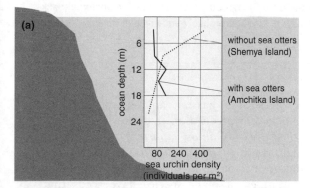

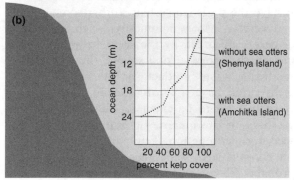

Figure 7.4 The effect of sea otters on sea urchin density and kelp cover at Shemya Island (otters absent) and Amchitka Island (otters present), Aleutian Islands. Without sea otters preying on sea urchins numbers of urchins increase and exert a strong grazing pressure on kelp. With sea otters, urchin numbers are controlled, and kelp is allowed to flourish. Kelp is the basis of an important subtidal ecosystem. Sea otters are the keystone species in top-down control of the ecosystem.

7.3.2 Dispersal and migration

Dispersal needs to be examined at both the local and the broader geographical scale. Local dispersal involves the generally seasonal spread of spores, seeds and juvenile animals. Sometimes such dispersal is very local indeed, but in the context of wind dispersal and the use of moving water – fluvial or marine – relatively long distances can be travelled. There is therefore overlap with broader-scale dispersal, which in turn can take the form of, again, seasonal movements or migration, or over a longer period of time an extension of the species' geographical range.

7.3.2.1 Seed dispersal and dispersal of juvenile animals

In plants, dispersal serves to spread seeds or spores over as wide an area as possible to avoid

---

ISSUES BOX 7.3

Flagship species

Another important kind of species in conservation is that of the *flagship species*. These are usually rare and often have little importance to ecological functioning, but they have a resonance with the public and are therefore invaluable for raising support, including money, for specific rescue conservation projects that have a more general conservation value: protect the flagship species' habitat and you protect the habitat of perhaps hundreds of other vulnerable species.

Flagship species tend to be 'attractive' in some way. Examples include the panda (*Ailuropoda melanoleuca*), used as the logo for the World Wide Fund for Nature/World Wildlife Fund, and the avocet (*Recurvirostra avosetta*), a black-and-white wading bird used by the Royal Society for the Protection of Birds. Neither of these animals is a crucial component of any community.

Other species may be more important in the ecological community, for example the tiger (*Panthera tigris*) (Save the Tiger Fund) and that symbol of the USA, the bald eagle (*Haliaeetus leucocephalus*).

'Save the bushdog' does not have the same clarion call about it, even though *Speothos venaticus*, a nocturnal pack-hunting, rodent-eating Latin American member of the dog family, is rare and probably endangered: it simply is not known and therefore uncared about.

---

intraspecific competition with both parent and fellow offspring, and to offer the maximum chance (for chance it is) of finding an appropriate unoccupied space for germination. Different mechanisms have evolved to accomplish this, from the use of small light seed with feathery appendages to take advantage of wind – as with dandelion (*Taraxacum*), willowherb (*Epilobium* and *Chamerion* species), and all grasses – to the explosive scatter of plants such as the balsams touch-me-not (*Impatiens non-tangere*) and Himalayan balsam (*I. glandulifera*), and even heavier seeds such as those of broom (*Cytisus scoparius*). Some plants adopt a system akin to a priest's senser, which releases the seeds when shaken by wind or passing animal, for example ragged robin (*Lychnis flos-cuculi*) and species of poppy. Heavy tree seeds using wind dispersal, such as those of sycamore (*Acer pseudoplatanus*), ash (*Fraxinus* spp.) and elms (*Ulmus* spp.), are generally flattened to maximise the surface that can be carried by the wind.

Seed dispersal may be achieved using animals (*zoochory*) either externally or following consumption. External transport is facilitated by the seeds or seed cases being covered with small hooks or burrs that are picked up on the fur or feathers of a passing animal and subsequently knocked or preened off. Examples are cleavers, or goosegrass (*Galium aparine*), and enchanter's nightshade (*Circaea lucetiana*). Seeds are an important source of food for many animals, and a number of plant species have seeds that can survive the digestive system so that some emerge in excreta. More commonly, such means of dispersal are aided by the seeds being contained in fruit that are the food source, the seeds representing a waste product for the animal. These seeds often have a hard protective layer. Some actually need to be eaten for digestive juices or crushing in the gizzard of birds to prepare the seed for germination. Fruit and frugivore have often co-evolved, sometimes dangerously so. It is probable that seeds of the rare endemic tree *Calvaria major* on Mauritius had become dependent on being crushed in the gizzards of the dodo (*Raphanus cucullatus*); with the dodo's extinction in 1681, the plant lost its only chance of germinating. Temple (1977) fed seventeen *Calvaria* seeds to domestic turkeys as a dodo substitute: ten passed through the bird successfully and three subsequently germinated – probably the first seeds of this plant to do so for over three centuries.

Seeds can also be transported by animals for individual burial or storage in caches for later consumption: many oak, hazel, beech and pine trees have grown from seed buried in such a manner. Birds such as jays and acorn woodpeckers, however, store seeds in tree trunks, which is of no use to the parent tree. Ants are also important seed storers, especially of leguminous plants such as gorse (*Ulex*) and broom, such dispersal being called *myrmecochory*.

Unlike pollination using animals, which is often directed, with 'reward' (nectar) on delivery, seed dispersal provides 'payment in advance' and no guarantee that the seed will end up in a suitable location for germination and subsequent success. Many seeds possess a *dormancy* which will allow them to remain in, for example, soil for a number of years as a seed bank in anticipation of an appropriate environmental trigger that will initiate germination. Such triggers are light and temperature (important for many woodland plants) and water (crucial for desert plants), and are often effected following disturbance, such as a treefall in woodland or fire in heathland. Most seeds remain viable for no more than ten years, and often less, but some legumes have been reported as germinating after 50 years, and with freezing even longer. Lupin seeds, for example, 10 000 years old, have reputedly germinated after having been found in frozen lemming burrows in cold, dry Russian tundra (Fitter, 1987).

Many parallels can be drawn with dispersal in animals. Eggs of some parasitic animals may be eaten, transported and egested just as with seed, and other small animals are typically transported on the bodies of larger species (*phoresy*). Propagule dispersal from many *sessile* (fixed) intertidal animals is a chance affair involving tides and currents, with most offspring not finding a suitable substrate upon which to settle and develop. For most vertebrates, however, postnatal dispersal owes less to chance and, especially in mammals, often involves male juveniles.

Post-natal movements may serve to disperse a growing population so that local resources are not overexploited. Another reason is to prevent inbreeding by allowing populations to mix and in this way retain high genetic variability. Dispersal is a risky activity, partly because animals on the

move tend to be at greater risk of predation, partly because the animal is perhaps literally moving into unknown territory: there is no guarantee that suitable habitat will be found or that suitable habitat will not already be fully occupied and defended. It makes sense, therefore, to expect that dispersal movements be made by individuals with low reproductive value, which in turn implies juvenile males – juvenile because their fitness and reproductive skills have yet to be demonstrated, and males because the viability of a population depends more on the number of eggs than the number of sources of sperm. This is exactly the scenario in many dispersing bird and mammal species.

Local dispersal may be triggered by density factors in relation to carrying capacity, as was shown in the case of lemmings (see Ecology Box 5.3). In aphids, many species are able to produce low-fecundity winged forms (*alates*) when population pressure is high, which allows them to disperse, subsequently to revert to wingless morphs, which have higher fertility rates. Dispersal may also be triggered by environmental factors. These may reflect the inherent 'risk' properties of an environment. In the UK, for example, 64% of diving beetles from temporary ponds can fly, while only 25% of those from permanent water bodies can do so, presumably because the need to disperse in less. Environmental triggers can also be extrinsic factors such as flooding or drought, sometimes seasonal and predictable, often not.

7.3.2.2 Migration

Where environmental constraints are predictable, dispersal also becomes a predictable solution to avoiding such stresses, and evolution has facilitated the ability of many animals to travel great distances. Such migration is characteristically seasonal and involves return migration when the stress is lifted. Many temperate breeding birds, for example, are actually summer visitors: each autumn they migrate to warmer environments where food is available, then return to temperate latitudes in spring to breed. Winter visitors to cool temperate regions similarly travel from polar regions: many geese do this, for example, as do large mammals such as the musk ox (*Ovibos moschatus*) and caribou/reindeer (*Rangifer tarandus*).

Salmon and eels are good examples of fish that not only migrate, but do so when young from fresh water to the sea then, when ready to spawn, from sea back to fresh water – indeed, to the natal river.

Such migrating animals need to build up massive reserves of fat to use in energetically exhausting long-distance travel. Migrating birds and insects must suffer the vagaries of wind, and huge flocks and swarms provide a predictable and massive supply of food for predatory animals, which therefore present another danger.

Some migration routes are well travelled by a range of species, for example the movement across the Gulf of Mexico from North to South America (although many birds and insects take the longer but perhaps safer land route through Central America or island-hop from Florida to the Yucatán Peninsula via Cuba), and the movement of birds from North and Western Europe via Gibraltar to various parts of Africa. The greatest distance travelled by a bird during migration is that of the Arctic tern (*Sterna paradisaea*), which travels from pole to pole, but other long-distance migrant birds are the Manx shearwater (*Puffinus puffinus*), greater shearwater (*P. gravis*) and Wilson's petrel (*Oceanites oceanicus*) (Figure 7.5).

It should also be pointed out that, having bred, many species of albatross travel great distances out at sea over most of the year. The wandering albatross (*Diamedea exulans*), for example, takes advantage of the almost continuous westerly winds to fly without resting in the region of 40° S. At this latitude, the distance around the globe is about 32 000 km.

Other migrations reflect animals' movements away from drought to lusher pastures, perhaps best exemplified by the distances covered by hoofed animals of the East African plains, where huge multi-species herds including giraffes

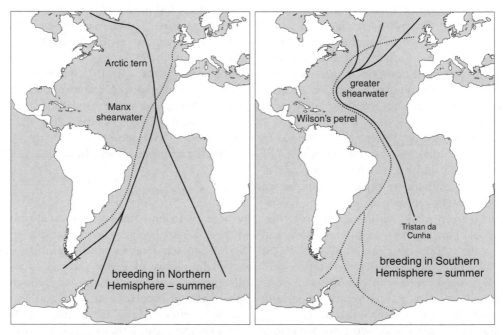

Figure 7.5 Migration of Arctic terns, Manx shearwaters, greater shearwaters and Wilson's petrels. A number of sea birds travel enormous distances twice a year in order to live in perpetual spring and summer. Some, notably the Manx shearwater and the Arctic tern, breed in the summer of the Northern Hemisphere and fly south to spend the summer in the Southern Hemisphere. In contrast, the greater shearwater and Wilson's petrel nest on the Southern Hemisphere. But they too make enormous migration journeys.

(*Giraffa camelopardalus*), plains zebras (*Equus burchelli*), wildebeest (*Connochaetes taurinus*) and a variety of antelopes follow the rains in search of fresh pastures. And as the grazers move, so too do many of their predators, especially the big cats – lions (*Panthera leo*), leopards (*P. pardus*) and cheetahs (*Acinonyx jubata*).

Animals generally migrate in groups for a number of reasons, including defence, safety in numbers, taking advantage of experienced individuals (and gaining that experience), and efficient flight (seen for example in the V-formation used by many waterfowl). Homing ability is often phenomenal, so that birds such as the swallow (*Hirundo rustica*) and the swift (*Apus apus*) not only return from their African wintering quarters to the same localities in Europe but even to their former nest sites. Navigation is achieved by using the Earth's magnetic field or the celestial (stars) map for long flights, then using visible landmarks and smell when in the general homing area (Street, 1976).

7.3.3 Colonisation

Dispersing propagules of plants and juvenile animals may, often fortuitously, find an available and appropriate space upon which to settle and develop. Availability implies that a potentially competing individual (not necessarily of a different species) is not yet present, and that environmental conditions are suitable. If the organism, or better still a population, is able to grow and successfully reproduce, then colonisation has taken place.

Sites that are freshly colonised may be spatial gaps in an already existing community. The more impoverished the community in terms of species, numbers and functional linkages the more susceptible it might be to colonisation. Examples of such gaps are treefall sites in woodland and burnt areas in heathland or savanna. Regrowth in such areas by plants can partly be from remaining shoots, but it is likely that new plants will also enter the site, either from outside (current dispersal) or from the seed bank (reflecting prior dispersal). *Fugitive species* are those unable to compete with other species, but they can colonise gaps quickly, grow and reproduce, and if gap creation is sufficiently frequent in space and time then they can persist in the overall community as a metapopulation. Pre-emption of space is also important: the first coloniser can establish itself to such an extent that it can exclude or reduce the vigour of another, later-arriving species that, in other circumstances, would be an equal or even superior competitor.

There are many circumstances when a bare, inorganic substrate such as rock, mud or sand is colonised, and colonising species must therefore be able to withstand extreme environmental conditions such as exposure, fluctuations in water availability and an absence of nutrients or food. These *pioneer species* must first of all possess the means to disperse and perhaps also characteristically be able to do so in high numbers in a procedure fraught with danger and reliant on chance. They must also be able to settle securely on an inhospitable substrate. Pioneers therefore tend either to be habitat specialists, with a narrow but appropriate range of tolerance for potentially limiting factors, or eurytopic generalists that can, for example, tolerate drought conditions yet take up water immediately and effectively on its perhaps brief and unpredictable availability.

7.3.4 Zonation

On a stable substrate such as a rocky seashore there is, quite literally, an environmental gradient – not only in the sense of there being a slope but also in terms of degree of exposure to tidal movement of water, from being submerged for most of the time to being out of the water except for spring high tides. Because different plant and animal species have different ranges of tolerance (see Section 4.3.1), we should expect to see different species colonising different sections of the rock. Most species found on rocky seashores are essentially marine: they require salt water in order to function, and when the tide is out they cease activity until it returns. Seaweeds reduce metabolic activity to a minimum; bivalves such as mussels close their shells; gastropods such as periwinkles and, very effectively, limpets clamp down on the rocks; barnacles close their upper plates; the tentacles of sea anemones are withdrawn, and so on. The greatest abiotic environmental risk is desiccation, but each organism can tolerate different levels of exposure to air, reflecting different tolerance levels to combinations of temperature, light, salinity and submergence. They will each grow where they can, provided that they can colonise the location and that they are not out-competed for that space.

Species that succeed in extreme conditions such as rocky shorelines tend to be specialists with narrow ranges of tolerance. If we plotted the range of tolerance for each species along the environmental gradient in the absence of competition we might get a pattern such as in Figure 7.6a, where ten species are distributed with overlapping ranges of tolerance, narrower ranges being found at the environmentally more extreme upper and lower ends of the gradient. In practice, however, competition might sharpen the boundaries of where the species are actually found on the slope, species at the edges of their tolerance threshold being excluded by species for which that position is closer to optimal: distribution is thus a matter of environmental tolerance moderated by competitive exclusion, and a pattern rather like that in Figure 7.6b may emerge. Species with narrower ranges of tolerance in the more extreme locations are likely to exclude less tolerant species entirely; those with broader ranges of tolerance in less extreme (*mesotopic*) conditions will be more likely to show coexistence and therefore overlapping distributions. One therefore tends to get single-species (*monospecific*) or species-poor (*oligospecific*) stands in the one case, *polyspecific* communities in the other. In mesotopic parts, one community may merge into the next, with many species in common but with differences in abundance. In extreme conditions, there will be sharp boundaries between the single-species or species-poor stands, and these boundaries are often visible to the eye. These boundaries separate discrete zones. This spatial pattern along an environmental gradient is *zonation*. The environment provides opportunities and constraints to species and communities, and the controlling

abiotic factors are therefore external, *allogenic* or *exogenous* – three terms in this context meaning essentially the same.

This can be exemplified by transposing Figure 7.6b on to a real-life situation such as the salt marsh shown in Figure 7.6c. At the seaward margin we might find *Enteromorpha*, a green macroalga that is essentially submerged all the time. Eelgrass (*Zostera*) can withstand brief emergence, while glasswort (*Salicornia*) is a terrestrial species that can withstand frequent submergence, as can cordgrass (*Spartina*) but not by as much. These are therefore plants that tolerate extreme environmental conditions, and they tend to form monospecific stands. Further upshore, a mixture of species is found, although some found lower down – such as sea purslane (*Halimione portulacoides*) may disappear upslope, where other salt-tolerant species such as thrift (or sea pink, *Armeria maritima*) may enter instead, so a lower and upper general salt marsh community might be distinguishable. Finally, conditions become less driven by salt water inundation and first rushes then grasses that can tolerate a salt-rich damp soil but are rarely flooded by the tide may form a meadow.

On rocky shores, the upper limit of a particular zone is in practice often determined by physical factors, the lower limit by competition. An example of zonation in seaweed species at Filey Brigg on the Yorkshire coast is shown on Figure 7.7, where plotting presence/abundance against position shows a replacement series: channel wrack (*Pelvetia canaliculata*, the only brown seaweed that can tolerate long periods of emergence) at the upper margins overlaps slightly with flat wrack (*Fucus spiralis*) downslope, which shows a sharp boundary with knotted wrack (*Ascophyllum nodosum*) at just under 12 hours emergence (based on low water mark ordinary spring tide); bladder wrack (*F. vesiculosus*) and serrated wrack (*F. serratus*) and the subtidal kelps (*Laminaria saccharina* and *L. hyperborea*) then follow, the last not tolerating more than 3 hours emergence at the lowest of spring tides. Experimental removal of bladder wrack and knotted wrack allows flat wrack to extend its distribution seawards, demonstrating that the lower limit of flat wrack is fixed by the presence of superior

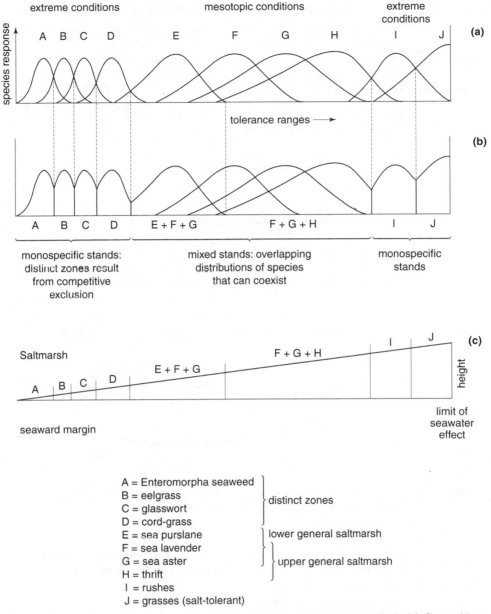

extreme conditions   mesotopic conditions   extreme conditions

A   B   C   D   E   F   G   H   I   J   (a)

species response

tolerance ranges ⟶

(b)

A   B   C   D   E + F + G   F + G + H   I   J

monospecific stands: distinct zones result from competitive exclusion   mixed stands: overlapping distributions of species that can coexist   monospecific stands

(c)

Saltmarsh   F + G + H   I   J

E + F + G

height

A   B   C   D

seaward margin   limit of seawater effect

A = Enteromorpha seaweed ⎫
B = eelgrass   ⎬ distinct zones
C = glasswort
D = cord-grass ⎭
E = sea purslane ⎫ lower general saltmarsh
F = sea lavender ⎭
G = sea aster ⎫ upper general saltmarsh
H = thrift   ⎭
I = rushes
J = grasses (salt-tolerant)

Figure 7.6 (a) Overlapping ranges of tolerance along an environmental gradient. (b) Competitive exclusion leads to zonation at the extreme parts of the environmental gradient. (c) Zonation and coexistence along a salt marsh gradient.

competitors rather than by an inability to tolerate conditions of deeper water. Zonation of plants (seaweeds) on the shore is paralleled by that of animal species and communities.

Zonation is also evident at larger scales of study, in particular as vegetation changes in relation to altitude and boundaries of varying degrees of sharpness are evident as one moves up the slopes of certainly the taller mountains. Globally, the effect of latitude has to be taken into account, and equivalent zones are therefore found at higher altitudes the closer one gets to the Equator (Figure 7.8). This is especially evident in the altitudinal location of the treeline (Table 7.7).

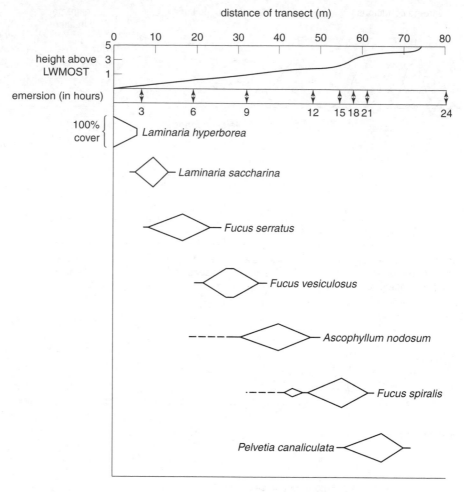

Figure 7.7 Zonation of major seaweed species on the rocky shore at Filey Brigg, East Yorkshire, UK, in relation to length of submergence/emergence.

Another use of the word 'zonation' is in relation to the broadly latitudinal belts of vegetation types that recapitulate the broadly latitudinal belts of climate. The tundra zone, for example, is followed in a general way by the coniferous forest zone as one moves towards the Equator, which in turn is followed by the mixed forest zone, broadleaved deciduous forest zone, and so on. Vegetation types not following this latitudinal pattern, but still reflecting climate, are called *interzonal*, for example west coast American mediterranean-type vegetation (chaparral in California, matorral in Chile). Where factors other than climate are critical in establishing vegetation types, these latter are called *azonal*, for example

salt marshes (responding to tides) and heathlands (responding to fire or grazing).

7.3.5 Succession

The tidal and wave dynamics of rocky shores ensure that environmental conditions remain the same over time. Where such forces are absent, colonising plants are able to effect environmental changes, which in turn feed back into changes in the character of the vegetation itself.

A bare rock surface, for example, may be colonised by lichens and mosses. Lichens are in fact two organisms, an alga and a fungus, that live

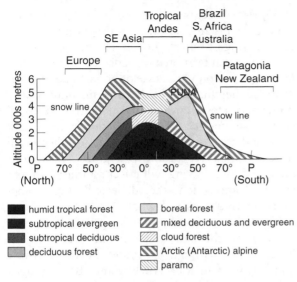

Figure 7.8 Diagrammatic north–south global cross-section illustrating variation in altitude of main vegetation zones.

together as one, a form of obligatory *mutualism* called a *symbiosis*. Mosses are bryophytes, which are true plants. These pioneer organisms are able to colonise rocks because they do not need a root system but instead superficially penetrate the surface using very small hair-like growths – fungal hyphae and moss rhizinae.

Rocks are subject to *physical weathering*, where tiny fragments are worn off by the abrasive action of particle-laden wind and water and (in cold climates) by freeze–thaw action. Some of the weathered material may remain trapped in crevices in the rock. Precipitation may be mildly acidic, and this too can etch away at the rock, a form of *chemical weathering*. And hyphae and rhizinae also penetrate and fragment the rock surface as a form of *biological weathering*. Gradually, then, a film of inorganic material may accumulate over parts of the rock. The plants themselves not only live and grow, they also die, and dead fragments are subjected to processes of decomposition. In this way, small amounts of organic matter are added to the inorganic material.

This is the beginning of a soil. Environmental conditions have changed, for there is now a shallow rooting layer containing nutrients and better able to hold moisture. The *habitat potential*, that is the potential of the habitat to sustain a more complex vegetation, has become greater. Whereas before only lichens and mosses could colonise, now it might be possible for shallow-rooting plants such as grasses to establish themselves. The process continues, the second suite of plants improving the habitat potential yet further,

Table 7.7 Altitude of tree line (with main species) at different locations

Location		Altitude (m)	Main species
63°N	Sweden	1000	Birch (*Betula pubescens*)
60°N	Alaska	900	Sitka spruce (*Picea sitchensis*)
50°N	British Columbia	1850–1900	*Abies lasiocarpa* (krummholz to 2500)
50°N	Rockies (Alberta)	2150–2300	Englemann spruce (*P. engelmannii*)
47°N	Switzerland	1900–2000	*Pinus cembra* and *P. abies*
41–44°N	Caucasus	up to 2500	*Betula verrucosa*
38°N	S. Nevada	3300	*Pinus albicaulis* (krummholz to 3750)
28°N	E. Himalayan	3800	*Larix griffithii*
19°N	Mexico	mean 3950	
		max. 4100	*Pinus hartweggi*
9°S	Andes	4100	*Polylepi*
6°S	New Guinea	3900–4100	*Podocarpus compactus*
19°S	N. Chile	4900	*Polylepi tomentella*
36°S	Snowy Mts (Aust.)	1850–2000	*Eucalyptus niphophila*
42°S	South Island (NZ)	1200–1300	*Nothafagus menziesii*

and further waves of species can enter the changing plant community.

There thus exists a series of successive stages of vegetation, a process undertaken in the context of the overall physical environment (climate, substrate, etc.) but which is essentially regulated by the plants themselves. This process is known as *succession*, and each stage is called a *sere*. (In practice, stages may merge into each other through time and any distinction of sere boundaries is notional.) There comes a point, however, when the vegetation is in equilibrium with its environment, and no further changes in the essential character of the community will take place. Succession ceases, and a *climax community* has been reached.

At a very broad continental scale, climate is usually the key environmental factor in relation to which the vegetation has reached a state of equilibrium, hence the parallels between climatic zones and those of vegetation. But climate is not the only possible environmental variable effecting a particular climax vegetation and – especially at regional and local scales – particular examples of climax vegetation could reflect such factors as wind, fire, grazing, slope, flooding and, of course, human activity.

A *prisere* occurs where succession takes place from an inorganic substrate right through to the climax stage. Often, however, the process of succession is interrupted or deflected, in particular (although not only) because of human activity. For example, heathland is likely to be maintained at a pre-climax stage through burning, the 'arrested' stage sometimes referred to as a *subclimax*. Chalk grassland that is grazed by rabbits or sheep will have a similar vegetation to ungrazed calcareous grassland, but grazing will effect a rather different species composition, the 'deflected' stage sometimes referred to as a *plagioclimax*.

Figure 7.9 notionally shows a prisere from bare chalk rock through to a climax vegetation of beech wood, as might be found on the North or South Downs in southern England. Beech (*Fagus sylvatica*) is often the dominant climax tree on such sites because it is not only tolerant of the alkaline conditions but, unlike other large native trees such as oak, is able to extend its roots laterally in the thin chalk soils. Chalk grassland is generally species-rich, especially in the later stages where plant cover is complete, but preferential grazing by rabbits or sheep selects for some species, against others, so the resulting grassland

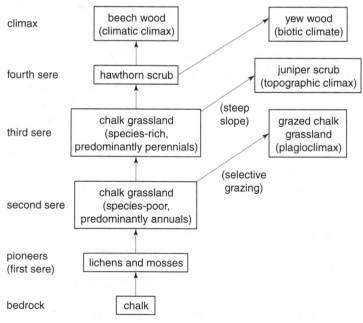

Figure 7.9 Primary succession from chalk to climax beech wood and other end-points in southern England.

differs in the contribution that different species make to the community. Grazing suppresses invasion by scrub, so the deflected grazing stage may be thought of as a plagioclimax. When rabbit numbers crashed following myxomatosis in 1953 many downland areas saw hawthorn (*Crataegus monogyna*) and other scrub species entering the vegetation, and succession was able to continue towards woodland. On some steep slopes, juniper (*Juniperus communis*) and box (*Buxus sempervirens*) become typical, and the steepness prevents trees from entering, so a topographic climax is found. If yew (*Taxus baccata*) establishes itself, the intense shade and toxic litter prevents anything from growing under a full canopy, and a biotic climax is reached.

The example given above of succession starting from a rock surface is that of a *lithosere*. A succession based on sand – where sand couch-grass (*Elytrigia repens arenosa*) and marram grass (*Ammophila arenaria*) are characteristic pioneers – is known as a *psammosere*. Where the substrate lies under water we have hydroseres, although it is useful to distinguish between freshwater *hydroseres* and saltwater *haloseres*. Clearly, the pioneer species and early communities will differ greatly between all these kinds of seral development. Succession beginning from an inorganic substrate is called *primary succession*. Where the starting point is vegetation free but with a soil in place, for example after a fire, this is referred to as *secondary succession*. Early views were that, whatever the starting point, successional sequences tended to converge towards a *climatic climax*.

However, recent work has criticised the ideas of directional, predictable succession and the climax. First, it is argued that vegetation at a so-called climax stage can still change: it is in a state of *dynamic equilibrium*, and the equilibrium can be altered by, for example, disease, pest outbreaks, invasive species or changes in herbivore pressure, never mind climate change itself. Second, not all climax states have the same ecological status, with contrasts being made between climatic climaxes and, say, edaphic climaxes, where soil is the crucial environmental factor. Third, there are occasions where succession, and hence the (temporary) climax end-point are not predictable, depending on chance: which parti-cular pioneer species arrive first, and which particular secondary species subsequently arrive.

A number of ecological characteristics change as succession proceeds. Contrasts between early (developmental) and mature stages are shown in Table 7.8. Whether or not species diversity increases as the plant community develops depends on the community (Figure 7.10). At the pioneer stage, for example, species richness (but not abundance, biomass or equitability) can be high, with a few individuals of a large number of species. For instance, in a lithosere the rock can be colonised by a low number of many different lichen species. Species diversity may then decline as more nutrient-demanding, more competitive species are able to enter. This is not generally the case, for example, in a psammosere or halosere. As the habitat potential increases with autogenic processes leading to succession, so too species diversity tends to increase. Ash–oak wood will tend to have a number of tree and shrub species and a rich field and ground layer. The greater shade and more slowly decaying litter of beech means that fewer species can survive under this tree species, a situation all the more pronounced in coniferous forests and the deep shade of yew wood (such as at Kingley Vale on the South Downs of Sussex), where little else can grow. As succession proceeds, biomass increases with time, usually levelling out at an asymptote when the climax stage is reached.

Horn (1981) has argued that the stages of succession might be predictable if we know what the initial species composition is and, for each species, the probability that within a particular time period an individual would be replaced by another of the same or of a different species. In modelling such a set of probabilities he suggests that, given time, vegetation does converge towards a single kind of stable community.

Connell and Slatyer (1977) proposed a model that takes into account the most likely mechanisms behind succession, which they termed 'facilitation', 'tolerance' and 'inhibition' (Figure 7.11). Facilitation provides the classical explanation for succession, with changes in the abiotic environment being imposed by the developing plant community. The earlier stages facilitate the success of the later ones. Facilitation seems to be the best explanation for most kinds of primary succession. The tole-

Table 7.8 Ecological succession: trends to be expected in the development of ecosystems*

Ecosystem attributes	Developmental stages	Mature stages
Community energetics		
1. Gross production/community respiration (P/R ratio)	Greater or less than 1	Approaches 1
2. Gross production/standing crop biomass (P/B ratio)	High	Low
3. Biomass supported/unit energy flow (B/E ratio)	Low	High
4. Net community production (yield)	High	Low
5. Food chains	Linear, predominantly grazing	Weblike, predominantly detritus
Community structure		
6. Total organic matter	Small	Large
7. Inorganic nutrients	Extrabiotic	Intrabiotic
8. Species diversity – variety component	Low	High
9. Species diversity – equitability component	Low	High
10. Biochemical diversity	Low	High
11. Stratification and spatial heterogeneity (pattern diversity)	Poorly organised	Well organised
Life history		
12. Niche specialization	Broad	Narrow
13. Size of organism	Small	Large
14. Life cycles	Short, simple	Long, complex
Nutrient cycling		
15. Mineral cycles	Open	Closed
16. Nutrient exchange rate, between organisms and environment	Rapid	Slow
17. Role of detritus in nutrient regeneration	Unimportant	Important
Selection pressure		
18. Growth form	For rapid growth ('r selection')	For feedback control ('K' selection)
19. Production	Quantity	Quality
Overall homeostasis		
20. Internal symbiosis	Undeveloped	Developed
21. Nutrient conservation	Poor	Good
22. Stability (resistance to external perturbations)	Poor	Good
23. Entropy	High	Low
24. Information	Low	High

*From E.P. Odum, in *Science, 164*: 262–70, April 18, 1969. Copyright 1969 by the American Association for the Advancement of Science.

rance model suggests that a predictable succession occurs because different species have different strategies for exploiting resources. Species entering the community at later stages can tolerate lower resource levels and are successful in the presence of earlier arrivals, which they eventually out-compete. This appears to be what happens in examples of secondary succession such as abandoned fields. The inhibition model proposes that species arrive in a secondary succession by chance, but once established they are able to resist invasion by later arrivals, which can only enter the community on the death of an earlier-established species. Such pre-emption of space was mentioned in Section 7.3.3. In the facilitation and tolerance models, plants die because they are out-competed for resources such as light and nutrients by later, better-adapted arrivals. In the inhibition model, early species are killed by external forces such as frost or a grazing animal.

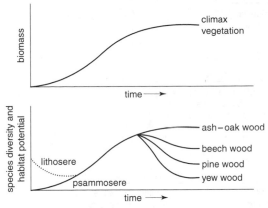

Figure 7.10   Changes in biomass, species diversity and habitat potential through primary succession.

Where succession is driven by the plant community itself, as with the facilitation model, changes are referred to as *autogenic* or *endogenous* – the changes come from the community itself. Where changes are effected or heavily affected by abiotic factors they are *allogenic*, as described in the previous section on zonation.

Succession has been examined in the context of plant communities. Does succession occur in animal communities? If a prerequisite for succession is that change is autogenic, then in most cases the answer is no, for changes in animal communities are generally a response to changes in plant communities. The insect community of a moss-strewn rock is different from that on the same site hundreds of years later under an old-growth forest, but the animals themselves have not effected that change. In a few cases, however, animals may effect autogenic changes with subsequent differences in community composition and structure. One example is in the insect community of dung. Early visitors include the yellow dungfly (*Scatophaga stercoraria*), which lay eggs in the faecal material. The grubs that emerge not only eat the dung, they also themselves excrete. The nature of the dung alters physically as it dries out, but many other physical and chemical changes in the material are the result of its use by insects, the early arrivals modifying it for later-feeding species, although it is true that bacterial and fungal activity is also important.

In a sense, succession is akin to zonation through time, the environmental gradient being reflected by a shift from low to high habitat potential evident, for example, in a change from a thin, largely inorganic, nutrient-poor substrate to a developed, nutrient-rich soil high in organic matter.

Zonation and succession can take place at the same location, but the former reflects allogenic processes, the latter autogenic ones. With the salt marsh example of Figure 7.6c, the zonation will tend to shift in a seaward direction. Tidal waters bring in particles of silt and mud, some of which are deposited as they are trapped by plant roots. Some plant material, meanwhile, will accumulate *in situ* as death and decomposition occur. Thus inorganic and organic material build up and the relative height of the substrate increases in relation to the tides. A particular location is inundated that little bit less, and the environmental conditions thus eventually favour a species more tolerant of greater emersion. This happens along the whole topographic long-section profile, so over time the zonation of plants shifts downslope as, within each zone, succession takes place. In practice, some salt marshes do just this; in other cases, accretion is countered by tidal scour, so the marsh remains in equilibrium, or indeed may actually erode.

7.4 Issues in environmental management

7.4.1 Conservation management goals and carrying capacity

All effective management is goal-oriented, and this is readily shown in the case of nature conservation. For example, decisions have to be made as to whether an area should be strictly protected and any human activity limited, as in the case of Antarctica, or, at the other extreme, whether an area should be managed for public amenity where unlimited access is permissible. Most conservation management goals lie somewhere in between. It is also important not to ignore the needs of indigenous people in an eagerness to preserve threatened species, and in 1996 the World Wide Fund for Nature and the World Conservation Union agreed new policies to safeguard exactly these needs (Edwards, 1997).

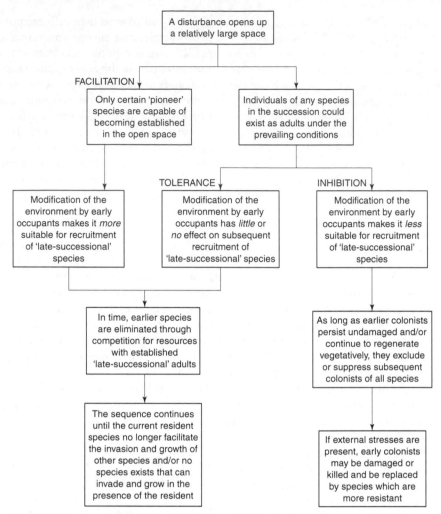

Figure 7.11 Connell and Slatyer's (1977) model of facilitation, tolerance and inhibition as explanations of succession.

There is also an issue of what to conserve, not only in terms of species but also community and habitat. Ponds and lakes silt up, for example, and component habitats disappear as succession takes place. Non-intervention would permit such losses, yet in many cases it is important to retain these to encourage a diversity that might, in Britain for example, include rare bird species such as the bittern (*Botaurus stellaris*) and the water rail (*Rallus aquaticus*), or habitats such as reed swamp and carr, the latter being an uncommon scrub/low tree habitat characterised by such species as alder buckthorn (*Frangula alnus*) and willows (*Salix* spp.) sometimes found between swamp and woodland where soil remains waterlogged for much of the year. Here management would involve preventing a natural ecological process, succession, from taking place, as has been the successful policy at Wicken Fen, Cambridgeshire, a site of great conservation value but one that also caters for the educational and recreational needs of 30 000 visitors each year (Friday, 1997).

A similar problem is found with some anthropogenic habitats that have become important substitute habitats for rare wildlife, for example a form of non-intensively managed coastal meadow found in Ireland and Scotland, and known in the latter as *machair*, which is the last retreat for the corncrake (*Crex crex*) in the British Isles. Machair is a declining habitat, a traditional land use now little in favour but which contains a wealth of wild flowers as well as wildlife and which it is important to preserve. And while it is understandable that farmers do not want their arable land infested with weeds, a consequence is that many plants of the field are now uncommon in the UK, for instance the corncockle (*Agrostemma githago*) and the cornflower (*Centaurea solstitialis*).

Management plans must therefore identify the primary and secondary goals: to maintain biodiversity, for example, or protect an identified rare species; to promote wilderness or ecotourism; to ensure a surplus of game animals or to afford absolute protection; to allow nature to take its course or to intervene. Conservation is usually to some extent or other interventionist: it is ironic that management is often required to maintain areas in an apparently natural state.

Threats to landscapes and their species can come from economic developments such as roads, pipelines, mining, quarrying, buildings or simply changes in land use. In most countries in the Western world such economic developments must now by law be accompanied by an *environmental impact statement*, which determines the economic, social and environmental costs and benefits of a particular proposal, and which must be open to public scrutiny and debate. However, there remains the problem of defining acceptable loss, and this again depends on what goals are set.

If an area subject to conservation management is also to be used by people it is almost certainly necessary to impose some kind of contraint on use, but to do this there has to be a clear idea of the nature of the environment, including its fragility and susceptibility to being used as a resource, together with an understanding of how its use could adversely affect the inherent character and characteristics of that environment. A useful concept here is that of *carrying capacity*: similar to the situation discussed in Section 5.3.4 in the context of population ceilings in relation to their environment, this idea can also be used to identify how many people undertaking particular kinds of activity an environment can support while maintaining ecosystem integrity and not leading to a decline in environmental quality. If there are too many people, for instance, walking across chalk downland there is a risk of trampling damage to wildflowers, distur-

bance to wildlife and path erosion. The problems are in identifying the carrying capacity by accurate predictions of different levels and kinds of activity, and in deciding on appropriate management tools and controls. These are major issues in using natural or semi-natural areas for amenity, recreation and tourism.

7.4.2 Amenity, recreation and tourism

A site with a high amenity value is one valued by the public for its attractiveness or use. A public park, for instance, will have lawns upon which to walk, flower beds and ponds to admire and, often today, areas such as wildflower meadows, which again might give an aesthetic pleasure but which also have ecological value. Recreation generally involves some kind of activity, from walking through riding and canoeing to exploiting the resources of an area, for example fishing and hunting. Amenity and recreation often overlap, such as where people are walking through a visually attractive landscape.

Whether we are considering people visiting a single site, such as a coastal sand dune, or a whole wilderness area, many problems are essentially the same, for example soil and water pollution, litter, trampling and disturbance (Edington and Edington, 1986; Liddle, 1998). In some ways, disturbance is often offset by the fact that people tend to keep to tracks, whether walking, riding, cycling or using off-road vehicles, but an inevitable consequence is damage to those tracks, with erosion a major issue. Some habitats are extremely fragile, for example sand dunes. Woodland and, perhaps surprisingly, heath are also vulnerable to trampling, grassland generally rather less so. Trails often have to be augmented or protected by boardwalks, stone paving or even concrete and tarmac. Slopes are particularly vulnerable to trampling pressure, especially under wet conditions, trampling destroying vegetation cover, and soil and indeed rock opened to the consequences not only of feet, hooves and wheels but also of running water, with gully erosion not infrequent. It is not just a matter of how many feet are doing the trampling. There will be different consequences of, say, a thousand people walking over a site in one day, one month or one year: the last will probably cause little damage, unlike the first.

Managers must therefore make decisions, for example whether people are to be allowed only limited access to an area of downland in order to give as much protection to wildflowers as possible; whether more people might be allowed greater access, and a decline in plant diversity accepted as the cost; or whether people might be allowed unlimited access where, indeed, some repair and replanting with resistant grasses might be required. Carrying capacity is therefore not an absolute, for it is clearly goal-dependent. Decisions on how to manage must involve people-oriented aims as well as those aimed at the conservation of plants, wildlife and indeed the landscape itself. Conservation involves the allocation of resources. Decisions may in part be based on an understanding of ecology but in essence they are political.

Some recreational activities are inimical to nature conservation and can be mutually exclusive, so management must here decide what is to be allowed where and when, and be able to monitor and police the implementation of any decision. An example might be on a freshwater lake that contains valuable fringing reed swamp and a sizeable and varied waterfowl population, but that is also in demand for fishing, canoeing, yachting, wind-surfing, power-boat racing and water-skiing, recreational activities that are not all compatible with each other. A large enough lake might be able to accommodate all of these, but part of the shoreline and nearshore waters might be off-limit to people during the birds' breeding season, and indeed that part could be permanently distinguished as a nature reserve. Fishing, too, would only be allowed during prescribed times of the year. Power-boat use and water-skiing may be limited to central areas away from yachting, while canoeing and wind-surfing might again be restricted to certain zones. Accommodation of all needs thus requires zoning in both space and time, and this in turn needs management and regulations to be enforced.

Parts of some of the more popular national parks in the UK have, during peak times of the year, limits on the number of cars entering, an approach to maintaining an appropriate level of use also evident in most wilderness parks in the

USA. These areas need facilities for visitors, including access routes, picnic areas, camp sites, toilets and shops. The US Park Service spends $900 million each year on these facilities, recouping only about $100 million in entrance fees, but food, lodging and other concessions bring in perhaps $700 million each year. In 1995, nearly 270 million visitors entered the US national parks, by far the most popular being Great Smoky Mountains in Tennessee and North Carolina, where over 9 million people were recorded. The Grand Canyon saw 4.6 million, Yosemite 3.9 million and Yellowstone 3.1 million people (Raven *et al.*, 1998). Wilderness is big business.

In the less developed countries, national parks and game reserves face other difficulties, chief of which are poachers and illegal use of resources such as wood by local people.

7.4.2.1 Hunting, shooting and fishing

Hunting mammals, shooting waterfowl and fishing are also important sporting activities in many countries, and although generally regulated by season and the need for permits, with restrictions of equipment and a limit on bag size, it is evident that abuse of the various systems has placed some animal populations at risk. In North America, many waterfowl are migratory, breeding in Canada then in autumn migrating to or through the USA along more-or-less regular routes, or *flyways* (Figure 7.12). Since 1972, the estimated breeding population of North American ducks has declined by 38%, not so much because of shooting but mostly because of prolonged drought in many key breeding areas and in particular through a deterioration of wetland and grazing habitat because of agricultural activities.

Some conservation measures are possible, including the construction of artificial ponds and nesting sites. Over three-quarters of the USA's federal wildlife reserves are wetlands used by migratory waterfowl. In 1986, the USA and Canada agreed on a scheme to double the number of breeding ducks by investing $1.6 billion over a 16-year period. This has involved the purchase of new waterfowl habitat and improvement and better protection of existing ones.

Other forms of hunting are unregulated and

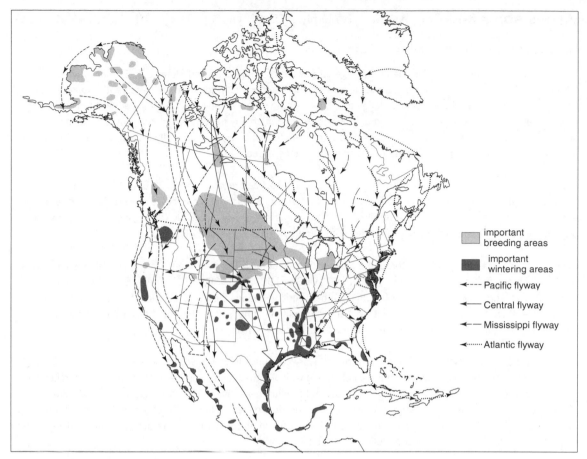

Figure 7.12 Principal breeding and wintering areas and autumn migration flyways used by migratory waterfowl in the USA.

inevitably take their toll. This includes the shooting of songbirds 'for the pot' in many southern European countries. In Italy, it is permissible to enter private land with shotgun under arm and an intent to kill birds. Many shot birds are migrating, afforded protection at both ends of their migratory journey but not *en route*.

7.4.2.2 Poaching and illegal trade

Legal hunting and collecting have driven many species to extinction – such as the thylacine (*Thylacinus cynocephalus*), sometimes called the Tasmanian wolf or Tasmanian tiger, extinct since 1936 – or close to extinction. Illegal hunting and poaching are all the more dangerous to wildlife since by definition it is unregulated. Tigers (*Panthera tigris*) were once hunted just for the

thrill; now they are big business, a tiger fur coat costing perhaps £200 000, tiger bones selling for vast amounts to be ground down and used in Chinese medicine. In 1990, freshly acquired ivory was banned in an attempt to reduce poaching on African elephants (*Loxondota africana*; see Issues Box 7.4), but in early 1999 some southern African countries were pushing hard to have the ban lifted. The irony is that the more endangered an animal or plant the higher the price it will fetch on the black market, and the more worthwhile it is for poachers or illegal collectors to risk their freedom or indeed lives.

It is not only terrestrial plants and animals that are at risk. Some areas of coral reef are under pressure both from disturbance by scuba divers and from collecting. In the Philippines, for example, the collection of reef fish for the aquarium trade has

---

ISSUES BOX 7.4

CITES and the ivory trade

The Convention on International Trade in Endangered Species of Wild Fauna and Flora (CITES) was launched by the IUCN in 1973 in an attempt to regulate the capture of, and international trade in, endangered and threatened species. By 1989, 95 nations had become signatories to the terms drawn up whereby rare species are placed in one of three lists. Appendix I lists about 675 plant and animal species for which any trade is *prohibited*, while Appendix II lists around 2350 species of animal and 24 000 species of plant for which trade is carefully *regulated*. Appendix III (rarely used) allows countries to prohibit trade in nationally threatened species.

Parties to the Convention must submit annual reports, including trade records, to the CITES–UNEP Secretariat in Switzerland. It is difficult to identify the true impact of international trade on a particular species. Some for example, can be imported and re-exported by a number of countries in a single year. Mortality (during capture, transport and quarantine), illegal trade and trade to countries not bound by CITES also muddy the figures.

CITES was instrumental in pushing through a ban on the sale of fresh ivory, prompted by an evident crash in numbers of African elephants from 1.3 million in 1979 to 625 000 in 1989. In 1989, CITES voted 76–11 to move the elephant from Appendix II to Appendix I. Some southern African nations filed a 'reservation' to the Convention that would allow them to continue exports, but the ban was eventually imposed, helped by the stand taken by Japan, which imported 24% of the world's ivory, to agree to a full ban on fresh ivory.

It has been apparent, however, that illegally acquired ivory continues to be traded, and in early 1999 Botswana, Namibia and Zimbabwe were among potential exporters which argued for a reinstatement of limited, controlled trade in fresh ivory. Critics of the ban argue that the problem lies with ineffective wildlife management, and that ivory should be used as a renewable resource. While numbers of African elephants may have declined overall, in Botswana, Zimbabwe and South Africa numbers were stable or increasing, in places herds were putting pressure on local natural vegetation and farmland, and selective culling would be appropriate.

---

lacked regulation and has led to some environmentally devastating practices such as the use of sodium cyanide to stun the fish but with the incidental consequence of killing much of the coral – not just the coral species but a whole habitat. The corals themselves and some of the more spectacular shells are also being over-collected in many localities in the Indian and Pacific Oceans.

Regulation of the trade in species at risk has to a large extent been achieved through the Convention on International Trade in Endangered Species (CITES), which has been ratified by around 100 nations since 1973 (Issues Box 7.4). Whether CITES has been successful has been challenged, and certainly a number of trade bans have in practice been ignored. The global tiger population, for example, currently around 7000, appears to be declining rapidly despite an Appendix I listing. Some people view CITES as

being too restrictive, it having been hijacked (in the view of Eugene Lapointe, secretary-general of CITES until he left in 1990) by animal rights extremists from rich countries, who are 'more interested in making developing countries a natural history museum than in trying to feed people' (Pearce, 1997b: 14).

7.4.2.3 Ecotourism

The safari experience in East and southern Africa has focused more on seeing animals alive in their natural habitat than dead on a trophy wall, and going on a game shoot these days thus tends to involve camera rather than rifle. Not surprisingly, it is the large animal community that attracts greatest attention, in particular mammals but also, increasingly, birds. It is estimated that 50% of Americans and 84% of Canadians spend time (and dollars) each year in bird watching, wildlife photography and other outdoor recreational activities involving wildlife without killing them. A global figure of $12 billion generated annually by ecotourism has been suggested (Miller, 2000), and much of this is income generated for less developed countries.

Over 700 000 visitors bring much needed cash to Kenya, for example, by spending $500 million in national parks and game reserves, making ecotourism this country's biggest earner. All income generated by Kenya's parks and reserves system remains under the control of the Kenyan Wildlife Service and is essentially ploughed back into conservation management. Perhaps 500 mountain gorillas remain in the Virunga Mountains across the borders of Rwanda, Zaire and Uganda, in all of which countries they have been afforded a degree of protection by the establishment of reserves. Tourism was a crucial element in saving this gorilla from extinction following poaching and habitat loss in Rwanda, the Karisoke Research Centre bringing $4 million annually into a desperately impoverished country – a revenue now lost, with much else, as a consequence of the civil unrest and bloodshed of the 1990s.

7.4.3 Reclamation, restoration, revegetation and habitat creation

Different industries have disturbed land both by excavation (for example mines, quarries and gravel extraction) and by subsequent dumping of waste material (spoil tips of various kinds), and landfill sites also incorporate industrial with domestic waste material. Such sites are commonly viewed as eyesores and they are of no use for leisure, recreation or wildlife – at least not without reclamation and restoration. A 1988 survey recorded 40 500 ha of derelict land in England (0.3% of the area), disused spoil tips being the most common form (11 900 ha). Around 78% of derelict land was considered by local authorities to justify reclamation, and between 1982 and 1988 14 000 ha was reclaimed: 63% eventually used for sport and recreation, public open space, agriculture and forestry, 27% for housing, industry and commerce, and the remaining 10% for miscellaneous uses.

Figures for Wales were 20 580 ha of derelict land, being reclaimed at a rate averaging 330 ha each year. Scotland had nearly 7400 ha of derelict land, with over 300 ha being reclaimed in 1988 and 1989 together (Brown, 1992).

The term 'reclamation' is often used where a new use of the land is involved. 'Restoration' is strictly used to describe the process by which land is returned to its original state. 'Revegetation' is confined to situations where the original vegetation has been destroyed and an attempt is made to re-establish it or to encourage its return. In practice, restoration has come to be used 'as a blanket term to describe all activities which serve to upgrade damaged land or re-create land that has been destroyed and to bring it back into beneficial use, in a form in which the biological potential is restored' (Bradshaw and Chadwick, 1980: 3).

A key problem with restoration often lies with the nature of the substrate. Topsoil has often been removed, and with extractive industries one is often left with bare rock. With spoil tips, a range of toxic waste material is often incorporated, as is also the case with landfill sites. Spoil tips are steeply sloped and often unstable. They may be exceedingly porous or, alternatively, compacted into near impermeability. Exposure, instability, lack of organic matter, lack of nutrients, lack of soil organisms and toxicity represent inimical conditions for natural colonisation by pioneer plants or for deliberate planting.

Effective restoration is thus a management option that requires, once again, clear goals, clear methodologies and clear costings. End-uses can include nature conservation. Opportunities for the latter are many, and indeed 75 Sites of Special Scientific Interest in the UK are actually former quarries and mineral workings. In the USA, areas have been planted on former strip mines in the Tennessee Valley specifically to encourage wildlife, and similar ventures have been successful on former bauxite mines in Australia (Majer and Nichols, 1998).

The Norfolk Broads in East Anglia are actually flooded medieval peat cuttings – derelict land abandoned in about AD 1500 and now an important mosaic of habitats ranging from open water through reed swamp, marsh, fen and willow scrub. It is also an area used for a variety of recreational activities, including bird watching, and recreation and conservation must be managed hand in hand. Many gravel pits have been deliberately flooded and used as a focus for water sports, fishing and wildlife. Sevenoaks in Kent and the string of flooded pits west of London are major bird reserves, as is the Attenborough nature reserve on former open-cast mining west of Nottingham. Sandbach Flashes in Cheshire and Doxey Marshes adjoining Stafford are both former brine workings that now support large numbers of a variety of bird species.

These are examples of the restoration of individual sites, but whole landscapes have also been subjected to restoration attempts. One of the earliest communities where management aimed at restoration were those of the North American prairies. A major experiment has been undertaken since 1936 on former farmland at the Curtis and Greene Prairies at the University of Wisconsin–Madison Arboretum in which the goal has been to establish the structure, species composition and interacting characteristics of a functioning prairie system (Cottam, 1987). Prairie restoration can involve upgrading an existing degraded community or establishing the community on sites where prairie has disappeared. Major problems are the need to increase populations of desirable and characteristic but less successful species, getting rid of introduced herbaceous species (including competitive grasses), and preventing invasion by woody species. In general, it is assumed that with the restored plant community will come an appropriate animal community, and for many animals this is what happens, but some key components often need introducing, for instance mound-building ants, which are important for turning over the soil in tallgrass prairie and which provide small-scale disturbances crucial for the establishment of some plants (Kline and Howell, 1987).

Where prairie and indeed other communities are planted where they have disappeared or not previously existed, this essentially involves 'habitat creation'. This is an important tool in the greening of many derelict sites and it has become a valuable landscaping device in many urban areas. Habitat creation has focused on the establishment of ponds and lakes and on wildflower meadows, but recently much work has also been undertaken on other communities, in particular urban woodlands

(with particular attention being paid to enhancement of the field layer) and, in rural areas, heathland. Heathland can become degraded, and restoration can involve the control of invasive trees or bracken (Marrs, Johnson and Le Duc, 1998), but true habitat creation or translocation is needed on old field sites and on former mineral workings (Aerts *et al.*, 1995; Free and Kitson, 1992; Putwain and Rae, 1988; Pywell *et al.*, 1996).

A major problem on derelict sites is often the absence of a soil or, if present, the need to take into account the toxic material (commonly, heavy metals) that remain from previous dumping. Ironically, another problem in many urban sites where meadow is planned is a soil that is too nutrient-rich, and topsoil generally needs stripping. Nutrient enrichment from earlier agricultural activity is a common general problem in heathland restoration as well. Nutrient-rich soils encourage the colonisation and dominance of competitive plants, which reduce species diversity and exclude desirable species.

Reclamation is not only possible on metal-polluted sites using metal-tolerant plant species or varieties, but such plantings may actually help in detoxifying the soil, allowing less tolerant species to enter the community. Recent work on transgenic engineering points to further possibilities. A bacterium has been discovered that produces an enzyme which reduces toxic mercury ions to a form that can evaporate. By transferring the appropriate gene, *merA*, to a fast-growing tree, yellow poplar (*Liriodendron tulipifera*), mercury is taken up from the soil and released into the atmosphere. This allows a visually attractive means of vegetating toxic landfill sites, but it begs the question of increasing atmospheric pollution by the release of mercury vapour into air (Pearce, 1998c).

Related to restoration are techniques of stabilisation using plant cover. This is of particular value in stabilising sand dunes in areas eroded by foot or wind, especially by establishing marram grass (*Ammophila arenaria*) in Europe, beachgrass (*A. breviligulata*) in North America and sand spinifex (*Spinifex hirsutus*) in warmer climates. Similarly, the reduction of estuarine silting has been achieved by planting cord grass (*Spartina*), which traps and retains much of the mud and silt being moved by tidal and estuarine water movements.

7.4.4 *In situ* and *ex situ* conservation

We have already seen that the best way to conserve endangered species is to ensure that their habitat is secure. Habitats and their communities are also worthy of conservation in their own right. Conservation of species and habitats in their natural environment is called *in situ* conservation.

Sometimes, however, it is necessary to take precautionary conservation measures by maintaining captive breeding populations in zoos and parks in the case of endangered animals, and maintenance in botanical gardens or as seed banks in the case of threatened plants. This is *ex situ* conservation. There have been a number of cases where a species has only survived because of such measures. Père David's deer (*Elaphurus davidiensis*) became extinct in the wild, but animals have been reintroduced to their native range in China from stock that had been kept at Woburn in Bedfordshire. The Arabian oryx (*Oryx leucoryx*) is another success, after having been overhunted in Jordan and Oman, and the reintroduced population now numbers around 150 individuals. The Hawaiian goose, or nene (*Branta sandvicensis*), has been restocked (and genetic heterogeneity increased) from birds reared at the Wildfowl and Wetlands Trust at Slimbridge, Gloucestershire. Whooping cranes (*Grus americana*) in North America had declined to a mere fifteen birds by 1941, but a captive breeding programme has resulted in a re-established flock that, wintering as it does almost exclusively at the Arkansas National Wildlife Refuge in coastal Texas, in 1996 numbered 158 birds, and the number of chicks being produced in the wild should ensure continued population growth.

There is no point in reintroducing animals or plants into their natural range if the ecological and environmental circumstances that led to their rarity or local extinction in the first place are still present. Reintroduction programmes must therefore ensure that such threats are no longer present, and this again means goal-oriented management. Finally, there is no point in reintroducing animals from captive breeding stock where they do not have a sufficiently broad gene pool or indeed even a viable breeding population; nor is there any point in release where animals have not acquired the behavioural repertoire that would be needed for surviving, for example hunting skills in predatory birds and mammals.

7.5 Conclusions

In many ways, conservation (which among other goals aims at minimising the likelihood that a population declines to extinction), harvesting (which aims at maintaining exploited populations at sustainable and productive levels) and pest control (which aims at decreasing the numbers of a pest below some kind of damage threshold) are three aspects of the same general problem – population management (Shea *et al.*, 1998).

Any conservation programme must have clearly defined goals to allow appropriate measures to be identified, appropriate monitoring to be introduced and appropriate achievements to be assessed. Goals, however, are often difficult to agree, partly because of the uncertainties of the science involved, partly because of the common obligation to include human wants (such as tourism and amenity) and needs (such as indigenous agriculture or forestry), and partly because of issues of resource allocation, of which money is a key feature. While some species and some environments need absolute protection (for example in Antarctica), in the majority of cases the most appropriate planning and management are geared towards compatible and complementary land uses. Conservation thus becomes a component in multi-purpose land use, sometimes a minor component, sometimes a highly significant one.

Further reading

Alerstam, T. (1990) *Bird migration* (Cambridge: Cambridge University Press).

Cadieux, C.L. (1991) *Wildlife extinction* (Washington DC: Stone Wall Press).

Dingle, H. (1996) *Migration: the biology of life on the move* (Oxford: Oxford University Press).

Fogg, G.E. (1998) *The biology of polar habitats* (Oxford: Oxford University Press).

Gilbert, O.L. and Anderson, P. (1998) *Habitat creation and repair* (Oxford: Oxford University Press).

Hansom, J. and Gordon, J. (1998) *Antarctic environments and resources: a geographical perspective* (Harlow: Longman).

Harris, J., Birch, P. and Palmer, J. (1996) *Land restoration and reclamation* (Harlow: Longman).

Jordan III, W.R., Gilpin, M.E. and Aber, J.D. (eds) (1987) *Restoration ecology: a synthetic approach to ecological research* (Cambridge: Cambridge University Press).

Luken, J.O. (1990) *Directing ecological succession* (London: Chapman & Hall).

Mace, G.M., Balmford, A. and Ginsberg, J.R. (eds) (1998) *Conservation in a changing world* (Cambridge: Cambridge University Press).

Oelschlaeger, M. (ed.) (1992). *The wilderness condition* (Washington DC: Island Press).

Pimm, S.J. (1991) *The balance of nature? Ecological issues in the conservation of species and communities* (Chicago: University of Chicago Press).

Runte, A. (1979) *National parks: the American experience* (Lincoln: University of Nebraska Press).

Western, D. and Pearl, M. (1989) *Conservation in the twenty-first century* (Oxford: Oxford University Press).

QUESTIONS BASED ON CHAPTER 7

Q1. Why does succession not usually take place in hot deserts?

Q2. What kinds of evidence might you consider to demonstrate that a woodland was, or was likely to be, ancient? (In the UK, ancient woodlands are those known or believed to have been in existence since AD 1600.)

Q3. What damaging or nuisance effects might feet, off-road motor vehicles, mountain bikes and horses have on upland habitats?

Q4. Are humans a keystone species? Give reasons for your answer.

Q5. Is the ideal way to conserve an endangered species to maintain it in safety in a botanical garden or as part of a captive breeding programme in a zoo?

ANSWERS

A1. The extreme environment means that exogenous (allogenic) factors completely dominate endogenous (autogenic) community factors. Ephemeral plant species germinate after a rainfall event, grow rapidly, flower and seed in a matter of weeks. Seeds are scattered to await the next rainfall event, and the flowers die down. Lack of permanent vegetation makes succession impossible. Perennial desert plants such as cacti, succulents and creosote bush are scattered (any competition tends to be below ground), and there is no facilitative opportunity for improvements in habitat potential. Community processes that reflect succession, such as accumulation of standing crop biomass and high net community production (yield), and ecosystem processes such as soil development, are not generally associated with deserts.

A2. Evidence could include measurement or estimation of tree age (e.g. counting rings on felled specimens or in trunk cores; measurement of girth at 1 m (3 feet) height, where each 2.5 cm (1 inch) roughly corresponds to one year in age; height is a poor estimate of age by itself); floristic indicators (plants such as bluebells and dog's mercury are good indicators of ancient woodland); historical (e.g. documents or maps); and archaeological (e.g. pollen analysis of soil cores, evidence from soil cores or on the ground of charcoal burning).

A3. Some of these uses may come into conflict with or pose dangers to each other. Tyres and hooves churn up the soil, making walking difficult. Too many feet damage vegetation and cause soil erosion, but damage and erosion are more frequently associated with, are often more pronounced with, and happen sooner following vehicular or horse activities. Wildlife may be disturbed by trampling and by noise. Trampling and disturbance may affect the status of rare or endangered plants and animals.

ANSWERS (cont)

A4. Humans dominate many ecosystems, and some would alter dramatically if humans were to disappear. Some, indeed, rely entirely on humans for their origin and maintenance, for example urban ecosystems, agro-ecosystems, and many lowland heaths in Europe. In these cases, then, the answer is 'yes', and humans exercise a top-down control. In other ecosystems, however, even where humans currently have some control over species content and ecosystem processes, little would change were people no longer around. With these examples the answer is either 'maybe' or categorically 'no'. The world, and most of its ecosystems, could easily survive without us. We, however, cannot survive without the rest of the world.

A5. No. Botanical gardens and zoos are useful back-ups to reduce the chances of extinction, and some reintroduction programmes have been successful. They also provide us with opportunities to learn a little more about the ecology of the species. But there is no substitute for improving and protecting the species' native environment, which in any case are prerequisites for any reintroduction programme.

Discussion topics

D1. The UK's 1981 Wildlife and Countryside Act favoured voluntary rather than compulsory compliance with measures aimed at protecting Sites of Special Scientific Interest. What have been the advantages and disadvantages of this?

D2. A proposal has been made to convert a landfill site into farmland. What would the advantages, disadvantages and risks be of such an exercise? What would be the advantages, disadvantages and risks were the proposal to have been for amenity grassland in an urban area?

D3. What potential conflicts of interest might there be, both environmentally and in terms of human use, of planning for and managing recreational activities in:

a 10 ha urban park
an area of lowland heath
an ancient woodland close to a large built-up area
an area of coastal duneland

D4. What arguments would you use to address the concerns of local people when proposing to establish a nature reserve aimed at protecting a dangerous animal such as a tiger?

D5. Developers may be allowed to destroy a habitat if they protect, restore or create a similar one of similar size in mitigation. What support, if any, would you give to such a scheme? What are the risks and disadvantages of mitigation?

EXERCISES

E1. As the manager of an urban park you have been told that no more money is available to buy new plants. Draw up a plan and schedule of how you might nevertheless increase the biodiversity of the park using the labour force as your only external resource.

E2. Visit a local derelict urban site or a recently abandoned arable field where plants have been able to colonise. (Make sure you have obtained permission for access and that safety precautions are taken.) Identify as many plant species as possible, using a flora if you have one. What are the characteristics that have allowed these colonising species to arrive and grow at the site? Is succession taking place? How do you know? Does the site, or will it, have any value for nature conservation?

E3. Conservation is a land use that often has to compete with other land uses on which a social or cash value can be placed, for example housing or agriculture. One of the problems in nature conservation is therefore quantifying the 'value' of species and landscapes, whether in terms of cash value equivalents or by quantifying desirable attributes. Think of ways in which quantitative values could be allocated to landscapes. Test your ideas on a public open space (whether or not it is a reserve) close to your home or educational institution.

Chapter 8

Biological invasions, competition and the niche

Summary

Biological invasions are organisms that have arrived in a region, whether naturally or through human action, where they have not previously been found, at least in historical times, and where they are able to survive, reproduce, spread and functionally participate in the communities they have penetrated. The 'tens rule' suggests that the probability of successfully making the transition from imported status to that of a true introduction (deliberately or accidentally transported by humans and found in the wild) is about 10%, and again there is about a 10% chance of changing from introduced status to that of established or naturalised (self-sustaining populations and a significant contribution to community dynamics). Similarly, about one in ten naturalised species becomes a weed or pest (although not all weeds and pests are introduced species), and issues of management for control of such species are outlined. Naturalised invaders succeed by taking the opportunity of using available niche space, or by displacing or replacing other species, in the latter cases sometimes causing local or complete species extinctions. Island biotas are particularly vulnerable to biological invasions, partly because they often contain fewer and evolutionarily specialised species in simpler communities than on the mainland, as illustrated with the examples of Hawaii, the Galapagos Islands and Guam. Comments on habitat classification are followed by observations on stress-tolerant, disturbance-tolerant and competitive strategies in plants. The concept of the niche is linked with ranges of tolerance and the idea of resource axes defined in multi-dimensional space. A distinction is drawn between fundamental niche and realised niche. The idea of the niche is used both as a framework for considering why the extent of species packing can vary and as a means of examining ideas of intra- and interspecific competition. Interference competition is distinguished from exploitation competition. Resource partitioning reduces or avoids niche overlap and is one of the mechanisms of coexistence. Island biogeography theory is examined in terms of species–area relationships, geographical attributes such as island area, shape and distance from mainland, species turnover rate, and equilibrium number of species, and applications of island biogeography theory to the design of nature reserves are critically assessed.

8.1 Biological invasions

Communities are not fixed in time or space. Species enter and disappear, population sizes and structures fluctuate, and changes are evident in the way individuals, populations and species interact. A species entering a community for the first time, or after an absence, usually does so from neighbouring or nearby populations within its current geographical range, having spread by natural means.

From time to time, though, a species arrives in a region where it has not previously been found as part of the species pool, at least not in historical times. If it is able to survive, reproduce and spread then it will have become a successful example of *biological invasion*. An understanding of biological invasions is important not only in terms of species distributions but also with respect to changes in community dynamics, since any invasive species can only be successful by becoming part of, and therefore affecting, a community or communities.

Some biological invasions take place using natural means of dispersal. The collared dove (*Streptopelia decaocto*), for example, has steadily spread northwards and westwards from the Near East since the 1930s. Between 1933 and 1972, its breeding range extended into most parts of cool temperate Europe and parts of north-west Africa, effectively increasing its range by 2.5 million km². Only some drier parts of the Mediterranean and arctic–alpine parts of Fennoscandia remain uncolonised. It is suspected that climatic changes that allowed a long breeding period were associated with an increase in fecundity (to three to five broods per breeding season), and it may have helped that the species seems to be attracted to human settlements.

Another bird that has recently extended its range in Europe is the pochard (*Aythya ferina*). During the second half of the twentieth century this duck has colonised Iceland, southern Sweden, the Benelux countries, south-west Germany, France and Ireland, as well as increasing in numbers in places where it had already been present, for example in the UK, where it had been an occasional and partial migrant. This expansion may also have had a climatic explanation (a drying out of its habitat in Central Asia), but it is more likely that this species has simply taken advantage of an increase in the number of reservoirs, flooded gravel pits and other water bodies, allowing it to overwinter and breed in regions from which it had previously been excluded.

Excluding range extensions for unknown reasons, Isenmann (1990) distinguishes between four invasion types for birds in Western Europe: (1) response to climatic fluctuations (see Section 4.2.2.6); (2) creation of new habitats and/or new natural feeding resources; (3) increasing artificial food resources, for example landfill sites allowing scavengers such as black-headed gulls (*Larus ridibundus*) and herring gulls (*L. argentatus*) to move away from the coast to inland sites; and (4) introductions.

Introductions are a special case of biological invaders. An introduced species is one that has moved (or has been transported) from one discrete region to another region, often but not necessarily geographically separated, through the deliberate or accidental agency of humans. Species have been deliberately moved from one part of the world to another because humans have viewed them as being useful, attractive or in some other way valuable (Jarvis, 1979). Domestic stock, crops, garden plants and forestry trees are obvious examples, although most livestock, crops and horticultural specimens cannot survive in the wild and are therefore not truly invasive.

A few such, however, have become so. A number of exotic pasture grasses, for example, have invaded the prairie rangelands of North America, such as Bermuda grass (*Cynodon dactylon*), Lehmann lovegrass (*Eragrostis lehmanniana*), and buffelgrass (*Pennisetum ciliare*). Rabbits (*Oryctolagus cuniculus*) were originally introduced beyond their native southern European range as a food animal. Grey squirrels (*Sciurus carolinensis*) were brought into the British Isles during the nineteenth century as parkland ornamentals, also the reason for a number of exotic deer species in Britain, and for birds such as Canada goose (*Branta canadensis*) and mandarin duck (*Aix galericulata*). Many European species were introduced into Australia and New Zealand during the nineteenth century because they reminded the settlers of home. The Acclimatization Society of New Zealand, for example, introduced songbirds such as the blackbird (*Turdus merula*), robin (*Erithacus rubecula*) and chaffinch (*Fringilla coelebs*), and plants such as gorse (*Ulex europaeus*), broom (*Cytisus scoparius*) and bramble (*Rubus fruticosus*), because of this sentiment. The house sparrow (*Passer domesticus*) and starling (*Sturnus vulgaris*) are examples of birds introduced from Europe to the USA for similar reasons.

Sailors formerly released food animals such as pigs (*Sus scrofa*) and goats (*Capra hircus*) on remote islands in the Indian and Pacific Oceans as future reserves of fresh meat. Salmon, trout and a host of other fish species have been intro-duced to many waters from their natural range in order to expand sports fishery opportunities, and in many instances they have come to dominate their water bodies. Ornamental plants, too, have often escaped from horticulture into surrounding countryside, for example pontic rhododendron (*Rhododendron ponticum*) and Japanese knotweed (*Reynoutria japonica*) in Western Europe.

Species have also been transported from region to region by accident. Rodents such as the house mouse (*Mus domesticus*), black (or ship) rat (*Rattus rattus*) and brown rat (*R. norvegicus*) are now found throughout the world, the house mouse being the only mammal, humans apart, found in Antarctica. Seeds and plant fragments are easily moved from place to place on or in clothing and other materials, including packing. Dumped ballast has been responsible for the arrival of a number of species. Microbial organisms must not be forgotten, and despite screening and quarantine many pathogenic organisms still move around the globe.

In the face of so many examples that can be cited of introduced species it must be emphasised that by far the majority fail to establish themselves, because they do not possess a breeding population, because environmental conditions are not conducive to or appropriate for success, or because they cannot successfully enter an existing community. Williamson (1996) describes four levels of success in exotic species.

1. **Imported species** are all the species brought into a country (or new region), whether they survive or not, and if they do whether or not they need constant human intervention. These would, for example, include the thousands of ornamental plants grown in gardens, which have no chance of success in the wild.

2. **Introduced species** are found in the wild, even if only as casual members of a community, and including garden escapes and feral animals.

3. **Established species** are introduced species with a self-sustaining population, and which have become an integral part of a community. Another term for such species is *natura-lised*.

Table 8.1 British angiosperms and the 'tens rule'

	Number	Percentage
Total imported	12 507	
Total casual or more	1642	13.1
Total established	210	12.8
All weeds	39	18.6 (of 210)
Severe weeds	14	6.7 (of 210)

Source: Williamson (1996)

4. **Pest species** are successful in terms of population size, competitive vigour or other characteristics that makes them have an adverse impact either on economic activity or desirable conservation goals (see Section 5.2.2).

Williamson notes that an imported species has about a one-in-ten chance of success, i.e. the probability of the transition from imported to introduced status is around 10% (although in practice this tends to be between 5% and 20%). Thus about one in ten imported species finds itself living in the wild; of these introductions, about one in ten then becomes established; and around one in ten established species reaches pest (or weed) status. Williamson calls this generalised relationship the 'tens rule'. As an example, he cites the case of British angiosperm plants (Table 8.1).

To succeed, biological invaders – whether arriving naturally or as introductions – must be able to produce a sufficient number of offspring, whether from selfing or as propagules, to ensure establishment and spread. They must also find an appropriate habitat and an opportunity to function within a community. Once established, invasive species may spread rapidly, slowly or hardly at all. Not all communities are readily invadable. Biological invasions may fit into existing communities with little obvious impact, they may displace one or a few species (or reduce their abundance), or they may come to dominate. While there are a few attributes that tend to make invasion successful (Table 8.2), predictions are difficult to make concerning the eventual success of any particular species.

Similarly, it is difficult to predict what the impact of an invading species might be on the invaded community or ecosystem. Certainly, a number of introductions have caused extinctions whose effects have cascaded through the community. There are three particular circumstances where severe impacts are likely:

Table 8.2 Some attributes associated with successful biological invaders

Ecological/physiological	Morphological/behavioural	Genetic/demographic
Broad niche	Small body size	*r*-selected
Non-specialised germination and regeneration	High vagility (tendency to move from home area)	High fecundity
Non-specialised germination	High mobility	Rapid population growth
Dormancy	Highly resistant spores	Short and simple life cycle
Rapid growth	Phoretic (animals transported on another organism)	High genetic variation
High resource allocation to reproduction		Uniparental reproduction
Longevity of seeds permits seed banks	Seed morphology appropriate for long dispersal by wind (anemochory), e.g. plumed or winged, or animals (zoochory), e.g. spiny or sticky	Polyploidy (chromosome multiplication)
Edible fruits and seeds dispersed by animals		

Source: di Castri (1990)

1. where species are introduced to areas where predators are absent, for example introducing large herbivores to islands where there are no external constraints on feeding activity or population growth, or where top predators (which are not themselves preyed upon) are brought in. Similarly, severe perturbations will tend to occur where an introduction has no competitors.
2. where polyphagous (food generalist) animals are introduced, since their wide-ranging diet will tend to affect more food species, whether plants or animals, and compete with a greater number of other animals for that food.
3. where species are introduced into relatively simple communities, where it might be easier to usurp the functional roles of existing members and where any removal (local extinction) of a few species – especially plants – will reverberate throughout the community, possibly leading to its collapse.

All these effects have been seen in New Zealand, for example, where the introduction of many plant species has led to major changes in vegetation – the spread of woody plants such as gorse, broom and bramble in open country, for instance; where the introduction of large domestic (sheep and goats) and non-domestic (red deer, *Cervus elaphus*) grazing and browsing animals has similarly led to major changes in vegetation; where the arrival of the Australian brushtail possum (*Trichosurus vulpecula*) heralded major changes in the ecology of forests and forest plantations; and perhaps most serious of all, where the introduction of a wide range of predatory mammals – e.g. stoats (*Mustela erminea*), weasels (*M. nivalis*), red foxes (*Vulpes vulpes*) and cats (*Felis catus*) – has put at risk much of the native ground-dwelling and ground-nesting fauna, which has evolved in the complete absence of any mammal other than bats (King, 1984).

Island biotas and communities are particularly vulnerable to the adverse effects of biological invasions (see Section 8.2.2), effects that are exacerbated by other consequences of human activity such as habitat destruction. The interactive effects of habitat loss and introductions are suggested in Figure 8.1, which indicates a hypothetical situation, but one akin to New Zealand. As introductions put competitive or predatory pressures on native species so populations of the latter need greater amounts of habitat to survive in order to dilute, deflect or avoid these

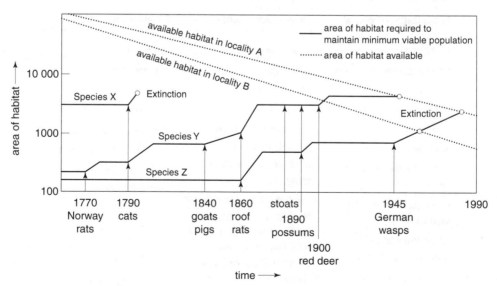

Figure 8.1   Hypothetical model of the relationship between introduced animals and habitat loss in leading to extinctions of native species (after Miller, 2000).

pressures. Yet habitat may actually be decreasing in extent. Species X becomes extinct as a result (in this example) of predation by cats. Species Y and Z come under greater and greater pressure as more and more introductions enter the system, but extinction comes sooner to both where amount of habitat is less, or is declining at a faster rate (locality B).

8.2 Key environmental issues: introductions and the vulnerability of oceanic islands

8.2.1 Introductions as weeds and pests

Most introduced species do not persist, or if they do, have minimal impact in their country of adoption (tens rule), and by no means all serious weeds and pests are introductions, but it is evident that many of the world's worst weeds and pests are indeed biological invasions. This is not so surprising. Comparing some of the attributes of weeds and pests outlined in Section 5.2.2 and Table 8.2, many characteristics do overlap, for instance *r* selection, high fecundity, high genetic variation, high mobility, persistence and competitive vigour. Species that are weeds or pests in their country of origin, however, need not be so in their country of adoption. The tortricid moth (*Epiphyas (Tortrix) postvittana*), for instance, is a pest of fruit trees in its native Australia, but in the UK, where it has been established for some time, it has neither spread much nor become a nuisance.

Introductions are particularly successful and intrusive in anthropogenically simplified communities, often dominated by a single species, such as are found in agriculture, forestry and other economic enterprises. Feeding habit is an important factor in the successful spread and economic impact of alien pests. Introduced species that have a broad diet tend to be more successful than those specialising on a few or a single host. Nevertheless, it is not unusual for specialist feeders to be the most serious pests of crops.

While under 10% of all pest species associated with cotton, coffee, cocoa and sugar cane are introductions, this percentage does represent nearly 500 taxa, including the most serious ones. Taking the 350 agricultural pests considered by the Commonwealth Institute of Entomology to be of greatest economic importance, over 63% are introductions (Jarvis, 1979).

Estimates of the world's most serious agricultural weeds highlight the importance of introductions, many being persistent grasses such as cogon grass (*Imperata cylindrica*), an aggressive, rhizomatous annual introduced throughout much of the tropics and subtropics, especially in Asia, but also in the southern USA, where it invades pastures, plantations, ruderal communities and lawns.

Natural communities are also invaded by introduced plants and animals, again often with devastating effects. In the Florida peninsula, for example, ecologists debate which introduced tree will take over first, the Brazilian peppertree (*Schinus terebinthus*) or the Australian *Melaleuca leucadendron*, although the latter may just have the edge (Bodle *et al.*, 1994; Lodge, 1994). Both invade, out-compete and take over from natural vegetation, leaving huge monospecific stands and so being of major conservation concern, and they both also produce pollen that is a respiratory irritant to humans, the sap causes blistering and skin rash, and peppertree fruit can kill horses, deer and other animals. Melaleuca, introduced for its soil-drying properties, has become too successful in this respect, threatening parts of the Everglades.

Five reasons why so many introductions become troublesome are:

1. inherent autecological attributes that allow them to invade existing communities.
2. pre-adaptation to the general environmental conditions of their host country, for example climate will tend to be similar to that of the home region.
3. the vulnerability and invadability of the host community in terms of its intrinsic stability.
4. the absence in the host country of environmental constraints (such as temperature) or ecological constraints (such as particular diseases, predators or competitors) that keep

numbers and activities in check in the country of origin.

5. the opportunities taken by the invading species to exploit the 'ecological space' of the host community by replacing or displacing existing species or by finding new ways of utilising the resources of the community and its ecosystem. This introduces the idea of the niche, which is explored in Section 8.3.2.

8.2.2 Vulnerability of oceanic islands to species introductions

Discrete areas of land surrounded by marine waters are colonised over time by plants, animals and microbial organisms. Chance dispersal occurs as individuals or groups that are blown by wind or drift on ocean currents. The latter includes the possibility of *rafting*, where clumps of vegetation containing and sustaining living organisms break away from the mainland to be washed ashore elsewhere. In many ways, island biotas are samples of the biotas found on the source regions (mainland), but also the processes of evolution take place in isolation, so that over time island communities will generally contain many species that are genetically, morphologically and behaviourally – in a word, taxonomically – very different from the *founder populations* that comprised the original colonists. Islands therefore contain many endemics, and ecological relationships build up that may be unique to each island. Adaptations emerge which reflect the unique conditions and assemblages, and which ignore any environmental and ecological constraints that no longer affect the communities and their members. *Adaptive radiation* commonly occurs whereby species diversify as adaptations to different ways of life. For example, the Galapagos finches (*Geospiza*), form an endemic subfamily, the Geospizinae, which have diversified from an ancestral seed eater to become fruit eaters, foliage insectivores, bark gleaners and wood excavators.

Island biotas tend to have few or indeed no large predators. On Hawaii, for instance, the only predatory land vertebrates that have colonised the islands naturally are the Hawaiian hawk (*Buteo solitarius*) and the short-eared owl

(*Asio flammeus*). Non-flying mammals are also uncommon on islands: the only native mammals of New Zealand, for instance, are bats, a group of animals that for a long time were also the only mammals to be found on Krakatau after its eruption in 1883. One consequence is that many birds become flightless and ground-nesting. The wings of insects, too, often become redundant, and again flightless forms evolve.

In the absence of mammals disturbing the ground, plants associated with such habitats are often poorly represented on islands. Nor are plants much adapted to grazing or browsing, so physical and chemical defences are absent: there is simply no need for such energetically costly products.

Another common characteristic of island biotas is *ecological release* – the expansion of niche space (see Section 8.3.2) by the occupation of more habitats and/or the use of a greater range of resources in the absence of strong competition. Compared with mainland taxa, island species often compensate for a relatively impoverished flora and fauna by becoming more habitat generalist.

Possessing these biotic characteristics, it is not surprising that island communities and ecosystems are particularly susceptible to biological invasions, for they often have little or no defence against ecologically aggressive invaders. This susceptibility, however, is aggravated by human activities, such as agriculture, forestry and road building, which disturb the ground so that ruderal plants can invade and dominate. Habitat modification and destruction can also disturb and (through habitat fragmentation) isolate populations, making them vulnerable to dangers associated with minimal viable threshold sizes (see Section 5.3.6). And humans also bring in diseases that affect plants and animals possessing no immunity whatsoever. Three examples illustrate this vulnerability: the Hawaiian archipelago, the Galapagos Islands and Guam (Figure 8.2).

8.2.2.1 The Hawaiian archipelago

The Hawaiian archipelago comprises a set of volcanic islands, atolls and reefs in a chain

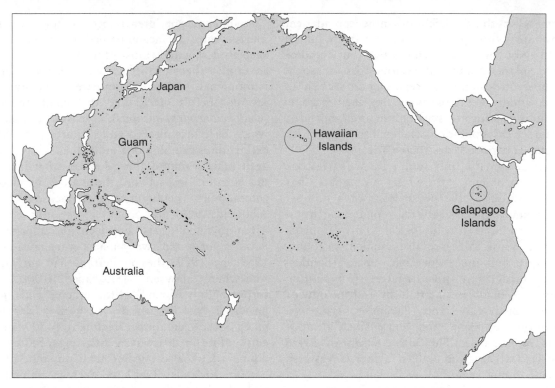

Figure 8.2   The Pacific Ocean, showing the location of the Hawaiian Islands, Galapagos Islands and Guam.

2450 km in length between 19° N and 22° 30′ N in the humid tropical Pacific. About 95% of the plant and animal species are unique to these islands, probably the highest degree of endemism for any comparable area. It is estimated that the 1200–1300 species of native flowering plants have derived from around 270 ancestral forms. A thousand land snail endemics have speciated from 22–24 colonisations, while 300–400 arthropod species (animals with articulated legs such as insects, spiders, millipedes and crabs) have evolved to produce over 6000 descendant species. A single ancestral finch species has radiated to produce 47 species and subspecies (Carlquist, 1980; Cuddihy and Stone, 1990; Stone and Scott, 1985; Stone and Stone, 1989).

When visited by Captain Cook in 1778, these islands had already lost many species as a result of colonisation by Polynesian people. Rates of environmental disturbance and species extinctions, however, have greatly increased following European settlement, the most important factors being habitat destruction and the introduction of alien plants and animals. Over 600 exotic plants have become established in the wild, at least 86 of which have become serious weeds.

The firetree (*Myrica faya*), for example, a native of the Canary Islands in the Atlantic, and introduced before 1900, can invade intact native plant communities and has particularly come to dominate many damp and volcanic ash sites on all of the main islands, the ability of its roots to fix nitrogen giving it a competitive edge. Another nitrogen-fixing plant, 'koa haole' (*Leucaena leucocephala*), introduced from the Neotropics before 1837, forms dense stands that crowd out other species in many lowland habitats. Banana poka (*Passiflora mollissima*), introduced in 1921 and now covering over 500 km^2, is a climbing plant from the Andes whose seeds are spread by introduced pigs (*Sus scrofa*), which eat the fruit and excrete the seed on to ground disturbed by snout and trotter, and the plant now grows into and smothers the foliage of native forest trees. Broomsedge (*Andropogon virginicus*), introduced from the south-east USA, has now spread over many areas once covered by moist mountain forest. Not only does this sedge out-compete native plants but also during its seasonal dormancy it does not extract water from the soil, which under wet conditions can then become saturated, leading to slope failure and landslides, and under dry conditions can exacerbate the risk and consequences of destructive fire.

Pigs are not the only feral (escaped) livestock causing problems. Browsing by goats has seriously reduced the populations of a number of endemic plants. Feral cats, mongooses (ironically introduced for biological control), black rats and house mice are also problem introductions preying on vulnerable, often flightless native birds and invertebrates. Competition exists, too, between native birds and introduced species such as the Japanese white-eye (*Zosterops japonica*) and house finch (*Carpodacus mexicanus*). The introduction of avian malaria and avian pox has further devastated the indigenous avifauna.

Once established, extermination or even reduction of the *keystone exotics* is nigh on impossible. Since European settlement, thirteen species of Hawaiian land bird have become extinct, and 30 others are now endangered, with populations of fewer than 100 individuals.

8.2.2.2 The Galapagos Islands

The Galapagos Islands lie on the Equator 1000 km west of South America and include a range of habitats from arid lava flows to humid upland forest. The native biota, largely derived from South America, is highly endemic: over 42% of the 541 native plants, all of the native reptiles and mammals and most of the indigenous birds are found only on these islands. Several plant and animal genera show highly developed and often elaborate patterns of adaptive radiation. About 90% of the non-peopled parts of the islands were declared a national park in 1959, and in 1964 the Charles Darwin Research Station was established on Santa Cruz Island to coordinate research and conservation activities. Tourism is today the major source of income, with over 20 000 visitors a year.

Despite recent great care – for example, tourists must be accompanied by a guide and keep to designated trails – human activities have adversely affected the ecology of the islands. Hunting has reduced or eliminated populations of several species, including the giant tortoises (*Geochelone elephantopus*), at least three races of which have disappeared and a fourth doomed to extinction, since only one individual survives. But again it is a suite of introductions that has had the greatest impact on the native biota and communities (Eckhardt, 1972; Jackson, 1985; Schofield, 1989).

Eat-anything goats are a major culprit. On Pinta, a male and two females were released in 1959; by 1979, the population had grown to somewhere between 5000 and 10 000. Not surprisingly here, and on the other islands, goat browsing has destroyed or severely damaged much of the vegetation, affecting over 70% of the native flora in this way. Cattle, pigs, horses and donkeys have also become feral on some of the inhabited islands. Rats have overrun many areas and have led to the extinction of native rice rats. Invasive plants also alter the vegetation drastically, important examples being guava (*Psidium guajava*; also a problem on Hawaii), lantana (*Lantana camara*), and the wind-blown quinine tree (*Cinchona succiruba*).

8.2.2.3 The snake that ate Guam

A good example of the impact of a keystone exotic comes from Guam, the largest island of Micronesia in the north-west Pacific. The Australasian brown tree snake (*Boiga irregularis*) was accidentally introduced in around 1950 and initiated a cascade of extinctions that Fritts and Rodda (1998) believe has been unprecedented among historical extinction events in both its severity and the range of species affected.

The brown tree snake was not the only introduced animal species in Guam to have had an impact on the island's biota. The musk shrew (*Suncus marinus*), for example, may have been responsible for the disappearance of two species of lizard, the pelagic gecko (*Nactus pelagicus*) and the Mariana skink (*Emoia slevini*), and was probably (and more valuably) the cause of an order of magnitude decline in house mice during the 1960s. The strongly territorial and aggressive black drongo (*Dicrurus macrocercus*) is a bird that was introduced to control pest insects in the late 1930s and may have reduced numbers of smaller, native bird species until its own decline in recent years. And an introduced lizard, the curious skink (*Carlia* cf. *fusca*), also increased dramatically in numbers following its introduction in the early 1950s: it probably had little effect on native lizard species, and ironically its major significance to the ecology of the island may have been its role as the major prey item to the brown tree snake.

This snake is a voracious, generalist predator that can climb trees and can strike prey in total darkness. It has been held responsible for the extirpation or decline of virtually all native forest birds, as well as many of those from other habitats; for the near extinction of a subspecies of the Mariana fruit bat (*Pteropus marianus marianus*), and possibly of two other bat species; and for the demise and decline of some, at least, of the indigenous reptile fauna.

The impoverishment of the native fauna has resulted from a combination of factors:

- Guam has a particularly vulnerable ecology, being an island with a moderate climate and an abundance and variety of prey;
- a lack of co-evolution between predators and prey: resident species evolved in an essentially predator-free environment and so lacked anti-predator defences;
- the autecology of the tree snake makes it an effective generalist predator;
- the abundance of prey species (primarily other introductions) increased brown tree snake numbers so much that native species, taken opportunistically, could not persist; and
- introduced species are most successful in disturbed and anthropogenic habitats, and habitat loss and decline in habitat quality predisposed native species to suffer all the more from further perturbation.

While the brown tree snake would not have reached such high densities were it not for the large, vulnerable prey base of other introductions, it was clearly the key to the dramatic impact that biological invaders had on native fauna, and in many ways it was indeed 'the snake that ate Guam' (Pimm, 1987).

8.3 Ecological concepts

- Habitat classification
- Niches
- Resource axes and species packing
- Competition and coexistence
- Island biogeography theory

8.3.1 Habitat classification

If ecosystems represent the functional interrelationships between living organisms and their environment, then *habitat* represents the arenas in which such interactions take place. In Section 1.3.3 it was noted that communities exist in habitats, which are the areas in which organisms live, defined in terms of space and the environmental characteristics of that space. Habitats can therefore only be examined from the point of view of the organism. The habitat provides a template for species (Southwood, 1977), which may be more or less constant but which can vary through time, especially seasonally. Species have become morphologically and behaviourally adapted to particular habitats, even where these are patchy, ephemeral or unpredictable.

Habitats can be classified according to their physical characteristics. Figure 8.3, for example, classifies freshwater habitats according to size and speed (if any) of flow. Although the boundaries of both size and water flow can only be drawn subjectively, because these are continuous attributes, the resultant groupings are useful in separating often clearly different kinds of habitat, the environments of which will contain very different kinds of species and communities, with different sets of adaptations.

Habitats can also be distinguished in terms of the pressures placed on the species they contain. A good example of this uses the ideas of stress, disturbance and resource availability introduced

	A very small	B small	C medium	D large	E very large
1. Still	tree-hole	small pond <20 sq. yd (17 m²)	pond <1 acre (0.4 ha)	large pool or tarn <100 acres (40 ha)	lake or sea
2. Slow	trickle, shallow stream	ditch, field dyke	canal, river backwater		
3. Medium	trickle, shallow stream	lowland brook or small stream	lowland river	lowland large river	river estuary
4. Fast	spring	upland small torrent stream	large torrent stream		
5. Vertical or steep	water drip, pipe outlet, cascade	small weir or waterfall	large weir or medium waterfall	large waterfall	

Figure 8.3   Water bodies classified by size and speed of flow (after Elton, 1966).

in Section 6.3.2. In the context of plants, *stress* has been defined as 'the external constraints which limit the rate of dry matter production of all or part of the vegetation' (Grime, 1979: 21). Stress-tolerant (S) plants are therefore those that can withstand environmental factors leading to a reduction in productivity. Disturbance-tolerant plants are known as *ruderals* (R), disturbance being any environmental factor that in some way damages or destroys plant tissue. *Competitive* (C) species are those that are especially effective at acquiring resources such as light, water and nutrients, and which in so doing can out-compete less competitive species. Generalised characteristics of C-, S- and R-selected plants are outlined in Table 8.3.

Nutrient acquisition and efficient use of energy are often keys to the success of competitive species, rapid uptake of nutrients from the soil or the use of energy and nutrients stored in overwintering rhizomes, corms or bulbs allowing such plants to grow rapidly in early spring, outshading their neighbours. In this way, they acquire more than their share of sunlight with

which to photosynthesise, and this in turn accentuates their growth advantages. Root systems, too, tend to be more extensive and efficient at acquiring soil resources throughout the growing season, again giving an advantage.

Levels of stress and disturbance can be plotted against two axes (Figure 8.4a), which can then be angled (since axes need not be set at right angles to each other) to produce what is in effect a third axis, that of resource availability and therefore level of competitiveness (Figure 8.4b) (Grime, 1974; 1979). In areas of high stress but low disturbance, for example hot deserts and tundra (although the latter may be subject to frost heaving), one would clearly expect to find *S-selected* plants. Similarly, in areas of high disturbance and low stress, for example in ploughed fields, *R-selected* plants would be expected. In areas of high productivity (low stress) that were also undisturbed, *C-selected* plants would be characteristic. Mixed strategies can also be accommodated by this system, for example CR strategies where disturbed but productive sites are found (Figure 8.5).

Table 8.3   Some general characteristics of competitive, stress-tolerant and ruderal plants

	Competitive	Stress-tolerant	Ruderal
Morphology			
1 Lifeforms	Herbs, shrubs and trees	Lichens, herbs, shrubs, trees	Herbs
2 Shoot morphology	Dense leaf canopy; extensive lateral spread above and below ground	Very wide range	Small stature with limited lateral spread
Life history			
3 Longevity of mature plants	Long or relatively short	Long	Very short
4 Longevity of leaves and roots	Relatively short	Long	Short
5 Seasonal patterns of leafing (leaf phenology)	Well-defined peaks of leaf production coinciding with period(s) of maximum potential productivity	Evergreens	Short period of leaf production in period of high potential productivity
6 Seasonal patterns of flowering (flowering frequency and phenology)	Flowers usually produced after periods of maximum potential productivity	Intermittent flowering, with no general relationship between season and phenology	High frequency, with flowers produced early in the life history
7 Proportion of annual production devoted to seeds	Small	Small	Large
8 Reproductive strategy	Vegetative, seasonal regeneration in vegetation gaps, numerous wind-dispersed seeds, or persistent seed bank	Vegetative, or persistent seedling bank	Seasonal regeneration in vegetation gaps, numerous wind-dispersed seeds, or persistent seed bank
Physiology			
9 Maximum potential relative growth rate	Rapid	Slow	Rapid
10 Photosynthesis and uptake of mineral nutrients	Strongly seasonal, coinciding with long period of vegetative growth	Opportunistic, often uncoupled from vegetative growth	Opportunistic, coinciding with vegetative growth
11 Storage of photosynthate and mineral nutrients	Most rapidly incorporated into vegetative structure but some is stored to form the basis for expansion of growth during the following growing season	Storage system in leaves, stems and/or roots	Seeds only

Source: after Grime (1979)

The beauty of this system is that we can group together or compare different species of plant in terms of their habitat requirements, and categorise responses at different stages of their life history (for example a germinating plant may be located in a different part of the diagram from a plant in its reproductive phase). The scheme also allows comparison between the habitats themselves according to the environmental attributes that are found there (Figure 8.6).

(a)

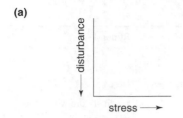

(b)

Figure 8.4 (a) Graph showing 90° axes of disturbance and stress; (b) graph showing 60° axes of disturbance and stress, to which an axis showing resource availability (competitiveness) can be joined.

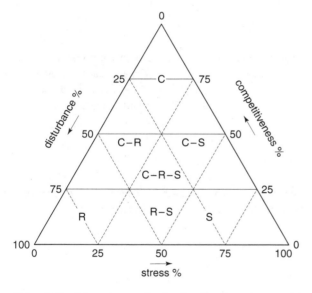

Figure 8.5 Triangular graph showing location of pure and mixed C, R and S strategies.

8.3.2 Niches

The environment within a habitat may provide a gradient of environmental conditions, for example of temperature or salinity, and in Section 4.3.1 it was shown how species have

limits of tolerance for such environmental factors. Species may have limits, or preferences, for other environmental attributes, for example vegetation height or water depth. And finally, species may have requirements or preferences for food type, not only for particular species of food but also for such characteristics as prey size, plant tissue moisture or nutrient content. All of these environmental attributes needed by an organism in order to survive can be thought of as *resource gradients*, ranging from low values (or low value) to high.

The particular suite of resources used by an organism, together (often) with the manner in which the resource is utilised and (sometimes) the time of day or season it is utilised, defines the very specific ecological demands of that organism and characterises its *niche*. The niche of a species can be thought of in terms of ecological space and may be conceptualised as the position occupied within a matrix of resource gradients, as shown in Figure 8.7a–f.

Figures 8.7a and 8.7b show how the range of tolerance of a species translates into *niche breadth* as defined in one dimension. A stenotopic species (see Section 4.3.1) will have a narrow niche breadth, a eurytopic species a wide breadth. Species response along a second axis can be constructed in exactly the same way (Figure 8.7c), the resource gradient here shown on the *y*-axis rather than the *x*-axis.

In Figure 8.7d it is evident that, because of its environmental requirements, the species can only be found within the part of the diagram designated E, since A is too wet and too cold; B is too wet (although temperature conditions are appropriate); C is too wet and too hot; D is too cold (although water conditions are appropriate); F is too hot; G is too dry and too cold; H is too dry; and I is too dry and too hot. We have defined the *niche space* of the species in two dimensions according to its tolerance of two physical environmental conditions.

Two species might live in the same habitat but occupy different niches, even at this simple level of discrimination, for example willows (*Salix* spp.) might be found in damp parts of a deciduous woodland, while hazel (*Corylus avellana*) might be associated with dry ground. Similarly,

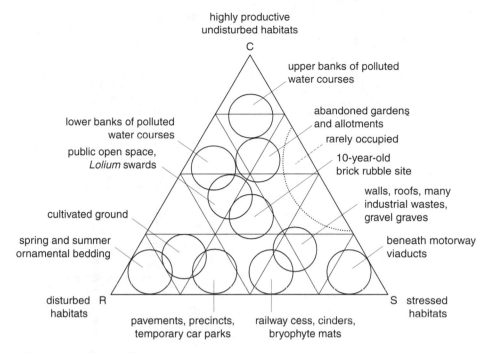

Figure 8.6 Grime's C–R–S model used to characterise some urban habitats (after Gilbert, 1989).

wracks (*Fucus*) and kelps (*Laminaria*) occupy different levels of tidal submersion on rocky shores (see Section 7.3.4). In both cases, the taxa can coexist in the habitat because they 'occupy' different positions along a single resource axis. Even where species demonstrate *niche overlap* along any one axis, consideration of the two axes together indicates that niche separation (or certainly great reduction in overlap) is possible even in two dimensions (Figure 8.8). Nevertheless, many species still have essentially identical niches when these are defined along two axes, yet one of the key axioms of ecology is that *no two species can occupy the same niche*, for theory dictates, and some experimental work shows, that one such species would eventually outcompete and exclude the other. Competition may be one outcome of such niche overlap, but there are other ways in which species can coexist (see Section 8.3.4).

Also, there is no reason to define niche space only in two dimensions. By adding a third resource axis, the niche of a species can be characterised, and plotted, in three dimensions (Figure 8.7e), and it might be this third dimension

of resource use that allows one species to coexist with another that shares the requirements of the first two resources. And why stop at three dimensions? While it is impossible to visualise, there is no conceptual or mathematical reason not to extend the definition of niche into multi-dimensional space. Niche space is indeed often thought of in this way, as a hypervolume defined in *n*-dimensional space, *n* representing the number of axes used.

The unique ecological requirements of most organisms, however, can usually be defined using no more than five or six axes, and often fewer. This is particularly the case when using resource axes to determine niche space in communities with only one component of a species' needs being considered, for example in delimiting a feeding niche, where the axes will refer to environmental components pertaining only to food or feeding (Figure 8.9).

In practice, the theoretical maximum niche space of a species is rarely completely occupied. There are two main reasons for this. First, if they can, individuals of a species try to avoid the extremes of the resource axes, for example

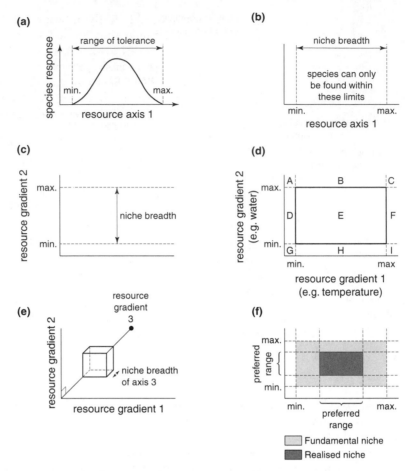

Figure 8.7 The idea of the niche: (a) limits of tolerance have been defined along one dimension; (b) simplified version of (a) to indicate niche breadth defined in one dimension; (c) the axes can be reversed so that the resource axis is vertical. This might represent a second resource (axis 2); (d) combining axes 1 and 2 defines the niche space (E) in two dimensions; (e) adding a third axis defines the niche space in three dimensions; (f) realised niche as a component of the fundamental niche.

temperature conditions close to their absolute limits of tolerance. Thus Figure 8.7d should more realistically be represented as shown in Figure 8.7f. Preferred niche space can thus be distinguished from tolerated but non-preferred space by differences in density or frequency of activity, as shown in Figure 8.9, where the feeding niche of the blue-grey gnatcatcher (*Polioptila caerulea*) is represented not by absolute limits but by a series of feeding frequency contours. Ideally, in the case of this bird, prey are sought 3–5 mm in length at tree heights of 3–7 m above the ground,

where feeding frequency is greatest. Beyond these size and height ranges feeding rates decline, and although prey over 12 mm can be taken (at the preferred foraging height), handling these larger items takes up a large amount of time (and energy), so feeding rate drops to a lower rate probably not offset by the greater biomass and energy value of the food.

A second reason for species occupying less than their maximum possible niche space is competition (see Section 8.3.4). Competition can be *intraspecific* in that at low densities a population

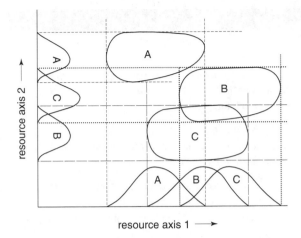

Figure 8.8 Although species A, B and C show overlap along each axis, when plotted against both, niche overlap is minimised (species B and C) or indeed niche separation is effected (species A and B, and A and C).

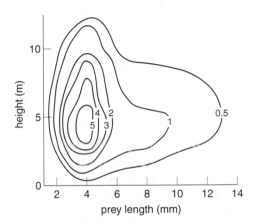

Figure 8.9 Feeding niche of blue-grey gnatcatcher during the incubation period (July–August) in California, defined in terms of percentage of the total diet for the two niche axes. The maximum response level lies within the 5% contour line.

of a competitively inferior species the superior will exclude the inferior from that part of the resource axis (or area) where there is overlap, in this way restricting the niche space of the inferior species. This is *competitive exclusion*. These two reasons for a reduction in occupied niche space overlap, since a species at the edge of its range of tolerance is unlikely to be competitively vigorous.

To accommodate these ideas, Hutchinson (1959) importantly distinguished between the *fundamental niche* of a species, which is the niche space it can theoretically occupy in the absence of competition, and the *realised niche*, which is the space actually occupied by the species when restricted by competitive interactions.

The niche is thus a representation of the ecological requirements of a species and in many ways reflects its role in the community and position in an ecosystem (Ecology Box 8.1). Organisms may occupy different niche spaces during different stages of their life cycle. For example, the ecological requirements of a tadpole are completely different from those of an adult frog, so the same species will, at different times, occupy different niches, as well as a different range of habitats.

One means of using essentially the same resources in the same environment may be through adopting behavioural differences in using or acquiring those resources. Treecreepers (*Certhia familiaris*), for example, tend to search for invertebrate prey by moving *up* the trunk of a tree, in contrast to the nuthatch (*Sitta europaea*), which seeks insects by travelling *down* the trunk. In this way, both species can coexist on the same habitat feature and on much the same food, an example of resource partitioning which is explored further in the next section.

8.3.3 Resource axes and species packing

Using the concept of the niche goes some way towards explaining why communities contain the species they do, why some communities are more species-rich than others, and how such species interact in terms of competition and coexistence. Other things being equal, greater species richness is found where

will not need to occupy non-preferred ecological space at the extremes of the ranges of tolerance of that species, but at high densities some individuals may be forced to live under conditions near the boundaries of their tolerance range for at least one resource component, and will do so under competitive pressure from conspecifics. More usually, perhaps, competition is *interspecific*. If the resource demands of a competitively superior species overlap with the demands

ECOLOGY BOX 8.1

Developments in the idea of the niche

Joseph Grinnell (1917) suggested that the niche should be regarded as a subdivision of an environment occupied by a species, 'the ultimate distributional unit within which each species is held by its structural and functional limitations.' This, however, is perhaps better viewed as a definition of habitat.

More usefully, **Charles Elton** (1927) viewed the niche as the fundamental role of the organism in its community – what is does, what its food comprises, and how it relates to competitors and enemies. Elton considered the niche to represent the organism's profession, while habitat was seen as equivalent to its address.

Evelyn Hutchinson (1958), however, defined the niche in the context of the total range of physical environmental conditions under which the organism lived and reproduced. By adding biological variables such as competition, this idea of the niche is extended to include both the organism's environment and its function in the community.

Eugene Odum (1959) defined the niche as 'the position or status of an organism within its community and ecosystem resulting from the organism's structural adaptations, physiological responses and specific behavior (inherited and/or learned). The ecological niche of an organism depends not only on where it lives but also on what it does.'

Robert Whittaker and co-workers (1973) also distinguished between the habitat, referring to the distributional response of an organism at different places in the landscape, and the niche of an organism, which reflects its functional relationships within a community. Habitat and niche can be combined into the term 'ecotope', which is 'the species' response to the full range of environmental variables to which it is exposed.'

Eric Pianka (1978) defined the niche as 'all the various ways in which a given organismic unit [individual, population or species] conforms to its particular environment.'

Useful reviews of how ideas about the niche have changed are given in Vandermeer (1972) and Schoener (1989).

- the extent or range of resources is greater. Even when considering just one resource axis, the more extended the axis, the greater the number of species that may be found along it (Figure 8.10a).
- species have more specialist resource requirements or narrower ranges of tolerance, and therefore narrower niche breadths (Figure 8.10b).
- species have a greater degree of overlap with their 'neighbours' along the resource axis (assuming mechanisms of coexistence or differentiation along other niche dimensions) (Figure 8.10c).
- more of the resource axis is exploited (Figure 8.10d).

More productive habitats will thus tend to contain a greater number of interacting species (greater *species packing*) as well as individuals, since resources are likely to be greater in extent (resource axis length) as well as amount (reflected in the resource exploitation 'height'), and possibly also greater in variety (arguably relating to the actual number of relevant resource axes). Species interactions include plant–herbivore and predator–prey interactions. They also include competition and coexistence.

8.3.4 Competition and coexistence

When individuals of the same species compete for the same resource this is known as intraspecific competition. This in turn may be intra- or intersexual, usually in the context of mating behaviour, for example males competing for territories or fighting for access to females are participating in male intrasexual competition, while they are undertaking intersexual behaviour when they perform courtship displays to the female. Intra-

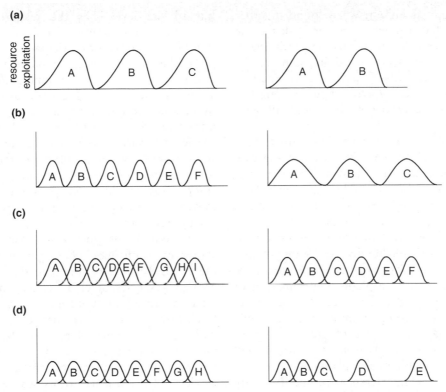

Figure 8.10   Resource axes and species packing: (a) species have non-overlapping niches of equal breadth. More species are found along the left-hand resource axis simply because the extent of the resource (axis length) is greater; (b) resource axes are of equal extent, but more species are found when they have narrower niche breadths; (c) more species are found where the degree of niche overlap is greater; (d) more species are found where the resource axis is fully exploited.

specific competition is an important underlying feature of population dynamics, affecting mate selection, fecundity, reproductive success, mortality and growth (see Chapter 5). It is also important in driving natural selection, since individuals that can acquire more or better resources, or can gain these more efficiently or less energetically expensive, will have greater fitness: more of their offspring will survive to contribute more of their parental genes to the next generation. In this way, particular genetic traits enhancing survival and reproductive success are more likely to persist, and distinct behavioural and morphological differentiation might result (see Section 6.3.1.1).

Interspecific competition occurs when individuals of different species compete for resources. We have seen earlier (Section 8.3.2) that one species may compete more effectively than another (asymmetrical competition), leading to a restriction in use of a resource axis. One option for the less competitive species is to change its location or its behaviour, but this is not always possible, so through time it may, via natural selection, adapt morphologically or physiologically to less competitive conditions, in effect shifting its range of tolerance along the resource axis, a process called *character displacement*.

Related to this, a species may adopt characters that allow it to specialise more than it would in the absence of competition. By specialising it exploits a narrower range of the resource but does so more efficiently. On the Galapagos Islands, for example, two species of Darwin's finch, *Geospiza fortis* and *G. fuliginosa*, have similar beak sizes when occurring on an island where the other is absent; when found together, *G. fuliginosa* has a much narrower beak than its congeneric, allowing it to use an admittedly smaller range of seed sizes but doing so more efficiently and so effectively having a competitive advantage over *G. fortis*. This is another mechanism reducing competition and allowing coexistence.

Interference competition involves direct interactions, in animals perhaps literally fighting over territory or for an item of food, or interfering with each others' behaviour by disturbing prey. Time and energy are spent in such interactions, and injury is possible, so anticipated benefits must exceed such costs. Interference competition in animals is usually, but by no means always, intraspecific. Intensity of interaction tends to increase with density. In plants, vigorous root or leaf growth will tend to gain access to resources more efficiently in competition with more slowly growing plants, and release of growth-suppressing chemicals (auxins) from the roots will adversely affect neighbouring plants.

Two forms of interference competition are contest and scramble competition. In *contest competition*, there are immediately clear winners and losers, the winners acquiring all the resource. In *scramble competition*, there is an initial random exploitation of a resource, but chance winners gain relative fitness and so can acquire resources more effectively, and will gradually emerge as the winners. An example of scramble competition is when maggots hatch in a piece of meat. At first all maggots have an equal chance of survival, but only a few will predominate and will eventually be able to pupate and emerge as adults. All the meat will have been eaten, however, a large amount of its energy having been 'wasted' on non-surviving maggots. The eventual winners will have consumed only a fraction of the total energy originally available.

Exploitation competition is indirect. The quantity or quality of a resource will be reduced simply by being exploited. Again, this can happen intraspecifically when the density of a population increases, with more individuals seeking a finite amount of some resource. Exploitation competition, however, is often interspecific, and the organisms respond not to each other's presence but to the level that the resource has been depleted by the action of one or the other or indeed any number of participants.

Another form of indirect interaction is where two prey species share the same predator and, in so doing, increase the local predator population by making the food rewards of the habitat more attractive. The interactive effect on the two prey species populations is much the same as if they were competing, even although they could be using entirely different resources. This *apparent competition* can be avoided by one prey species moving away from the vicinity of the other into enemy-free space.

An example of this is seen on some rocky shores of California, where gastropod snails of the genus *Tegula* are found in the same general area as a species of clam, *Chama arcana*. Both taxa are preyed on by lobsters. At a microhabitat level, however, clams are particularly associated with locations where large boulders provide a number of hiding places, while the gastropods are mostly found on substrates where there are few crevices. Experiments translocating clams to gastropod-dominated substrates resulted in increased overall rates of predation and a reduction in density of both prey taxa. The natural pattern of distribution thus seems to be maintained by predation rather than by resource use. Once again, a mechanism has been found to permit coexistence through differential microhabitat selection and niche differentation, here along the environmental resource axis of crevice availability.

Species with similar ecological requirements can thus coexist through *resource partitioning*. Resources are partitioned to reduce or avoid competition in a variety of ways, for example:

- **By utilising different microhabitats**, as with the gastropods and clams mentioned above. Similarly, many woodland birds forage for essentially the same food items but in different parts of a tree. Blue tits (*Parus caeruleus*), for example, tend to search for insect larvae in the leaves and small twigs near the tops of trees, while the marsh tit (*P. palustris*) forages closer to the trunk at mid-tree heights, and great tits (*P. major*) prefer lower and larger branches:

the food resource offered by the tree is partitioned spatially in three dimensions.

Similarly, in New England, five species of insectivorous wood warbler all feed in the same tall firs and spruces but do so in sufficiently different parts of the tree to reduce or avoid competition and thus coexist (Figure 8.11a.). The yellow-rumped warbler (*Dendroica coronata*), for example, spends most of its foraging time in the base of the tree, while the Cape May warbler (*D. tigrina*) favours the tree top, rather like the Blackburnian warbler (*D. fusca*), the latter, however, preferring the outer part of the tree top and being prepared to move to mid-height parts. In turn, the black-throated green warbler (*D. virens*) favours mid-height feeding sites but clearly prefers the outer parts, in contrast to bay-breasted warbler (*D. castanea*) which seeks its insect prey more in the interior needles. Not surprisingly, these species partition their preferred nesting heights in a similar manner to their feeding locations (Figure 8.11b) (MacArthur, 1958).

Partitioning of habitat space is also seen in plants, for example by varying the kinds of root (tap, fibrous, rhizomatous, etc.) and depth of rooting, which reduces competition in the soil for water and nutrients, as seen for example in the desert grasslands of southern Arizona (Burgess, 1995) (Figure 8.12).

- **By utilising the same habitat in different ways.** Even when the New England wood warblers feed in the same parts of the tree there are some differences in feeding technique, *D. virens* for example seeking stationary prey hiding cryptically, in contrast to the flying prey largely captured by its congenerics. In finches, bill size tends to increase with preferred seed size: as examples, redpolls (*Acanthis flammea*) possess relatively small bills and take the smallest seeds, followed by linnets (*A. cannabina*), greenfinches (*Carduelis chloris*), bullfinches (*Pyrrhula pyrrhula*) and hawfinches (*Coccothraustes coccothraustes*), which have very chunky beaks and take the largest seeds. The different direction of movement on the tree trunk adopted by treecreepers and nuthatches mentioned earlier is

another example, and woodpeckers feed on bark insects in yet another manner, hammering their bills into the wood. Similarly, diving and dabbling ducks use ponds and rivers in different ways as well as at different depths, and different species of seabird will seek fish at different depths and at different distances from the coastline.

- **By using resources at different times.** A group of animals, for instance, may use the same feeding methods and general prey but at different times of the day, for example diurnally hunting birds of prey such as hawks and nocturnally hunting birds such as owls. Plants in the same community may germinate, leaf, flower and seed at different times of the year, as seen in the spring, early and late summer, and autumn phenologies of the ground flora of many temperate woodlands, and in the grasses and herbs of prairies and steppes.

An example of niche separation in Malaysian squirrels is shown in Ecology Box 8.2, in which the animals partition microhabitat, food and time of day.

- **By using resources in a way that minimises costs.** The corolla of a flower refers to the petals as a whole, especially when these are joined together. Long tongued bees such as the bumble bees *Bombus pascuorum* and *B. hortorum* can feed on nectar from flowers with both short and long corollas, but short-tongued bees such as honey bees (*Apis mellifera*) can only feed from short corollas. Long-tongued bees, however, tend to avoid short corollas because they would then be in competition with short-tongued species, not necessarily directly (interference competition) but indirectly (exploitation competition), since a limited supply of nectar would be sought by the whole nectarivorous bee community. It therefore pays the long-tongued bees to specialise on long-corolla flowers, reducing the time and energy costs of interspecific competition, and avoid short corollas even although they are physically capable of feeding from these

Competition is indeed costly in terms of time, energy and lost opportunity to maximise (or at least optimise) the resources of a habitat.

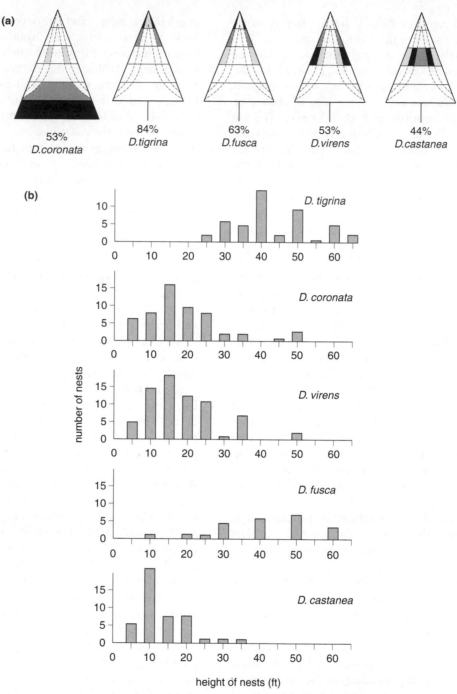

Figure 8.11 (a) The zones of the trees where the five warblers studied by MacArthur (1958) spent most of their time feeding. For each of the five species, the solid black areas show the zone where the birds were most likely to be found, the hatched areas show the second most popular zone, and the dotted areas show the third most popular zone. The figures at the bases of the trees show the percentage of the time that the birds spent in these three zones when feeding in trees. (b) The heights at which the five species of warbler made their nest.

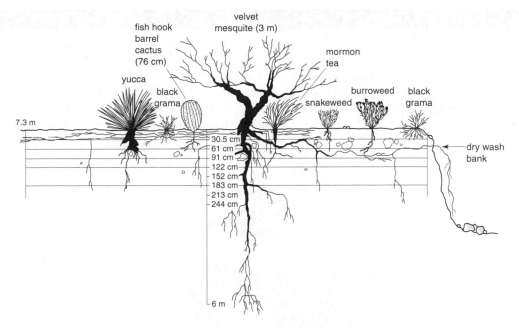

Figure 8.12 Root distribution of common plants in desert grasslands of sourthern Arizona. Black grama (*Bouteloua eriopoda*) and snakeweed (*Gutierrezia sarothrae*) are intensive exploiters. Velvet mesquite (*Prosopis velutina*) and Mormon tea (*Ephedra* spp.) are extensive exploiters. Burroweed (*Isocoma tenuisecta*) uses an intermediate strategy. Fish hook barrel cactus (*Ferocactus wislizenii*) and yucca (*Yucca* spp.) are water storers.

Mechanisms of coexistence reduce these costs and ensure that, other things being equal, environmental resources are used in as many ways by as many individuals or as many species as possible. This is mediated by various kinds of niche differentiation. The critical threshold of differentiation in the way a resource is used is known as the *limiting similarity*. This does not exclude overlap

ECOLOGY BOX 8.2

Niche separation in Malaysian tree squirrels

Different species of tree squirrel can coexist in the tropical moist forests of the Malaysian Peninsula by partitioning the habitat, types of food and time. By adopting different diets and feeding in different parts of the canopy or forest floor, and by being active either during the daytime or at night, at least seventeen species can be found in the same general area.

The three-striped ground squirrel, for example, preferably feeds on leaves and insects at ground level, including from fallen branches; the slender squirrel is active on the lowest parts of tree trunks consuming bark and sap; and the tufted ground squirrel takes fruit and nuts from the lower reaches of the forest. Further up the tree trunks are the bark-feeding Low's squirrel and the insectivorous pygmy squirrel. In mid-canopy, black-banded and plantain squirrels have varied diets, food being taken opportunistically, while the horse-tailed squirrel is a seed specialist. Prevost's squirrel and the black giant squirrel feast on the abundant fruits and nuts found in the upper canopy, foods also eaten by cream giant squirrels, which take insects as well. These eleven squirrels are all diurnal, and a further six species – all flying squirrels – become active at night, again feeding at different levels and on different foods. The larger species tend to live at greater heights and eat a greater proportion of leaves than smaller species, which take mainly fruit.

ECOLOGY BOX 8.2 (cont)

Partitioning of the food resource is particularly evident when food is abundant and the squirrels can concentrate on their preferred food items, but in times of scarcity the diet of each species becomes more generalist (relying heavily on bark and sap) and therefore there is more dietary overlap and competition. In the daytime canopy, the black giant squirrel and Prevost's squirrel often feed on the same fruit trees, but while the former has the competitive advantage of size its metabolism is energetically more expensive. Thus Prevost's squirrel, although smaller and also selecting a smaller range of fruits, can afford to spend less time feeding each day and can travel further to find food trees than the larger animal.

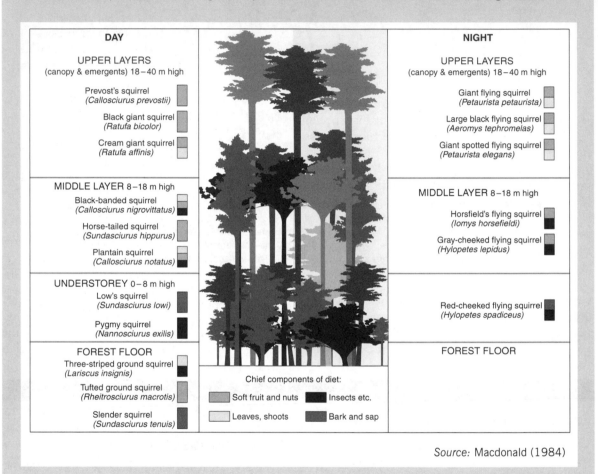

Source: Macdonald (1984)

along niche axes, but again there is a critical threshold for each pair or group of species for each resource related to the intensity of competition where overlap does occur.

By including a suite of organisms that maximally exploit the environmental resources of the habitat by resource partitioning and through overlapping niches, communities can accommodate a great number and range of species. The membership of and interactions within a community, however, are not fixed. New species enter, while other species may become locally extinct. This is particularly evident in communities that exist within clearly defined boundaries such as islands, and in well-developed communities it might be that an equilibrium number of species exists. This is one of the ideas explored in island biogeography theory.

8.3.5 Island biogeography theory

Island biogeography theory rests on three related sets of ideas: species–area relationships, the geographical disposition of island to mainland, and the equilibrium number of species associated with rates of immigration and local extinction.

8.3.5.1 Species–area relationships

We might intuitively expect the number of species on an island to increase with the size of the island. In general terms, such a species–area relationship does indeed exist. Plotting species number against area produces a more-or-less curved line, with the number of species increasing more slowly as size increases. This can be represented by the equation $S = cA^z$, where S is species number, A is area, and c and z are dimensionless parameters whose values need to be fitted for each set of species–area data (Figure 8.13a).

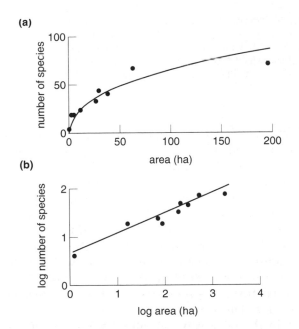

Figure 8.13 (a) an example of a species–area relation: the number of breeding bird species in different–size plots of North American deciduous forest; (b) The species–area relation in (a) plotted on logarithmic axes.

Transferring area into log values, however, generally results in a straight line. In fact, area and species number are often both transformed to log value, and again a straight line – a regression line, or line of best fit – can be fitted to the data. The above equation can now be written as $\log S = c + z . \log A$, where c is a constant representing the theoretical base value of S when plotted as a regression line when A is zero, and z is a measure of the slope of the regression line (Figure 8.13b). In practice, the slopes (values of z) of log–log plots usually fall within the range 0.24–0.34.

The resulting graphs relating species number to area vary in slope and goodness of fit between island groups and organisms, but as a crude approximation species numbers nearly double with every increase in area by an order of magnitude (Figure 8.14). Thus, if an island of 1 ha contains ten species, we might expect an island of equivalent environment of 10 ha to possess nearly twenty species and a 100 ha island to support a little under forty species. To some extent a size effect might be expected simply in terms of geater available space, but it is also the case that the larger the island the greater the variety of habitats or microhabitats, and the greater the opportunity for species packing. Furthermore, larger islands can support larger populations of any one species, so minimum viable population sizes are more likely to be exceeded, and species persistence is therefore more likely.

8.3.5.2 Geographical attributes

A newly created island such as the volcanic Surtsey, which emerged from the North Atlantic a few kilometres south of Iceland over the period 1963–67, or a denuded island such as Krakatau, which erupted in 1883, will be colonised by species from nearby sources – other islands or the mainland. A number of geographical attributes will affect the rate of immigration. For plants and for passively drifting or weak-flying animals the speed and direction of wind and ocean currents are important. Soo too are distance from the mainland, and the size, shape and orientation of the island (Figure 8.15).

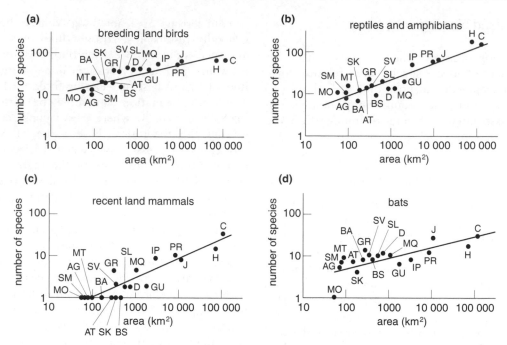

Figure 8.14 Species–area relations of four major vertebrate taxa on the same West Indian islands. The relative differences in the observed z values follow from taxon-specific colonisation and extinction rates. They suggest that consequences of habitat loss and insularisation depend on metabolic rate, body size and dispersal ability. Species–area curves fitted by linear regression are as follows: (a) $S = 6.1A^{0.24}$, (b) $S = 1.6A^{0.38}$, (c) $S = 0.1A^{0.48}$. (d) $S = 1.6A^{0.24}$. (C) Cuba, (H) Hispaniola, (J) Jamaica, (PR) Puerto Rico, (IP) Isle of Pines, (GU) Guadeloupe, (MQ) Martinique, (D) Dominica, (SL) St Lucia, (SV) St Vincent, (BS) Barbados, (GR) Grenada, (AT) Antigua, (SK) St Kitts, (BA) Barbuda, (MT) Montserrat, (AG) Anguilla, (SM) St Martin, (MO) Mona. Recent land mammals include living and recently extinct native mammals. Many of the present mammal faunas include exotic species that have replaced native species.

8.3.5.3 Rates of immigration and extinction, and equilibrium numbers of species

Arrival on an island is no guarantee of an individual's survival or a species' persistence. The newly arrived organism must find a suitable habitat, acquire nutrients, avoid being eaten or out-competed, and be able to reproduce. Plants capable of vegetative reproduction or self-fertilisation, and parthenogenic animals, may have an initial advantage. For sexually reproducing organisms, clearly at least one fertile member of each sex needs to be present, and preferably rather more than this to minimise the dangers of inbreeding.

For any one island, the rate of immigration of new species will decline with time and with the number of species already present, i.e. for each

new individual arriving on the island the chances of this individual representing a species already present increases with time, and the chances of it being a new species decreases. Also, the species pool of the mainland is finite, so the more species that arrive on the island, the fewer new species are actually available for colonisation from the mainland. Furthermore, islands closer to the mainland, as well as larger islands, will tend to have higher rates of immigration because of the proximity and size effects noted in the previous section (Figure 8.16a).

In the same way, not all species that colonise will persist. Local extinction may occur not only by chance or through genetic problems associated with minimum viable population thresholds (see Section 5.3.6) but also because as more and more

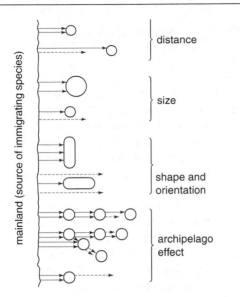

species colonise so competition for resources intensifies and many species will be completely out-competed, or food webs become more complex and some species may be eaten to extinction. The more species that are present on an island, therefore, the greater the rate of local extinction, and the smaller the island the more that rate will rise (Figure 8.16b).

The number of species on an island thus reflects the relationship between rate of immigration and extinction. The number of species may change through time, but even when it remains more or less the same the actual floristic and faunistic make-up may alter (*species turnover*). The rate at which one species is lost and a replacement species is gained is the *turnover rate*. The equilibrium number of species (S^*) occurs where the rates of immigration and extinction are equal (Figure 8.16c).

Figure 8.15   Effects of island geography on number of colonising species.

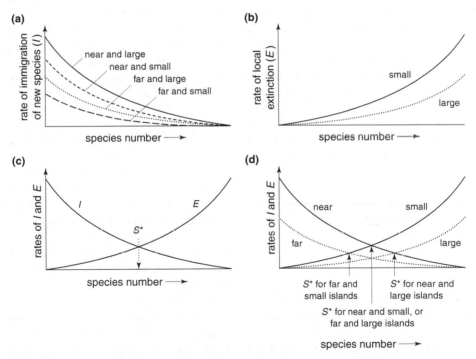

Figure 8.16   Rates of immigration, extinction and equilibrium number of species on small and large, and near and distant, islands. (a) Rates of immigration (I) dependent on size and proximity of island to the mainland. Numbers on near and small islands may be similar to those on distant but large islands. (b) Rates of local extinction (E) dependent on size of island. (c) Equilibrium number of species (S^*) where rates of I and E are equal. (d) S^* will vary according to size and distance of island. Large islands close to the mainland will tend to have most species, small islands far from the mainland the least.

The value of S^* will tend to vary according to the factors of mainland proximity and island size, a large island close to the mainland having a higher equilibrium number of species than small islands far from the mainland (Figure 8.16d).

8.3.5.4 Habitat islands

Island biogeography theory has not only been applied to oceanic islands. Any habitat surrounded by a quite different habitat can be viewed as an island, and similar relationships between species number and island size, for example, have been noted for bird species in woodland islands in a sea of agriculture, or for invertebrates in tufts of grass surrounded by bare ground in semi-arid regions.

Island biogeography, too, has also been used in the design of nature reserves, a notion that is explored in Section 8.4.3. One of the problems here is the more general one that while island biogeography theory is useful in providing a unifying theory that describes the interactions of a wide range of independent variables such as area, isolation and habitat complexity, it is rarely possible to use it in a specifically predictive manner. The theory ceases to be 'a general abstraction of the elements common to all island communities, and becomes merely a framework of narrative descriptions of each situation' (Cox and Moore, 1993: 149).

8.4 Issues in environmental management

8.4.1 Prevention, eradication and control of introduced weeds, pests and diseases

The Position Statement of the International Union for Conservation of Nature and Natural Resources is firm: 'Introduction of an alien species should only be considered if clear and well defined benefits to man [sic] or natural communities can be foreseen [and] if no native species is considered suitable for the purpose for which the introduction is being made' (IUCN,

1987: 3). Assessment of likely ecological impact, however, is fraught with difficulty.

The very qualities that lead to competitive success in biological invasions make them difficult to eradicate once they have become established. Until well into the twentieth century there was often no constraint on introducing plants or animals, and indeed there was the general encouragement to introduce any species, other than the obviously dangerous, believed to be valuable, interesting or of sentimental value. Recently, however, there has been a presumption against deliberate introduction and greater care in the prevention of accidental introductions. Prevention of accidental introductions has been achieved by means of better hygiene, by more rigorous searches of incoming sea and air traffic, and by *quarantine*.

Failure to disinfect imported timber led to the introduction of the fungus *Ceratocystis ulmi* in the UK in the 1960s. This fungus causes Dutch elm disease, and its transmission from tree to tree is facilitated by its vectors, the European elm-bark beetle (*Scolytus scolytus*), which burrows into the living tree, readily transmitting spores of the yeast-like pathogen. Most elms in the British landscape died as a consequence of this invasive fungus. Control was virtually impossible, since felling a diseased tree without immediately burning it allowed the adult beetle simply to fly to another standing tree.

An effective quarantine law with respect to domestic pets has almost certainly been the reason why rabies has not entered the UK, although the current near–eradication of the red fox reservoir of this disease in continental Europe together with proposals for the certification of health of incoming animals means that quarantine requirements are (at the time of writing) likely to be lifted.

Most successful introductions have withstood attempts at their control, but some have eventually been extirpated. The story of the coypu is salutary in this respect (Issues Box 8.1) and shows the need for determination and persistence, together with an understanding of the ecological requirements and population dynamics of the target species.

In practice, management of nuisance introductions tends to be pragmatic, and control rather

ISSUES BOX 8.1

The coypu in England

The coypu (*Myocastor coypus*) is a large semi-aquatic herbivorous rodent native to South America. It was brought into England in 1929 when fur (nutria) farms were established in Sussex, Hampshire, Devon and Norfolk. During the 1930s, many animals escaped from captivity, and while most were caught soon after, or small colonies exterminated, coypus in Norfolk persisted in the waterways of the Broads and neighbouring rivers, streams, dykes, ponds and flooded gravel pits.

Coypus breed continuously, and two litters of two–nine young can emerge in a single year. Numbers therefore increased rapidly, with plentiful food and (for adults) an absence of non-human predators. At first they were tolerated in Norfolk, but as numbers built up the extent of their damage became greater and their threats to freshwater ecosystems more apparent, their grazing habit destroying large patches of reed swamp (itself a critical but already declining habitat for a variety of plants and wildlife, many local and rare) and their burrowing habit leading to the collapse of river banks. Coypus also eat green vegetables and cereal and root crops, so they also became an agricultural pest.

By 1960, it was estimated that around 200 000 coypus were living in East Anglia, and a major culling campaign began. By the end of 1961, 97 000 coypus had been exterminated, and in 1962 a further 40 000 were killed. The harsh winter of 1962–63 further reduced numbers. By 1970, an estimated 2000 animals were thought to have survived, but culling had been reduced to a workforce of six men, and five consecutive mild winters allowed numbers to increase again, so that by 1975 there were at least 12 000 and possibly 20 000 coypus at large. A severe winter in 1978, together with the reintroduction of culling (with twenty trappers) led to a drop to perhaps 6000 by the end of that year.

In 1978, too, the Coypu Strategy Group, which advised the Ministry of Agriculture, recommended an eradication campaign, and a 10-year intensive trapping programme began in 1981. The coypu population fell from perhaps 5000 in 1981 to 40 by 1986. It was feared that as numbers declined the remaining few would be harder to trap, but in fact males began to travel further in order to find increasingly dispersed females, and so were more likely to be caught. This in turn meant that more females failed to find mates and breed. The last breeding group was caught on the Great Ouse in April 1987. Traps continued to be set for a further two years, and two old males were killed in road accidents. The last coypu was trapped in December 1989, with no definite sightings since.

It is undoubtedly appropriate that, on balance, coypus should have been exterminated as an unwelcome biological invasion, but not unwelcome to everyone: the warden of a nature reserve in Norfolk has reported that 'many visitors would go home happier having seen one coypu than ten avocets' (Addison, 1980).

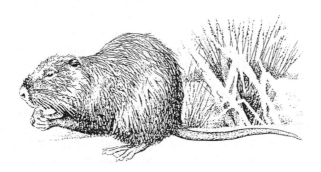

Sources: Gosling and Baker (1989); Smith (1995)

than extermination is generally sought, reducing numbers to what are perceived to be acceptable levels and keeping the invasive species out of particularly sensitive areas such as nature reserves, and away from endangered species.

Ironically, many agents of control are themselves introductions, for it makes sense to identify whether there are species in the country of origin, or indeed elsewhere, which can be targeted at the invasive species. The constraints on such biological control have already been outlined (see section 5.4.2.2), and in particular there is a need to ensure that any introduced agent does not itself become a pest, for example by ignoring the target invasive species and putting non-target native species at risk.

An example of recent efforts at biological control is seen with purple loosestrife (*Lythrum salicaria*), a member of riverside, marsh and fen communities in its native Europe. In North America, where it was introduced 200 years ago, it has become a weed. It grows rampantly, displacing sedges, rushes and a range of other wetland plants that in turn are hosts to, and provide habitat for, a complex indigenous fauna. North American purple loosestrife plants are 30% taller than European specimens, weigh 30% more and have much larger leaves. It is likely that leaving their natural enemies back in Europe has allowed the American plants to reallocate to growth resources what they would otherwise have spent in producing chemical defences against herbivorous insects. However, this leaves them particularly vulnerable were these herbivores to arrive and, following laboratory trials in the UK and Switzerland over the period 1986 to 1996, preliminary results from field trials at 500 sites across the USA and Canada suggest that both adults and larvae of a leaf-eating beetle, *Galerucella calmariensis*, may indeed be able to keep this invasive weed at bay (Coughlan, 1997).

8.4.2 Beneficial introductions and wildlife conservation

Discussion and exemplification of introduced species have so far stressed the deleterious effects such species have on biota, communities and ecosystems. Natural communities and native species have a high priority in nature conservation, and artificial communities and introduced species generally have low priority. On balance, it seems axiomatic that introduced species should be discouraged from establishing themselves, certainly in natural and semi-natural communities.

> [Yet] it is important to get both the magnitude and seriousness of these problems into perspective. The very great majority of species introduced into Great Britain or any other country have caused no problems whatsover ... Of the few species which have become successfully naturalised even fewer have become pests; most have fitted so unobtrusively into our natural ecosystems as to be readily mistaken for natives if their history were not known. The little owl *Athene noctua* and evening primrose *Oenothera biennis* are good examples ... Introduced species like the forestry conifers, the pheasant and many others have brought much financial benefit, and through enriching the flora and fauna, given much pleasure.
>
> (Anon. 1979: 2)

Some introduced species might therefore be encouraged: forestry, agriculture and game species of economic or amenity importance; agents of biological control; and a suite of species that have, perhaps counter-intuitively, been important for the conservation of native wildlife (Jarvis, 1983).

In Central America, for example, over fifteen genera of large frugivorous herbivores became extinct 10 000 years ago – part of the great Pleistocene megafaunal extinctions, in part probably a consequence of overhunting by primitive peoples. These extinctions affected the seed dispersal and subsequent distribution of a number of plant species, and indeed many such plants themselves became extinct for want of effective germination or transport. The introduction of horses and cattle by Europeans 500 years ago, however, may in part have restored the local ranges of such trees as jicaro (*Crescentia alata*) and guanacaste (*Enterolobium cyclocarpum*), these animals being substitutes for, or analogues of, the large mammals that formerly had acted as agents of dispersal (Janzen and Martin, 1982).

Similarly, two of the three most important food plants of the endangered Seychelles black parrot

(*Coracopsis nigra barklyi*) are introductions – cucumber tree (*Averrhoa bilimbi*) and mango (*Mangifera indica*). Indeed, nine out of sixteen food plant species are introductions, and a conservation strategy to improve the status of this parrot includes planting more introduced fruit trees such as cucumber tree (Evans, 1979).

By dispersing the population of a species, introductions can also lessen the risk of extinction, as happened with Père David's deer (*Elaphurus davidianus*), which became extinct in its native China. Reintroduction in the 1980s was possible only because of the breeding herd that had been established in the early 1800s in an estate in Oxfordshire. This kind of example, however, leads into issues of captive breeding for conservation, which is a related but different issue.

preferable to an irregularly shaped area (high ratio) or a long thin reserve, which would, as it were, be all 'edge'. This has led to the kind of judgements indicated in Issues Box 8.2.

These prescriptions have to be viewed critically, however. There are circumstances, for example, where linear reserves are very important, for instance reserves where rivers or riparian habitats are important, or in towns where again rivers, canals, railway cuttings and embankments, hedgerows, and linear relict scrub and woodland may provide important informal nature areas worthy of protection.

Size alone is not a guarantee of habitat quality or habitat heterogeneity. One large reserve may be vulnerable to chance extinctions in a way that several small reserves would not (Kobayashi, 1985). Again, a single large reserve may actually

8.4.3 Island biogeography and the design of nature reserves

On the premise that a nature reserve will contain a sample of the biota of the surrounding or adjacent area, it has been suggested that some of the ideas behind island biogeography theory might be useful in the design and distribution of nature reserves (Diamond, 1975; Simberloff and Abele, 1976; 1982; Higgs, 1981; Margules *et al.*, 1982). Certainly, a number of relationships might be expected to exist, for example that larger areas would tend to contain larger populations and a greater number of species, and that anything that facilitates the arrival of fresh genetic material into a reserve (such as proximity of source or habitat corridors) is desirable. Conversely, a small reserve may witness many local extinctions, whether because of human disturbance, chance fluctuations in population size or minimum population size thresholds not being reached, and an isolated reserve will tend to limit the extent to which in-migration of species or genes is possible. Shape, too, might be significant in that 'core' areas will tend to be more protected against outside disturbances to which 'periphery' or 'edge' areas will be more prone. Thus the smaller the ratio of circumference to area the better: a circular shape (possessing the minimum ratio) is, in theory,

ISSUES BOX 8.2

Theoretical patterns in nature reserve design

Character	Worse	Better	Reason
Size	o	◯	Larger area holds more species and larger populations.
Proximity	o o	o o	Proximity facilities inter-reserve linkage, e.g. increasing the extent of genetic viability.
Fragmentation	o o o o	◡	A coherent site is better than several smaller sites, even if total area is the same (but see text comments on SLOSS).
Spatial relationships	⬦⋯⬦	⬦	Three-way linkage is facilitated by clumping rather than by a linear pattern.
Linkage	o o	△	Habitat corridors facilitate movement between reserves
Shape	small core area / no core area / large core area		Irregular and linear shapes have less (or no) core area compared with circular shapes

contain fewer species overall than several small ones. For example, in their study of breeding birds in Illinois, Blake and Karr (1984) found that two woodland blocks of a particular size usually supported more species than a single woodland of equal total size. The debate over single large or several small reserves (the SLOSS debate) has exercised the minds of conservationists for a couple of decades. Similarly, Blouin and Connor (1985) found no significant difference in species number with different island shapes.

There is no single answer, for decisions cannot be made in an ecological vacuum. Large predators and large grazing herd animals, for example, must have large reserves on grounds of feeding habits alone, as evident in the grassland nature and game reserves of East and southern Africa. The dispersal ability of species particularly targeted for protection is another factor. There are also planning judgements and political decisions to be made. Some issues also relate to the idea of critical faunas discussed in Section 6.4.2.

8.5 Conclusions

Competition and the niche are, together with the community and the ecosystem, four of the most important concepts in ecology (see Table 9.1). Different kinds of resource partitioning allow many species to coexist in a community, and ultimately mechanisms of coexistence leading to niche separation and minimum niche overlap may be more important in understanding community structure and dynamics than those of competition. Nevertheless, this chapter has also demonstrated how organisms can successfully invade and become functionally involved in communities by being competitively vigorous, as well as by exploiting available niche space. Where such biological invasion takes place on islands the competitiveness and feeding habits of the introductions can drastically alter island ecosystems and lead to the extinction of many native species, including a high proportion of endemics. Competition, niche, community and ecosystem are therefore also critical concepts to understand in the context of conservation.

Further reading

Bell, S.S., McCoy, E.D. and Mushinsky, H.R. (1991) *Habitat structure: the physical arrangement of objects in space* (London: Chapman & Hall).

Drake, J.A. and six others (1989) *Biological invasions: a global perspective* (Chichester: Wiley).

Mueller-Dombois, D., Bridges, K.W. and Carson, H.C. (eds) (1981) *Island ecosystems* (London: Academic Press).

Whittaker, R. (1998) *Island biogeography* (Oxford: Oxford University Press).

QUESTIONS BASED ON CHAPTER 8

Q1. Why are introduced species rarely successful in the wild?

Q2. Why is biological control often more successful on a small island than in a large continental region?

Q3. What strategy or strategies, according to Grime's C-R-S model, would plants in the following habitats be likely to possess?
Arable field — Salt marsh
Shingle bank — Chalk grassland
Fire-prone savanna grassland

Q4. Indicate some of the adaptations that allow cacti to live in stressful hot desert environments.

Q5. Animals also have morphologies and behaviours that allow them to tolerate stressful environments. Indicate some of the adaptations that polar bears have to help them live on the Arctic ice cap.

ANSWERS

A1. There are often physical environmental constraints (e.g. an unsuitable climate); biological and ecological constraints (e.g. competition, predation, lack of suitable food, disease); and demographic and genetic constraints (e.g. lack of sexual partners and genetic problems of founder populations).

A2. In general terms it is easier to target the weed or pest problem, identify likely control organisms, and monitor the consequences of control. A small, enclosed arena (the island) enhances the chances of success, and again makes it easier to monitor progress. Islands tend to have fewer species, fewer species interactions and simpler ecosystems than an area of equivalent size on the mainland, which again might facilitate control.

A3. Arable field – competitive–ruderal: the soil would be highly productive, but periodic ploughing acts as a disturbance.
Salt marsh – stress-tolerant: salt water and tidal flooding are stressful.
Shingle bank – ruderal–stress-tolerant: Storm surges periodically shift the shingle around, providing a disturbance, while the substrate is nutrient-low and provides a poor rooting medium, which are stresses.
Chalk grassland – stress-tolerant: the thin, calcareous soils provide a relatively harsh environment for plants, and such areas are often species-rich since no one species can dominate.
Fire-prone savanna grassland – competitive stress-tolerant: underlying soil is fertile, and nutrients are returned to the soil following fires, but the fires themselves provide a major stress.

A4. Absorbent internal tissues allow water storage in the stem. Long tap roots can penetrate the water table, but also finer near-surface 'rain roots' can take up water quickly following rainfall. Fluting of the stem will channel water down to the roots effectively and create small pockets of turbulence in a light breeze, which cools the surface. Photosynthesis (CAM) is undertaken by the stem not the leaves. Leaves are reduced to spines, which minimise water loss by evapotranspiration and provide a physical defence against large browsing animals. Water stored in the tissue is often toxic to animals. Cladodes (leaf pads) often face where the sun rises and sets, reducing heat stress by presenting minimum leaf surface to the sun at midday.

A5. Large body (high ratio of volume to surface area means heat loss is slower than in a smaller animal). Small ears and tail (reduces skin area vulnerable to freezing). Thick layer of fat (insulation). White colour (camouflage). Large paws (facilitates movement on snow and ice). Large claws (provides grip on ice as well as making it an effective killer). Carnivorous (since there are no plants to eat).

Discussion topics

D1. What parts of our (human) fundamental niche are we occupying today? To what extent, and why, is our realised niche changing?

D2. How appropriate is it to manage a nature reserve as if it were an ecological island?

D3. The ruddy duck is a North American species introduced to the British Isles, where for a while it was considered as an interesting addition to local bird faunas. From Britain it spread to the European continent. During the 1990s, it was realised that migratory ruddy ducks were interbreeding with a congeneric species, the rare white-headed duck, in the Iberian Peninsula, with ruddy ducks the more dominant bird. Survival of the white headed duck as a species was thus at risk as hybridisation became more and more common. One consequence was a campaign in Britain to cull ruddy ducks and to prevent breeding. Do you believe that such a campaign was needed on conservation grounds? How would you argue the case for culling to someone wanting to keep this duck as a member of the UK avifauna? How would you argue the case for someone who wanted to exterminate all British specimens?

EXERCISES

E1. Identify a habitat island near to where you live or study and determine which plants, birds and insects are most vulnerable to local extinction. Are the reasons for this vulnerability the same, similar or different?

E2. Using a deep seed tray filled with non-peat compost, mix and sow roughly equivalent numbers (or volumes if seed sizes are obviously different) of two wildflower species (available from most garden centres or seed merchants). Place outside or in a greenhouse, and make sure the tray is adequately watered. Keep a daily diary of numbers of plants germinating, distinguishing between the species as soon as this is possible. Do not worry if eventually there are too many plants to count accurately. These plants will be in strong competition with each other, intraspecifically and interspecifically. What happens to plant growth under such strong competition? What happens to plant numbers as density gets too great for all specimens to survive? Do the species coexist or does one out-compete the other – how and why? What conclusions can you draw from this experiment about competition in the wild.

Chapter 9

Important concepts in ecology and global environmental issues

As a way of rounding off the book, this chapter notes the perceived importance of some of the ecological principles that have been explored and exemplified, and provides an overview on how we might approach some of the environmental issues raised. A useful commentary, 'Common themes for ecologists in global issues', was presented to the annual conference of the British Ecological Society in January 1998 by the environmental director of the World Bank and chair of the Intergovernmental Panel on Climate Change (Watson, 1999), who emphasised the needs to alleviate poverty, increase biodiversity, turn the tide against habitat destruction and reduce the rate at which climatic changes are taking place.

9.1 Ecological principles

In 1986, members of the British Ecological Society were sent a questionnaire asking their views on which ten concepts out of a choice of 50 they felt had been most important in the development of ecology. Some 645 completed forms were returned, a response rate of 14.7%. Subsequent ranking (Cherrett, 1989) showed the data summarised in Table 9.1.

Apart from the 3/2 thinning law (a form of self-regulation of density in plants) and socio-ecology, all of these important concepts – together with many others – are examined in this book, although some such as species packing and parasite–host interaction only in passing. This is not a book on behavioural ecology as such, so territoriality and feeding guilds are mentioned

from time to time in other contexts and sometimes using different terms.

9.2 Environmental issues

Many politicians, economists and technologists feel that the environment can take care of itself and that predictions of population explosions and dwindling resources are the mere fancies of scaremongers. Certainly, the world *as a whole* is growing more prosperous, and more people (although nowhere near all people) have higher qualities of life than at any other time in the past. The populations of developed countries are stabilising (although problems of an ageing population then emerge), and those of the developing world should do so during the twenty-first century. And the dire predictions of the Club of Rome's *Limits to Growth* (1972) have not materialised, nor indeed the earlier ones of Thomas Malthus of population size outstripping food. Health and hygiene have improved, and many killer diseases are now under control. The scientific and technological advances of the second half of the twentieth century are coming into their own, with the consequences of microchip technology, global communications, molecular biology, genetic engineering and even space exploration all trickling into the day-to-day lives of more and more people. The people of the world are therefore benefiting from better environmental and resource management, better food, better health and, in a phrase, better lives. And all this, as a generalisation, is absolutely true.

Table 9.1 Ranking the fifty most important concepts in ecology

Rank	Concept	Rank	Concept
1	The ecosystem	26	Natural disturbance
2	Succession	27	Habitat restoration
3	Energy flow	28	The managed nature reserve
4	Conservation of resources	29	Indicator organisms
5	Competition	30	Competition and the conditions for species exclusion
6	Niche	31	Trophic level
7	Materials cycling	32	Pattern
8	The community	33	r and K selection
9	Life-history strategies	34	Plant/animal coevolution
10	Ecosystem fragility	35	The diversity/stability hypothesis
11	Food webs	36	Socio-ecology
12	Ecological adaptation	37	Optimal foraging
13	Environmental heterogeneity	38	Parasite–host interactions
14	Species diversity	39	Species–area relationships
15	Density-dependent regulation	40	The ecotype
16	Limiting factors	41	Climax
17	Carrying capacity	42	Territoriality
18	Maximum sustainable yield	43	Allocation theory
19	Population cycles	44	Intrinsic regulation
20	Predator–prey interactions	45	Pyramid of numbers
21	Plant–herbivore interactions	46	Keystone species
22	Island biogeography theory	47	The biome
23	Bioaccumulation in food chains	48	Species packing
24	Coevolution	49	The 3/2 thinning law
25	Stochastic processes (chance/time processes)	50	The guild

Nevertheless, most evidence from a closer scrutiny of what is happening to the environment makes it clear that the world is in trouble. 'The most serious potential consequence of global environmental change is the erosion of Earth's life-support system ... Our burgeoning numbers, technology and consumption are overloading Earth's capacity to absorb, replenish and repair' (McMichael, 1993). Malthus and the Club of Rome might have got their timing wrong, but the basic predictions were apposite. Southwick (1996) usefully presents an agenda for rational and sustainable environmental management that includes a set of necessary actions, divided into ecological, professional and personal responsibilities.

Of ecological priorities, the prevention of nuclear war is clearly crucial if we are to have a planet to save at all, but a general reduction and indeed prevention of regional conflicts is also important on environmental as well as humanitarian and political grounds. For example, the devastating consequences to the environment of the Vietnam War (with the effects of saturation chemical defoliation on the tropical moist forest) and the Gulf War (massive oil spillage and burning) have been well documented. Possible future flashpoints may centre around such environmental issues as the availability of good-quality fresh water, already a concern of many geopoliticians regarding further political instability in the Middle East.

Stabilisation of world population growth is also seen as a crucial element in the sustainable use of the world's resources and protection of its natural environment. This is partly to do with the provision of food, but the implications of rapid urbanisation also need to be assessed, and the 'ecological footprint' of cities – the total area of land and water needed to support each example – needs to be reviewed (Rogers, 1997).

We also need to promote conservation in the broadest sense of this word – the conservation of species and habitats, certainly, but also the conservation of resources generally, and the conservation of, and improvement in, quality of life in all the various ways that this can be defined. This includes reduction in waste and pollution, reduction in deforestation and desertification, reduction in loss of biodiversity, and ultimately reduction in social and economic disparities between and within the countries of the world.

Professional responsibilities include the need to make scientific and technological advances, but to temper these with common sense and ethical responsibility, for example in terms of genetic engineering and cloning. Planners and engineers, farmers and foresters, all need to incorporate ideas of sustainability into their work, to plan not for tomorrow but beyond tomorrow, and to avoid the irrationality of compulsory competitive tendering, which merely promotes short-termism, shoddiness and cheapness at the expense of quality and value. Cost is an understandably important factor in any decision making, but there are costs other than the financial, and ideas of 'best available technology not involving excessive cost' and (more simply) 'best value' have been incorporated into many decisions affecting the environment in recent years. National and local government need to identify appropriate environmental policies and find both the means to achieve these and the will to do so. Lip service to Rio is not enough. Professional inputs also extend into education, from instilling a respect for the environment in junior schoolchildren to technological training in environmental practice at post-degree level.

Finally, each of us has a personal responsibility in caring for the environment, in avoiding waste, in becoming a 'green' user of the resources offered by the planet. Reduce, reuse, recycle. Think globally, act locally. These are truisms because they are true. They work. Such responsibility comes from a knowledge and understanding of *what* needs to be done, *why* it needs to be done and *how* it can be achieved. This knowledge and understanding includes the need to be at the very least aware of the ecological principles underlying such crucial environmental issues.

Further reading

Bormann, F.H. and Kellert, S.R. (eds) *Ecology, economics, ethics* (New Haven, Conn: Yale University Press).

Botkin, D.B. (1990) *Discordant harmonies: a new ecology for the 21st century* (Oxford: Oxford University Press).

Brown, L.R., Flaven, C. and Postel, S. (1994) *Saving the planet: how to create an environmentally sustainable economy* (New York: W.W. Norton).

Gleick, P.H. (ed.) (1993) *Water in crisis* (Oxford: Oxford University Press).

Mayo, D.G. and Hollander, R. (eds) *Acceptable evidence: science and values in risk management* (Oxford: Oxford University Press).

Nash, R.F. (1989) *The rights of nature: a history of environmental ethics.* (Madison: University of Wisconsin Press).

Odum, E.P. (1989) *Ecology and our endangered life support system* (Sunderland, Mass.: Sinauer).

Phillips, M. and Mighall, R. (1998) *Society and exploitation through nature* (Harlow: Longman).

Vandeveer, D. and Pierce, C. (1994) *The environmental ethics and policy book* (Belmont, Calif.: Wadsworth).

Discussion topics

D1. Identify and discuss an environmental problem or issue for which a good deal of scientific (including ecological) evidence is available, and which has received extensive media coverage, yet remains unsolved or unresolved.

D2. Surveys that correlate population growth, increasing production of consumer goods, depletion of non-renewable resources, non-sustainable use of renewable resources and pollution all point to the inevitable destruction of the environment. Yet economists, politicians and multinational companies continue to measure success in terms of increasing growth. Why are these rational and responsible people leading the world to the brink of such environmental catastrophe?

References

Ackery, P.R. and Vane-Wright, R.I. (1984) *Milkweed butterflies* (London: British Museum of Natural History).

Addison, G. (1980) Yes to the coypu. *Ecos: A Review of Conservation*, 2: 26–7.

Aerts, R., Huiszoon, A.M., van Oostrum, J.H.A., van de Vijver, C.A.D.M. and Willems, J.H. (1995) The potential for heathland restoration on formerly arable land at a site in Drenthe, the Netherlands. *Journal of Applied Ecology*, 32: 827–35.

Agricultural Research Council (1965) *Nutrient requirements of farm livestock. 2. Ruminants* (London: HMSO).

Allee, W.C. (1931) *Animal aggregation: a study in general sociology* (Chicago: University of Chicago Press).

Angerbjörn, A., Tannerfeldt, M. and Erlinge, S. (1999) Predator–prey relationships: arctic foxes and lemmings. *Journal of Animal Ecology*, 68: 34–49.

Anon. (1979) *Wildlife introductions to Great Britain*. Report by the Working Group on Introductions of the UK Committee for International Nature Conservation (London: Nature Conservancy Council).

Barney, G., Pickering, T.R. and Speth, G. (1982) *The Global 2000 Report to the President* (Washington DC: Government Printing Office).

Barrow, C.J. (1995) *Developing the environment: problems and management* (Harlow: Longman Scientific & Technical).

Bartlein, P.J. and Prentice, I.C. (1989) Orbital variations, climate and palaeoecology. *Trends in Ecology & Evolution*, 4: 195–9.

Batzli, F.O., White, R.G., MacLean, S.F. *et al.* (1980) The herbivore based trophic system. In J. Brown, P.C. Miller, L.L. Tieszen and F.L. Bunnel (eds) *An Arctic ecosystem: the coastal tundra at Barrow, Alaska* (Stroundsburg, Pa.: Dowden, Hutchinson and Ross): 335–410.

Bazzaz, F.A. (1975) Plant species diversity in old-field successional ecosystems in southern Illinois. *Ecology*, 56: 485–8.

Bazzaz, F.A. (1990) The response of natural ecosystems to the rising global CO_2 levels. *Annual Review of Ecology and Systematics*, 21: 167–96.

Beck, U. (1992) *Risk society: towards a new modernity* (trans. M. Ritter) (London: Sage).

Beeby, A. and Brennan, A.-M. (1997) *First ecology* (London: Chapman & Hall).

Begon, M., Harper, J.L. and Townsend, C.R. (1996) *Ecology: individuals, populations and communities* (third edition) (Oxford: Blackwell Scientific).

Bezemer, T.M., Thompson, L.J. and Jones, T.H. (1998) *Poa annua* shows inter-generational differences in response to elevated CO_2. *Global Change Biology*, 4: 687–91.

Bibby, C.J., Crosby, M.J., Heath, M.F. *et al.* (1992) *Putting biodiversity on the map: global priorities for conservation* (Cambridge: International Council for Bird Preservation).

Blake, J.G. and Karr, J.R. (1984) Species composition of bird communities and the conservation benefit of large versus small reserves. *Biological Conservation*, 30: 173–87.

Blouin, M.S. and Connor, E.F. (1985) Is there a best shape for nature reserves? *Biological Conservation*, 32: 277–88.

Bodle, M.J., Ferriter, A.P. and Thayer, D.D. (1994) The biology, distribution, and ecological consequences of *Melaleuca quinquenervia* in the Everglades. In S.M. Davis and J.C. Ogden (eds) *Everglades: the ecosystem and its restoration* (Delray Beach, Fla.: St Lucie Press): 341–55.

Boer, M.M. and de Groot, R.S. (eds) (1990) *Landscape-ecological impact of climatic change* (Amsterdam: IOS Press).

Boorman, L.A. (1990) Impact of sea level changes on coastal areas. In M.M. Boer and R.S. de Groot (eds) *Landscape-ecological impact of climatic change*. (Amsterdam: IOS Press): 379–91.

Borger, J. and Bates, S. (1999) Why Americans are happy to swallow the GM food experiment. *The Guardian*, 20 February: 4–5.

Botkin, D.B. and Keller, E.A. (1995) *Environmental science: Earth as a living planet* (Chichester: Wiley).

Botkin, D.B., Woodby, A. and Nisbet, R.A. (1991) Kirtland's warbler habitats: a possible early indicator of climatic warming. *Biological Conservation*, 56: 63–78.

Bowen, H.J.M. (1977) Residence times of heavy metals in the environment. In *Proceedings of the International Conference on heavy metals in the environment. Vol. 1* (Toronto: Institute for Environmental Studies, University of Toronto): 1–19.

Bradley, R. and Jones, P. (eds) (1994) *Climate since AD 1500* (London: Routledge).

Bradshaw, A.D. and Chadwick, M.J. (1980) *The restoration of land* (Oxford: Blackwell Scientific).

Brand, D. (1998) Opportunities generated by the Kyoto Protocol in the forest sector. *Commonwealth Forestry Review*, 77: 164–9.

Bromley, D.W. (1992) The commons, common property and environmental policy. *Environmental and Resource Economics*, **2**: 1–18.

Brown, A. (ed.) (1992) *The UK environment* (London: HMSO).

Brown, K. and Adger, N. (1993) Estimating national greenhouse gas emissions under the Climate Change Convention. *Global Environmental Change*, **3**: 149–58.

Brown, L.R. *et al.* (1993) *State of the World, 1993* (New York: W.W. Norton).

Brown, L.R. *et al.* (1994) *State of the World, 1994* (New York: W.W. Norton).

Brown, R.G.B. (1991) Marine birds and climatic warming in the northern Atlantic. *Occasional Paper, Canadian Wildlife Service*, **68**: 49–78.

Burgess, T.L. (1995) Desert grassland, mixed shrub, savanna, shrub steppe or semidesert scrub. The dilemma of coexisting growth forms. In M.P. McClaran and T.R. van Devender (eds) *The desert grassland* (Tucson: University of Arizona Press): 31–67.

Buschbaum, R. (1948) *Animals without backbones* (revised edition) (Harmondsworth: Penguin).

Campbell, B.D., Stafford Smith, D.M. and McKeon, G.M. (1997) Elevated CO_2 and water supply interactions in grasslands: a pastures and rangelands management perspective. *Global Change Biology*, **3**: 177–97.

Cao, M. and Woodward, F.I. (1998) Net primary and ecosystem production and carbon stocks of terrestrial ecosystems and their reponses to climate change. *Global Change Biology*, **4**: 185–98.

Carlquist, S. (1980) *Hawaii: a natural history* (Honolulu: Pacific Tropical Botanic Garden).

Carruthers, K., Fe, Q., Cloutier, D. and Smith, D.L. (1998) Intercropping corn with soybean, lupin and forages: weed control by intercrops combined with interrow cultivation. *European Journal of Agronomy*, **8**: 225–38.

CCIRG (Climate Change Impacts Review Group) (1996) *The potential effects of climate change in the United Kingdom* (London: HMSO).

Chapin III, F.S. and Starfield, A.M. (1997) Time lags and novel ecosystems in response to transient climatic change in Arctic Alaska. *Climatic Change*, **35**: 449–61.

Chapin III, F.S., Torn, M.S. and Tateno, M. (1996) Principles of ecosystem sustainability. *American Naturalist*, **148**: 1016–37.

Cherrett, J.M. (1989) Key concepts: the results of a survey of our members' opinions. In J.M. Cherrett (ed.) *Ecological concepts: the contribution of ecology to an understanding of the natural world* (Oxford: Blackwell Scientific): 1–16.

Cohen, Y. and Pastor, J. (1991) The responses of a forest model to serial correlations of global warming. *Ecology*, **72**: 1161–5.

Cole, H.S.D. *et al.* (1973) *Models of doom: a critique of 'The limits to growth'* (New York: Universe Books).

Coleman, D.C., Andrews, R., Ellis, J.E. and Singh, J.S. (1976) Energy flow and partitioning in selected man-made and natural ecosystems. *Agro-ecosystems*, **3**: 45–54.

Coleman, D.C. and Hendrix, P.F. (1988) Agroecosystem processes. In L.R. Pomeroy and J.J. Alberts (eds) *Concepts of ecosystem ecology: a comparative view* (New York: Springer-Verlag): 149–70.

Collins, F.H. and Paskewitz, S.M. (1995) Malaria: current and future prospects for control. *Annual Review of Entomology*, **40**: 195–219.

Collins, N.M. and Morris, M.G. (1985) *Threatened swallowtail butterflies of the world. The IUCN Red Data Book* (Cambridge: IUCN).

Connell, J.H. and Slatyer, R.O. (1977) Mechanisms of succession in natural communities and their role in community stability and organisation. *American Naturalist*, **111**: 1119–44.

Conway, G.R. (1987) The properties of agroecosystems. *Agricultural Systems*, **24**: 95–117.

Conway, G. (1997) *The doubly green revolution: food for all in the 21st century* (Harmondsworth: Penguin).

Cottam, G. (1987) Community dynamics on an artificial prairie. In W.R. Jordan III, M.E. Gilpin and J.D. Aber (eds) *Restoration ecology: a synthetic approach to ecological research* (Cambridge: Cambridge University Press): 257–70.

Coughlan, A. (1997) Beetles on the attack. *New Scientist*, 9 August: 20.

Coull, J.R. (1993) *World fisheries resources* (London: Routledge).

Cox, C.B. and Moore, P.D. (1993) *Biogeography: an ecological and evolutionary approach* (fifth edition) (Oxford: Blackwell Scientific).

Cross, M. and Hamer, M. (1992) How to seal a supertanker. *New Scientist*, 14 March: 40–4.

Cuddihy, L.W. and Stone, C.P. (1990) *Alteration of native Hawaiian vegetation: effect of humans, their activities and introductions* (Honolulu: University of Hawaii).

Currie, D.J. (1991) Energy and large-scale patterns of animal- and plant-species richness. *American Naturalist*, **137**: 27–49.

Darden, T.R. (1972) Respiratory adaptations of a fossorial mammal, the pocket gopher (*Thomomys bottae*). *Journal of Comparative Physiology*, **78**: 121–37.

Davidson, J., Myers, D. and Chakraborty, M. (1992) *No time to waste: poverty and the global environment* (Oxford: Oxfam).

Davis, S.D., Droop, S.J.M., Gregerson, P. *et al.* (1986) *Plants in danger: what do we know?* (Gland, Switzerland: Gland).

Dayton, L. (1989) Pathologists chart poisonous punch of Alaskan slick. *New Scientist*, 3 June: 27.

de Jong, W.W. (1998) Molecules remodel the mammalian tree. *Trends in Ecology & Evolution*, **13**: 270–5.

Department of the Environment (1994) *Biodiversity: the UK Action Plan* (London: HMSO).

Diamond, J.M. (1975) The island dilemma: lessons of modern biogeography studies for the design of nature preserves. *Biological Conservation*, **7**: 129–46.

di Castri, F. (1990) On invading species and invaded ecosystems: the interplay of historical change and biological necessity. In F. di Castri, A.J. Hansen and M. Debussche (eds) *Biological invasions in Europe and the Mediterranean Basin* (Dordrecht: Kluwer): 1–16.

Dilz, K. (1988) Efficiency of uptake and utilization of fertilizer nitrogen by plants. In D.S. Jenkinson and K.A. Smith (eds) *Nitrogen efficiency in agricultural soils* (London: Elsevier Applied Science): 1–26.

Doak, D.F., Bigger, D., Harding, E.K., Marvier, M.A., O'Malley, R.E. and Thomson, D. (1998) The statistical inevitability of stability–diversity relationships in community ecology. *American Naturalist*, **151**: 264–76.

Dobzhansky, E.S. (1950) Evolution in the tropics. *American Scientist*, **38**: 209–21.

Dover, M. and Talbot, L.M. (1987) *To feed the Earth: agro-ecology for sustainable development.* (Washington DC: World Resources Institute).

Dufrêne, M. and Legendre, P. (1997) Species assemblages and indicator species: the need for a flexible asymmetrical approach. *Ecological Monographs*, **67**: 345–66.

Dury, D.J., Good, J.E.G., Perrins, C.M. *et al.* (1998) The effects of increasing CO_2 and temperature on oak leaf palatability and the implications for herbivorous insects. *Global Change Biology*, **4**: 55–61.

Eckhardt, R.C. (1972) Introduced plants and animals in the Galapagos Islands. *BioScience*, **22**: 585–90.

Edington, J.M. and Edington, M.A. (1986) *Ecology, recreation and tourism* (London: Croom Helm).

Edwards, R. (1997) Beware green imperialists. *New Scientist*, 31 May: 14–15.

Elton, C.S. (1927) *Animal ecology* (London: Sidgwick & Jackson).

Elton, C.S. (1966) *The pattern of animal communities* (London: Methuen).

Engelberg, J. and Boyarsky, L.L. (1979) The noncybernetic nature of ecosystems. *American Naturalist*, **114**: 317–24.

Erhardt, A. and Rusterholz, H.-P. (1997) Effects of elevated CO_2 on flowering phenology and nectar production. *Acta Oecologica*, **18**: 249–53.

Estes, J.A. and Duggins, D.O. (1995) Sea otters and kelp forests in Alaska: generality and variation in a community ecological paradigm. *Ecological Monographs*, **65**: 75–100.

Evans, P.G.H. (1979) Status and conservation of the Seychelles black parrot. *Biological Conservation*, **16**: 233–40.

Falkenmark, M. (1990) Hydrological shifts as part of landscape ecological impacts of climatic change. In M.M. Boer and R.S. de Groot (eds) *Landscape-ecological impact of climatic change* (Amsterdam: IOS Press): 194–217.

FAO (1992a) *The state of food and agriculture, 1992* (Rome: Food and Agriculture Organisation).

FAO (1992b) Marine fisheries and the Law of the Sea: a decade of change. In *The state of food and agriculture* (Rome: Food and Agriculture Organisation): 129–94.

Field, C., Chapin III, F.S., Matson, P.A. and Mooney, H.A. (1992) Responses of terrestrial ecosystems to the changing atmosphere: a resource-based approach. *Annual Review of Ecology and Systematics*, **23**: 201–35.

Fischer, G. (1990) Heat pollution and global warming. *Environmental Conservation*, **17**: 117–22.

Fischlin, A. and Gyalistras, D. (1997) Assessing impacts of climate change on forests in the Alps. *Global Ecology and Biogeography*, **6**: 19–37.

Fitter, A. (1987) *New generation guide to the wild flowers of Britain and northern Europe* (London: Collins).

Forman, R.T.T. (1964) Growth under controlled conditions to explain the hierarchical distribution of a moss, *Tetraphis pellucida*. *Ecological Monographs*, **34**: 1–25.

Free, T. and Kitson, M.T. (eds) (1992) *Heathland habitat creation* (Sizewell: Nuclear Electric).

Freeman, C. and Jahoda, M. (eds). (1978) *World futures: the great debate* (Oxford: Martin Robertson).

Friday, L. (ed.) (1997) *Wicken Fen: the making of a wetland nature reserve* (Colchester: Harley Books).

Fritts, T.H. and Rodda, G.H. (1998) The role of introduced species in the degradation of island ecosystems: a case history of Guam. *Annual Review of Ecology and Systematics*, **29**: 113–40.

Furness, R.W., Greenwood, J.J.D. and Jarvis, P.J. (1993) Can birds be used to monitor the environment? In R.W. Furness and J.J.D. Greenwood (eds) *Birds as monitors of environmental change* (London: Chapman & Hall): 1–41.

Galt, J.A., Lehr, W.J. and Payton, D.L. (1991) Fate and transport of the *Exxon Valdez* oil spill. *Environmental Science and Technology*, **25**: 202–9.

Garrott, R.A., Eberhardt, L.L. and Burn, D.M. (1993) Mortality of sea otters in Prince William Sound following the *Exxon Valdez* oil spill. *Marine Mammal Science*, **9**: 343–59.

Gaston, K.J. (1996) Species richness: measure and measurement. In K.J. Gaston (ed.) *Biodiversity: a biology of numbers and difference* (Oxford: Blackwell Science): 77–113.

Gates, D.M. (1962) *Energy exchange in the biosphere* (New York: Harper & Row).

Giddings, G. (1998) Tansley Review No. 99. The release of genetically engineered micro-organisms and viruses into the environment. *New Phytologist*, **140**: 173–84.

Gifford, R.M. (1979) Growth and yield of CO_2-enriched wheat under water-limited conditions. *Australian Journal of Plant Physiology*, **6**: 367–78.

Gitay, H. and Noble, I.R. (1997) What are functional types and how should we seek them? In T.M. Smith, H.H. Shugart and F.I. Woodward (eds) *Plant functional types: their relevance to ecosystem properties and global change* (Cambridge: Cambridge University Press): 3–19.

Givnish, T.J. (1999) On the causes of gradients in tropical tree diversity. *Journal of Ecology*, **87**: 193–210.

Glenn, E.P. and O'Leary, J.W. (1984) Relationship between salt accumulation and water content of dicotyledonous halophytes. *Plant, Cell and Environment*, **7**: 253–61.

Goldsmith, E., Allan, R., Allaby, M., David, J. and Lawrence, S. (1972) Blueprint for survival. *The Ecologist*, **2**: 1–43 (reprinted 1972. Harmondsworth: Penguin).

Goldsmith, F.B. (ed.) (1991) *Monitoring for conservation and ecology* (London: Chapman & Hall).

Gopal, B. (1987) *Aquatic plant studies 1: water hyacinth* (Amsterdam: Elsevier Science).

Gosling, L.M. and Baker, S.J. (1989) The eradication of muskrats and coypus from Britain. *Biological Journal of the Linnean Society*, **38**: 39–51.

Graham, R.W. and Grimm, E.C. (1990) Effect of global climatic change on the pattern of terrestrial biological communities. *Trends in Ecology & Evolution*, **5**: 289–92.

Graves, J. and Reavey, D. (1996) *Global environmental change: plants, animals and communities* (Harlow: Longman).

Grayson, A.J. (1998) Introduction: forestry and carbon storage. *Commonwealth Forestry Review*, **77**: 161–3.

Greenwood, J.J.D., Baillie, S.R., Gregory, R.D., Peach, W.J. and Fuller, R.J. (1995) Some new approaches to conservation monitoring of British breeding birds. *Ibis*, **137** (Supplement): 16–28.

Grime, J.P. (1974) Vegetation classification by reference to strategies. *Nature*, **250**: 26–31.

Grime, J.P. (1979) *Plant strategies and vegetation processes* (Chichester: Wiley).

Grinnell, J. (1917) The niche relationships of the California thrasher. *Auk*, **34**: 427–33.

Hakala, K. (1998) Growth and yield potential of spring wheat in a simulated changed climate with increased CO_2 and higher temperature. *European Journal of Agronomy*, **9**: 41–52.

Halliday, T.R. (1980) The extinction of the passenger pigeon *Ectopistes migratorius* and its relevance to contemporary conservation. *Biological Conservation*, **17**: 157–62.

Hamilton, W.A. (1988) Microbial energetics and metabolism. In J.M. Lynch and J.E. Hobbie (eds) *Microorganisms in action: concepts and applications in microbial ecology* (Oxford: Blackwell Scientific): 75–100.

Hardin, G. (1968) The tragedy of the commons. *Science*, **162**(3859): 1243–8.

Harmon, D., Paden, M. and Henniger, N. (1990) Forests and rangelands. In World Resources Institute, *World resources, 1990–91* (Oxford: Oxford University Press), 101–120 (especially Box 7.1 – Forest politics in Brazil: 105).

Hattenschwiler, S., Miglietta, F., Raschi, A. and Korner, C. (1997) Morphological adjustments of mature *Quercus ilex* trees to elevated CO_2. *Acta Oecologica*, **18**: 361–5.

Hayden, B.P. (1998) Ecosystem feedbacks on climate at the landscape scale. *Philosophical Transactions of the Royal Society of London, Series B, Biological Sciences*, **353**(1365): 5–18.

Hayman, D.S. and Mosse, B. (1972) Plant growth responses to vesicular arbuscular mycorrhiza. III. Increased uptake of labile phosphorus from soil. *New Phytologist*: **71**: 41–7.

Heino, R. (1978) Climatic change in Finland during the last hundred years. *Fennia*, **150**: 3–13.

Hellawell, J.M. (1991) Development of a rationale for monitoring. In F.B. Goldsmith (ed.) *Monitoring for conservation and ecology* (London: Chapman & Hall): 1–14.

Henderson, N. (1992) Wilderness and the nature conservation ideal: Britain, Canada and the United States contrasted. *Ambio*, **21**: 394–9.

Henderson-Sellars, A. (1990) Modelling and monitoring 'greenhouse' warming. *Trends in Ecology & Evolution*: **5**: 270–5.

Hengeveld, R. (1990) Theories on species responses to variable climates. In M.M. Boer and R.S. de Groot (eds) *Landscape-ecological impact of climatic change* (Amsterdam: IOS Press): 274–89.

Herren, H.R. (1996) Cassava and cowpea in Africa. In G.J. Persley (ed.) *Biotechnology and integrated pest management* (Wallingford: CAB International): 136–149.

Higgs, A.J. (1981) Island biogeography theory and nature reserve design. J*ournal of Biogeography*, **8**: 117–24.

Hoffmann, A.A. and Blows, M.W. (1994) Species borders: ecological and evolutionary perspectives. *Trends in Ecology & Evolution*, **9**: 223–7.

Holdgate, M.W. (1979) *A perspective of environmental pollution* (Cambridge: Cambridge University Press).

Holdridge, L. (1967) *Life zone ecology* (San Jose, Costa Rica: Tropical Science Center).

Holling, C.S. (1959) Some characteristics of simple types of predation and parasitism. *Canadian Entomologist*, **91**: 385–98.

Holling, C.S. (1973) Resilience and stability of ecological systems. *Annual Review of Ecology and Systematics*, **4**: 1–23.

Holmberg, J.,Thomson, K. and Timberlake, L. (1993) *Facing the future: beyond the Earth Summit* (London: Earthscan).

Holt, R.D. (1990) The microevolutionary consequences of climatic change. *Trends in Ecology & Evolution*, **5**: 311–15.

Horn, H.S. (1981) Succession. In R.M. May (ed.) *Theoretical ecology: principles and applications* (Oxford: Blackwell Scientific): 253–71.

Houghton, J.T., Jenkins, G.J. and Ephraums, J.J. (1990) *Climatic change: the IPCC scientific assessment* (Cambridge: Cambridge University Press).

Hungate, B.A., Holland, E.A., Jackson, R.B. *et al.* (1997) The fate of carbon in grasslands under carbon dioxide enrichment. *Nature*, **388**(6642): 576–9.

Hunt, E.G. and Bischoff, A.I. (1960) Inimical effects on wildlife of periodic DDT applications to Clear Lake. *California Fish and Game Bulletin*, **46**: 91–6.

Huntley, B. (1995) Plant species' response to climate change: implications for the conservation of European birds. *Ibis*, **127**(Supplement 1): S127–38.

Hurst, P. (1990) *Rainforest politics: ecological destruction in South-east Asia* (London: Zed Books) (Chapter 1, Indonesia: 1–45).

Hutchinson, G.E. (1958) Concluding remarks. *Cold Spring Harbor Symposia in Quantitative Biology*, **22**: 415–27.

Huxley, T. (1974) Wilderness. In A. Warren and F.B. Goldsmith (eds) *Conservation in practice* (London: Wiley): 361–74.

IFPRI (1994) *Annual Report* (Washington DC: International Food Policy Research Institute).

Independent Commission on International Development Issues (1980) *North–South: a programme for survival* (London: Pan).

IPCC (Intergovernmental Panel on Climate Change) (1996) *Climate Change 1995 – the science of climate change* (Cambridge: Cambridge University Press).

Isenmann, P. (1990) Some recent bird invasions in Europe and the Mediterranean Basin. In F. di Castri, A.J. Hansen and M. Debussche (eds) *Biological invasions in Europe and the Mediterranean Basin* (Dordrecht: Kluwer): 245–61.

IUCN (1987) *Translocation of living organisms* (Gland, Switzerland: IUCN).

IUCN, UNEP and WWF (1980) *World conservation strategy: living resources for sustainable development* (Gland, Switzerland: IUCN).

IUCN, UNEP and WWF (1991) *Caring for the Earth: a strategy for sustainable living* (Gland, Switzerland: IUCN).

Jackson, M.H. (1985) *Galapagos: a natural history guide* (Calgary, Alberta; University of Calgary Press).

Jacobs, J. (1975) Diversity, stability and maturity in ecosystems influenced by human activities. In W.H. van Dobben and R.H. Lowe-McConnell (eds) *Unifying concepts in ecology* (The Hague: dr W. Junk bv): 187–207.

Janzen, D.H. (1970) Herbivores and the number of tree species in tropical forests. *American Naturalist*, **104**: 501–28.

Janzen. D.H. and Martin, P.H. (1982) Neotropical anachronisms: the fruits the gomphotheres ate. *Science*, **215**: 19–27.

Järvinen, O. and Väisänen, R.A. (1979) Climatic changes, habitat changes, and competition: dynamics of geographical overlap in two pairs of congeneric birds in Finland. *Oikos*, **33**: 261–71.

Jarvis, P.J. (1979) The ecology of plant and animal introductions. *Progress in Physical Geography*, **3**: 187–214.

Jarvis, P.J. (1983) Introduced species and nature conservation. University of Birmingham, Department of Geography, Working Paper 23.

Jarvis, P.J. (1993) Environmental changes. In R.W. Furness and J.J.D. Greenwood (eds) *Birds as monitors of environmental change* (London: Chapman & Hall): 42–85.

Jarvis, S.C. (1978) Copper uptake and accumulation by perennial ryegrass grown in soil and culture solution. *Journal of the Science of Food and Agriculture*, **29**: 12–18.

Jenkinson, D.S. and Smith, K.A. (1988) *Nitrogen efficiency in agricultural soils* (London: Elsevier Applied Science).

Jenny, H. (1941) *Factors of soil formation* (New York: McGraw-Hill).

Jermy, A.C., Long, D., Sands, M.J.S., Stork, N.E and Winser, S. (1995) *Biodiversity assessment: a guide to good practice* (London: DoE/HMSO).

Juday, C. (1940) The annual energy budget of an inland lake. *Ecology*, **21**: 438–50.

Keith, L.B. (1983) Role of food in hare population cycles. *Oikos*, **40**: 385–95.

Kempe, S. (1979) Carbon in the rock cycle. In B. Bolin, E.T. Degens, P. Davigneaud and S. Kempe (eds) *The global carbon cycle. SCOPE 13* (Chichester: Wiley): 343–78.

Kendall, H. and Pimentel, D. (1994) Constraints on the expansion of the global food supply. *Ambio*, **23**: 198–205.

Kenmore, P.E. (1996) Integrated pest management in rice. In G.J. Persley (ed.) *Biotechnology and integrated pest management* (Wallingford: CAB International): 76–97.

Kienast, F., Wildi, O. and Brzeziecki, B. (1997) Potential impacts of climate change on species richness in mountain forests – an ecological risk assessment. *Biological Conservation*, **83**: 291–305.

King, C. (1984) *Immigrant killers: introduced predators and the conservation of birds in New Zealand* (Oxford: Oxford University Press).

Kirschbaum, M.U.F., Medlyn, B.E., King, D.A. *et al.* (1998) Modelling forest-growth responses to increasing CO_2 concentration in relation to various factors affecting nutrient supply. *Global Change Biology*, **4**: 23–41.

Kleiber, M. (1947) Body size and metabolic rate. *Physiological Review*, **27**: 511–41.

Kline, V.M. and Howell, E.A. (1987) Prairies. In W.R. Jordan III, M.E. Gilpin and J.D. Aber (eds) *Restoration ecology: a synthetic approach to ecological research* (Cambridge: Cambridge University Press): 75–83.

Kobayashi, S. (1985) Species diversity preserved in different numbers of nature reserves of the same total area. *Research on Population Ecology*, **27**: 137–43.

Koch, M. and Grubb, M. (1993) Agenda 21. In M. Grubb (ed.) *The 'Earth Summit agreements': a guide and assessment* (London: Earthscan). Reprinted in L. Owen and T. Unwin (eds) (1997) *Environmental management: readings and case studies* (Oxford: Blackwell): 455–9.

Kullman, L. (1991) Cataclysmic response to recent cooling of a natural boreal pine (*Pinus sylvestris* L.) forest in northern Sweden. *New Phytologist*, **117**: 351–60.

Laine, K. and Henttonen, H. (1983) The role of plant production in microtine cycles in north Fennoscandia. *Oikos*, **40**: 407–18.

Laurance, W.F. (1998) A crisis in the making: responses of the Amazon forests to land use and climatic change. *Trends in Ecology & Evolution*, **13**: 411–15.

Leighton, F.A., Butler, R.G. and Peakall, D.B. (1985) Oil and Arctic marine birds: an assessment of risk. In F.R. Engelhardt (ed.) *Petroleum effects in the Arctic environment* (London: Elsevier): 183–215.

Lennard, J. (1999) Washington risks global pact to govern GM trade. *The Guardian*, 23 February: 14.

Levine, J.S. (1991) *Global biomass burning: atmospheric, climatic and biospheric implications* (Cambridge, Mass.: MIT Press).

Liddle, M. (1998) *Recreation ecology: the ecological impact of outdoor recreation and ecotourism* (London: Chapman & Hall).

Liebig, J. (1840) *Chemistry in its application to agriculture and physiology* (fourth edition in translation, 1847) (London: Taylor & Walton).

Lim Guan Soon (1996) Integrated pest management in developing countries. In G.J. Persley (ed.) *Biotechnology and integrated pest management* (Wallingford: CAB International): 61–75.

Lindeman, R.L. (1942) The trophic-dynamic aspect of ecology. *Ecology*, **23**: 399–418.

Lloyd, H.G. (1980) *The red fox* (London: Batsford).

Lodge, T.E. (1994) *The Everglades handbook: understanding the ecosystem* (Delray Beach, Fla.: St Lucie Press).

Loucks, O.L. (1977) Emergence of research on agro-ecosystems. *Annual Review of Ecology and Systematics*, **8**: 173–92.

Lucas, G. and Synge, H. (1978) *The IUCN plant red data book* (Morges, Switzerland: IUCN).

MacArthur, R.H. (1958) Population ecology of some warblers of northeastern coniferous forests. *Ecology*, **39**: 599–619.

MacArthur, R.H. and Wilson, E.O. (1967). *The theory of island biogeography* (Princeton, NJ: Princeton University Press).

MacDonald, D. (ed.) (1984) *The encyclopedia of mammals* (Oxford: Andromeda).

MacKinnon, J.A. (1972) *The behaviour and ecology of the orang utan* (Pongo pygmaeus). Unpublished DPhil thesis, University of Oxford; cited in Longman and Jenik (1987).

Magnuson, J.J., Webster, K.E., Assel, R.A. *et al.* (1997) Potential effects of climate changes on aquatic systems: Laurentian Great Lakes and Precambrian Shield region. *Hydrological Processes*, **11**: 825–71.

Majer, J.D. and Nichols, O.G. (1998) Long-term recolonization patterns of ants in Western Australian rehabilitated bauxite mines with reference to their use as indicators of restoration success. *Journal of Applied Ecology*, **35**: 161–82.

Margules, C., Higgs, A.J. and Rafe, R.W. (1982) Modern biogeographic theory: are there any lessons for nature reserve design? *Biological Conservation*, **24**: 115–28.

Marrs, R.H., Johnson, S.W. and Le Duc M.G. (1998) Control of bracken and restoration of heathland. VIII. The regeneration of the heathland community after 18 years of continued bracken control or 6 years of control followed by recovery. *Journal of Applied Ecology*, **35**: 857–70.

Mather, A.S. and Chapman, K. (1995) *Environmental resources* (Harlow: Longman Scientific & Technical).

Mauseth, J.D. (1991) *Botany: an introduction to plant biology* (international edition) (Orlando, Fla.: Saunders College Publishing/Holt, Rinehart & Winston).

May, R.M. (1975) Stability in ecosystems: some comments. In W.H. van Dobben and R.H. Lowe-McConnell (eds) *Unifying concepts in ecology* (The Hague: dr W. Junk bv): 161–8.

McCann, S. (1994) Food and agriculture. In World Resources Institute, *World resources 1994–95* (Oxford: Oxford University Press).

McCredie, S. (1994) Focus on marine fisheries. In World Resources Institute, *World Resources, 1994–95* (Oxford: Oxford University Press): 184–94.

McKinney, M.L. and Schoch, R.M. (1996) *Environmental science: systems and solutions* (St Paul, Minn.: West Publishing).

McMichael, A.J. (1993) *Planetary overload: global environmental change and the health of the human species* (Cambridge: Cambridge University Press).

McNulty, S.G., Vose, J.M. and Swank, W.T. (1996) Potential climate change effects on loblolly pine forest productivity and drainage across the southern United States. *Ambio*, **25**: 449–53.

Meadows, D.H., Meadows, D.L., Randers, J. and Behrens III, W.W. (1972) *The limits to growth. (A report for the Club of Rome's project on the predicament of mankind)* (New York: Universal).

Meadows, D.H, Meadows, D.L. and Randers, J. (1992) *Beyond the limits: confronting global collapse and envisioning a sustainable future* (London: Earthscan).

Michener, W.K., Blood, E.R., Bildstein, K.L. *et al.* (1997) Climate change, hurricanes and tropical storms, and rising sea levels in coastal wetlands. *Ecological Applications*, **7**: 770–801.

Miller Jr, G.T. (2000) *Living in the environment* (eleventh Edition) (Pacific Grove, Calif.: Brooks/Cole Publishing).

Mitchell, R.B. (1995) Lessons from intentional oil pollution. *Environment*, **37**: 10–15, 36–41. Reprinted (1997) in L. Owen and T. Unwin (eds) *Environmental management: readings and case studies* (Oxford: Blackwell): 283–97.

Montieth, J.L., Scott, R.K. and Unsworth, M.H. (1994) *Resource capture by crops* (Nottingham: University of Nottingham Press).

Moore, M.V., Pace, M.L., Mather, J.R. *et al.* (1997) Potential effects of climate change on freshwater ecosystems of the New England/Mid Atlantic region. *Hydrological Processes*, **11**: 925–47.

Moss, S. (1998) Predictions of the effects of global climate changes on British birds. *British Birds*, **91**: 307–25.

Muck, P. (1989) Major trends in the pelagic ecosystem off Peru and their implications for management. In D. Pauly *et al.* (eds) *The Peruvian upwelling ecosystem: dynamics and interactions* (Callao: Instituto del Mar del Peru): 392–400.

Myers, N. (1981) The hamburger connection: how Central America's forests became North America's hamburgers. *Ambio*, **10**: 3–8.

Myers, N. (1988) Threatened biotas: 'hot spots' in tropical forest. *Environmentalist*, **8**: 187–208.

Myers, N. (1990) The biodiversity challenge: expanded hot-spots analysis. *Environmentalist*, **10**: 243–56.

National Research Council (1991) *Tanker spills: prevention by design* (Washington DC: National Academy Press).

Nelson, S.M. and Roline, R.A. (1998) Evaluation of the sensitivity of rapid toxicity tests relative to daphnid acute lethality tests. *Bulletin of Environmental Contamination and Toxicology*, **60**: 292–9.

Nelson-Smith, A. (1968) The effects of oil pollution and emulsifier cleansing on shore life in south-west Britain. *Journal of Applied Ecology*, **5**: 97–107.

Nelson-Smith, A. (1972) *Oil pollution and marine ecology* (London: Paul Elek Scientific).

Newman, E.I. (1993) *Applied ecology* (Oxford: Blackwell Scientific).

Newson, M. (1992) *Managing the human impact on the natural environment: patterns and processes.* (London: Belhaven).

Niemi, G.J., Hanowski, J.M., Lima, A.R., Nicholls, T. and Weiland, N. (1997) A critical analysis on the use of indicator species in management. *Journal of Wildlife Management*, **61**: 1240–52.

Nobel, P.S. (1991) Environmental productivity indices and productivity for *Opuntia ficus-indica* under current and elevated atmospheric CO_2 levels. *Plant, Cell and Environment*, **14**: 637–46.

Nonhebel, S. (1996) Effects of temperature rise and increase in CO_2 concentration on simulated wheat yields in Europe. *Climatic Change*, **26**: 73–90.

Noss, R.F. (1990) Indicators for monitoring biodiversity: a hierarchical approach. *Conservation Biology*, **4**: 355–64.

Nriagu, J.O. (1979) The global copper cycle. In J.O. Nriagu (ed.) *Copper in the environment. Part I. Ecological cycling* (Chichester: Wiley): 1–17.

Nykvist, N. (1997) Total distribution of plant nutrients in a tropical rainforest ecosystem, Sabah, Malaysia. *Ambio*, **26**: 152–7.

Odum, E.P. (1959) *Fundamentals of ecology* (first edition) (Philadelphia: Saunders).

Odum, E.P. (1971) *Fundamentals of ecology* (third edition) (Philadelphia: Saunders).

Odum, E.P. (1984) Properties of agroecosystems. In G.J. House, R. Lowrance and B. Stinner (eds) *Agricultural ecosystems – unifying concept* (New York: Wiley/Interscience): 5–11.

Orians, G.H. (1975) Diversity, stability and maturity in natural ecosystems. In W.H. van Dobben and R.H. Lowe-McConnell (eds) *Unifying concepts in ecology* (The Hague: dr W. Junk bv): 139–50.

O'Riordan, T. (1976) *Environmentalism* (London: Pion).

Orr, M.R. and Smith, T.B. (1998) Ecology and speciation. *Trends in Ecology & Evolution*, **13**: 502–6.

Ostrom, E. (1990) *Governing the commons: the evolution of institutions for collective action* (Cambridge: Cambridge University Press).

Pain, S. (1993) The two faces of the Exxon disaster. *New Scientist*, 22 May: 11–12.

Park, C. (1997) *The environment: principles and applications* (London: Routledge).

Parry, M. (1990) *Climate change and world agriculture* (London: Earthscan).

Pearce, D.W. (1991) *Blueprint 2: greening the world economy* (London: Earthscan).

Pearce, D.W., Markandya, A. and Barber, E.B. (1989) *Blueprint for a green economy* (London: Earthscan).

Pearce, D.W. and Turner, R.K. (1990) *Economics of natural resources and the environment* (Hemel Hempstead: Harvester Wheatsheaf).

Pearce, F. (1992) A plague on global warming. *New Scientist*, 19/26 December: 12.

Pearce, F. (1997a) Northern exposure. *New Scientist*, 31 May: 24–7.

Pearce, F. (1997b) Changing the game. *New Scientist*, 7 June: 14–15.

Pearce, F. (1997c) Trading places/A rotten prospect for the tropics. *New Scientist*, 13 December: 7.

Pearce, F. (1997d) Dirty dealings. *New Scientist*, 20/27 December: 10.

Pearce, F. (1998a) Playing with fire. *New Scientist*, 21 March: 36–9.

Pearce, F. (1998b) Burnt out. *New Scientist*, 25 July: 13.

Pearce, F. (1998c) Blown away: metal-munching poplars could clear toxic dumps. *New Scientist*, 3 October: 11.

Penuelas, J. and Estiarte, M. (1998) Can elevated CO_2 affect secondary metabolism and ecosystem function? *Trends in Ecology & Evolution*, **13**: 20–4.

Peters, R.H. (1983) *The ecological implications of body size* (Cambridge: Cambridge University Press).

Peters, R.L. (1990) Effects of global warming on forests. *Forest Ecology and Management*, **35**: 13–33.

Pianka, E.R. (1970) On r- and K-selection. *American Naturalist*, **104**: 592–7.

Pianka, E.R. (1978) *Evolutionary ecology* (second edition) (New York: Harper & Row).

Piatt, J.R., Lensink, C.J., Butler, W., Kenziorek, M. and Nysewander, D.R. (1990) Immediate impact of the 'Exxon Valdez' oil spill on marine birds. *Auk*, **107**: 387–97.

Pimm, S.L. (1989) The snake that ate Guam. *Trends in Ecology & Evolution*, **2**: 293–5.

Pinard, M.A. and Putz, F.E. (1996) Retaining forest biomass by reducing logging damage. *Biotropica*, **28**: 278–95.

Pirazolli, P.A. (1989) Present and near-future global sea-level changes. *Palaeogeography, Palaeoclimatology, Palaeoecology*, **75**: 241–58.

Prendergast, J.R., Quinn, R.M., Lawson, J.H., Eversham, B.C. and Gibbons, D.W. (1993) Rare species, the coincidence of diversity hotspots and conservation strategies. *Nature*, **365**(6444): 335–7.

Pretty, J.N. and Howes, R. (1993) *Sustainable agriculture in Britain: recent achievements and new policy changes*. IIED Research Series, Volume 2(1) (London: IIED).

Putwain, P.D. and Rae, P.A.A. (1988) *Heathland restoration: a handbook of techniques* (Liverpool: Environmental Advisory Unit, Liverpool University).

Pywell, R.F., Putwain, P.D. and Webb, N.R. (1996) Establishment of heathland vegetation on mineral workings. *Aspects of Applied Biology*, 44: 149–56.

Rankama, K. and Sahama, T.G. (1950) *Geochemistry* (Chicago: University of Chicago Press).

Rapport, D.J., Costanza, R. and McMichael, A.J. (1998) Assessing ecosystem health. *Trends in Ecology & Evolution*, 13: 397–402.

Ratcliffe, D.A. (1967) Decrease in eggshell weight in certain birds of prey. *Nature*, 215: 208–10.

Ratcliffe, D.A. (1970) Changes attributed to pesticides in egg breakage frequency and eggshell thickness in some British birds. *Journal of Applied Ecology*, 7: 67–115.

Raven, P. H., Berg, L.R. and Johnson, G.B. (1998) *Environment* (second edition) (Orlando, Fla: Saunders College Publishing/Harcourt Brace).

Rayner, A. (1997) *Degrees of freedom: living in dynamic boundaries* (London: Imperial College Press).

Reed, D.J. (1990) The impact of sea-level rise on coastal salt marshes. *Progress in Physical Geography*, 14: 465–81.

Reid, W.V. (1998) Biodiversity hotspots. *Trends in Ecology & Evolution*, 13: 275–80.

Reiss, M.J. (1989) *The allometry of growth and reproduction* (Cambridge: Cambridge University Press).

Rey, A. and Jarvis, P.G. (1997) Growth response of young birch trees (*Betula pendula* Roth) after four and a half years of CO_2 exposure. *Annals of Botany*, 80: 809–16.

Rigler, F.H. (1961) The relationship between concentration of food and feeding rate of *Daphnia magna* Straus. *Canadian Journal of Zoology*, 39: 857–68.

Robinson, D. (1991) Roots and resource fluxes in plants and communities. In D. Atkinson (ed.) *Plant root growth: an ecological perspective* (Oxford: Blackwell Scientific): 103–30.

Robinson, M. (editor-in-chief) (1996) *Chambers 21st century dictionary* (Edinburgh: Chambers).

Rodenhouse, N.I. (1992) Potential effects of climatic change on a neotropical migrant landbird. *Conservation Biology*, 6: 263–72.

Rogers, R. (1997) *Cities for a small planet* (London: Faber and Faber).

Rosswall, T. (1983) The nitrogen cycle. In B. Bolin and R.B. Cook (eds) *The major biogeochemical cycles and their interactions. SCOPE 21* (Chichester: Wiley): 46–50.

Rouse, W.R., Douglas, M.S.V., Hecky, R.E. *et al.* (1997) Effect of climatic change on the freshwaters of Arctic and Subarctic North America. *Hydrological Processes*, 11: 873–902.

Rudd, R.I. (1975) Pesticides. In W.W. Murdoch (ed.) *Environment: resources, pollution and society* (Sunderland, Mass.: Sinauer Associates): 325–53.

Russell, J.S. (1991) Likely climatic changes and their impact on the northern pastoral industry. *Tropical Grasslands*, 25: 211–18.

Rusterholz, H.-P. and Erhardt, A. (1998) Effects of elevated CO_2 on flowering phenology and nectar production of nectar plants important for butterflies of calcareous grasslands. *Oecologia*, 113: 341–9.

Sanderson, M.G. (1996) Biomass of termites and their emission of methane and carbon dioxide: a global database. *Global Biogeochemical Cycles*, 10: 543–57.

Schenk, U., Jäger, H.-J. and Weigel, H.-J. (1997) The response of perennial ryegrass/white clover mini-swards to elevated atmospheric CO_2 concentrations: effects on yield and fodder quality. *Grass and Forage Science*, 52: 232–41.

Schindler, D.W., Beaty, K.G., Fee, E.J. *et al.* (1990) Effects of climatic warmings on lakes of the central boreal forest. *Science*, 250: 967–70.

Schofield, E.K. (1989) Effects of introduced plants and animals on island vegetation: examples from the Galapagos archipelago. *Conservation Biology*, 3: 227–38.

Schulz, A.M. (1964) The nutrient recovery hypothesis for arctic microtine cycles. II. Ecosystem variables in relation to arctic microtine cycles. In D.J. Crisp (ed.) *Grazing in terrestrial and marine environments* (Oxford: Blackwell Scientific): 57–68.

Scurlock, J.M.O. and Hall, D.O. (1998) The global carbon sink: a grassland perspective. *Global Change Biology*, 4: 229–33.

Sharp, B.E. (1996) Post-release survival of oiled, cleaned seabirds in North America. *Ibis*, 138: 222–8.

Shaw, D.G. and Bader, H.R. (1996) Environmental science in a legal context: the *Exxon Valdez* experience. *Ambio*, 25: 430–4.

Shea, K. and the NCEAS Working Group on Population Management (1998) Management of populations in conservation, harvesting and control. *Trends in Ecology & Evolution*, 13: 371–5.

Shelford, V.E. (1913) *Animal communities in temperate America* (Chicago: University of Chicago Press).

Shelford, V.E. (1943) The abundance of the collared lemming (*Dicrostonyx groenlandicus* (Tr) var *richardsoni* Mer.) in the Churchill area, 1929–1940. *Ecology*, **24**: 472–84.

Shiva, V. (1991) *The violence of the green revolution: Third World agriculture, ecology and politics* (London: Zed Books).

Shoener, T.W. (1989) The ecological niche. In J.M. Cherrett (ed.) *Ecological concepts: the contribution of ecology to an understanding of the natural world* (Oxford: Blackwell Scientific): 79–113.

Shrivastrava, P. (1992) *Bhopal: anatomy of a crisis* (second edition) (London: Paul Chapman).

Shugart, H.H. (1990) Using ecosystem models to assess potential consequences of global climatic change. *Trends in Ecology & Evolution*, **5**: 303–7.

Simberloff, D. and Abele, L.G. (1976) Island biogeography theory and conservation practice. *Science*, **191**: 285–6.

Simberloff, D. and Abele, L.G. (1982) Refuge design and island biogeography theory. *American Naturalist*, **120**: 41–50.

Sitarz, D. (ed.) (1993) *Agenda 21: the Earth Summit strategy to save our planet* (Boulder, Colo.: Earth Press).

Smith, D.F. and Hill, D.M. (1975) Natural agricultural ecosystems. *Journal of Environmental Quality*, **4**: 143–5.

Smith, S. (1995) The coypu in Britain. *British Wildlife*, 6: 279–85.

Sousa, W.P. (1985) The role of disturbance in natural communities. *Annual Review of Ecology and Systematics*, **15**: 353–91.

Southwick, C.H. (1996) *Global ecology in human perspective* (Oxford: Oxford University Press).

Southwood, T.R.E. (1977) Habitat, the templet for ecological strategies? *Journal of Animal Ecology*, **46**: 337–65.

Spellerberg, I.F. (1991) *Monitoring ecological change* (Cambridge: Cambridge University Press).

Stewart, G.R. (1991) The comparative ecophysiology of plant nitrogen metabolism. In J.R. Porter and D.W. Lawlor (eds) *Plant growth: interactions with nutrition and environment* (Society for Experimental Biology, Seminar Series 43) (Cambridge: Cambridge University Press): 81–97.

Stigliani, W.M. (1990) Climate change and its potential effects on the retention and release of hazardous chemicals in soils and sediments. In M.M. Boer and R.S. de Groot (eds) *Landscape-ecological impact of climatic change* (Amsterdam: IOS Press): 361–78.

Stone, C.P. and Scott, J.M. (eds) (1985) *Hawaii's terrestrial ecosystems: preservation and management* (Honolulu: University of Hawaii).

Stone, C.P. and Stone, D.B. (eds) (1989) *Conservation biology in Hawaii* (Honolulu: University of Hawaii).

Strahler, A.N. (1969) *Physical geography* (third edition) (London: Wiley).

Street, P. (1976) *Animal migration and navigation* (Newton Abbot: David and Charles).

Synge, H. (ed.) (1981) *The biological aspects of rare plant conservation* (London: Wiley).

Szaboles, I. (1990) Effects of predicted climatic changes on European soils, with particular regard to salinization. In M.M. Boer and R.S. de Groot (eds) *Landscape-ecological impact of climatic change* (Amsterdam: IOS Press): 177–93.

Tansley, A.G. (1935) The use and abuse of vegetational concepts and terms. *Ecology*, **16**: 284–307.

Tate, K.R. and Ross, D.J. (1997) Elevated CO_2 and moisture effects on soil carbon storage and cycling in temperate grasslands. *Global Change Biology*, **3**: 225–35.

Tatton, J.O. and Ruzicka, J.H.A. (1967) Organochlorine pesticides in Antarctica. *Nature*, **215**: 346–8.

Taylor, R.H. and Wilson, P.R. (1990) Recent increases and southern expansion of Adelie penguin populations in the Ross Sea, Antarctica, related to climatic warming. *New Zealand Journal of Ecology*, **14**: 25–9.

Taylor, W.P. (1934) Significance of extreme or intermittent conditions in distribution of species and management of natural resources, with a restatement of Liebig's law of the minimum. *Ecology*, **15**: 274–379.

Temple, S.A. (1977) Plant–animal mutualism: coevolution with dodo leads to near extinction of plants. *Science*, **197**: 885–6.

Thomas, C. (1992) *The environment in international relations* (London: Royal Institute of International Affairs).

Thomas, M.B. and Willis, A.J. (1998) Biocontrol – risky but necessary? *Trends in Ecology & Evolution*, **13**: 325–29.

Thornley, J.H.M. and Cannell, M.G.R. (1997) Temperate grassland responses to climatic change: an analysis using the Hurley Pasture Model. *Annals of Botany*, **80**: 205–21.

Thornton, I. (1979) Copper in soil and sediment. In J.O. Nriagu (ed.) *Copper in the environment. Part I. Ecological cycling* (Chichester: Wiley): 171–216.

Tissue, D.T., Thomas, R.B. and Stain, B.R. (1997) Atmospheric CO_2 enrichment increases growth and photosynthesis of *Pinus taeda*: a 4 year experiment in the field. *Plant, Cell and Environment*, **20**: 1123–34.

Tivy, J. (1990) *Agricultural ecology* (Harlow: Longman Scientific & Technical).

Turner, R.K. (1993) Sustainability: principles and practice. In R.K. Turner (ed.) *Sustainable environmental economics and management: principles and practice* (London: Bellhaven). Reprinted in L. Owen and T. Unwin (eds) (1997) *Environmental management: readings and case studies* (Oxford: Blackwell): 412–26.

UK Biodiversity Group (1998) *Tranche 2 Action Plans. Volume 1 – Vertebrates and vascular plants* (Peterborough: English Nature).

UNEP (1991) *Human development report 1991* (Oxford: Oxford University Press).

United Nations (1993) *Report of the United Nations Conference on Environment and Development* (three volumes) (New York: United Nations).

United Nations Population Fund (1998) *The state of world population* (New York: United Nations).

Usher, M.B. (1991) Scientific requirements of a monitoring programme. In F.B. Goldsmith (ed.) *Monitoring for conservation and ecology* (London: Chapman & Hall): 15–32.

van Valen, L. (1973) A new evolutionary law. *Evolutionary Theory*, **1**: 1–30.

Vandermeer, J.H. (1972) Niche theory. *Annual Review of Ecology and Systematics*, **3**: 107–32.

Vane-Wright, R.I., Humphries, C.J. and Williams, P.H. (1992) What to protect? Systematics and the agony of choice. *Biological Conservation*, **55**: 235–54.

Vernadsky, V. (1926, translated 1997) *The biosphere* (New York: Copernicus).

von Haartman, L. (1978) Changes in the bird fauna in Finland during the last hundred years. *Fennia*, **150**: 25–32.

Wallen, C.C. (1986) Impact of present century climatic fluctuations in the Northern Hemisphere. *Geografiska Annaler, Series A*, **68A**: 245–78.

Warkowska-Dratnal, H. and Stenseth, N.C. (1985) Dispersal and the microtine cycle: comparison of two hypotheses. *Oecologia*, **65**: 468–77.

Watson, R. (1999) Common themes for ecologists in global issues. *Journal of Applied Ecology*, **36**: 1–10.

Watson, R.T., Meira Filho, L.G., Sanhueza, E. and Janetos, A. (1992) Sources and sinks. In J.T. Houghton, B.A. Callander and S.K. Varney (eds) *Climate change 1992: the supplementary report to the IPCC Scientific Assessment* (Cambridge: Cambridge University Press): 25–46.

Weiner, A., Berg, C., Gerlach, T., Grunblatt, J., Holbrook, K. and Kuwada, M. (1997) The *Exxon Valdez* oil spill: habitat protection as a restoration strategy. *Restoration Ecology*, **5**: 44–55.

Weir, D. (1988). *The Bhopal syndrome* (London: Earthscan).

Whitmore, T.C. (1975) *Tropical rain forests of the Far East* (Oxford: Clarendon Press).

Whittaker, R.H. (1975) *Communities and ecosystems* (London: Collier Macmillan).

Whittaker, R.H., Levin, S.A. and Root, R.B. (1973) Niche, habitat, and ecotope. *American Naturalist*, **107**: 321–38.

Whitten, M.J., Jefferson, R.A. and Dall, D. (1996) Needs and opportunities. In G.J. Persley (ed.) *Biotechnology and integrated pest management* (Wallingford: CAB International): 1–36.

Wieser, W. (1979) The flow of copper through a terrestrial food web. In J.O. Nriagu (ed.) *Copper in the environment. Part I. Ecological cycling* (Chichester: Wiley): 325–55.

Wigley, T.M.L. (1983) The pre-industrial carbon dioxide level. *Climatic Change*, **5**: 315–20.

Wilcox, B. (ed.) (1988) *1988 IUCN red list of threatened animals* (Gland, Switzerland: IUCN).

Wilkinson, D.M. (1999) Plants on the move. *New Scientist*, 20 March – insert: *Inside Science* **19**: 4.

Williams, P., Gibbons, D., Margules, C., Rebelo, A., Humphries, C. and Pressey, R.A. (1996) Comparison of richness hotspots, rarity hotspots and complementary areas for conserving diversity of British birds. *Conservation Biology*, **10**: 155–74.

Williams, P.H. and Gaston, K.J. (1994) Measuring more of biodiversity: can higher taxon richness predict wholesale species richness? *Biological Conservation*, **67**: 211–17.

Williamson, M. (1996) *Biological invasions* (London: Chapman & Hall).

Williamson, P. and Holligan, P.M. (1990) Ocean productivity and climatic change. *Trends in Ecology & Evolution*, **5**: 299–303.

Willis, J.C. (1922) *Age and area* (Cambridge: Cambridge University Press).

Winstanley, D. (1973) Rainfall patterns and general atmospheric circulation. *Nature*, **245**: 190–4.

Woodward, F.I. (1987) *Climate and plant distribution* (Cambridge: Cambridge University Press).

Woodward, F.I. (1990) Global change: translating plant ecophysiological responses to ecosystems. *Trends in Ecology & Evolution*, **5**: 308–11.

Woodward, F.I., Lomas, M.R., Botts, R.A. *et al.* (1998) Vegetation–climate feedbacks in a greenhouse world. *Philosophical Transactions of the Royal Society, Series B, Biological Sciences*, **353**(1365): 29–39.

World Bank (1985) *Population change and economic development* (Oxford: Oxford University Press).

World Commission on Environment and Development (1987) *Our common future* (Oxford: Oxford University Press).

World Conservation Monitoring Centre (1992) *Global biodiversity: status of the Earth's living resources* (London: Chapman & Hall).

World Resources Institute (1994) *World Resources 1994–95* (Oxford: Oxford University Press).

Wynne, G., Avery, M, Campbell, L. *et al.* (1995) *Biodiversity challenge: an agenda for conservation action in the UK* (second edition) (Sandy: RSPB).

Index

stability, 25, 27, 41, 59, 63, 71, 73–4, 86–8, 167, 232, 249, 278
starling (Sturnus vulgaris), 246
steppe, 16, 20, 107, 263
stick insect (Carausius), 139, 145
stoat (Mustela erminea), 248
Stockholm Conference, 60, 62
stone plant (Lithops), 139
stonefly, 15, 150
strangler vine, 19, 24
strawberry (Fragaria), 145
stress tolerance, 254–7
succession, 59, 71, 74, 228–34, 278
Sudan, 38
sulphur (dioxide), 57, 73
Sumatra, 5, 30
sunflower (Helianthus annuus), 111
surplus yield, 163, 166
Surtsey, 267
sustainability, 25, 28, 31, 36–7, 61–7, 71–3, 89, 138, 207, 279
swallow (Hirundo rustica), 225
swallowtail butterfly, 196
swamp cypress (Taxodium), 120
Sweden, 220, 229, 245
swift (Apus apus), 225
Switzerland, 130, 220, 229, 272
symbiosis 3, 42, 54, 56

tadpole, 122, 150, 259
Tanzania, 177, 196
taxonomy, 3–4, 175, 183, 191
teak (Tectona grandis), 4
Tegula (snail), 262
Tennessee, 236, 239
termite, 18, 23–4, 101–2
tern, Arctic (Sterna paradisaea), 224
Tetraphis pellucida (moss), 122–3
Thailand, 5, 7, 58, 170, 217
Thetford Forest, 182
Thiobacillus, 53
thorn scrub, 16, 23, 27
thrips, banana rust, 170
thrush, song (Turdus), 139, 197
tidal activity, 122, 128, 225–8, 233, 240
tiger (Panthera tigris), 24, 222, 237–8
tit (Parus), 50, 262–3
toad, 150
    cane (Bufo marinus), 169
    spadefoot (Scaphiopus), 122–3
tolerance limits, 112, 117–22, 195, 225–7, 256, 259
tolerance model (succession), 231, 234
toluene, 77–8

tomato, 139
Torrey Canyon, 78–9, 93
tortoise, giant (Geochelone), 252
touch-me-not (Impatiens), 222
tourism, 30, 79, 209, 217, 234–5, 238–9, 241, 252
tragedy of the commons, 128–9, 135
transgenic engineering, 201, 203
transpiration, 9, 11, 18, 22 (see also evapotranspiration)
treecreeper (Certhia familiaris), 259
treefall gap, 24, 27, 190, 223, 225
treeline, 107, 227, 229
trophic level, 40–51, 89, 219, 278
trout, lake (Salvelinus), 103
trypanosomiasis, 125
tsetse fly (Glossina), 125, 141
tundra, 14, 16–17, 46, 107, 159, 179, 223, 228, 254
turtle, leatherback (Dermochelys), 149
two,4–D (2,4-D) and 2,4,5-T, 81, 143

Uganda, 198, 239
UK, 104, 111–12, 125, 167, 180–3, 185, 195–6, 200, 213–18, 220, 223, 234, 236, 239, 245, 249
Ukraine, 130, 217
ultraviolet radiation, 73, 115, 117–8
UN Conference on Environment and Development (see Rio Conference)
urban habitat, 58, 115, 176, 180, 196, 235, 239–40, 257, 273, 278
USA, 37, 66–67, 103, 117, 127, 130, 167–8, 178–9, 191, 200, 202–3, 208–14, 217, 220, 222, 236–7, 239, 246
Utah, 210

Venezuela, 178, 199, 217
vesicular-arbuscular mycorrhizae, 56
viceroy butterfly (Limenitis), 139
Vietnam War, 278
vine, grape (Vitis vinifera), 99, 169
Virunga mountains, 239
vole, 50, 159

warbler
    willow (Phylloscopus), 197
    wood (Dendroica), 112, 263–4
wasp, 139, 170, 248
water flea (Daphnia), 75, 139, 155
water hyacinth (Eichhornia), 141–4
weasel (Mustela), 25, 47, 50, 248
weed, 57–58, 63–65, 81, 112–13, 138, 141–4, 152, 234, 246–53
    control, 167–71
weevil, 143, 170
West Midlands (England), 180, 218